STRATEGIC
FLEXIBILITY

STRATEGIC THINKING
Leadership and the Management of Change
Edited by
JOHN HENDRY AND GERRY JOHNSON
WITH JULIA NEWTON

COMPETENCE-BASED COMPETITION
Edited by
GARY HAMEL AND AIMÉ HEENE

BUILDING THE STRATEGICALLY-RESPONSIVE ORGANIZATION
Edited by
HOWARD THOMAS, DON O'NEAL, ROD WHITE AND DAVID HURST

STRATEGIC RENAISSANCE AND BUSINESS TRANSFORMATION
Edited by
HOWARD THOMAS, DON O'NEAL AND JAMES KELLY

COMPETENCE-BASED STRATEGIC MANAGEMENT
Edited by
AIMÉ HEENE AND RON SANCHEZ

STRATEGIC LEARNING AND KNOWLEDGE MANAGEMENT
Edited by
RON SANCHEZ AND AIMÉ HEENE

STRATEGY STRUCTURE AND STYLE
Edited by
HOWARD THOMAS, DON O'NEAL AND MICHEL GHERTMAN

STRATEGIC INTEGRATION
Edited by
HOWARD THOMAS AND DON O'NEAL

STRATEGIC DISCOVERY
Edited by
HOWARD THOMAS, DON O'NEAL AND RAUL ALVARADO

MANAGING STRATEGICALLY IN AN INTERCONNECTED WORLD
Edited by
MICHAEL A. HITT, JOAN E. RICART AND ROBERT D. NIXON

NEW MANAGERIAL MINDSETS
Edited by
MICHAEL A. HITT, JOAN E. RICART AND ROBERT D. NIXON

Further titles in preparation

STRATEGIC FLEXIBILITY

Managing in a Turbulent Environment

Edited by

GARY HAMEL, C. K. PRAHALAD,
HOWARD THOMAS AND DON O'NEAL

JOHN WILEY & SONS

Chichester · New York · Weinheim · Brisbane · Singapore · Toronto

Other Wiley Editorial Offices

John Wiley & Sons, Inc., 605 Third Avenue,
New York, NY 10158-0012, USA

WILEY-VCH Verlag GmbH, Pappelallee 3,
D-69469 Weinheim, Germany

Jacaranda Wiley Ltd, 33 Park Road, Milton,
Queensland 4064, Australia

John Wiley & Sons (Canada) Ltd, 22 Worcester Road,
Rexdale, Ontario M9W 1L1, Canada

John Wiley & Sons (Asia) Pte Ltd, 2 Clementi Loop #02-01,
Jin Xing Distripark, Singapore 129809

Library of Congress Cataloging-in-Publication Data

Strategic flexibility : managing in a turbulent environment/edited by Gary Hamel, C.K. Prahalad,
Howard Thomas and Don O'Neal.
   p.   cm. — (The strategic management series)
   The 16th International Conference of the Strategic Management
Society, held in Phoenix, Arizona, November 10–13, 1996; entitled
"Competing in the new economy: managing out of bounds."
   Includes bibliographical references and index.
   ISBN 0 471 98473 6 (cloth)
   1. Industrial management—Congresses.   2. Technological
innovations—Congresses.   3. Knowledge management—Congresses.
4. Competition, International—Congresses.   I. Thomas, Howard,
1943– .   II. O'Neal, Don.   III. International Strategic Management
Society Conference (16th : 1996 : Phoenix, Ariz.)   IV. Series.
HD31.S6963887   1998
658—dc21
                                                    96–16680
                                                      CIP

British Library Cataloguing in Publication Data

A catalogue record for this book is available from the British Library

ISBN 0-471-98473-6

Typeset in 10/12pt Palatino by Footnote Graphics, Warminster, Wiltshire.
Printed and bound by Antony Rowe Ltd, Eastbourne
This book is printed on acid-free paper responsibly manufactured from sustainable forestry,
in which at least two trees are planted for each one used in paper production.

Contents

Contributors

CHARLES BADEN-FULLER
City University Business School, Frobisher Crescent, Barbican Centre, London EC2Y 8HB, UK

WILLIAM C. BOGNER
Department of Management, Georgia State University, PO Box 4014, Atlanta, GA 30302-4014, USA

DONG SUNG CHO
Seoul National University, Shinlim-Dong, Kwanak-Ku, Seoul 151, Korea

JAMES A. CHRISTIANSEN
INSEAD, 6 rue Castex, 75004 Paris, France

WUJIN CHU
Seoul National University, Shinlim-Dong, Kwanak-Ku, Seoul 151, Korea

PATRICE COOPER
Department of Management and Marketing, University College Cork, Ireland

THOMAS DURAND
Ecole Centrale Paris, Grande Voie des Vignes, F-92295, Châteney Malabry Cédex, France

JEFFREY H. DYER
Wharton School, University of Pennsylvania, 2000 Steinberg–Dietrich Hall, Philadelphia, PA 19104–6370, USA

STEVEN FLOYD
University of Connecticut, 368 Fairfield Road, U-41M, Storrs, CT 06269-2041, USA

Dennis M. Garvis
Department of Management, Georgia State University, PO Box 4014, Atlanta, GA 30302-4014, USA

George W. Giusti
Small Business Consultants, 215 Lassen Drive, PO Box 1289, San Bruno, CA 94066-1289, USA

Paul C. Godfrey
Department of Organizational Leadership and Strategy, Marriott School of Management, Brigham Young University, 789 TNRB, Provo, UT 84602, USA

Sebastian Green
Department of Management and Marketing, University College Cork, Ireland

Hal B. Gregersen
Marriott School of Management, Brigham Young University, 789 TNRB, Provo, UT 84602, USA

Karsten Heppner
Universität zu Köln, Albertus-Magnus-Platz, 50923 Koln, Germany

Anne Sigismund Huff
University of Colorado at Boulder, University of Colorado, Box 419, Boulder, CO 80309-0419, USA

Mulumdi Jayaram
Department of Marketing and Supply Chain Management, Eli Broad Graduate School of Management, Michigan State University, East Lansing, MI 48824, USA

Gerry Johnson
Centre for Strategic Management and Organisational Change, Cranfield School of Management, Cranfield University, Cranfield, Bedfordshire MK43 0AL, UK

Stanley J. Kowalczyk
Department of Management, San Francisco State University, 1600 Holloway Avenue, San Francisco, CA 94132, USA

Michael Lubatkin
University of Connecticut, 368 Fairfield Road, U-41M, Storrs, CT 06269-2041, USA

John McGee
Warwick Business School, University of Warwick, Coventry CV4 7AL, UK

RITA GUNTHER MCGRATH
Graduate School of Business, Columbia University, 703 Uris Hall, New York, NY 10027, USA

YASMIN MERALI
Warwick Business School, University of Warwick, Coventry CV4 7AL, UK

GRANT MILES
Department of Management, College of Business Administration, University of North Texas, PO Box 305429, Denton, TX 76203-5429, USA

RAYMOND E. MILES
Haas School of Business, 545 Student Services Building, University of California, Berkeley, CA 94720-1900, USA

CAROLINE MOTHE
Paris X Nanterre University, 200 avenue de la Republique, 92000 Nanterre, France

PANCHO NUNES
Groupe ESC Lyon, 23, avenue Guy de Collongue, G9132 Ecully cédex, France

DON O'NEAL
Department of Management, L53 University of Illinois at Springfield, Springfield, IL 62794-9243, USA

KENNETH D. PRITSKER
Strategic Reengineering Institute, 2304 Eldridge Street, Suite 200, Pittsburgh, PA 15217, USA

BERTRAND QUÉLIN
HEC Paris School of Management, Corporate Strategy Group, 1, rue de la Liberation, 78351 Jouy en Josas, France

PAUL RAIMOND
City University Business School, Frobisher Crescent, Barbican, London EC2Y 8HB, UK

CHARLES C. SNOW
Department of Management and Organization, The Smeal College of Business Administration, Pennsylvania State University, 411 Bean BAB, University Park, PA 16802-1914, USA

J. L. STIMPERT
Department of Economics and Business, Colorado College, Colorado Springs, CO 80903, USA

HOWARD THOMAS
College of Commerce and Business Administration, University of Illinois at Urbana-Champaign, 260 Commerce West, 1206 South Sixth Street, Champaign, IL 61820, USA

TRACY A. THOMPSON
Business Administration Program, University of Washington, Tacoma, Box 358420, 1900 Commerce Street, Tacoma, WA 98402-3100, USA

KATHLEEN L. VALLEY
Graduate School of Business Administration, Harvard University, Boston, MA 92163, USA

HENK W. VOLBERDA
Department of Strategic Management and Business Environment, Rotterdam School of Management, Erasmus University, PO Box 1738, 3000 DR Rotterdam, The Netherlands

MICHAEL E. WASSERMAN
School of Management, George Mason University, Fairfax, VA 22030, USA

DAVID A. WHETTEN
Marriott School of Management, Brigham Young University, 789 TNRB, Provo, UT 84602, USA

Series Preface

The Strategic Management Society was created to bring together, on a worldwide basis, academics, business practitioners, and consultants interested in strategic management. The aim of the Society is the development and dissemination of information, achieved through its sponsorship of the annual international conference, special interest workshops, the *Strategic Management Journal*, and other publications.

The Society's annual conference is a truly international meeting, held in recent years in Stockholm, Barcelona, Toronto, London, Chicago, Paris, and Mexico City. Each conference deals with a broad, current theme, within which specific sub-themes are addressed through keynote speeches and discussion panels featuring leading experts from around the world.

This volume is the sixth in the series representing Strategic Management Society annual conferences. Papers and panel discussions presented at these conferences address not just the conference themes but, more importantly, discuss "live" issues—those that are currently confronting the Society and its members. In this context presenters feel more freedom to step outside the "boilerplate"-type issues that sometimes discourage dialectic discussion, and utilize these conferences as opportunities to take chances—to address issues that are more "interesting," though perhaps less conventional.

This type of conference format provides the editors with a broader range of ideas, thoughts, and themes from which to select papers, and the opportunity to make available an interesting and intriguing selection of conversations to anyone interested in joining the dialog or in just reading about the discussions.

Attending a conference at which a number of presentations are occurring simultaneously requires attendees to make choices and, in the process, inevitably miss some presentations that they may have found interesting and useful. This results in most conference presentations playing to only a few or, at most a few dozen, of those who might be interested. This volume, as do others in the series, offers the opportunity for hundreds of interested individuals to, in effect, attend a number of thought-provoking conference presentations. At the same time it offers much wider exposure to a selection of papers deemed likely to be of interest to a broader audience.

This conference,* entitled "Competing in the New Economy: Managing Out of Bounds," was intended to expand our understanding of the strategic opportunites presented by the far-reaching developments unfolding in the rapidly changing world economy.

The Conference Steering Committee reviewed several hundred papers, ultimately selecting around 200 for presentation at the conference, along with around 20 panel discussions. We believe that the wisdom contained in the rich body of research and experience benefited all the participants, and will be a major contribution to better understanding the significance of the contributions of strategic management.

With so many worthwhile contributions to consider, a decision was made early in the editorial process not to attempt to select a set of "best" papers from the conference. Judging which presentations are best is highly subjective and, moreover, is unlikely to provide the balance of content that will make the volume interesting and useful to a broad range of Society members.

With that in mind, a theme was selected that is consistent not only with the theme of the conference but also with the mission of the Society. Presentations were selected with the additional consideration that they represent some of the more significant issues currently facing business strategists. The result is, we feel, an interesting and effective integration of strategic perspectives that exemplifies many of the most important issues facing strategic management, both now and in the future.

An eclectic ensemble of contributors, including academics, business executives, and consultants, addresses one of the Society's primary concerns—building and maintaining bridges between management theory and business practice.

Editorial commentary provides integration among contributions, resulting in a volume that is more than a collection of currently-relevant discussions, to be read once and perhaps forgotten. It is, instead, a collection of thoughts on and approaches to management issues that are timeless in their nature and importance.

HOWARD THOMAS
Series Editor

* The 16th International Conference of the Strategic Management Society, held in Phoenix, Arizona, 10–13 November 1996, was attended by several hundred delegates from both the academic and the business worlds.

Introduction

In *Beyond Uncertainty* (1995) Charles Handy foresees the world moving into a period of change as significant as that brought about by the invention of the printing press, which allowed people, for the first time, to read and interpret the Bible for themselves rather than having it interpreted by representatives of the church. The ability to make up their own minds and take charge of their own destinies gave people the incentive to break free from the authority of the church and other institutions, and the resulting burst of individual freedom may have been the genesis of the Renaissance.

Handy sees the nascent information age as the modern equivalent of the printing press, in which people will be freed from the constraints of the office and the formal organization, and organizations will become more like communities than properties, and people more like members than employees. This type of change—of the magnitude defined by Schumpeter as "creative destruction"—represents great uncertainty and will be viewed, as was the printing press, as a time of great opportunity by some, and as ominous and threatening by others. This turbulence will require different perspectives on organizations, different styles of leadership and, perhaps most importantly, the strategic flexibility on which this volume focuses.

This perspective was inherent in the objectives outlined by co-chairs Gary Hamel and C.K. Prahalad in designing the program for the Phoenix Conference:

> Developing a program of ideas—new ideas, new theory, new applications, new concepts—that are relevant to a manager facing the new millenium . . . . To do that we need to escape old constraints, old thinking, old questions, and address everything that is new. We hope that . . . we can work together to help set the research agenda for the field of strategic management in the year 2000 and beyond. Let's break out of old paradigms; let's challenge received dogma; let's have the courage to ask new questions; let's rekindle our passion for relevance.

Although it is impossible to include in one volume the full breadth of ideas under discussion in the area of strategic management, the editors have selected contributions that effectively exemplify the objectives set forth by the conference co-chairs, and that offer interesting food for thought in five currently crucial strategic conversations:

1. Innovation. Chapters in this section discuss moving from a strategy of low-cost leadership to one of innovation, utilizing pockets of innovation, technological development from R&D consortia, and the influence of strategic trajectories on technological innovation.
2. Organization. Chapters in this section examine deliberate and emergent corporate cultures, value-creation as a function of organizational form, strategic reengineering as a framework for understanding industries, and changing organizational structure to enhance organizational knowledge.
3. Leadership. Chapters in this section discuss good ethics vs. good business, the role of leaders in managing knowledge, the influence of corporate headquarters on organizational learning, measuring board performance, and where strategic ideas come from.
4. Partnership. Chapters in this section address managing supplier relationships, and understanding the knowledge structures of European managers.
5. Competence. Chapters in this section describe a renewed model of competence, determining optimal organizational form in MNCs, an empirical analysis of the value of having/developing core competences, and mechanisms for matching firm-level competences with industry-level sources of competitive advantage.

Section I

Innovation

"Innovation," Peter Drucker tells us, "is the specific tool of entrepreneurs, the means by which they exploit change as an opportunity for a different business or a different service. It is capable of being presented as a discipline, capable of being learned, capable of being practiced" (*Innovation and Entrepreneurship*, 1985, p. 19).

Although we often associate entrepreneurship with innovative individuals who start up their own businesses, it is also the primary driver of innovation in many larger organizations. Popularly visualized in the context of the invention of high-tech products, innovation also adds value to organizations in many other areas (e.g. management, production processes), as demonstrated by the chapters in this section.

Christiansen examines how managers in a European firm dealt with the problem of changing the firm's basic competitive strategy from low-cost leadership to innovation. Beginning with simple, project-focused changes and progressing to more complex, system-wide changes, managers in four different divisions all accomplished the changeover, but in different ways.

Arguing that local innovativeness is a critical pool of new ideas that is likely to be overlooked by traditional ideas about research and development, Johnson and Huff examine how and why pockets of innovation develop, and how innovative ideas from these sources can be nourished and utilized to a firm's competitive advantage.

Based on more than 300 partners in a European consortium, Mothe and Quélin empirically analyse the different types of technological developments stemming from R&D consortia and examine the impact of partners' characteristics and organizational forms on the types of resources and new products created.

Stimpert, Wasserman and Jayaram develop the concept of *strategic trajectory* to explain the dynamic, path-dependent nature of decision making. They then use the pattern of innovation pursued by US railroad

companies during the 25 years following World War II to bolster the
argument that decisions about technological innovation are strongly
influenced by these strategic trajectories.

1

Improving Innovation Performance in Older Firms: The General Manager's Role

JAMES A. CHRISTIANSEN

INTRODUCTION

This chapter focuses on a problem faced by general managers in some large, diversified firms. Suppose that a firm has used low-cost strategies for decades. All of its systems are oriented toward achieving low cost. All of its people have been trained to achieve that goal and work together effectively. But changes in its market have made this low-cost strategy untenable.

The firm's senior management has determined that the firm must offer an increasing variety of value-added products. To do this, the firm must increase its innovation performance: it must increase its output of new and improved products. The problem is that no one knows how. The managers who must implement the change grew up in the old system. They know how to manage for low cost, but not how to manage for high innovation performance. The problem is: given these conditions, how do they get a change process started, and how do they sustain change over time?

Using a grounded theory methodology, I look in detail at how managers in four divisions of a large European firm, MGE (a pseudonym), dealt with

Strategic Flexibility: Managing in a Turbulent Environment. Edited by G. Hamel, C.K. Prahalad, H. Thomas and D. O'Neal.

this problem during the period 1988–1994. In 1988, the managers of the Pharmaceutical division decided that their division had to increase its innovation performance. In 1990, corporate management decided that three other divisions, Industrial Chemicals, Lawn & Garden, and Advanced Materials, had to do the same. From 1990 to 1994 (1988 to 1994 in the Pharmaceutical division), managers in all four divisions made sustained efforts to increase innovation performance. I collected detailed case histories of their efforts in each division, and analysed these to identify how the management of each division got change started.

Since the four MGE divisions did not all change in the same way, I looked at the evolution of four comparison companies over ten years (1984–1994): USChem (chemicals), USMfg (a diversified manufacturer), EurAuto (a motor vehicle assembler) and ConPro (a consumer products manufacturer). The eight organizations (four MGE divisions and four comparison companies) fell neatly into two groups. Four (two MGE divisions and two comparison companies) emphasized *increased diversification capacity* in their efforts to improve innovation performance. The four others emphasized *increased innovation system efficiency* in their efforts to improve innovation performance.

In the next section I describe the overall patterns of change; that is, how managers of the four MGE divisions began and continued their change efforts, how they began moving from a low-cost to a differentiation strategy. In the following section I describe the two different paths of change.

THE OVERALL PATTERN OF CHANGE: HOW MGE MANAGERS CHANGED THE MGE SYSTEM

MGE's general managers embarked on a programme of innovation performance improvement, despite the fact that they were embedded in a non-innovative system, and despite the fact that they had never worked in a more highly innovative system. They began by defining the problem as "finding ways to increase innovation performance". They quickly latched onto two simple and obvious solutions which promised to help fix the problem without totally solving it. These solutions were the following. First, they greatly increased the budgets of a number of existing projects. This solved the immediate problem that such projects had been starved of resources under the old system. Second, they greatly increased the prominence of these projects by having them report to the highest officers in their divisions and in the corporation as a whole. This assured that the projects would continue to receive sufficient resources. It also functioned as a signal to the corporation's managers that innovation would continue to be one of their highest priorities for the foreseeable future.

One feature of these simple and obvious solutions was that they were safe. Little harm could be done to the corporation, or to other projects, by increasing one project's budget. MGE was still rich enough that giving one project more money did not necessarily cause a reduction in anyone else's budget. Changing reporting relationships involved a reallocation of senior management time, but the change was marginal. Neither of these actions bore much risk of undesirable secondary effects. The interactions between one project and another were not sufficient to warrant much concern. As a result, these simple, obvious solutions could be implemented quickly and without any worry about their long-term effects.

But the simple solutions were not enough. Managers had to look at more systemic reforms of the project management system and of overall business management systems in order to make further progress in addressing the problem. The problem was that reforms of the project management system would have much wider impacts than simple changes in the status or budgets of individual projects. Such reforms could not be undertaken without serious prior thought about how they would affect all existing and future projects. Business system reforms, which impacted operating units as well as projects, demanded even more serious reflection. The company could not afford to restructure the business units without serious thought about how the changes would affect the business units' ability to continue producing short-term profits. Thus, after implementing the simple, obvious solutions, MGE managers spent some time reflecting about what to do next. It took some time for MGE's managers to determine their next steps.

Managers in the Industrial Chemicals division looked at things that had gone wrong in the division's past. Key projects had been starved of funds in their early years. Clearly something was wrong with the division's project funding system. After identifying the problem, division management analysed what had gone wrong and designed a new project funding system which would not be subject to the same problems. Once the design was completed, they quickly implemented the system.

Similarly, Industrial Chemicals management observed that some well-funded projects were not being run well. They determined that the old system of selecting project managers did not work. They developed a new profile of the ideal project manager and selected people who fit it to run projects. In addition, they recognized that they had to devise some way of spreading knowledge about effective project management methods. To solve this, they set up new training programmes for all project managers.

This incremental process continued as division management went through successive cycles of problem definition, learning, designing a solution, implementing the solution and training others how to run the new system. The next major step was an organizational reform which involved a radical revision of organization structure and communication flows throughout the division. Here Industrial Chemicals management brought in consultants to accelerate their learning and expand their experience base. The sequence of events—problem definition, learning, solution design, training and implementation—followed the pattern observed in the other reforms.

The learning and adjustment process was similar, with variations, in the other divisions. The Pharmaceutical division used consultants much earlier and also brought in new hires. The new hires, experienced at managing more effective innovation systems elsewhere, were confident of their own knowledge. They implemented reforms without having to rely solely on Pharmaceuticals' own experience. Pharmaceuticals management thus moved more quickly than Industrial Chemicals management in making project management and business system reforms.

One side effect of Pharmaceuticals' willingness to move quickly was that subordinate managers had trouble keeping up. Senior Pharmaceuticals managers had to remove numerous managers at middle levels. They were not adapting quickly enough to changes. Senior managers in the other divisions removed fewer people, a sign that the changes were occurring slowly enough that most people could keep up.

The pattern at Lawn & Garden also had its unique aspects. Besides increasing project budgets and changing project reporting relationships, Lawn & Garden management hit upon one other simple solution. They would, for nearly three years, run important projects themselves. This intervention did not work. Senior division management did not know the territory as well as the project team. Chastised by experience, division management backed off from micro-management, proposed a number of changes in project and business management systems (including decentralization of their own power) and asked subordinate managers to discuss the proposal. Six months of discussion and planning followed. Subordinate managers accepted the proposals as their own and filled in many details. Implementation went quickly and smoothly.

The Advanced Materials story is a hybrid of several of the others. As in Lawn & Garden, management stuck to single-project solutions for a long period. But when reforms came, they looked much like the reforms in Industrial Chemicals. They were accompanied by training programmes designed to teach people how to manage the new system.

To summarize, there was a common pattern in the methods MGE managers used to improve innovation performance. Despite the fact that they were embedded in the old system, and were unfamiliar with more innovative systems, they were still able to identify a few simple and obvious methods of improving the firm's innovation performance. These methods included increasing project funding and increasing the prominence of projects. To go beyond these simple and obvious methods, they had to learn more about how to construct and manage a more innovative system.

They learned through several means. They looked at problems that had occurred in the past. They designed tentative solutions to these problems, thought about any interaction effects, and then implemented the solutions. In some cases, they adjusted the solutions as they gained more experience. In the case of particularly complex reforms (such as organizational restructurings), they brought in consultants to expand their experience base. Some reforms involved large numbers of people. In these cases, they set up training programmes to teach people how to run the new systems. The result was workable, though not perfect, transitions. In Pharmaceuticals, the division which moved fastest, a number of middle-level managers had to be replaced, as they were not willing or able to change as fast as the systems were changing.

TWO PATHS OF CHANGE

In the previous section, I looked at how managers of the four MGE divisions had begun to improve their divisions' new product development systems. Starting with systems which emphasized low cost, they began building systems that could more effectively generate, fund and develop new product ideas. In this section, I look more closely at how the systems changed. To cite the extremes, the changes made at Industrial Chemicals were quite different from those made at Pharmaceuticals. In the broader sample of eight organizations, four followed the Industrial Chemicals pattern and four followed the Pharmaceuticals pattern.

BUILDING DIVERSIFICATION CAPACITY AT INDUSTRIAL CHEMICALS

Before 1990, the Industrial Chemicals division had few new product development projects. Those which existed were often poorly funded. Management's efforts after 1990 focused largely on developing the ability to generate more ideas and to develop a wider range of products. I call this developing "diversification capacity", or "creativity".

To summarize what happened, Industrial Chemical management used two key methods to build the divisions' ability to generate and explore new ideas.

First, they loosened up the funding system so that a wider variety of ideas could find funding. They did this in two ways, one of which involved ending the monopoly over innovation project funding formerly enjoyed by business unit managers. They ended the monopoly by providing funds at the division level as well. Projects which fell between business units, or which otherwise did not fit nearly into a single business unit's area, could be covered by division-level funds. In addition, through a process of signalling, corporate management began to make it clear that they would support speculative product innovation projects. While business unit managers were slow to believe this, division-level management picked up the signal quite quickly and began putting division-level funds into innovation within months of top management giving the signal.

The second method of increasing the division's diversification capacity involved increasing idea generation itself. After fixing the funding system, division management believed, doubtless correctly, that the division simply wasn't generating sufficient new business ideas. The solution they found to this problem was organizational. Through a reorganization, they set up new communications paths linking the technical side of business units much more closely with the marketing side and with customers. In addition, they set up new links between business units—links which allowed the division to look for synergies across its technologies.

In addition to building the division's diversification capacity, division management tried to build efficiency by improving project management methods. These effects involved replacement of ineffective project managers, training in project management methods and more effective supervision of project managers' work. Far more extensive efforts were made to improve efficiency in the Pharmaceuticals division, however (see below).

Three other organizations in the sample evolved much like Industrial Chemicals. Each of them was already diversified, and wished to become more diversified through new product development. MGE's Advanced Materials division implemented much the same kinds of reform as Industrial Chemicals. USChem began its innovation reform efforts earlier. But, like the two MGE divisions, it built idea generation capacity by multiplying horizontal links across functions and business units, and with customers. It also multiplied and diversified funding sources to broaden the range of projects it could shepherd through its system. USMfg already had multiple funding sources in 1984. It multiplied and tightened its links with customers in the ensuing decade in an effort to be able to generate and efficiently execute a wider variety of ideas.

BUILDING INNOVATION SYSTEM EFFICIENCY AT PHARMACEUTICALS

Industrial Chemicals managers focused on developing diversification capacity. Pharmaceuticals managers had a quite different focus. Even in

1988, they had plenty of ideas for new pharmaceutical products. The problem was that they were not bringing the ideas they had to fruition. To fix this, they focused on increasing innovation system efficiency.

The key techniques used at Pharmaceuticals to increase innovation system efficiency should be understood in the context of the pharmaceutical industry. Three issues are key in that industry.

First, the profitable life of a product is limited by the length of time during which it is protected by a patent. Since products must be patented very early in the development process, this puts a high premium on completing development early. Each year spent in development is one year less the product can be profitably sold.

Second, for every ten compounds entering development, perhaps one will successfully pass all the regulatory tests and become a commercial product. Of these, only a few will be unique products which become highly profitable. Any which are not unique, but which copy something already on the market ("me-too" products) are unlikely to make much money. As a result, there is usually a much higher payoff for developing one unique product than for developing a number of "me-too"s.

Third, once a compound is put into development, the tasks needed to develop it can be specified well in advance. While there is uncertainty about the outcome of the project (whether the compound will pass all the tests), there is little uncertainty about what will have to be done to test and develop the compound. This is the case because the regulatory regime prescribes most of what must be done during development. With the tasks being known in advance, it is possible to plan and rationalize the whole development process without worrying that the plans will be upset by some unexpected quirk in the technology or by a change in the marketplace.

The fixed term of patents encouraged Pharmaceuticals management to speed up development. To speed up development, it was necessary to invest more money in each project. But only a fixed amount of money was available. As a result, the number of projects had to be cut so that more money could be invested in the rest.

The high payoff for uniqueness also encouraged Pharmaceuticals management to cut the number of projects and to raise the criteria for funding new projects. Quick development of the few potentially unique compounds was seen as a far better bet than slower development of a mixture of unique and me-too compounds.

Meanwhile, the relatively fixed and predictable nature of the tasks involved in pharmaceutical development facilitated the rationalization of the process. Once the number of projects was cut, Pharmaceuticals management focused on process rationalization. The first step was to carefully identify and specify the tasks to be accomplished. The next was to determine what sequence they needed to be done in. The third was to find the critical path (or paths) and to find ways to shorten it by overlapping tasks or reducing the time needed to perform tasks.

As Pharmaceuticals began overlapping development tasks, the functions had to cooperate far more than in the past. The laboratory functions had to build working relationships so that development work could be coordinated on an ongoing basis. The different laboratory functions had never before needed a common project tracking system, since they had always worked independently. But with the different functions coordinating their work, a common tracking system was needed.

As cross-functional relationships and methods of overlapping tasks were developed within a lead project, Pharmaceuticals management saw a need to replicate the system elsewhere. Tools such as a standard project plan were developed to facilitate replication. In addition, the R&D head began dividing development into large, multi-project teams to facilitate the formation and maintenance of cross-functional working relationships.

To summarize, the earliest reforms tried were essentially budgetary. Pharmaceuticals management terminated many projects, while increasing the budgets of the rest. The next reforms focused on project management. Management and project teams together developed a standard project plan. With the tasks in the plan identified and specified, they began looking for ways to rationalize and speed up the system. This resulted in a great increase in cross-functional work.

Finally, management pushed through a broader-scale organizational re-form in an effort to institutionalize cross-functional working relationships. To reform involved setting up permanent, multi-project teams. This increased efficiency by eliminating the need to build up new cross-functional relationships with each project.

Pharmaceuticals' evolutionary path was not unique. MGE's Lawn & Garden also developed new chemical compounds in an area subject to a large amount of regulation. Some of the reforms which occurred there involved speeding project completion by strengthening project managers and increasing their ability to plan and execute parallel work. In addition, facing more uncertainty about market acceptance of new products, Lawn & Garden management tightened the links between R&D functions, operating units and their customers.

EurAuto was in a very different industry. Because of the complex nature of its product, many different tasks had to be performed to develop a new version of the product. Since the overall architecture of the product was stable, the tasks that had to be performed could be predicted in advance and varied relatively little from one project to the next. As a result, innovation performance improvement efforts at EurAuto focused on rationalizing the system: increasing the amount of parallel work and speeding up the development process.

ConPro also developed products in a regulated environment. The regulations were far less demanding than those in pharmaceuticals. Nonetheless, most development tasks could be foreseen and planned in advance. Already by 1984, ConPro had done much to rationalize its development system. Management had set up a number of specialized, cross-functional teams to push new products through development quickly. Here, even more than at the other sites, innovation was a daily, routinized process involving parallel work by multiple functions.

CONCLUSION

Managers in MGE's four divisions faced a difficult task in the late 1980s and early 1990s. MGE had never previously emphasized new product development. But in the late 1980s it became evident that the firm would have to put more emphasis on product innovation in all areas. The firm's managers began to improve innovation performance by taking small, obvious steps first, such as increasing budgets. After additional reflection and experience, managers were able to make more complex changes, first in project management systems and later in overall business management systems. The state of managers' knowledge, both of their own systems and of alternative systems, was key to these more complex changes.

The task of change was complicated by the fact that not all innovation systems are alike. Each MGE division had to adapt its innovation system to the contingencies inherent in its industry, and to the strategy the division was pursuing in that industry. Managers faced not just the task of learning how to manage innovation overall, but also the more complicated problem of determining what type of innovation system best fit the conditions present in their industry and the strategy they were pursuing in that industry.

The lessons to managers are the following. First, if you want to improve your firm's innovation performance, learn about how innovation is managed, not only in your firm, but in the best firms in your business and in other businesses. Build your knowledge base before attempting any complex reforms like major organizational changes. Use the expertise of consultants and/or experienced managers from more innovative firms when you attempt such changes. Second, if you have trouble getting a change process started, look for simple, obvious, locally controllable ways to begin. Increased budgets and changes in reporting relationships can draw attention to the need to improve innovation performance. Third, pay attention to the fit between your strategy, your industry and your innovation system. If you are pursuing a diversification strategy, the appropriate model is a diversified form, not a pharmaceutical company. If, on the other hand, you are very focused and you mainly want to speed up innovation, then a pharmaceutical company would be a good benchmark.

2

Everyday Innovation/ Everyday Strategy

GERRY JOHNSON, ANNE SIGISMUND HUFF

We argue that traditional ideas about research and development are likely to overlook and/or distort key aspects of "everyday innovation". Yet, local innovativeness is a critical gene pool of new ideas, especially for corporations dependent on innovation for strategic advance. Why and how pockets of innovation develop, how these can be distinguished from less innovative behaviour and locales, how meritorious ideas can be nourished, refined and disseminated to promote the firm's competitive advantage, are questions of interest. Also of concern is the facilitating/dampening effect of local and central management on day to day innovation.

In conceptualizing our ideas about these relatively neglected but important topics we build on (i) the work around "everyday cognition", which describes individuals as reflective, theorising practitioners, (ii) explanations of how the knowledge of individuals contributes to and forms organizational knowledge and (iii) work that looks to individual and organizational emotion for insight into why some parts of organizations are more enthusiastically innovative than others. This chapter brings together these different themes to develop an explanatory model of innovation throughout the organization and we give special attention to its managerial implications because we feel further understanding can not advance without involving those in organizations. This chapter also argues that other issues of strategic importance are rooted in day to day activity and must be examined at a micro level largely unfamiliar to strategy researchers.

Strategic Flexibility: Managing in a Turbulent Environment. Edited by G. Hamel, C.K. Prahalad, H. Thomas and D. O'Neal.
Copyright © 1998 John Wiley & Sons Ltd.

BACKGROUND

There is a convergence of interest between the practical concerns of managers in organizations operating in dynamic international business environments, and an emerging paradox in research in strategic management. Consider, for example, a global corporation operating in fast-changing technology-intensive industry environments faced with the challenges of sustaining innovation to meet expectations of growth. As with other companies operating on a global scale, it also faces the challenges of managing a "transnational" organization that can give simultaneous attention to local flexibility and central coordination (Bartlett and Ghoshal, 1989).

In dealing with these challenges company executives report that innovation often originates from the "periphery" of their organization, through everyday behaviour, rather than being centrally planned or masterminded. Their concerns are that they are not clear how this happens or how it can be cultivated, and they suspect that many potential innovations are not detected, fostered or diffused. "Everyday innovation" has become a major challenge for this corporation. Indeed, it has already dedicated management personnel to considering the issues, and their prior attention informs our thinking on the subject.

A key concern is that natural innovation does not occur in ways that have become familiar in a separate R&D facility; by extension, it also seems logical that insightful management of everyday innovation will differ in significant ways from that taken when innovation is a centralized activity used to keep the organization at the forefront of science. Once everyday innovation is the subject of interest, the corporate centre must be concerned with how it is able to identify diverse sources of innovation across the organization, respond rapidly and constructively to nurture useful innovative ideas, and adapt these to quite different settings. These issues guide the theoretical problems and research questions that are the focus of this chapter.

However, our broader argument is that the challenges of leveraging innovation more widely across the organization are of central strategic importance for all organizations. If the unique complexity of a firm can be more fully harnessed, their processes and products will be harder for other firms to match. This possibility relates everyday innovation to developing literatures on the creation and maintenance of competitive advantage and the processes of strategic development in firms.

THEORETICAL DIMENSIONS

A diversity of theoretical perspectives is necessary to explain problems in the strategic management of innovation. Traditionally the notion of strategic management has been associated with formal planning, centralized control and top-down management; strategy is formulated centrally and implemented "down the line". Much writing has emphasized how top management should manage strategy, or has attempted to analyse the relationship between management decisions and performance, on the assumption that if such relationships can be improved then top managers will be able to make better decisions. Recently these traditional notions of strategic management have been challenged by two schools of research.

Those who have been interested in processes of strategic management have shown that strategies develop in organizations not so much through formal planning orchestrated by top managers, but more through the day to day routine of management better described in terms of social and political behaviour (Mintzberg, Raisinghani & Theoret, 1976; Pettigrew, 1985; Johnson, 1987). Further, managers draw on mental models based on past experience to make sense of complex situations (Duhaime & Schwenk, 1985; Fiol & Huff, 1992; Dutton, 1993). Such explanations are potentially useful in describing organizational responses to technological change and innovation (Henderson & Clark, 1990) but they have made achieving innovation problematic to understand theoretically and practically.

Economists who have attempted to understand how organizations achieve competitive advantage also do not appear to have tools to explain innovation adequately. They have emphasized the need to analyse markets carefully and develop organizational strategy to fit market need, and latterly have shown that successful organizations build strategies on unique resources or assets not easily imitable by other organizations (Collis & Montgomery, 1995). It is becoming clear, however, that some of the most difficult aspects of organizations to imitate are the routines and behaviours lodged in practice and experience (Barney, 1986). This is an uncomfortable finding, first because it is difficult to pin down precisely what experience means; second because experience is difficult to manage in a top-down fashion; and third because routine behaviour and "taken for granted" aspects of organizations can also be inertial forces in firms that jeopardize sustained high performance (Johnson, 1988).

Our concern with the day to day aspects of strategy is also reflected in the experience of transnational corporations. Innovation and the diffusion of innovation in the transnational cannot be explained solely in terms of top-down planning and control but is likely to be dependent upon highly localized, often tacit, behaviour and cooperation among different parts of the organization. The issue of cooperation is, indeed, a key one in managing

FIGURE 2.1   A convergence of concepts in strategic management

transnationals, yet it is difficult to conceptualize and to operationalize. It manifests itself, again, in the everyday behaviour of individuals.

Our argument, in short, is that process/behavioural research and economics/resource based theory pose challenges to the traditional notion of strategy as the province of top management and the product of grand plans. Rather, there is a need to conceive of strategy development as the province of experience, routine everyday behaviour and culture. In this chapter we take the theme of the management of innovation in organizations as a means of bringing together the different topics illustrated in FIGURE 2.1. The firm we describe initially faces the processual problems of managing strategy across the world on the basis of innovation as a core competence. This chapter argues that in order for management to understand how innovative processes can be better managed, there is a need to "unpack" the notion of everyday organizational behaviour within a strategic context. It further argues that there is a body of emerging theory and research that can inform this exercise, but which has yet to be used systematically to do so.

EVERYDAY BEHAVIOUR, KNOWLEDGE AND INNOVATION

If we are to understand how everyday processes of organizational behaviour contribute to innovation, there is a need to begin at the micro-behavioural level. We do so by considering the knowledge of individuals as it takes form in activities, and go on to discuss how such knowledge in practice exists and develops between individuals and in groups. This is summarized in FIGURE 2.2. As the discussion proceeds the chapter also

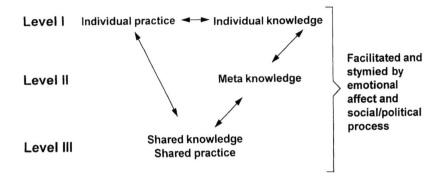

FIGURE 2.2   A descriptive framework of everyday behaviour

considers how behaviour and knowledge at different levels might develop, what the "generative mechanisms" to galvanize this might be, and what behaviours indicate the kind of innovation that might result.

We begin at the individual level by noting that the separation of knowledge and action has been questioned in the management literature (Weick, 1979). Managers have been described from this perspective as theorising in their everyday work, as "reflective practitioners" (Schon, 1983). More broadly we argue that all individuals in the organization might be described as "knowing more than they know" and enacting this knowledge in practice. Their *everyday cognition* is more insightful and powerful than most researchers (or managers) recognize. Consider work on supermarket shoppers who are incapable of doing relatively simple arithmetic in laboratory settings, but exhibit much greater levels of expertise as they shop (Rogoff & Lave, 1984). Their competence is only apparent at the point of execution, and there is a strong structuring effect of highly localized environments. Thus, individuals may be very vague about brand choices and prices at the beginning of a supermarket aisle, but in front of a specific display can recall changes in prices over a long period of time, and are able to describe in detail their reasons for making a specific brand choice.

This kind of knowledge is represented as level I in FIGURE 2.2. Extrapolating from work on everyday cognition, we believe management research on the individual's capacity to innovate must become not just a matter of considering knowledge of practice but knowledge *in* practice. Similarly, we cannot expect to manage the contribution of the individual to innovation by considering what the individual knows, or explains what he or she knows or does; we need to observe what he or she does and therefore knows in practice.

Based on prior work on everyday cognition, and our direct observation in organizations, we expect that there will often be a high degree of assurance and expertise within context. Assured individuals with experience within their contexts are not only competent performers, they are often prepared to indulge in rule bending, playing or even fooling the system. This raises questions about the management of everyday cognition in context, identifying and fostering assurance as a potential precursor to useful innovation, and the acceptance of the notion of games and play (Dandridge, 1986) as important aspects of innovative behaviour.

However, innovation in the organization does not typically take place at the individual level; it is the product of the interaction of individuals both cognitively and in action. Individual localized knowledge is often so context-bound that it is of little organizational use, and there is the potential that the individual will deny or not recognize such knowledge outside of its context. More broadly, organizational knowledge cannot be thought of as just the aggregation of individual knowledge; we also have to explain how the knowledge of many individuals coalesces to form a body of organizational knowledge.

Meta knowledge (Larsen & Christensen, 1993), the second level of FIGURE 2.2, is concerned with knowing what others know. This is not to say that we know all that others know, but that we know something of what they know as it relates to ourselves; that we have relevant understanding of others' knowledge. Daniels, Johnson & de Chernatony (1994) have shown that managers, often working in close relationships, do not hold the same views about who their competitors are. However, they have the facility to recognize their colleagues' logic of who competitors are. Managers similarly may differ in how they see other competitive issues, but we expect they will often have the facility to recognize and understand their colleagues' perceptions and rationales. This meta knowledge may be of an explicit nature, perhaps as a result of formal training, but it is more likely to do with direct experience and observation of others; it may be explicit but it is more likely to be of a tacit nature (Polanyi, 1966), built up through shared experience.

Thus, the existence of meta knowledge is likely to be dependent on the extent of shared discourse and experience. It is likely to be enhanced by a diversity of groups within which individuals have different knowledge but can draw on the knowledge of others. Meta knowledge may facilitate cooperation; it may also lead to competition and more effective political manoeuvring. Meta knowledge may be aided by putting together groups within which individuals have relevant but different experience. It is likely that the time dimension will be important, and unlikely that meta knowledge will emerge rapidly, although crisis or conflict might be effective "pressure cookers".

Level III in FIGURE 2.2 goes beyond meta knowledge. It suggests that if we are to understand innovation as a process in motion throughout organizations, we have to understand how meta knowledge becomes shared knowledge. Nonaka & Takeuchi (1995) call tacit shared knowledge "sympathized knowledge". An important feature of sympathized knowledge is that it is not achieved purely cognitively. Edwards & Middleton (1986) discuss how remembering becomes common through discourse. Seely-Brown & Duguid (1991) and Nonaka & Takeuchi (1995) demonstrate how groups concerned with problem solving and innovation rely heavily on informal socialization processes and discourse in knowledge sharing. Weick & Roberts (1993) show how organizational knowledge is built on heedful interaction. Johnson (1987) shows how shared assumptions of managers are reinforced and supported by a web of cultural artefacts, including organizational routines, rituals, stories and symbols which embed assumptions in social interaction. Taken together, we have a description of how individuals working with other individuals pool their knowledge not only by knowing what others know (meta knowledge) but by paying careful attention to what they do (heedful interaction), and by learning from them at the tacit level through socialization processes. We need to recognize that at level III shared knowledge is inextricably linked to, indeed defined in terms of, shared practice.

The emphasis is on the links between understanding and activity in the creation and maintenance of organizational knowledge. It is to do with interdependence among individuals in knowledge creation. It is likely to be context specific. It is unlikely to come about rapidly. Thus facilitating shared knowledge is likely to be dependent on the extent to which managers can create interdependence, be sensitive to context and allow time for shared understanding to develop. There are questions as to the extent to which the cultural context of such interaction can be managed deliberately to create knowledge sharing as suggested by Nonaka & Takeuchi (1995); these questions can only be answered by micro-level research.

We also need to explain *why* individuals are motivated to work within groups to share knowledge and experience, and, further, why in some settings individuals and groups leverage that knowledge and experience in innovative ways. Nor do we understand enough about why individuals do not share, and at times are motivated to work against the organization. Finding answers, we suggest, involves understanding more about emotion. The idea behind this emerging area of social science research is that our models have been overly rational. Even as attention has moved from rational assumptions to considering the impact of uncertainty, complexity and even chaos, work on social systems in general and management systems more particularly has been curiously inhuman. The understanding of the role of *emotion* (Parkinson, 1996) in relation to cognition (Ortony,

Gerald & Collins, 1988) and with regard to individual and group processes (Rom, 1986) is still in its infancy in management research, but highly relevant to understanding strategy as a micro-process.

Innovation in organizations is carried out by human beings, in interaction with each other and the work environment. The complexities of today's organizational and external environments have their own effects on this interaction. Weick (1995, p. 45) suggests that because individuals in close contact with each other in work situations know less about each other than in some other settings "organizational life generates stronger feelings, both positive and negative than is true of other settings". Considering emotional response as a key part of context is surely necessary to explain why some organizations or parts of organizations are more innovative than others. Presumably innovation would be more evident where excitement, assurance and commitment dominate rather than boredom, fear or concern with the consequences of innovation. Emotion, then, is shown as a factor influencing the previous three levels in FIGURE 2.2.

MODELLING THE OCCURRENCE OF EVERYDAY INNOVATION

Everyday innovation often arises because the formal systems available in the organizational setting cannot cover all contingencies individuals experience on their jobs, or because the individuals using formal systems cannot or will not use them to do so. TABLE 2.1 summarizes the discussion so far and gives examples, at the three levels of behaviour we have been discussing, of innovations of interest to the organization. For example:

Consider the following scenarios, as outlined in the last column of the table:
- A skilled worker begins to take "shortcuts" with standard procedures that do not appreciably affect outcomes.
- When expected resources are not at hand, a self-assured worker invents a needed tool from available materials.
- An employee playfully changes standard procedures.
- A bored worker looks for problems, hopefully devising solutions, but possibly sabotaging the system.

Each of these scenarios, which occur in virtually all organizations, identifies an innovation that might be more broadly useful (or harmful), but in most cases their presence will go unnoticed. When other individuals are aware of such innovations, additional activity may ensue, and these activities are likely to have a longer life span within the organization:

- "Chat" about experiences can lead to the discovery of new ways of doing things, with positive or negative effects.

TABLE 2.1   A model of everyday innovation

Level	Characteristics	Generative conditions and mechanisms	Examples of informal innovation
Everyday standard cognition	Context-specific	Experience	Variation around
	expertise	Assurance	operating procedures
		Play	Adaptation of material at
	"Playing the system"	Boredom	hand when expected
		Anger	resources are not
available			
	"Bending the rules"		Search for novel problems and solutions
	Potential denial		Sabotage
Meta-knowledge	Potentially explicit but reliance on shared discourse and experience	Interaction Training Shared discourse Trust/distrust Time Cooperative diversity	Simplification of standard operating procedures Competitive "one-upmanship" to increase (or retard) process speeds, provide (or shirk) service, etc.
	Facilitates diversity and cooperation		Bending rules as a favour for clients, suppliers, distributors, etc.
Shared procedures knowledge	Where "heedful" a basis of efficiency and effectiveness	Interdependence Heedful interaction Time Trust	Tacit operating Shared, locally devised tools Response to unofficial, unspoken cues
	Context-specific	Share cultural artefacts	Enduring, unique "fixes" for shared problems
	Built up over time		

- In response to shared stories of acceptable outcomes, the standard operating procedures in daily use may become more elaborate or more streamlined.
- When people know what others know, competitive "one-upsmanship" may lead to new outcomes. For example, individuals or groups may work to increase (or retard) process speeds, provide additional services or shirk prescribed standards.
- Boundary spanners who are aware of the knowledge and needs of various stakeholders (clients, suppliers, distributors, etc.) may bend official rules.

At our third level of analysis, when innovation occurs on the basis of shared knowledge rather than mere awareness, everyday innovations are likely to be even more far-reaching. For example:

- When individuals within a work group pool their knowledge, new behaviour operating at a more tacit level can emerge.
- Locally appropriate tools are more likely to be created, shared and passed on to more distant colleagues and/or newcomers.
- The needs of clients and other stakeholders are more likely to be met on the basis of cues that are not formally specified and may not even be verbalized (though in unhealthy organizations subtle cues can also trigger negative behaviours).
- Generalized solutions to problems experienced at multiple points in the local system are likely to be created.

All of these are meant to be merely suggestive, raising important but insufficiently understood issues. The challenge for researchers is to observe such examples of everyday innovation, understand more about the circumstances that lead to their occurrence, and then consider the contextual factors that affect the evaluation, diffusion and life history of innovation. The outcome, we contend, will be a richer inventory of innovation that can expand the capacity of even the most R&D intensive company.

MANAGEMENT CHALLENGES AND A DEVELOPING RESEARCH AGENDA

A particularly important challenge for researchers interested in innovation as it occurs throughout the organization is to explore the challenges this behaviour poses for managers. At the beginning of this chapter we observed that writings on strategic management traditionally have emphasized formalized planning, centralized control and top-down management. Indeed, much of the literature continues to put emphasis on formal systems of data capture, information building, tools of analysis and evaluation, job specification and the like. This work arises within the so-called *mechanistic* view of management.

It should be clear given our discussion above that objective measurement and analysis are not expected to foster everyday innovation in complex organizations (although they may well provide the circumstances that require such innovation). An alternative way of thinking can be found in the growing body of literature on *organizational learning* (Crossan *et al.*, 1994; Nonaka, 1994). This work, which has gained currency in both managerial and academic circles, has developed notions of organizations as open systems built on mutual trust; the organizations described are improvisory in nature (Weick, 1993) with ready exchange of information and less emphasis on formal systems. Descriptions of learning organizations show that they minimize hierarchical structures, devolve authority and often seek outsiders to extend internalized thinking. Managers are less figures of control and more facilitators of context, cooperation, even fun. While the literature in this field remains largely theoretical or descriptive and is only beginning to be specifically related to the context of sustained innovation, it does point to the importance of the frequency and quality of the linkages delineated in TABLE 2.1.

There are of course problems here. Many ways of managing (and teaching about management, accounting, finance etc.) still tend to emphasize formal, mechanistic systems of control. These have attractions, because control has been shown over time to generate positive outcomes in stable situations. Moreover the literature on learning, while attractive, contains little empirical evidence of its effectiveness or indeed its practicability. We argue that before there can be any serious advocacy of such an alternative model of management, there needs to be some serious questioning about its utility.

One approach with both practical and academic significance is to examine linkages and disconnects within the process of knowledge creation, sharing and innovation. This chapter identifies a number of these which appear to be critical in helping to create, expand or alternatively stifle new knowledge and innovation. The researcher *and* the manager are advised to look at:

- what an individual *knows* and what that individual *does* within a quite specific *context*.
- the *frequency, nature* and *quality* of *discourse and shared experience* among individuals.
- the ways in which individuals work together and *cooperate routinely* in ways which require *mutual reliance* on each other's *knowledge and skills*.
- the nature of and extent to which informal *socialization processes* occur within and between related work groups.
- the sources and means of transmitting the *emotional commitment* required to innovate.

At the same time we are also concerned about the long-term impact of managerial interventions on everyday innovation. In every set of innovations the manager identifies (with or without researcher help), there will be some innovations that are judged *not* to serve the best interests of the organization. We are convinced, in fact, that a serious search for everyday innovation will yield far more ideas than the organization can possibly pursue; consider the low yield ratio in formal R&D. Many innovations may not be stable over the range of circumstances likely to be encountered, for example; they may require more skill than the average worker possesses; they may be effective but legally and/or morally suspect. These judgements might reflect undesirable traditionalism on the part of the manager, but there is every reason to assume that many innovations will not be worth fostering. Nonetheless, lack of managerial support for many identified but unpursued innovations will almost certainly affect the willingness and interest of those in the organization to innovate further. The manager risks making necessary and worthwhile immediate decisions but eroding the organization's long term position in the war to gain competitive advantage.

There are equal risks in official attempts to foster innovations that are judged to be of merit. The annals of organization change attempts are littered with case histories of apparent compliance with new initiatives that were never supported by those asked to adopt new behaviours, and never successfully implemented. The conditions that lead to innovation (playfulness at the individual level, for example, or long-term association among a knowledge sharing group at the collective level) cannot be legislated. In a globalizing world that appears to require ongoing adaptiveness and innovation, formalistic adoption procedures are likely to be the kiss of death for a locally promising innovation.

These concerns suggest the need to understand the processes of everyday innovation and the adoption of everyday innovation more fully and intimately. The discussion so far has been largely theoretical. Do our figures explain what is found in practice? There is a need for observational, longitudinal, contextually-specific research. It is most important to pursue such research questions as topics of academic *and* practical interest. We need to bring together researchers interested in everyday innovation as it is embedded in organizational behaviour, with company executives directly involved in exploring such issues themselves. We believe it will be necessary to work together, both in theory building and in the field, to develop a richer understanding of innovation outside of the laboratory. For example, cooperation will be necessary to identify specific exemplar events and locations that merit study and to facilitate the ethnographic methods which the enquiry appears to demand.

We need to join practitioners to ask if the processes of innovation throughout the firm are capable of being managed. How can organizations encourage and develop a set of innovative behaviours within the organization? To what extent do commonly found systems of control such as target setting, budgeting, reward systems and the like have a part to play in innovation throughout the organization, or do they stymie it? TABLE 2.1 suggests that the characteristics, generative conditions and occurrence of innovation have to do with context, with the building of trust, the encouragement of play and the acceptance of the importance of time. Can evidence be gathered to suggest that managers taking one approach or the other better develop innovation as we are defining it? And to what extent could this be culturally specific? For example, are different management styles in relation to innovation more or less appropriate in the West versus the East?

There are also questions related to organizational size and structure. Arguably, the sort of processes described in TABLE 2.1 would be most suited to small, intimate units and less well suited to large complex corporations. The complex organization that initiated this study is dependent on innovation for sustained growth and recognizes the significance of innovation at the periphery. But does the structure of this and other large organizations inevitably militate against such innovation? We need to ask how to shelter, elaborate and disseminate innovative ideas from one site to other, quite different, locales. Again, there are control issues here; we suspect, too, that this is about how to transmit excitement across borders, cultures and organizational boundaries.

CONCLUSION

There are obvious parallels between the issues just raised and other themes developing in the management literature, as was pointed out at the beginning of the chapter. Specifically, the core competencies literature has moved towards a recognition of the importance of tacit knowledge and routines; the strategic change and leadership literature emphasizes symbolic aspects of management; the organizational learning literature emphasizes the importance of linkages within and outside the organization; studies of the transnational management of multinational organizations have highlighted the potential need for a reliance on cooperation, learning and top management coaches.

Thus, there is a need to look not just at everyday innovation, but at the everyday processes underlying every aspect of managing strategy. There is the everyday recognition of opportunities, or missed opportunities. Implementation of strategy certainly happens at the micro level, and so does the everyday slide back to old, less appropriate ways of doing things. Human resources are developed in everyday activities, and everyday activities are the reason human skills lie dormant, or flower outside the organization. As strategy researchers and managers, we have operated too long at a macro level. This chapter is a manifesto to look at day to day patterns of activity across the organization, to consider strategy with a small "s".

REFERENCES

Barney, J.B. (1986). Organisational culture: can it be a source of sustained competitive advantage? *Academy of Management Review*, 11(3), 656–665.

Bartlett, C. & Ghoshal, S. (1989). *Managing Across Borders: The Transnational Corporation.* Cambridge, MA: Harvard Business School Press.

Collis, D.J. & Montgomery, C.A. (1995). Competing on resources: strategy in the 1990s. *Harvard Business Review,* July/August, 118–128.

Crossan, M., Djurefeldt, T., Guatto, T., Lane, H. & White, R.E. (1994). Organisation learning citation search and annotated bibliography, WBS Working paper series no. 94-08R, The University of Western Ontario.

Dandridge, T.C. (1986). Ceremony as an integration of work and play. *Organisation Studies,* **7,** 159–170.

Daniels, K., Johnson, G. & de Chernatony, L. (1994). Differences in managerial cognitions of competition. *British Journal of Management,* **5** (special issue), 21–29.

Duhaime, I.M. & Schwenk, C.R. (1985). Conjectures on cognitive simplification in acquisition and divestment decision making. *Academy of Management Review,* **10**(2), 287–295.

Dutton, J.E. (1993). Interpretations on automatic: a different view of strategic issue diagnosis. *Journal of Management Studies,* **30**(3), 339–357.

Edwards, D. & Middleton, D. (1986). Joint remembering: constructing an account of shared experience through conversational discourse. *Discourse Processes,* **9,** 423–459.

Fiol, C.M. & Huff, A.S. (1992). Maps for managers. *Journal of Management Studies,* **29**(3).

Henderson, R.M. & Clark, K.B. (1990). Architectural innovation: the reconfiguration of existing product technologies and the failure of established firms. *Administrative Science Quarterly,* **35,** 9–30.

Johnson, G. (1987). *Strategic Change and the Management Process.* Oxford: Basil Blackwell.

Johnson, G. (1988). Re-thinking incrementalism. *Strategic Management Journal,* **9,** 75–91.

Larsen Jr, J.R. & Christensen, C. (1993). Groups as problem solving units: toward a new meaning of social cognition. *British Journal of Social Psychology,* **32,** 5–30.

Mintzberg, H., Raisinghani, O. & Theoret, A. (1976). The structure of unstructured decision processes. *Administrative Science Quarterly,* **21,** 246–275.

Nonaka, I. (1994). A dynamic theory of organisational knowledge creation. *Organisation Science,* **5**(1), 14–37.

Nonaka, I. & Takeuchi, H. (1995). *The Knowledge Creating Company.* Oxford: Oxford University Press.

Ortony, A., Gerald, L.C. & Collins, A. (1988). *The Cognitive Structure of Emotions.* Cambridge: Cambridge University Press.

Parkinson, B. (1996). Emotions are social. *British Journal of Psychology,* **87,** 663–683.

Pettigrew, A. (1985). *The Awakening Giant.* Oxford: Basil Blackwell.

Polanyi, M. (1966). *The Tacit Dimension.* London: Routledge and Kegan Paul.

Rogoff, B. & Lave, J. (eds) (1984). *Everyday Cognition: Its Development in Social Context.* Cambridge, MA: Harvard University Press.

Rom, H. (ed.) (1986). *The Social Construction of Emotions,* Oxford: Blackwell.

Schon, D. (1983). *The Reflective Practitioner.* New York: Basic Books.

Seely-Brown, J. & Duguid, P. (1991). Organisational learning and communities of practice: toward a unified view of working, learning and innovation. *Organisation Science,* **2,** 40–57.

Weick, K.E. (1979). *The Social Psychology of Organizing.* Reading, MA: Addison-Wesley.

Weick, K.E. (1993). Organisational redesign as improvisation. In G. Huber &

W. Glick (eds) *Organisational Redesign: Ideas and Insights for Improving Performance.* New York: Oxford University Press.

Weick, K.E. (1995). *Sensemaking in Organisations.* New York: Sage.

Weick, K.E. & Roberts, K.H. (1993). Collective mind in organisations: heedful interrelating on flight decks. *Administrative Science Quarterly,* **38,** 357–381.

3

Cooperative R&D and Competence Building

BERTRAND QUÉLIN, CAROLINE MOTHE

INTRODUCTION

The theory of the firm based on competences emphasizes the internal features of firms, in contrast to Porter's five forces model. This approach developed in parallel with voluminous works devoted to inter-firm cooperation. Certain works bring together the theory based on competences and analyses of cooperation (Teece, 1986; Hamel, 1991).

The topic of this chapter is R&D cooperation, extended as a privileged means to create new resources such as new products, patents and proto- types, as well as scientific and technological competences. The objective of this work is to understand the relations between the outcomes of co- operative R&D and the characteristics of firms involved in the cooperation. In more precise terms, this chapter analyses the type of resources co- developed within a R&D consortium in relation to the characteristics of firms and their involvement, thereby providing an empirical dimension to the resources and competences approach. It contributes to a precise knowledge of resources created during R&D cooperation by testing deter- minants of the creation of these new assets, and, more specifically, those relative to the creation of new products. Finally, it sheds new light upon inter-firm cooperation, a topic that still is not extensively covered in the great amount of literature devoted to this theme.

In the first section, we briefly analyse the major works dedicated to competences, inter-firm cooperation and R&D consortia. Later sections

Strategic Flexibility: Managing in a Turbulent Environment. Edited by G. Hamel, C.K. Prahalad, H. Thomas and D. O'Neal.
Copyright © 1998 John Wiley & Sons Ltd.

focus on the methodology adopted and on the statistical analysis of links between the characteristics of the firms involved and the types of resources created. Special consideration is given to the creation of new products. Finally, a certain number of strategic implications on how to manage cooperation in the R&D domain are highlighted.

COOPERATIVE R&D AND THE CREATION OF RESOURCES

RESOURCE-BASED THEORY AND CORE COMPETENCES

Thanks to the initial contributions by Penrose (1959), Nelson & Winter (1982) and Wernerfelt (1984), then the work of Teece (1986) and Pralahad & Hamel (1990), a theoretical and innovative line of thinking developed a conception of the firm based on resources and competences. These works pay particular attention to the firm's internal competences, and to its capabilities to develop new activities and to enter new markets (Barney, 1986; Dierickx & Cool, 1989; Hamel & Heene, 1994; Sanchez & Heene, 1996; Sanchez, Heene & Thomas, 1996).

Among the resources, core competences distinguish one firm from another and are the source of competitive advantage (Barney, 1991; Leonard-Barton, 1992; Amit & Schoemaker, 1993). Since they are specific, tacit, intangible, accumulated over time, durable and rare, these core competences are difficult to imitate by competitors. Following many researchers (Penrose, 1959; Wernerfelt, 1984; Barney, 1991; Amit & Schoemaker, 1993; Sanchez, Heene & Thomas, 1996), we define resources as assets that are possessed or controlled by the firm, be they tangible (such as machines, processes, capital, etc.) or intangible (such as brand names or technological know-how).

However, the theory of the competences-based firm still has not analysed, except in Nonaka *et al.* (1994), in a sufficiently thorough manner the process of new resource creation. Indeed, either these resources are submitted to a high risk of market failure or they cannot be bought or sold via traditional contracts. Hence, the creation of resources through inter-firm cooperation must be discussed.

INTER-FIRM COOPERATION

The analysis of inter-firm cooperation has already brought about extensive research on motivations, objectives sought and forms adopted (Contractor & Lorange, 1988; Hagedoorn, 1993). Other more specific works concentrated on the longitudinal analysis of American or Japanese R&D consortia (Evan & Olk, 1990). Case studies are available on MCC (Microelectronics and

Computer Technology Corporation), notably by Peck (1986); SEMATECH, created in 1987 and involved in the semiconductor industry in the United States, by Grindley, Mowery & Silverman (1994) and Browning, Beyer & Shelter (1995); and VLSI (Very Large Scale Integration) and the Fifth Generation Computer project by Kurozumi (1992) in Japan.

Numerous authors have developed the argument that firms use cooperation to acquire or to create new resources (Kogut, 1988; Pisano, 1990; Hamel, 1991; Kogut & Zander, 1993; Quélin, 1997). They confirm the need for firms to widen their bases of competences in order to succeed in their development, especially their technological development.

According to these works, inter-firm cooperation possesses three strategic attributes: it is a means to combine tacit or complementary competences (Teece, 1986; Hennart, 1988; Hamel, 1991); it is an organizational tool to acquire or to exchange without irreversible involvement (Pisano, 1990); and it is a choice to create value and to accelerate the adaptation of a firm to its environment (Teece, Pisano & Shuen, 1997).

Although literature on inter-firm cooperation abounds, it is still nonetheless focused principally on the motivations and the determinants of the cooperation. Analysis of the influence of the specific capabilities of each of the partners, the objectives sought and involvement in cooperation for the creation of new resources remain largely unexplored. Likewise, the question of the creation of knowledge, resources and competences is still given little consideration in the literature dedicated to R&D consortia. Yet, in the case of R&D consortia, it is important to understand which types of competences are created in common and to know which organizational form is adapted to the development of which resource or competence.

R&D CONSORTIA AND THE CREATION OF RESOURCES

A consortium is defined as a group of firms, linked by a cooperation agreement, conducting R&D together. It is thus an organized form of innovation activities. An R&D consortium is a specific organizational form that possesses two characteristics:

1. The consortium is not an organization that is completely detached from its parent companies (Osborn & Baughn, 1990).
2. The perimeter of the consortium changes over time: certain members leave and other join (Evan & Olk, 1990).

This cooperative form can be considered as an organizational tool necessary to gain access to resources that are difficult to transfer, that do not have a true market and the strong specificity of which makes their evaluation uncertain (Fusfeld & Haklisch, 1985; Link & Bauer, 1989). Thus, the three principal strategic objectives of R&D consortia are: (i) access to the partners' competences; (ii) creation of new competences and (iii) exploitation of the results of the cooperative process.

The partners of an R&D consortium ally with a view to conducting a certain activity, at the end of which results are obtained, shared and exploited according to modalities generally defined in the cooperative agreement (Ouchi & Bolton, 1988). In this case, not only is there a transfer of competences, but also a true creation of resources and value. This stresses that one of the principal reasons for firms to become involved in cooperation is to learn and to appropriate products from the R&D conducted together (Lyles, 1988; Nonaka, 1994; Nonaka & Takeuchi, 1995; Mothe, 1996).

One of the fundamental questions within an R&D consortium, then, is that of the results of this cooperation. Their evaluation and production are identified as management problems specific to the consortium. Among these outputs are generally cited *technical reports, display of research projects, products, testing of equipment, licensable technology, training programmes and product presentation* (Evan & Olk, 1990, p. 42).

All the same, the organizational dimension specific to cooperative R&D, previously evoked, frequently leads to a certain dissemination of resources and outputs. On the other hand, the members of a consortium expect a certain return on investments through the exploitation of the main results obtained, whether through the perception of being on the leading edge of technology, or, in a more tangible way, through new products or processes, patents or licences. It is therefore interesting to identify the elements linked to the firms themselves and to the R&D consortium that influence the creation of new resources (Khanna, Gulati & Nohria, 1995).

Hypotheses

Strategic Coherence

Numerous works insist upon the strategic importance of cooperations for the firm, particularly in advanced technology environments (Contractor and Lorange, 1988; Hagedoorn, 1993). In this case, becoming involved in common R&D projects requires a high degree of coherence with a firm's strategic objectives: if the project is essential to the firm, certain theoretical recommendations lean towards internalization (Kogut, 1988). It is necessary for the firm to confront its multiple options (Kogut & Zander, 1993) and for the R&D to be sufficiently far back in the value chain for the sharing of costs, and of financial and technical risks to be of interest. The strategic coherence is here considered across two aspects: (i) the importance of the project conducted in the technological strategy of the partner and, (ii) the objective sought from its participation in the consortium.

This leads us to the following hypotheses:

Hypothesis 1a: The more important the consortium project is in the technological strategy of a partner firm, the more significant the creation of resources for that partner.

Hypothesis 1b: The more the objective sought by a firm that becomes involved in a consortium is to increase sales, the more the creation of tangible resources is emphasized over the creation of intangible resources.

Hypothesis 1b': The more the objective sought by a firm that becomes involved in a consortium is to increase its knowledge, the more the creation of intangible resources is emphasized over the creation of tangible resources.

INTERNAL CAPABILITIES

Rosenberg (1976), Teece (1986) then Pisano (1990) emphasized the role of the complementarity of assets in the development of innovations, by demonstrating that this complementarity could justify the development of inter-firm cooperation to gain access to assets held by the partner. Cohen & Levinthal (1989) insisted on the learning capacity of the internally developed R&D, which they associate with the absorptive capacity. Notably, they state that this learning function gives the firm the capacity to identify and exploit the knowledge coming from its environment. These works stress the importance of the ability to choose partners with whom to cooperate well, and also to identify future links to develop between both internally held competences and those of the partners. More precisely, it appears necessary to possess specific competences in order to be an attractive partner in a cooperation. However, these competences are not entirely sufficient for a firm to conduct R&D on its own.

Therefore, we can consider that there is a link between the internal capacities of a firm and the resources that it is capable of creating while conducting R&D within a consortium:

Hypothesis 2a: The more the partner firm possesses assets linked to the development domain of the consortium, the more significant the creation of resources.

Hypothesis 2b: The more the partner firm conducts internal R&D projects linked to the domain of the consortium, the more significant the creation of resources.

INVOLVEMENT IN COOPERATION

The involvement of the firm in technological cooperation seems to be a condition for success. This involvement can be a signal for the establishment of long-term relationships (Osborn & Baughn, 1990). It essentially translates the determination of the consortium member firms to successfully accomplish the research, technical development and/or development of new products or services. The learning and exploitation capabilities of the partner firms vary as a function of their motivation and involvement in the project conducted by the consortium. As Cohen & Levinthal (1990) emphasized, the more significant the quantity of knowledge to assimilate, the stronger the motivation. The respective interest of firms in a R&D consortium can be different. The motivations are not the same depending on whether or not the activity of the consortium is *strategic* for the firm or if it is just one of many options for development.

The involvement can also vary according to the size of the firm. These asymmetric learning capacities were stressed by Doz (1988) in his study of technological partnerships between firms of different sizes. The larger the firm, the more it has the human and financial resources to invest in a consortium—and the means to invest in *non-strategic* projects. In contrast, SMEs intervene particularly in projects that are at the core of their activity and for which the objective of creating resources is important. One can develop the hypothesis that the more the firm is involved, the more it increases its absorption capacity and the higher the potential to create knowledge.

The involvement can thus be evaluated through the energy provided to develop the basis of cooperation in financial terms as well as in terms of managerial responsibilities—which often implies an involvement in terms of human resources—in a consortium.

Hypothesis 3a: The more a partner firm is involved in the organization and management of the R&D consortium, the more significant the creation of resources.

Hypothesis 3b: The more a partner firm is financially involved in the R&D consortium, the more significant the creation of resources.

FREQUENCY OF MEETINGS

The frequency of meetings between the parent firms and the joint ventures is often evoked as a means to create common managerial practices and therefore to accelerate organizational learning (Brown & Duguid, 1991; Inkpen, 1996). By extension, a similar argument can be developed in terms of relations between an R&D consortium's partners, particularly for the project's definition, the tracking of the cooperation's progress, and to confront with the partners' mobility (Grindley, Mowery & Silverman, 1994).

In the case of R&D efforts and technological development projects, individuals need to interact to develop new ideas, identify problems and find solutions to solve them. The intensity of these interactions can contribute to the creation of common knowledge, a common language, and even the sharing of a strategic vision. Hence, it is interesting to test this impact: does the frequency of meetings influence the creation of resources and competences during the cooperation, and the type of competences created? Rather than keeping track of the number of visits to sites, which is a dimension of industrial cooperation, we consider instead the number of meetings dedicated to the preparation, documentation and circulation of information necessary to conducting an R&D project. Since one of the characteristics of these consortia is to divide up the tasks between the different partners, the number of meetings is a good indicator of the need for coordination between them.

Hypothesis 4: The more frequently a partner firm meets with its partners in the consortium, the more significant the creation of resources.

RESOURCES CREATED AND ROLE PLAYED IN THE R&D CONSORTIUM

Contrary to works that are concerned with the dimensions or characteristics of knowledge (Winter, 1987; Zander & Kogut, 1995), we limit our study to the elements of resources and competences that can be observed and described by all the actors in the consortia using a common language.

We thus have a fairly complete spectrum of assets, which can be tangible or intangible, complex or simple, observable or not. For a given firm, a consortium dedicated to technological development can be important; it is therefore useful for the management of these cooperative efforts to know if the role played by a firm influences the type of resources and competences created or if it has an impact on the importance of this creation. We consider this question to be positioned more at the firm level than at the level of the involvement of its corporate management (Hedlund, 1994)—that is, in terms of leadership, of direction, of the consortium and of the involvement in the coordination of the different partners.

Hypothesis 5a: The importance of the resources created by a partner firm depends on its role in the consortium.

Hypothesis 5b: The type of resources created (tangible/intangible) by a partner firm depends on its role in the consortium.

RESEARCH METHODOLOGY

Our research is based on a sample of 317 industrial partners which participated in EUREKA consortia. In terms of methodology, the dependent and independent variables are measured using a questionnaire and are brought into relation with each other through statistical tests, essentially through linear correlation analyses.

The five hypotheses constitute a selective list of explanatory factors of the creation of resources in EUREKA consortia. Indeed, other elements linked to the internal organization of the R&D consortium (such as the specialization of tasks or the type of profit distribution agreement established in the contract) are not taken into account in this study, because access to elements confidential and relevant to industrial secrecy was denied.

SAMPLE OF EUROPEAN EUREKA CONSORTIA

Europe is fertile ground for studying R&D consortia, because many firms in different countries are concerned with the same technological developments. EUREKA was created in 1985, in parallel with other European R&D programmes (such as ESPRIT, RACE, BRITE, etc.) where there is a collaboration of several firms, in order to reinforce research in certain strategic activities in Europe. EUREKA inter-firm cooperative projects, often more practical in nature than other European Union subsidized consortia, receive partial financing from different participating countries. Among the large EUREKA projects, JESSI (semi-conductors) and HDTV (High Definition TeleVision) can be cited.

Twenty-two countries belong to EUREKA as of 1995: the 15 countries of the European Union, and Iceland, Norway, Switzerland, Hungary, Russia, Slovenia and Turkey. Purely national consortia were thus eliminated from the database in the aim of increasing the research's external validity. Likewise, R&D consortia for which there are no complete data were not considered in the sample.

EUREKA projects are not specialized in a specific industry, but operate in nine activity sectors. Furthermore, innovation can be achieved by varying actors in the industry (manufacturers, consumers, suppliers, etc.). The diversity of the activity sectors and of the members of the consortia led us to choose EUREKA. In the consortia studied, the partners choose each other mutually. They become involved in the cooperation on a voluntary and deliberate basis. Firms that are part of EUREKA can receive financial support from each consortium partner's country. The consortium forms are quite varied since the consortia studied cover either the totality of the phases of R&D processes or a specific step (fundamental research, applied research, co-development). The partners are industrial companies, public laboratories or university research centres.

This survey concerns only the results created by partners of finished projects. A total of 200 consortia, or 1260 participants (910 of which were firms), were completed as of 31 October, 1994 (TABLE 3.1). The survey conducted from September 1994 to December 1994 was addressed uniquely

TABLE 3.1   Structure of the final sample in terms of partners

Partners	EUREKA ($n = 1260$) (%)	Questionnaires ($n = 452$) (%)
Total cost (K ECUS)		
< 500	7	8
500–999	8	8
1000–1499	8	8
1500–2499	11	9
2500–4999	21	20
5000–9999	16	18
10 000–60 000	16	18
> 60 000	13	11
Number of partners		
2	5	4
3–5	32	35
6–10	26	24
11–15	13	13
≥ 16	25	24
Number of countries		
2	41	40
3–5	38	40
6–10	12	9
≥ 11	9	11
Start-up date		
Before 1987	23	19
1987	18	17
1988	15	16
1989	20	18
1990	15	18
1991 and after	9	12
EUREKA main area		
Biotechnologies	10	9
Communication	14	15
Energy	5	3
Environment	12	17
Information technologies	16	13
Laser	2	3
Materials	8	8
Robotics	27	28
Transport	6	4

to industrial members of a completed EUREKA consortium. Institutes or research and university laboratories were eliminated from our sample, as their objective is essentially to pursue fundamental research without the intention of exploiting the results commercially. The survey considered the judgements of member firms concerning the resources and competences stemming from the technological collaboration.

DATA AND MEASURES

The data used were obtained through the evaluation of EUREKA projects, conducted by the EUREKA Administration through the SOFRES Polling Institute at the end of 1994. Using the data of the EUREKA/SOFRES questionnaire implied a certain number of methodological constraints, but allowed us to introduce the necessary empirical variables to operational-ize the construct of the resource creation. Data was collected in most of the 22 countries belonging to EUREKA, and 317 usable questionnaires, representing a response rate of 35%, were received.

Dependent Variable

The dependent variable (the creation of resources) was separated, according to the Freeman (1982) and Hall (1993), typologies into:

- tangible results, measured on 10 dimensions: (1) improvement of existing products, (2) new products, (3) improvement of existing processes, (4) new processes, (5) prototypes, (6) patents, (7) licences, (8) norms/standards, (9) doctorates and (10) publications. A binary variable was used in the questionnaire for each item (1 = result attained, 0 = result not attained);
- intangible results, measured by four items: (1) improvement of know-how, (2) increase in scientific knowledge, (3) increase in technical knowledge and (4) increased personnel qualification.

Factor analysis of multiple correspondence on the variables shows that the resources can be described according to two independent groups of variables, denominated here as tangible and intangible.

These measures, developed specifically for this study, are based on previous evaluations of European consortia and on 21 interviews conducted with different R&D project managers in order to validate the questionnaire. The responses concerning the creation of intangible resources were registered on a Likert scale of 5 points, 1 being "unimportant effect" and 5 being "very important effect".

These dimensions thus cover a fairly complete spectrum of different assets associated with technological research and development. They reflect different possible dimensions, such as the tangible or intangible, concrete of non-concrete, or visible or invisible character of these assets.

Independent Variables

The measures of explanatory variables largely stem from existing literature.

Strategic Coherence

The importance of the project in the technological strategy is determined by the question: in the beginning, in terms of your technological strategy, was this project (1) essential, (2) important, or (3) marginal?

The objective pursued by a partner is a nominal variable, coded 1 for the increase of sales, 2 for the increase of knowledge and 3 for other objectives (such as improved image).

Internal Capabilities

The importance of the possession of complementary assets (Teece, 1986) was recognized for the creation of resources, but especially for the exploitation of results produced by technological innovation processes. Possessing—or not possessing—these assets depends largely on the position of the firm in the product's value chain: the more the firm is situated back in the production value chain, the more it has complementary assets, especially commercialization assets. Moreover, the closer the project is to the core activity of the firm, the more likely it is to possess complementary assets, allowing it to exploit and to offer on the market its R&D results. The indicator retained, represented by a binary variable (1: yes; 2: no), is therefore the fact that the firm is linked (or not) to the development of the product/process.

The internal R&D capability of the firm is directly linked to experience, and even to learning through practice. The cumulative character of learning allows us to approach the notion of experience in quantitative terms. Experience—and thus the internal R&D capability—is measured by the existence, within a firm, of research projects in the domain of the consortium, thanks to the question: does (or did) your firm have other research projects directly linked to this one? The codification is 1: yes, 2: no.

Involvement

Buckley & Casson (1988) confirm the importance of certain characteristics concerning the involvement of partners in cooperation. In particular, the involvement of partners will be higher if the result of the cooperation is strategically important, or if the distribution and division of results are seen as equitable by all parties. Thus, it is supposed that (1) the higher the firm's level of participation in an R&D consortium, the more it is involved and (2) its financial involvement also determines its motivation to pursue the project.

The organizational involvement is coded 1 when the firm is the major partner, 2 if it is a partner and 3 in all other cases (especially in the case of subcontracting). In terms of financial involvement, it is defined by the direct cost of the project for the firm (not including subsidies) and is noted 1: less than 200 000 ECUS; 2: between 200 000 and 600 000 ECUS; 3: between 600 000 and 1 500 000 ECUS (1 ECU ≈ $US1.3).

Frequency of Meetings

This variable is defined through the following question: during the project, how many times a year on average did you meet with your partners? Four answers are possible: fewer than twice a year, 3–5 times a year, 6–10 times a year, more than 10 times a year.

Resources and Role in the Consortium

Six main roles, non-exclusive of each other, were identified: (1) ensure the management, (2) undertake the technical development, (3) integrate, (4) test, (5) expertise, (6) advise. Each of these variables were noted either 1: the role was ensured by the firm, or 2: the role was not ensured by the firm.

RESULTS

FREQUENCY OF TANGIBLE AND INTANGIBLE RESULTS

Statistics concerning the creation of resources by members of the 149 consortia that participated in the survey tend to show that the tangible result most frequently obtained is a prototype (produced by 54% of the partners), followed by the improvement of existing products (45%) and by the production of new products (45%). Certain results, such as doctorates, standards and licences, were attained by a small number of firms (less than 10% of the sample). The importance of learning for the participants of a EUREKA consortium is attested by the frequency of intangible results: improvement of technical knowledge (for 77% of the industrial companies), increase of scientific knowledge (58%), improvement of know-how (55%) and increased qualification of the personnel (53%). These numbers can be explained by the fact that most of the firms in the EUREKA consortia concentrate on the applied part of research: the increase in knowledge leads to a similar increase in know-how and consequently in the qualification of the partner firm's personnel in the R&D consortium.

LINEAR CORRELATIONS AND TESTS

The discussion that follows will be based on statistics conducted in order to identify the most determining influences between each independent variable and each type of technological resource created by an R&D consortium. TABLE 3.2 illustrates descriptive statistics and correlations for variables. The strongest correlations ($p = 0$) were found between:

- the objective of increasing sales and (1) the internal capability of the partner firm linked to its participation in the development of the product and (2) the organizational involvement measured by the participation level in the consortium;
- the participation in the development and (1) organizational involvement and (2) the integrating role;
- organizational involvement and the roles of (1) management and (2) integration;
- management and integration roles, which explains the preceding result.

The correlations between dependent and independent variables support some of the hypotheses:

1. The coherence that emerges across the strategic importance of the R&D project tends to favour the creation of resources, except those linked to prototypes, publications and patents. Moreover, the type of resources created (tangible versus intangible) seems to depend on the main objective sought by the partner. As the objective of increasing sales (for 107 partners) is inversely correlated ($-.85$) to the objective of increasing knowledge (for 180 firms), only the first will be retained for further use in the statistical analyses (see TABLES 3.2 and 3.3).
2. Strong internal capabilities lead to the creation of more resources for that partner.
3. Organizational and managerial involvement seem to be more determinant than financial involvement in the creation of resources for that partner.
4. A high frequency of meetings between a firm and its partners in the R&D consortium is favourable to the creation of resources at the firm level.

TABLE 3.2 Correlations between independent variables

Variables[a]	1a	1b	2a	2b	3a	3b	4	5_1	5_2	5_3	5_5
1. Coherence											
a Project	1.0										
b Objective: sales	0.16***	1.0									
2. Capabilities											
a Assets/development	0.13**	0.21***	1.0								
b R&D projects	0.14**	–	–	1.0							
3. Involvement											
a Organizational	–	0.23***	0.26***	0.17***	1.0						
b Financial	0.13*	–	–	–	–	1.0					
4. Frequency of meetings	–	–	–	–	0.11*	–	1.0				
5. Role											
1 Manage	–	0.12*	–	0.12*	0.45***	–	0.16***	1.0			
2 Develop	0.13**	0.12*	–	–	–	0.13*	–	–	1.0		
3 Integrate	0.17***	–	0.25***	–	0.29***	0.16***	–	0.21***	–	1.0	
5 Evaluate	–	–	–0.12*	–	–	–	–	0.18***	0.14**	–	1.0
Mean	1.95	0.34	0.62	0.42	2.35	2.47	2.36	1.65	1.51	1.44	1.55
Standard deviation	0.76	0.48	0.49	0.49	0.58	1.15	0.99	0.48	0.50	0.50	0.50

[a] The objective of increase in knowledge (1b') as well as the roles of testing (5_4) and counselling (5_6) have been removed here.
* $p < 0.05$; ** $p < 0.025$; *** $p < 0.01$.

TABLE 3.3 Results of multiple regression analysis for new products, stepwise method

	Variables	New products
1a	Project important in technological strategy	0.04**
1b	Main objective of partner: increasing sales	0.06**
2a	Assets linked to the development	0.06***
2b	Internal R&D projects conducted by partner	0.06**
3a	Involvement in the organization and management	–
3b	Involvement financial	–
4	Frequency of meetings with partners	0.3***
5_1	Role of partner: manage	–
5_2	Role of partner: develop	–
5_3	Role of partner: integrate	–
5_5	Role of partner: evaluate	–
R^2		0.23
F		13.3***

Column entries are standardized regression coefficients. $n = 317$.
Only the significant variables ($p < 0.05$) appear in the optimized models.
* $p < 0.05$; ** $p < 0.025$; *** $p < 0.01$.

5. The type of role assumed by the firm in the cooperation seems to influence both the quantity and the type of resources created. As the partners responsible for testing or advising in the consortium do not seem to create a significant amount of resources, we eliminate these two roles in successive analyses (see TABLES 3.2 and 3.3).

These results are not surprising: as the partners that ensure the management and the integration are those that create the most resources, they seek to assume these two roles simultaneously. These firms are also the most involved in the consortium, i.e. that tend to be the project leader or main partner, and, most likely, are those that possess the capabilities to participate directly in the project's development. They are therefore capable of increasing future sales. This clarifies the link observed between the sales objective and capability as well as involvement.

MULTIPLE LINEAR REGRESSION FOR NEW PRODUCTS

The principal determinants of the creation of resources having been identified, we now focus our attention on the type of resources considered to be essential to the firm's future: new products (Prahalad & Hamel, 1990). In the regression model for new products, which summarizes the different hypotheses, several precautions were taken in order to reduce the collinearity problems between independent variables. Thus, a preselection of variables was made using the stepwise method.

The results of the linear regression, illustrated in TABLE 3.3, confirm those of the simple correlation tests and are in the expected direction for the hypotheses (that is to say, a positive sign for all the variables). The optimized model for all new products leads to a R^2 of 0.23, which is very satisfying in view of the limited choice of explanatory variables. The principal determinants of the creation of new products by a partner in a EUREKA consortium are thus:

- the internal capability to be linked to the development of the product (Student's t-test = 5.2);
- the frequency of meetings (t = 2.6);
- the main objective of increasing sales (t = 2.5);
- the importance of the project in the firm's strategy (t = 2.4);
- the existence of R&D projects conducted internally in the same domain as that of the consortium (t = 2.3).

DISCUSSION AND IMPLICATIONS FOR MANAGEMENT

The results from these empirical analyses are useful for both scholars and managers of R&D cooperation. They show that the factors favouring the creation of technological resources vary as a function of the type of output sought and of variables linked to the characteristics of partners. This chapter emphasizes the results of the R&D cooperation process, that is to say, the types of resources and competences created, both tangible and intangible. The different types of outputs of R&D consortia will be linked to certain characteristics of the partner firms involved in the collaboration.

The main question revolves around the position that the different types of outputs occupy in an R&D consortium. The basic hypothesis is that certain characteristics of partner firms favour, more than other characteristics, the creation of certain technological outputs.

IMPLICATIONS FOR THE MANAGEMENT OF COOPERATIVE R&D

The analysis shows that the resources created are essentially tangible when the project is central to the partner firm's technological strategy. New products and licences result from the cooperation: this collaboration thus has a direct economic impact on the firm, which can quickly exploit its innovation. The weak level of knowledge and intangible resources created by a partner for which the project is essential can be explained by the fact that, in this case, the objective of the partner is essentially that of direct impact on activity through increasing its sales. When the project is essential, the objective is to increase sales. When the project is marginal in the firm's strategy, its expectation towards the consortium is essentially an increase in knowledge.

One notes that the type of objective sought (Hypothesis 1b) has an impact on the creation of tangible resources, while there is none on intangible resources. New products, improvement of products and licences are results that seem to be most linked to the type of objective pursued. Thus, they are even more present when the objective sought is to increase sales. In contrast, the objective to improve knowledge does not lead to any specific creation of intangible resources. This type of creation seems to be related to the creation of tangible resources.

When a partner firm in a EUREKA consortium is linked to the development of an R&D project, it is likely that the activities of the project undertaken are positioned relatively forward in the value chain and close to the market. The firm is thus directly involved in the exploitation of the results generated by the consortium and normally has the complementary assets necessary to market the prototype developed through the consortium. The improvement and production of new products are accompanied by an increase of technical as well as scientific knowledge. In certain cases, the firm has also applied for patents and has sold licences. Since the firm is directly linked to the development of the product, quick exploitation is possible.

The fact that the partner firm conducts R&D projects (Hypothesis 2b) internally in the same domain as that of the EUREKA consortium attests that it has internal competences in R&D and that there already existed, before the beginning of the consortium, a determination to undertake research on a similar or related activity. It is likely that this (or these) competence(s) of the firm is (are) situated further back in the value chain. It essentially translates the fact that the firm which undertakes parallel or even complementary research creates intangible resources that can be integrated by its R&D team in order to obtain an improvement of scientific and technical knowledge and enhancement of know-how. Moreover, the strong link with norms seems to illustrate that the projects pursued in a EUREKA consortium are also concerned with the definition of standards for a specific industry or technology. All the same, the R&D conducted together is not limited to applied research but also leads to tangible results such as prototypes and new products.

The participation level (organizational involvement) explains some of the types of technological result that can be produced during the period of the R&D cooperation. In general, it can be observed that if a firm initiated the project, it tends to ensure a major role in the organization as well as in the technical accomplishment of the project. A highly involved partner firm would tend to protect innovation through intellectual property rights (patents) and to financially exploit its innovation by selling licences. The firm seems to have in this case a position that is relatively forward in the value chain. To complement, a high frequency of meetings between partners is characteristic of projects positioned back in the value chain, relatively far from the development stage and from the market. Firms need to meet regularly essentially to develop norms, to publish part of the results obtained, to apply for licences and to improve their know-how.

The role played by the firm in the cooperation statistically influences both the quantity and the type of resources created: thus, the management role in the consortium and the technical integration role favour the creation of very diverse results, while technical development results essentially in new products, and the expertise role relates uniquely to technological exploitation. In fact, certain roles are linked: among the firms assuming the management role (project leader or main partner) and those assuming the role of integration, many play both roles simultaneously. Finally, the management of a consortium does not seem to result in an improvement of either product or process, and technical integration does not necessarily lead to the creation of new products.

LIMITATIONS OF THE RESEARCH

This research was faced with a certain number of limits linked in part to the method and the object observed. First, the method leads to the questioning of actors involved in the management of the consortia. There is always a risk that these actors over-evaluate the results of the cooperation and, in certain ways, their own work. Nonetheless, the diversity of the persons questioned and the confidential character of the questionnaire, reinforced by qualitative interviews conducted prior to and after the dissemination of the questionnaire, led to credible results. Furthermore, the variety of firms in the sample, both in terms of their involvement and in terms of size and objectives, offers a supplementary guarantee against such a bias.

Second, the object observed is the type of resources and competences that the firm questioned considers to have recuperated from the R&D collaboration. This type of observation level does not allow us to understand completely the organizational dimension of the consortium. It would have been interesting to analyse the creation of new resources at the level of the consortium itself and to correlate its own results with its organizational form, the characteristics of its members and the period of the collaboration.

Third, we need in-depth analysis to challenge the financial involvement of partners. Indeed, it seems, in contrast with organizational involvement, that the financial involvement of the partner firm (Hypothesis 3b) has little weight on the significance of resources created. The direct cost is, strangely enough, not statistically linked to patents and prototypes. Thus, the more a firm is involved financially, the more it tends to create prototypes and the more it intends to protect the results legally through patents. At the same time, the larger the project is financially, the more it is likely that the time needed to transform the prototype into a new product will be lengthy. It is not certain that the survey can capture the information about whether the work conducted together leads to the need for internal development by one (or several) of the partners previously involved in the consortium.

Fourth, with regard to the frequency of meetings among partners, there could be a link between the type of organization that the consortium assumes (i.e. planning, timing and concrete functioning modes in terms of the frequency of formal meetings planned) and the type of R&D conducted by the consortium. The manner in which exchanges within the cooperation take place should also depend on this type of configuration. Different knowledge transfer mechanisms exist. Among them, meetings are a direct means of exchange (in contrast to more formal and impersonal mechanisms such as written documents, technical summaries, etc.).

Hence, the more the consortium is involved in R&D that is positioned back in the value chain, the more necessary it is to exchange ideas and to find a consensus on subjects that are still obscure. In contrast, the need to meet is not as strong for product development; in fact, in this case, parallel work—or individual work by each partner—preserves the characteristics of each of the end products and facilitates the separate exploitation of results, in so far as they are created separately by the firms of the consortium. These two points go against what one may have thought. A high frequency of meeting between partners does not significantly improve the competences and intangible resources. The utility of personal relations for the creation of intangible resources is not confirmed by the statistical tests. Finally, we need in-depth and complementary work about the governance structure and the organizational dimension to better explain these last three points.

Nevertheless, this research contributes precisely to the analysis of the outcomes of consortia for their members, considered on an individual basis. It facilitates detailed analysis of the types of resources and competences that firms are capable of extracting from an R&D cooperation. It thus sheds new light in a truly innovative manner on the creation of new resources and the management of coopertive R&D projects.

ACKNOWLEDGEMENTS

The authors would like to thank Thanh-Hà Lê for editing. Bertrand Quélin completed the text during his stay as Visiting Research Scholar at the

University of California, W. Haas School of Business at Berkeley. He would like to thank the HEC Foundation and FNEGE for financial support. Special thanks to the NATO Scientific Research Program for granting him a Research Fellowship.

REFERENCES

Amit, R. & Schoemaker, P.J.H. (1993). Strategic assets and organizational rent. *Strategic Management Journal*, **14**, 33–46.

Barney, J. (1986). Strategic factor markets: expectations, luck, and business strategy. *Management Science*, **32**, 1231–1241.

Barney, J. (1991). Firm resources and sustained competitive advantage. *Journal of Management*, **17**, 99–120.

Brown, J.S. & Duguid, P. (1991). Organizational learning and communities-of-practice. *Organization Science*, **2**, 40–57.

Browning, L.D., Beyer, J.M. & Shelter, J.C. (1995). Building cooperation in a competitive industry: SEMATECH and the semiconductor industry. *Academy of Management Journal*, **38**, 113–151.

Buckley, P.J. & Casson, A. (1988). A theory of cooperation in international business. In F.J. Contractor & P. Lorange (eds) *Cooperative Strategies in International Business*. Lexington, MA: Lexington Books, pp. 31–53.

Cohen, W.M. & Levinthal, D.A. (1989). Innovation and learning: the two faces of R&D. *The Economic Journal*, **99**, 569–596.

Cohen, W.M. & Levinthal, D.A. (1990). Absorptive capacity: a new perspective on learning and innovation. *Administrative Science Quarterly*, **35**, 128–152.

Contractor, F.J. & Lorange, P. (eds) (1988). *Cooperative Strategies in International Business*. Lexington, MA: Lexington Books.

Dierickx, I. & Cool, K. (1989). Asset stock accumulation and sustainability of competitive advantage. *Management Science*, **35**, 1505–1514.

Doz, Y.L. (1988). Technology partnerships between larger and smaller firms. *International Studies of Management and Organization*, **17**, 31–57.

Evan, W.M. & Olk, P. (1990). R&D Consortia: a new US organizational form. *Sloan Management Review*, Spring, 37–46.

Freeman, C. (1982). *The Economics of Industrial Innovation*. London: Pinter.

Fusfeld, H.I. & Haklisch, C.S. (1985). Cooperative R&D for competitors. *Harvard Business Review*, November/December, 60–76.

Grindley, P., Mowery, D.C. & Silverman, B. (1994). SEMATECH and collaborative research: lessons in the design of high-technology consortia. *Journal of Policy Analysis and Management*, **13**, 723–758.

Hagedoorn, J. (1993). Understanding the rationale of strategic technology partnering: inter-organizational modes of cooperation and sectoral differences. *Strategic Management Journal*, **14**, 371–385.

Hall, R. (1993). A framework linking intangible resources and capabilities to sustainable competitive advantage. *Strategic Management Journal*, **14**, 607–618.

Hamel, G. (1991). Competition for competence and inter-partner learning within international strategic alliances. *Strategic Management Journal*, **12** (special issue), 83–103.

Hamel, G. & Heene, A. (1994). *Competence-Based Competition*. Chichester: Wiley.

Hedlund, G. (1994). A model of knowledge management and the N-form Corporation. *Strategic Management Journal*, **15** (special issue), 73–90.

Hennart, J.F. (1988). A transaction cost theory of equity joint-ventures. *Strategic Management Journal*, **9**, 361–374.

Inkpen, A.C. (1996). Creating knowledge through collaboration. *California Management Review*, **39**, 123–140.

Khanna, T., Gulati, R. & Nohria, N. (1995). The dynamics of learning alliances: competition, cooperation and relative scope. Presented at the *Strategic Management Society Conference*, Mexico City.

Kogut, B. (1988). Joint ventures: theoretical and empirical perspectives. *Strategic Management Journal*, **9**, 319–322.

Kogut, B. & Zander, U. (1993). Knowledge of the firm and the evolutionary theory of the multinational corporation. *Journal of International Business Studies*, **24**, 625–645.

Kurozumi, T. (1992). Outline of the fifth-generation project and ICOT activities. In D.V. Gibson & R.W. Smilor (eds) *Technology Transfer in Consortia and Strategic Alliances*. Lanham, MD: Rowman and Littlefield, pp. 173–189.

Leonard-Barton, D. (1992). Core capabilities and core rigidities: a paradox in managing new product development. *Strategic Management Journal*, **13**(special issue), 111–125.

Link, A.N. & Bauer, L. (1989). *Cooperative Research in US Manufacturing*. Lexington, MA: Lexington Books.

Lyles, M.A. (1988). Learning among joint venture sophisticated firms. *Management International Review*, **28** (special issue), 85–98.

Mothe, C. (1996). Competition for result appropriation, working paper, Academy of Management Meeting, Cincinatti.

Nelson, R.R. & Winter, S. (1982). *An Evolutionary Theory of Economic Change*. Cambridge, MA: Harvard University Press.

Nonaka, I. (1994). A dynamic theory of organizational knowledge creation. *Organization Science*, **5**, 14–37.

Nonaka, I. & Takeuchi, H. (1995). *The Knowledge-Creating Company: How Japanese Companies Foster Creativity and Innovation for Competitive Advantage*. Oxford: Oxford University Press.

Nonaka, I., Byosiere, Ph., Borucki, C.C. & Konno, N. (1994). Organizational knowledge creation theory: a first comprehensive test. *International Business Review*, **3**, 337–351.

Osborn, R.N. & Baughn, C.C. (1990). Forms of inter-organizational governance for multinational alliances. *Academy of Management Journal*, **33**, 503–519.

Ouchi, W.G. & Bolton, M.K. (1988). The logic of joint research and development. *California Management Review*, **30**, 9–33.

Peck, M.J. (1986). Joint R&D: the case of Microelectronics and Computer Technology Corporation. *Research Policy*, **15**, 219–231.

Penrose, E. (1959). *The Theory of Growth of The Firm*. Oxford: Basil Blackwell.

Pisano, G. (1990). The R&D boundaries of the firm: an empirical analysis. *Administrative Science Quarterly*, **35**, 153–176.

Prahalad, C.K. & Hamel, G. (1990). The core competence of the corporation. *Harvard Business Review*, May/June, 79–91.

Quélin, B. (1997). Appropriability and the creation of new capabilities through strategic alliances. In R. Sanchez & A. Heene (eds) *Strategic Learning and Knowledge Management*. Chichester: Wiley, pp. 139–160.

Rosenberg, N. (1976). *Perspectives on Technology*. Cambridge: Cambridge University Press.

Sanchez, R. & Heene, A. (eds) (1996). *Strategic Learning and Knowledge Management*. Chichester: Wiley.

Sanchez, R., Heene, A. & Thomas, H. (eds) (1996). *Dynamics of Competence-based Competition*. Oxford: Pergamon.

Teece, D.J. (1986). Profiting from technological innovation: implications for integration, collaboration, licensing and public policy. *Research Policy*, **15**, 285–305.

Teece, D.J., Pisano, G. & Shuen, A. (1997). Dynamics capabilities and strategic management. *Strategic Management Journal*, **18**(7), 509–533.

Wernerfelt, B. (1984). A resource-based view of the firm. *Strategic Management Journal*, **5**, 171–180.

Winter, S.G. (1987). Knowledge and competence as strategic assets. In D.J. Teece (ed.) *The Competitive Challenge*. New York: Harper & Row, pp. 159–184.

Zander, U & Kogut, B. (1995). Knowledge and the speed of the transfer and imitation of organizational capabilities: an empirical test. *Organization Science*, **6**, 76–92.

Strategic Trajectories and Patterns of Innovation

J.L. STIMPERT, MICHAEL E. WASSERMAN, MULUMDI JAYARAM

Successful innovation is vital to organizational welfare, yet most firms find the management of innovation to be problematic. Search, risk taking, experimentation, and other activities associated with innovation are costly, and most firms demonstrate a preference for relying on old certainties, while evading the speculative unknown (March, 1991). Yet failure to innovate can also be very costly. Changes in customer demographics, product and service offerings, and technological developments can drastically alter the competitive landscape, and firms that fail to innovate can be left in untenable positions.

Garud & Nayyar (1994) have argued that firms need to develop "transformative capacity," which they define as the ability of organizations to restructure themselves successfully over time. Transformative capacity is thus a very desirable attribute, yet few firms find it easy to respond to changes in their competitive environments. In fact, one of the key paradoxes of organizational life is that despite considerable managerial talent, use of sophisticated forecasting and planning tools, and access to consulting services, firms are often quite slow in responding to changing business conditions (Barr, Stimpert & Huff, 1992).

In attempting to explain this paradox, researchers have suggested that top managers simply fail to notice changes in their business environments (Starbuck & Milliken, 1988). Other studies have demonstrated, however,

Strategic Flexibility: Managing in a Turbulent Environment. Edited by G. Hamel, C.K. Prahalad, H. Thomas and D. O'Neal.
Copyright © 1998 John Wiley & Sons Ltd.

that even when managers are aware of changes, they tend to respond only slowly or only when changes lead to organizational crises (Barr, Stimpert & Huff, 1992). Still other studies have shown that a firm's failure to adapt to changing conditions may result from strategies adopted years or even decades before it experiences calamity (Agenti, 1976; Barr, Stimpert & Huff, 1992; Hall, 1984). Hambrick & D'Aveni (1989) have shown that bankrupt firms experience significantly lower performance levels ten years or more before their eventual failure. Their managers are either unable or unwilling to reverse course, and these firms eventually find themselves on downward spirals from which they cannot escape. These studies suggest that firms can be locked into *trajectories* that exert considerable influence on strategic decision making and determine performance potential.

This chapter develops this concept of trajectory, which we define as the path delineated through a multidimensional competitive space by strategic decision making over time. The concept of trajectory serves as a way to operationalize Mintzberg's dynamic view of strategy as "patterns in streams of decisions" (Mintzberg, 1978). Trajectories therefore allow us to visualize the patterns or logic that emerge from these streams of strategic decision making.

Trajectory is a useful metaphor. It captures both the path-dependent and dynamic qualities of strategic decision making, offering a significant enhancement over the static, "snapshot" models that tend to dominate the business strategy literature. Such a dynamic, path-dependent perspective suggests that firms' trajectories are not only determined by, but also influence, the strategic decisions that ultimately determine performance outcomes.

THE DYNAMICS OF STRATEGIC TRAJECTORIES

A number of questions must be addressed in developing a business strategy framework or theory that embraces a dynamic, path-dependent perspective. We need to know, for example, how firms come to be on a particular trajectory, and how trajectories both influence and are influenced by strategic decision making. As illustrated in FIGURE 4.1, the key forces that shape trajectories are cognitive processes and firms' institutional contexts. We now turn to a discussion of existing theories that support our conceptualization.

COGNITION AND ORGANIZATIONAL LEARNING

An interpretive perspective (Weick, 1979) suggests that managers understand environmental stimuli through the lens of mental models that they

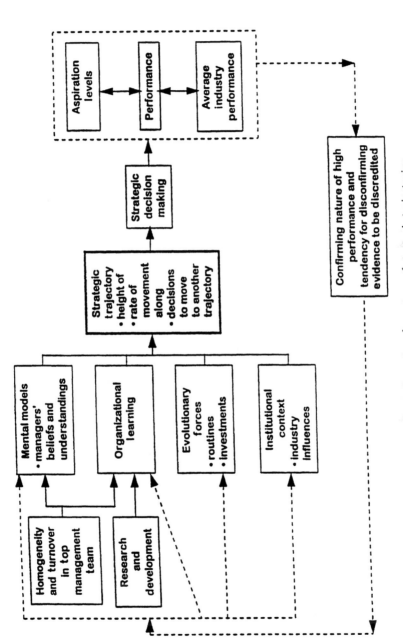

FIGURE 4.1 Factors influencing the nature of strategic trajectories

develop through their past experiences. Environments are therefore enacted as managers' schematic frameworks highlight some stimuli as important while allowing other stimuli to be ignored because they appear less important. Individual schemas also allow managers to "fill in" missing information to create comprehensible patterns (Nisbett & Ross, 1980). Schematic frameworks thus allow managers to make sense of what would otherwise be an overwhelming and bewildering array of stimuli (Daft & Weick, 1984). Managers' mental models also influence decision making by suggesting various policies or strategies that are deemed appropriate given the beliefs or understandings of cause and effect contained in their mental models (Gioia & Chittipeddi, 1991).

Despite the consistency or logic that characterizes the relationship between managerial thinking and organizational strategies, many researchers have noted the tendency for mental models that were used in interpreting and responding to past situations to be reused when new stimuli are encountered (Fiske & Taylor, 1991; Hall, 1984; Prahalad & Bettis, 1986). Kiesler & Sproull have noted that "[m]anagers operate on mental representations ... [that] are likely to be of historical environments rather than of current ones" (1982, p. 557). This observation helps explain why managers often fail to notice, mistakenly define, or poorly evaluate new trends, products, services, technologies, and even competitors (Starbuck & Milliken, 1988).

Managerial cognition therefore provides a theoretical explanation for strategic trajectories that lead to patterns of organizational decision making. Managers' beliefs and understandings of cause and effect influence the strategic decisions through which firm missions are defined, resources are accumulated, certain competencies are built, and patterns of innovation are delineated. Managerial cognition also explains much of the path-dependent nature of strategic trajectories: based on understandings developed in the past, managers make decisions today that will influence organizational effectiveness in the future.

Furthermore, individual mental models or schemas become tightly coupled with organizational routines and standard operating procedures. These routines, in turn, are reinforced by their successful application. Subsequent contracts and capital investments further solidify organizational routines, but also focus managerial attention on events that support these commitments and investments. As a result, even though organizations possess routines for assessing and responding to changes in their environments, they are more likely to trade speed, innovation, and the ability to respond to environmental changes for the reliable reproduction of existing routines and procedures (Nelson & Winter, 1982). Moreover, Nelson and Winter also suggested that routines and procedures push firms along a trajectory so that future technological advancements follow earlier advancements "in a way that appears somewhat 'inevitable' " (1977, pp. 56–57).

Ultimately, an organization's trajectory will influence its ability and willingness to learn, which will, in turn, influence its innovative activity. A key theme in the learning literature is the distinction made between low and higher levels of learning (Fiol & Lyles, 1985). Argyris (1976), for example, defined *single-loop learning* as simple error correction or a process adequate for dealing with routine, repetitive issues. *Double-loop learning*, in contrast, addresses fundamental systemic issues; it is a complex process, which is required for major organizational changes.

Levitt & March (1988) emphasized the importance of learning by doing and suggested that trial and error learning is a major way in which organizations develop routines and procedures that can be refined through subsequent experimentation or single-loop learning. But Levitt & March also identified a dangerous pitfall of learning by doing. Without the search for alternative practices—double-loop learning—organizations can become mired in *competency traps*, in which they find themselves increasingly adept at routines and procedures that are inappropriate given changes in their environments. The outcome is almost certainly suboptimal and may even be pathological. Levinthal & March (1981) have concluded that organizations fall into competency traps because low-level learning both improves performance and also reduces variability. Managers find these characteristics of low-level learning attractive, but reducing variability leads to less creativity, experimentation, and innovation—the very qualities that are required to avoid falling into competency traps.

FACTORS THAT STIMULATE CREATIVITY, INNOVATION, AND HIGHER LEVEL LEARNING IN ORGANIZATIONS

This discussion suggests a dilemma. The creativity and innovation associated with higher level learning, while essential for organizational effectiveness in the long run, are costly and speculative, while lower level learning leads to the refinement of current organizational routines and procedures, therefore offering short-run improvements in performance and reductions in variability. March (1991) concluded that balancing the twin objectives of *exploration*, which leads to new insights, and *exploitation* of existing knowledge is a key strategic consideration facing organizational executives. Research suggests that at least three factors influence how organizations balance the allocation of resources between low- and higher-level learning.

First, Cyert & March (1963) have suggested that higher-level learning is a product of *problemistic search*; in other words, when routine policies or procedures fail to deal effectively with organizational problems or crises, managers initiate search activity that leads to higher-level organizational learning. More recent studies (Cohen & Levinthal, 1990) have emphasized the relationship between aspiration levels and the rate of organizational learning. When organizational performance fails to match high aspiration levels, managers will be more likely to engage in problemistic search activity (Lant & Montgomery, 1987).

Second, March (1991) has modeled the important influence of turnover and workforce heterogeneity on organizational knowledge, and concluded that both contribute to greater organizational knowledge. March argued that the absence of turnover and workforce heterogeneity can lead to a situation in which all of an organization's members become well-versed in its routines and procedures. At some point, an information equilibrium is reached, and without new personnel, ideas for improving or changing organizational processes are not forthcoming and very little new knowledge accumulates.

Finally, Cohen & Levinthal suggested that organizational learning is a function of *absorptive capacity*, which they defined as the ability of firms to "recognize the value of new information, assimilate it, and apply it to commercial ends" (1990, p. 128). Thus, firms with high levels of absorptive capacity have the ability to scan their external environments, recognize the importance of developments such as an emerging technology, and then assimilate that knowledge into the organization.

INSTITUTIONAL INFLUENCES

DiMaggio and Powell (1983) have shown that as managers struggle to deal with various constraints and uncertainties, the structures of their firms' industries provide contexts that encourage imitation. Firms in the same industry develop a common language and similar understandings about how to compete. Executives of firms in the same industries are especially likely to possess a "common body of knowledge" (Hambrick, 1982), which is reinforced by reading the same publications, participating in professional networks and trade associations, and moving across firms. Strategy researchers have also commented on the industry and institutional influences that shape strategy formulation (Huff, 1982; Spender, 1989).

Institutional influences facilitate the emergence of industry standards, which inevitably influence future decisions about the types of technologies to be employed and the rate of technological change. Furthermore, by developing industry standards, these institutional influences also encourage consumer acceptance of products and services, but, again, these forces will later govern the amount and magnitude of change that consumers will come to expect in product or service offerings. Firms that deviate from these industry standards face considerable upside risks, but also significant downside risks. As a result, many firms choose the safer route of incremental changes in product or service offerings.

An organization's institutional context therefore exerts an important influence on its strategic trajectory. The institutional context serves to reinforce patterns of competition within industries because moving to different trajectories will typically require firms to contest industry norms. The institutional context also supports existing trajectories because the identification of and movement toward new trajectories is not a straight-forward process. Mintzberg's (1978) accounts of the struggles of organizations attempting to formulate new strategies that lead to wholesale, global changes in strategies—what we would view as movement to new strategic trajectories—suggest that the process is a painful one, character-ized by periods in which organizations are "groping" or "in flux," without a clear focus. As a result, firms may stay on old trajectories to avoid the uncertainty associated with delineating new trajectories.

FEEDBACK EFFECTS

Strategic decision making and organizational performance can be thought of as outcomes of strategic trajectories. Performance, in turn, provides feed-back that can influence the forces that shape a firm's trajectory, but prior research suggests that the influence of feedback effects will be moderated by a comparison of firm performance with managers' aspiration levels and average industry performance (Cohen & Levinthal, 1990; Lant & Montgomery, 1987). If performance compares favorably with managers' aspiration levels and average industry performance, then few changes in managers' mental models and organizational routines can be expected. Furthermore, organizational learning is likely to remain at a low level, focusing primarily on the exploitation of existing knowledge (March, 1991), and the firm is unlikely to seek to shift to a different strategic trajectory.

On the other hand, if firm performance compares unfavorably, at least two possible responses can be predicted. First, poor performance relative to managers' aspirations or other industry participants can initiate prob-lemistic search (Cyert & March, 1963). Through this searching activity, managers may come to new understandings, the organization may allocate more resources for exploring new developments, higher-level learning can ensue, and the organization can adopt new routines and procedures. Problemistic search can ultimately lead an organization to abandon its old strategic trajectory for a new, more viable, trajectory.

A less optimistic scenario is also plausible. Instead of prompting problemistic search, poor performance can be discounted or attributed to exogenous factors beyond the control of the firm's top managers. Existing beliefs, understandings, routines, and standard operating procedures may go unchanged or may even be reinforced if the poor performance suggests that the firm just needs to "try harder" (Nelson & Winter, 1982). Perhaps even more unsettling is the possibility that poor performance leads to what Senge (1992) calls "eroding goals," in which a failure to meet aspiration levels leads to pressure to lower the goals.

EXPLAINING THE PATTERN OF INNOVATION AMONG US RAILROADS, 1946–1970

The US railroad industry has a rich history that is closely intertwined with the nation's growth and industrial development (Chandler, 1962). Here, we apply the concept of trajectory to understand the decline of railroads in the post-War period from 1946 through 1970. We focus specifically on the pattern of innovation that accompanied and probably facilitated this decline. We will suggest that railroads engaged in active, but only low-level, learning, and that they developed and subsequently refined a set of routines and standard operating procedures that came to define their strategic trajectories during this entire 25-year time frame.

BACKGROUND

Our focus on the 25-year period following the end of World War II through 1970 is deliberate. Railroads emerged from the war as the dominant mode of freight transportation, moving over 66% of all intercity freight. By 1970, the railroads' market share had fallen to less than 40%, while trucks had more than doubled their share to 21%. Also, in 1970, the country was rocked by the collapse of the Penn Central and 13 other northeastern railroads. Following the oil crises of the 1970s, most utilities came to rely on coal for electricity generation, and the subsequent boom in coal traffic has led to a resurgence of the railroads.

At least three environmental changes contributed to the railroads' loss of pre-eminence in the intercity freight transportation market during the 25-year time frame of our study. First, the population and centers of industry shifted from large cities to suburban locations. Suburban factory or warehouse locations are often "off-line," not located along railroad tracks, and thus cannot be served directly by railroads. Second, the construction of the interstate highway system fostered the growth of the trucking industry by providing a national network of high quality roadways that improved the reliability of truck transportation. Finally, the freight service provided by motor carriers proved very attractive to shippers. Motor carrier shipments are typically loaded and then move directly to the receiver. In contrast, most railroad shipments move from the shipper's dock to a yard where they await classification for outbound train movements. These delays mean that rail shipments almost always have slower transit times and typically offer less reliable shipping schedules.

The response of railroad companies to these changes in their business environment certainly illustrates the paradox we described at the outset of this chapter: despite talented managers and vast resources, railroads failed to respond aggressively to the challenges posed by the emergence of motor carriers in the intercity freight transportation market.

Two observers of the railroad industry have placed the blame for decline squarely on managers' mistaken understandings of their competitive environment. Levitt (1960) argued that the major problem was one of market definition. In a now classic article, he suggested that railroad managers suffered from "marketing myopia": they saw themselves as competing in a *railroad industry* when they should have been focusing on the larger *transportation industry*, which was becoming increasingly intermodal and competitive. Wyckoff also implicated managers' beliefs and understandings of their competitive environment. Writing in 1976, he concluded that "[r]ailroad organizations have promoted continued, competitively insulated, 'monopoly thinking' in an increasingly . . . competitive environment" (1976, p. 171).

We will show that railroad managers did hold understandings of cause and effect that contributed to the decline of their companies. In addition, we will show how these beliefs and understandings conspired with institutional forces to place railroads on a suboptimal trajectory.

BELIEFS AND UNDERSTANDINGS OF CAUSALITY HELD BY RAILROAD MANAGERS

Many strategy researchers (Barr, Stimpert & Huff, 1992; Bettman & Weitz, 1983; Hall, 1984) have used Axelrod's (1976) techniques for mapping the causal beliefs found in archival documents to study the relationship between managerial thinking and strategic action. To examine railroad managers' understandings of cause and effect, we examined cognitive maps developed by Barr, Stimpert & Huff (1992), who analyzed the letters to shareholders of two railroad companies over a 25-year time frame that roughly corresponds to the time frame of our study. While a limited sample, the causal beliefs that we found in these cognitive maps are representative of views held by most railroad executives during this time period (Cottrell, 1970; Wyckoff, 1976).

Railroad Marketing Policy

Analysis of the cognitive maps developed by Barr, Stimpert & Huff (1992) reveals that railroad managers focused on two distinct policies (Axelrod, 1976). The first of these was a marketing or revenue policy which showed remarkably little variation over the time frame of our study. The cognitive maps suggest that, from the late 1940s through the late 1950s, managers held a view that revenues were positively influenced by two variables: (i) the ability of railroads to obtain permission from the Interstate Commerce Commission to increase freight rates, and (ii) overall traffic levels, which were largely determined by exogenous factors beyond the control of railroad managers (such as production levels and strikes in the industries served by the railroads, weather conditions, government farm policies, and the Korean War). The causal understandings associated with this marketing policy are illustrated in FIGURE 4.2.

By the late 1950s railroad managers began to develop a new understanding of the impact of freight rate increases. Causal assertions began to change from a view that rate increases raise revenues, toward a view that rate increases were causing an erosion in traffic levels as shippers were responding by diverting more traffic to trucks. This new perspective can be observed in the following passage from one railroad's 1957 letter to shareholders:

> The railroad industry as a whole has been suffering from a persistent erosion of its proportion of the total intercity revenue freight . . . . While there are many contributing causes . . . , not the least of these, in your management's opinion are the many railroad rates fixed at unrealistically high levels and without regard to competition. . . . there is much that we can and should do to retain or regain traffic from trucks and barges by fixing competitive rates . . .

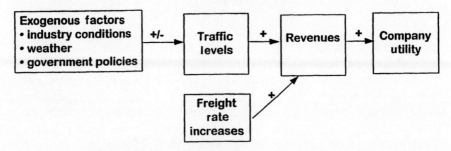

FIGURE 4.2   Railroad marketing policy: managers' understandings and beliefs, 1946 through late 1950s

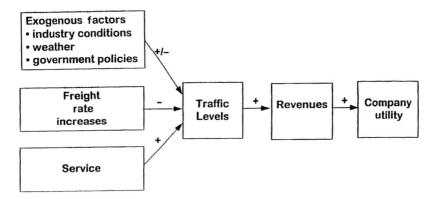

FIGURE 4.3   Railroad marketing policy: managers' understandings and beliefs, late 1950s through 1970

Furthermore, managers continued to see exogenous factors as important influences on traffic levels, but by the late 1950s they also began to assert that service levels were positively related to traffic volume. A map of these revised causal understandings associated with railroad marketing policy is illustrated in FIGURE 4.3.

Railroad Operating Policy

A second policy revealed by our analysis of the cognitive maps developed by Barr, Stimpert & Huff (1992) focused on railroad operating practices. Managers' beliefs and understandings about operating policies appear to have changed even less than the understandings associated with marketing policy. Rising wages, restrictive work rules, and the power of labor unions were associated with a view that labor costs were uncontrollable and that the only way to surmount this problem was to adopt labor saving or productivity enhancing equipment and operating practices. An excerpt from a 1956 letter to shareholders captures the essence of this operating policy:

> ... the basic problem of your railroad is to increase the productivity of all personnel through better supervision and through a high degree of mechanization.

Examples of specific labor substituting practices included dieselization of locomotive fleets, acquisition of higher capacity freight cars, laying heavier rail, and more mechanized track maintenance equipment. Managers believed that these innovations would lead to greater operating productivity and thus enhance company utility.

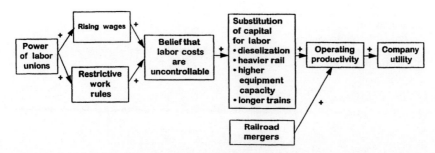

FIGURE 4.4   Railroad operating policy: managers' understandings and beliefs, 1946 through 1970

By 1960, another concept was added to the railroad operating policy. Managers began to see mergers with other railroads as an additional way to improve productivity. Instead of operating parallel, competing lines, railroads could realize economies by consolidating their operations and eliminating redundant services. The causal understandings associated with railroad operating policy from 1946 through 1970 are illustrated in FIGURE 4.4.

ORGANIZATIONAL LEARNING, ROUTINES, AND STANDARD OPERATING PROCEDURES

The adoption of innovations such as diesel locomotives, higher capacity freight cars, heavier rail, and more mechanized track maintenance equipment which began in the 1940s may have been significant enough to have shifted railroads to different and higher strategic trajectories. But after the introduction of these innovations, the next two decades were characterized by low-level learning, in which railroad companies continued to exploit the knowledge that these innovations could improve the efficiency and productivity of their operations. The 1950s and 1960s saw only continued, incremental adoption and diffusion of these productivity enhancing innovations, and few, if any, major innovative concepts, services, or technologies were introduced into the railroad industry.

With the adoption of labor saving innovations, railroads enjoyed considerable improvements in operating productivity. By the late 1950s, the dieselization of railroad locomotive fleets was largely complete. Dieselization allowed several locomotives to be coupled together, permitting railroads to increase the number of cars in each train. Increases in the length of trains corresponded with the rate of dieselization of locomotive fleets. Furthermore, throughout the entire post-War era, average freight car capacity increased, rising from just over 50 tons in 1946 to nearly 70 tons by 1970. Longer trains consisting of higher capacity freight cars caused average tons per train to nearly double, significantly improving the productivity of train crews. As a result, railroad employment fell sharply during the entire 25-year time frame. Railroad employment had long been falling from its peak of over two million employees in 1920. By 1946, railroad employment had already fallen to 1.36 million employees, but with the rapid diffusion and adoption of productivity enhancing innovations, railroad employment fell to a mere 566 000 employees by 1970. These trends are summarized in TABLE 4.1.

The tenacity with which railroads incorporated productivity enhancing innovations into their standard operating procedures is impressive, yet this

TABLE 4.1   The substitution of capital for labor in the railroad industry: some selected statistics, 1946–1970

Year	Diesel as a percentage of all locomotives	Average cars per train	Average freight car capacity (tons)	Average tons per train	Total railroad employees (000s)
1946	10	51.8	51.3	1086	1359
1947	14	52.2	51.5	1131	1352
1948	19	54.5	51.9	1176	1327
1949	27	56.8	52.4	1138	1192
1950	35	58.5	52.6	1225	1220
1951	44	59.0	52.9	1283	1276
1952	55	61.6	53.2	1296	1226
1953	64	63.2	53.5	1301	1206
1954	72	65.0	53.7	1287	1064
1955	79	65.5	53.7	1359	1058
1956	86	67.2	54.0	1422	1043
1957	90	68.6	54.5	1424	985
1958	93	70.1	54.8	1417	841
1959	95	69.0	55.0	1430	816
1960	97	69.6	55.4	1453	781
1961	98	70.4	55.7	1495	716
1962	98	70.5	56.3	1544	700
1963	98	70.3	56.8	1590	680
1964	98	69.7	58.3	1618	665
1965	98	69.6	59.7	1685	640
1966	99	69.3	61.4	1715	631
1967	99	70.5	63.4	1740	610
1968	99	70.1	64.3	1768	591
1969	99	70.0	65.8	1804	578
1970	99	70.0	67.1	1820	566

All data reported in this chapter were obtained from records compiled by the Interstate Commerce Commission.

dogged pursuit of incremental improvements in efficiency did little to slow the dramatic erosion of railroad market share. Railroads' strategic trajectories of the 1950s and 1960s provide what must be a classic illustration of the competency trap phenomenon. While their trajectories suggested strategies that produced major improvements in efficiency and pro- ductivity, these trajectories ultimately proved suboptimal. Railroad managers failed to engage in exploration or higher-level learning, which might have moved their companies to different trajectories. Beyond the incremental, efficiency enhancing innovations that were adopted during the entire time frame of this study, railroad companies probably needed to incorporate far more dramatic innovations that would have made them more viable competitors in the freight transportation market.

INDUSTRY INFLUENCES AND HOMOGENEITY IN RAILROAD MANAGEMENT TEAMS

A number of industry influences also reinforced management beliefs and the strategic trajectory pursued by the railroad companies. The railroad trade organization, the Association of American Railroads, has traditionally been very powerful, providing many services that facilitate the coordination of railroad operations. Because railroad companies are geographically dispersed, shipments may require the coordination of two or even several railroads. The Association of American Railroads establishes and enforces uniform procedures and standards that facilitate the movement of freight across different railroad companies. At the same time, the presence of this powerful industry trade association probably served to prevent or at least retard the adoption of any major innovations in railroad freight services. Because of the need to coordinate the activities of individual railroad companies, the Association would have to obtain the approval of all railroads before permitting any one railroad to introduce new freight equipment or train movement procedures.

Another important characteristic of the institutional context was the almost total absence of outside influences on railroad companies. Perhaps regulation by the Interstate Commerce Commission played a major role in the "monopoly thinking" observed by Wyckoff (1976). Whatever its antecedents, railroads became closed systems and were more or less unaffected by developments in other industries or other outside influences.

Perhaps this closed system is best illustrated by examining the homogeneity of the top management of railroad companies. Wyckoff (1976) analyzed data on railroad employment trends, and reported that during the period from 1885 through 1913, 18.4% of all senior managers in railroad companies had come from other industries. By 1940, however, only about

5% of all senior managers had come to railroad companies from other industries. Wyckoff argued that because of the tendency to promote from within:

> Outside inputs were often ignored and suppressed. Rather than being change seekers, the railroads attempted to accommodate the changing environment by retarding the change or accommodating the new situation with minimum change to the way business was conducted (p. 87).

Wyckoff also concluded that the tendency to promote from within had:

> contributed to an attitude of suspicion of any value or idea that is generated outside the system, and, as in many closed social systems, the belief that insiders are more worthy and trustworthy than outsiders and behavior that rejects anything "not invented here" (p. 99).

FEEDBACK FROM FIRM PERFORMANCE

As many dimensions of railroad performance began to deteriorate during the 1960s, it would seem logical that railroad managers would have been alerted to the inadequacies of their firms' strategic trajectories and engaged in problemistic search that might have resulted in new understandings, higher-level learning, and ultimately movement toward different traject-ories. Yet we noted in our earlier discussion of trajectories that the impact of organizational performance would be moderated by managers' com-parisons of their firm's performance with their aspiration levels and with the performance of other firms in the same industry.

In FIGURE 4.5, we compare average railroad industry return on investment with average return on investment for all manufacturing industries for each year of our study's time frame. This figure vividly illustrates that average railroad industry profitability was very low relative to average performance in other industries. Faced with such a large disparity between the perform-ance of their companies and the performance of firms in other industries, railroad managers may have adopted a sort of fortress mentality. From his observations, Wyckoff (1976) concluded that railroad managers did in fact develop a "defensive attitude" about the condition of their firms and the strategies they pursued. Wyckoff's observations reinforce the view that most railroad managers had low aspiration levels, and he offered little evidence to suggest that railroad managers engaged in problemistic search activities.

In addition to low aspiration levels, railroad managers also probably fell into the habit of discounting unfavorable performance data. Not only do the cognitive maps of railroad managers' beliefs about their companies'

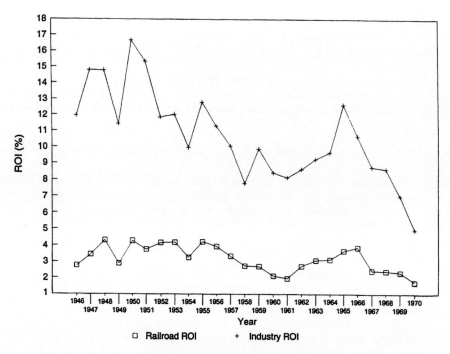

FIGURE 4.5   Average return on investment for all railroads compared with average return on investment for all manufacturing industries, 1946 through 1970

marketing policies suggest that they considered traffic levels to be largely determined by exogenous variables that were beyond their control, but they also had a good deal of positive productivity and efficiency data to offset negative performance data; the adoption of labor saving innovations *was* dramatically improving operating efficiency and productivity, as illustrated in TABLE 4.1.

Furthermore, railroad decline has been *relative* rather than *absolute*. Even as its share of the intercity freight transportation market declined during the 25-year time frame of our study, total railroad freight volume steadily increased. Even though this increase was far below overall increases in industrial production, railroad managers could at least console themselves by noting that their companies were transporting record volumes of freight with increasingly efficient operations. Moreover, in comparing the performance of their railroad with the performance of other railroads, any one company's managers would also observe that *all* railroads were losing market share and suffering relatively low levels of financial performance.

All of these moderating influences prevented low performance from prompting railroad executives to second-guess the appropriateness of their strategic trajectories. Little evidence of problemistic search exists. Railroad managers' beliefs, a low level of organizational learning, refinement of routines and procedures that emphasized productivity, and powerful industry influences (Huff, 1982) resulted in dogged pursuit of nearly identical strategic trajectories that promoted incremental innovations, while failing to suggest more dramatic innovations.

DYSFUNCTIONAL NATURE OF THE RAILROAD TRAJECTORY

While the incremental adoption of labor saving innovations did much to improve the efficiency of railroad operations, our analysis of the evidence suggests that these efficiency and productivity enhancing innovations did little to improve railroad service levels. Shipment transit times, for example, remained relatively unchanged over the entire 25-year time frame of our study. At the same time, competition from trucks—which generally offered not only faster but also more reliable shipping schedules—was intensifying. Furthermore, the move to higher capacity freight cars, which improved railroad efficiency and productivity, may have required shippers to transport lot sizes that were higher than those desired by shippers' traffic managers who were probably focused on controlling inventory carrying costs.

This suggests a fundamental incompatibility between railroad operating and marketing policies. Productivity enhancing policies succeeded in improving the efficiency of railroad operations, but in so doing, railroad service became less and less attractive relative to the service offered by trucks. Consistent with the path-dependent nature of trajectories, this outcome could almost have been predicted. Our analysis of managers' cognitive maps indicates that they held a belief that railroad traffic volume was largely a function of exogenous variables, such as industry activity, the weather, and government policies, which were beyond their control or influence. Even after cognitive maps began to indicate that railroad managers saw a connection between service quality and traffic volume, they continued to hold a view that exogenous factors were the key influence on traffic volume.

Such understandings probably did little to stimulate managers to question their companies' trajectories, even when confronted by declining market share. Unable to interpret correctly the seriousness of disconfirming performance indicators, railroad managers failed to appreciate the extent to which growing competition from trucks was eroding the railroad traffic base. As a result, managers simply failed to respond to the many changes in their environment. Problemistic search or higher-level learning did not occur.

DISCUSSION AND IMPLICATIONS

Hall (1984) likens organizational policy making to origami, in which successive folds in a piece of paper eventually produce a unique object. Origami conveys the dynamic and path-dependent nature that we believe characterizes the strategy formulation and strategic decision making processes. The concept of trajectory which we have introduced and developed in this chapter implies that the decisions an organization makes today are influenced by the decisions made in earlier time periods. Similarly, decisions made today will also have a profound impact on the array of opportunities a firm will face in the future. We believe the concept of trajectory has at least four important implications for academic research and management practice.

TWO DIFFERENT TYPES OF LEARNING

The academic literature has long distinguished between lower and higher level learning, yet academics have probably failed to convey to practising managers the important implications associated with distinguishing between these two types of learning, or perhaps the distinction between the two types of learning is only now becoming too important to ignore. As more and more industry environments take on high velocity characteristics (Eisenhardt, 1989), academics may need to develop the theory and engage in research that will enable them to suggest to practising managers how their firms can institutionalize higher-level learning while also balancing this exploration of the new with the need to exploit the known.

THE PROFOUND IMPACT OF DECISIONS MADE IN AN EARLIER TIME PERIOD

Unlike static conceptualizations of business strategy, we have emphasized the dynamic and path-dependent nature of strategic trajectories. While static conceptualizations of business strategy offer checklists of prescriptions, we have argued that the range of possible alternatives available to managers will be defined by the path of their firms' trajectories. While managers may elect to move their firms to different trajectories, here again the range of possible alternatives will have been shaped by firms' current paths.

Mistaken beliefs or the development of inefficient routines can place firms on suboptimal trajectories, and these firms may find it difficult to recover.

Compare, for example, two competing firms which early on find themselves on different trajectories. Even if the managers of the firm on the higher trajectory falter in subsequent time periods and the managers of the firm on the lower trajectory continue to improve their understanding of the environment and develop better routines and procedures, the firm on the lower trajectory may still never match the performance potential of its rival due to the rival's early advantage.

The path-dependent nature of strategic trajectories may require managers to develop more elaborate scenarios of possible future outcomes. They would then delay major decisions or resource commitments that could substantially influence the shape of their firms' trajectories until they have had opportunities to gain as much insight as possible about future environmental conditions. At the same time, they would have to avoid the tendency of waiting too long and missing opportunities to respond. Quinn (1980) has already suggested that this is one advantage of an incremental approach to strategy formulation, though he did not specifically suggest how firms could develop better scenario planning procedures. An article by Bowman & Hurry (1993) touted the advantages of viewing strategic commitments as financial options. Firms whose managers make a number of more general strategic "bets" are better positioned to respond to changing environmental conditions than firms whose managers focus on a single initiative.

Managers may also need to be more proactive in shaping their industries' futures. Rather than altering strategic trajectories in response to environmental changes, this recommendation would emphasize creative pioneering and blazing of new strategic trajectories through previously unknown portions of the competitive space.

THE IMPORTANCE OF MANAGERIAL HETEROGENEITY

Schneider (1987) has observed that many large organizations are caught in an "attraction–selection–attrition" (A-S-A) cycle that tends to promote homogeneity in managerial thinking. According to Schneider, only certain people are attracted to certain firms. Of those attracted, companies will select, primarily on the basis of "fit," an even more limited group of individuals to join their organizations. Over time, those employees who do not fit well will be more likely to leave. Schneider argues that this A-S-A cycle serves to homogenize the thinking of employees within their respective companies. As a result, those managers who are promoted to top management positions are likely to think very much alike.

As March (1991) has demonstrated, this "thinking alike" can be a serious problem. Without turnover and the introduction of new individuals with diverse perspectives into an organization, its pool of knowledge will fail to keep pace with changes in its business environment. Novices probably do not know as much as experts inside the organization; instead, their value is in the new, and possibly insightful, knowledge that they bring to the organization. Huff (1988) has argued that the knowledge of individuals who do not share the views of the dominant coalition may provide the insights that lead to future success. Certainly the dynamics of Schneider's (1987) A-S-A cycle were at work in the railroad industry.

TECHNIQUES FOR MAPPING MANAGERS' BELIEFS

Finally, if academic researchers could refine cognitive mapping techniques and further develop methodologies for charting strategic trajectories, then these tools could be applied in management practice to help top executives understand both the thinking that may be driving their firms' strategic trajectories and the likely strategic consequences of these trajectories. Managers would thus be equipped with the analytical tools that would allow them to make "real-time" adjustments to their beliefs and under-standings of cause and effect, as well as to evaluate the path of their firms' trajectories (Hall, 1984).

CONCLUSION

This chapter integrates several streams of literature to develop the concept of strategic trajectory. We have suggested that trajectories are the paths delineated by strategic decision making as firms move through a multi-dimensional competitive space over time. We have argued that because of the dynamic, path-dependent nature of trajectories, strategic decisions, including decisions about the assimilation and exploitation of innovations, will be strongly influenced by, and consistent with, firms' strategic traject-ories. Furthermore, we have identified managerial thinking, organizational learning, evolutionary forces, and institutional contexts as important influences on the shape of strategic trajectories, the rate at which firms move along their trajectories, and decisions to move to different trajectories.

We have applied the concept of strategic trajectory to understand the pattern of innovation that accompanied and probably accelerated the decline of railroads following World War II. Applying our trajectory frame-work, we focused on managers' beliefs, observing that managerial thinking emphasized the need to adopt productivity enhancing operating practices. During much of the post-War era, railroad managers also believed that traffic levels were largely a function of exogenous variables such as industry conditions, the weather, and government policies. Only later did managers come to appreciate that traffic volume would also be positively associated with service levels. By then, however, railroad companies were far along on a trajectory that was being shaped by routines and procedures that substituted capital for labor. While producing impressive efficiency gains, these routines probably decreased service levels. Like Hall (1984), we would associate decline with policies that may have been consistent with managerial thinking, but ultimately proved inappropriate.

By emphasizing the dynamic, path-dependent nature of strategic decision making, we are not asking managers or strategy researchers to resign to the teleology of environmental determinism. Rather, we are asking for a greater appreciation of the complexity and interdependency among strategic decisions made in the past, current options, and future positions in the competitive space. This suggests a major research agenda, focusing on the managerial thinking, organizational learning, and procedures that shape firms' trajectories and support the development of their innovation capabilities, which are becoming increasingly important to the development of competitive advantage and long-run organizational viability.

REFERENCES

Agenti, J. (1976). *Corporate Collapse: The Cause and Symptoms.* London: McGraw-Hill.

Argyris, C. (1976). Single-loop and double-loop models in research on decision-making. *Administrative Science Quarterly*, **21**, 363–377.

Axelrod, R. (1976). The cognitive mapping approach to decision making. In R. Axelrod (ed.) *Structure of Decision.* Princeton, NJ: Princeton University Press, pp. 221–250.

Barr, P.S., Stimpert, J.L. & Huff, A.S. (1992). Cognitive change, strategic action, and organizational renewal. *Strategic Management Journal*, **13**(special issue), 15–36.

Bettman, J.R. & Weitz, B.A. (1983). Attributions in the board room: causal reasoning in corporate annual reports. *Administrative Science Quarterly*, **28**, 165–183.

Bowman, E.H. & Hurry, D. (1993). Strategy through the option lens: an integrated view of resource investments and the incremental-choice process. *Academy of Management Review*, **18**, 760–782.

Chandler, A.D. (1962). *Strategy and Structure: Chapters in the History of the Industrial Enterprise.* Cambridge, MA: MIT Press.

Cohen, W.M. & Levinthal, D.A. (1990). Absorptive capacity: a new perspective on learning and innovation. *Administrative Science Quarterly*, **35**, 128–152.

Cottrell, W.F. (1970). *Technological Change and Labor in the Railroad Industry.* Lexington, MA: Lexington Books.

Cyert, R.M. & March, J.G. (1963). *A Behavioral Theory of the Firm.* Englewood Cliffs, NJ: Prentice Hall.

Daft, R. & Weick, K.E. (1984). Toward a model of organizations as interpretive systems. *Academy of Management Review*, **91**, 284–295.

DiMaggio, P.J. & Powell, W.W. (1983). The iron cage revisited: institutional iso-morphism and collective rationality in organizational fields. *American Sociological Review*, **48**, 147–160.

Eisenhardt, K.M. (1989). Making fast strategic decisions in high velocity environments. *Academy of Management Journal*, **32**, 543–576.

Fiol, C.M. & Lyles, M. (1985). Organizational learning. *Academy of Management Review*, **10**, 803–813.

Fiske, S.T. & Taylor, S.E. (1991). Social schemata. In S.T. Fiske & S.E. Taylor (eds) *Social cognition*, 2nd edn. New York: Random House, pp. 139–181.

Garud, R. & Nayyar, P.R. (1994). Transformative capacity: continual structuring by intertemporal technology transfer. *Strategic Management Journal*, **15**, 365–385.

Gioia, D.A. & Chittipeddi, K. (1991). Sensemaking and sensegiving in strategic change initiation. *Strategic Management Journal*, **12**, 433–448.

Hall, R.I. (1984). The natural logic of management policy making: its implications for the survival of an organization. *Management Science*, **30**, 905–927.

Hambrick, D.C. (1982). Environmental scanning and organizational strategy. *Strategic Management Journal*, **3**, 159–174.

Hambrick, D.C. & D'Aveni, R.A. (1989). Large corporate failures as downward spirals. *Administrative Science Quarterly*, **33**, 1–23.

Huff, A.S. (1982). Industry influences on strategy reformulation. *Strategic Management Journal*, **3**, 119–131.

Huff, A.S. (1988). Politics and argument as a means of coping with ambiguity and change. In L.R. Pondy, R.J. Boland, Jr. & H. Thomas (eds) *Mapping Ambiguity and Change*. New York: Wiley, pp. 79–90.

Kiesler, S. & Sproull, L. (1982). Managerial response to changing environments: perspectives on problem sensing from social cognition. *Administrative Science Quarterly*, **27**, 548–570.

Lant, T.K. & Montgomery, D.B. (1987). Learning from strategic success and failure. *Journal of Business Research*, **15**, 503–517.

Levinthal, D.A. & March, J.G. (1981). A model of adaptive organizational search. *Journal of Economic Behaviour and Organization*, **2**, 307–333.

Levitt, T. (1960). Marketing myopia. *Harvard Business Review*, **38**, 45–56.

Levitt, B. & March, J.G. (1988). Organizational learning. *Annual Review of Sociology*, **14**, 319–340.

March, J.G. (1991). Exploration and exploitation in organizational learning. *Organization Science*, **2**, 71–87.

Mintzberg, H. (1978). Patterns in strategy formation. *Management Science*, **24**, 934–948.

Nelson, R.R. & Winter, S.G. (1977). In search of a useful theory of innovations. *Research Policy*, **6**, 36–76.

Nelson, R.R. & Winter, S.G. (1982). *An Evolutionary Theory of Economic Change*. Cambridge, MA: Harvard University Press.

Nisbett, R.E. & Ross, L. (1980). *Human Inference*, Englewood Cliffs, NJ: Prentice Hall.

Prahalad, C.K. & Bettis, R.A. (1986). The dominant logic: a new linkage between diversity and performance. *Strategic Management Journal*, **7**, 485–502.

Quinn, J.B. (1980). *Strategies for Change: Logical Incrementalism*. Homewood, IL: Irwin.

Schneider, B. (1987). The people make the place. *Personnel Psychology*, **40**, 437–453.

Senge, P.M. (1992). *The Fifth Discipline: The Art and Practice of the Learning Organization*. New York: Doubleday/Currency.

Spender, J.-C. (1989). *Industry Recipes: An Enquiry into the Nature and Sources of Managerial Judgement*. Oxford: Basil Blackwell.

Starbuck, W.A. & Milliken, F.J. (1988). Executives' perceptual filters: what they notice and how they make sense. In D.C. Hambrick (ed.) *The Executive Effect: Concepts and Methods for Studying Top Managers*. Greenwich, CT: JAI Press, pp. 35–65.

Weick, K.E. (1979). *The Social Psychology of Organizing*, 2nd edn, New York: Random House.

Wyckoff, D.D. (1976). *Railroad Management*. Lexington, MA: Lexington Books.

Section II

Organization

Jay Lorsch describes the design elements of an organization as "the structure, rewards, and measurement practices intended to direct members' behavior toward the organization's goals, as well as the criteria used to select persons for the organization" (Note on Organization Design, Harvard Business School 476–094, 1975, p. 1) Lorsch suggests that managers have three goals in making organizational design decisions: (i) a permanent setting in which managers can influence individuals to do their particular jobs, (ii) to achieve the pattern of collaborative effort among individual employees that is necessary for organizational success, and (iii) to create a cost-effective organization. These objectives are readily apparent in the chapters in this section.

Kowalczyk and Giusti argue that organizational culture, like strategy, exists at two levels—deliberate and emergent. Using the Organizational Culture Profile to measure cultures at both levels in several divisions at Hewlett-Packard, the authors suggest that while there is a single deliberate culture that does not vary between divisions, there is, in each division, an emergent culture that is not only different than the deliberate strategy, but also different from emergent cultures in other divisions.

Miles, Miles and Snow suggest a theoretical framework to explain the value-creating properties of each of the major organizational forms, extend the economic justification provided for older forms to current forms, and offer a language and approach for the examination of future organizational forms from an integrated economic and behavioral perspective.

Pritsker offers strategic reengineering as a framework for understanding an industry in terms of its processes and value-added chain, utilizing the air transport industry to illustrate.

Thompson and Valley report on a longitudinal study of a large newspaper's attempts to enhance its performance and develop its employees' knowledge by restructuring into teams. The results suggest that productivity is enhanced by task-related interaction within teams, and that product quality is negatively influenced by high turnover within teams.

5

The H-P Way: An Application Using Deliberate and Emergent Corporate Cultures to Analyze Strategic Competitive Advantage

STANLEY J. KOWALCZYK, GEORGE W. GIUSTI

The primary perspective used to examine strategy has been economics. However, competitive advantage is not only position-based, but also capability-based. One capability is corporate culture. This is particularly significant in the case of Hewlett-Packard because the firm is universally recognized for the strength and excellence of its well-defined culture ("The H-P Way"). We accept that there are two types of strategies (deliberate and emergent) and argue that culture also exists at these two levels. Using an established instrument—the Organizational Culture Profile—we measured both cultures in several H-P divisions. The results suggest that there is a single deliberate culture that does not vary between divisions, and, in each division, an emergent culture different than the deliberate. These emergent cultures are also different from one another. We observe that these similarities and differences in culture should not necessarily be discouraged

Strategic Flexibility: Managing in a Turbulent Environment. Edited by G. Hamel, C.K. Prahalad, H. Thomas and D. O'Neal.
Copyright © 1998 John Wiley & Sons Ltd.

and, indeed, may actually be beneficial to an organization seeking to emulate H-P's success.

INTRODUCTION

The literature dealing with strategy suggests that strategy exists at several levels, including deliberate and emergent (Mintzberg, 1978, 1989, 1994a,b; Thompson & Strickland, 1995, 1996; Boyd, Carroll & Dess, 1995). This chapter has three purposes: (i) to argue that there is a link between an organization's culture and its strategy and, like strategy, culture also exists at several levels (including deliberate and emergent), (ii) to empirically test our arguments by assessing culture at these two levels in the Hewlett-Packard Corporation (H-P), and (iii) to offer discussion as to the extent to which an H-P published document called *The H-P Way* represents another level of culture and is consistent or inconsistent with our empirical assessment.

LITERATURE REVIEW

In the 1990s, the primary goal of a firm's strategy will be to match the competitive advantages of its global rivals (Hamel & Prahalad, 1989). Many variations of strategies have been utilized in the corporate environment, including cost control, technological innovation, and the use of physical resources (Porter, 1980). However, such position-based strategies are not the sole route to a competitive advantage (Hamel & Prahalad, 1989; Barney, 1997). Indeed, a more important method may lie in the socially complex capabilities of the organization. This resource-based view of competitive advantage identifies corporate culture as an important component of strategic competitive advantage (Barney, 1991, 1997; Peteraf, 1993; Pfeffer, 1994). Indeed, numerous studies have indicated that culture may even dictate the choice of strategy given a firm's unique characteristics (Barney, 1986; Prahalad & Hamel, 1990; Kotter & Heskett, 1992; Stalk, Evans & Shulman, 1992; Thompson & Strickland, 1995). One such study states that in an "innovative, adhocracy . . . such as Hewlett-Packard (H-P)," a culture-dominating strategy scenario will not only be a possibility but a likelihood (Mintzberg, 1989, pp. 217, 222). The former CEO of H-P, John Young, indicated his agreement with this argument when he stated, "[at] H-P . . . we could proceed with necessary changes in strategies *so long as they reflected* the basic values of the company" (emphasis added; Kotter & Heskett, 1992, p. 65). In fact, if strategy is allowed to dominate, the organization will face a "cultural risk." This "risk" is defined as the gap between strategy and culture. Such a situation will produce a competitive *dis*advantage or, possibly, the misfitting of the culture with the strategy (Schwartz & Davis, 1981; Barney, 1997). Research indicates that H-P's sustained superior performance may be due to its valuable, rare, and imperfectly imitable culture (Barney, 1986; Kotter & Heskett, 1992).

Among the many resources within H-P, culture has been extensively examined. Although there is little empirical evidence, researchers conclude that H-P's culture is strong and well-defined (Mintzberg, 1989; Kotter & Heskett, 1992). In fact, H-P has formalized the culture by publishing the document entitled *The H-P Way*, which specifies values (trust and respect for individuals, focus on a high level of achievement and contribution, conduct business with uncompromising integrity, achieve objectives through teamwork, flexibility and innovation), objectives (profit, customers, fields of interest, growth, our people, management, citizenship), and strategies (management by wandering around, management by objectives, open door policy, total quality control) (Hewlett-Packard, 1989).

Each employee is given a copy of these principles, and management is evaluated upon how specifically the principles are observed and followed (Packard, 1995).

One of the co-founders of the company, David Packard, expressed best how culture dictates strategy at H-P:

> Any organization, any group of people who have worked together for some time, develops a philosophy, a set of values, a series of traditions and customs. These, in total, are unique to the organization. So it is with Hewlett-Packard. We have a set of values—deeply held beliefs that guide us in meeting our objectives, in working with one another, and in dealing with our customers, shareholders, and others. *Our corporate objectives are built upon these values. The objectives serve as a day-to-day guide for decision making.* To help us meet our objectives, we employ (strategies) and practices. It is the combination of these elements—our values, objectives, (strategies) and practices—that forms the HP Way. (emphasis added; Packard, 1995, p. 85)

In examining an organization's strategy formulation process, Mintzberg contends that the process begins with an *intended* strategy (i.e. a strategy established by senior management). This strategy then bifurcates into two subdivisions: an *unrealized* strategy (that portion of the intended not adopted by the organization as a whole—a portion that "disappears" from the organization) and a *deliberate* strategy (the portion of intended that does get instituted by mid-level managers within the organization). In addition, another strategy is joined to the deliberate strategy. This strategy is called *emergent* and is defined as that strategy that was never intended by senior management but "emerges" from non-management employees. Together, the deliberate and emergent strategies constitute the *realized* strategy of the firm (Mintzberg, 1978; Mintzberg & McHugh, 1985; Green, 1988). This process is shown in FIGURE 5.1.

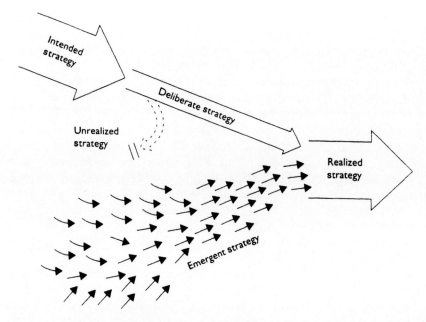

FIGURE 5.1   Strategy formulation process. *Source*: From *The Rise and Fall of Strategic Planning* by Henry Mintzberg. Copyright © 1994 by Henry Mintzberg. Reprinted with permission of The Free Press, a Division of Simon & Schuster

Several studies have proposed a similar path for the emergence of an organization's culture (Allaire & Firsirotu, 1984; Mintzberg & McHugh, 1985; Green, 1988; Meek, 1988; Thompson & Strickland, 1996). Of these different types of culture, we feel the most appropriate for our analysis are deliberate and emergent.

METHODOLOGY

We agree with Mintzberg and argue that H-P's culture is causal to the firm's strategy formulation. We propose that H-P's *intended* culture can be characterized by "The H-P Way" (i.e. the culture established by senior management). The *deliberate* culture becomes that portion of "The H-P Way" actually promulgated by mid-level management. Finally, the *emergent* culture will be that culture perceived by non-management employees. One of our purposes in this chapter is to determine whether there are distinct deliberate and emergent cultures. H-P is a diversified firm, consisting of numerous divisions operating in different geographical markets and manufacturing a wide array of products. Our objective was to determine whether the deliberate and emergent cultures in various divisions were similar to one another.

We focused on four divisions of H-P. Each division operated within a different geographical location and had a different product line. Further, each was faced with different industry demands. Division A produces analytical instrumentation. This represents a mature market and a product line that is quite different from the firm's core product line. The B Division, a manufacturer of computer peripherals, is often cited (internally and externally) as the most innovative operation within H-P and represents a significant portion of H-P's business. Division C is a relatively recent acquisition producing computer workstations. This is a highly competitive segment of the computer industry in which quick time to market is critical. This segment is generally thought to be one of the fastest growing parts of the company. Division D designs, manufactures, and markets electronic test and measurement instruments. It represents the historical core upon which H-P was founded.

To assess the various cultures at H-P, we administered the Organizational Culture Profile (OCP) to 156 employees: 37 mid-level managers and 119 non-managers (by division the breakdown was as follows: Division A—5 mid-level managers and 60 non-managers; Division B—10 mid-level managers and 27 non-managers; Division C—12 mid-level managers and 16 non-managers; Division D—10 mid-level managers and 16 non-managers). The OCP is an instrument based on a Q-sort methodology consisting of 54 value statements (Block, 1978; O'Reilly, Chatman & Caldwell, 1991). The statements describe attributes of the culture of an organization. The OCP is administered by asking the respondents to arrange the value statements into nine distinct categories, ranging from the statements that best describe an organization's culture to those least reflective of the culture. For instance, if a respondent placed the value statement "A willingness to experiment" in category 9 and "Predictability" in category 1, "A willingness to experiment" would score nine points and "Predictability" would score only one point. From this, we would surmise that this employee perceived that the culture emphasized experimentation among the employees, while predictability was not as valued. TABLE 5.1 lists the 54 OCP value statement items.

The outcome of this technique provides a symmetrical distribution, with most of the statements in the middle (or more "neutral" categories) and fewer on either extreme (most characteristic and least characteristic categories). In essence, the test provides a "forced" bell curve in the results.

In order to assess the deliberate culture, the mid-level managers in each division were asked to rank the value statements from the most *desired* characteristics of the firm (high score = 9) to the least desired characteristics (low score = 1) of H-P. An example of the form given to the managers is shown in FIGURE 5.2.

TABLE 5.1   Organizational Culture Profile (OCP) value statements

1.	Flexibility	28.	Action orientation
2.	Adaptability	29.	Taking initiative
3.	Stability	30.	Being reflective
4.	Predictability	31.	Achievement orientation
5.	Being innovative	32.	Being demanding
6.	Quick to use opportunities	33.	Take individual responsibility
7.	Willingness to experiment	34.	High expectations for performance
8.	Risk taking	35.	Opportunities for growth
9.	Being careful	36.	High pay for performance
10.	Autonomy	37.	Security of employment
11.	Being rule oriented	38.	Praise for performance
12.	Being analytical	39.	Low level of conflict
13.	Paying attention to detail	40.	Confronting conflict directly
14.	Being precise	41.	Developing friends at work
15.	Being team oriented	42.	Fitting in
16.	Sharing information	43.	Working in collaboration
17.	Emphasize single culture	44.	Enthusiasm for the job
18.	Being people oriented	45.	Working long hours
19.	Fairness	46.	Not being constrained by rules
20.	Respect of person's rights	47.	Emphasis on quality
21.	Tolerance	48.	Being different from others
22.	Informality	49.	Having a good reputation
23.	Being easy going	50.	Being socially responsible
24.	Being calm	51.	Being results oriented
25.	Being supportive	52.	Having clear guiding philosophy
26.	Being aggressive	53.	Being competitive
27.	Decisiveness	54.	Being highly organized

To ascertain the existence of an emergent culture within each division, a similar form was given to the non-managers. These individuals, however, were asked to rank the *actual* characteristics of H-P's culture. The following summarizes our link between Mintzberg's strategy categories and our study of H-P's culture:

Strategy	Culture	Measurement
Intended	The H-P Way	*The H-P Way* document
Deliberate	Desired	Mid-level managers (OCP)
Emergent	Actual	Non-managers (OCP)
Unrealized	Unrealized	Not measured
Realized	Realized	Not measured

While some researchers prefer to perform an analysis on each of the individual value statements (Hay Group, 1995), we decided a more efficient and robust method would be to perform a factor analysis on the overall data set. In order to be considered statistically rigorous, factor analysis requires

Recently, managers and researchers have noted the importance of corporate cultures. By culture we mean those things that are valued or rewarded within the organization. Important values may be expressed in the form of norms or shared expectations about what's important, how to behave, or what attitudes are appropriate.

We are interested in learning about your current organizational culture. To do this, we ask you to help us generate a profile of those attributes that you view as *most and least desirable* to your work environment. We have provided you with 54 attribute cards, each containing an attribute that might be important in defining your organization's culture. Also provided are 9 category cards, each describing a category ranging from most desirable to most undesirable. We would like you to sort the 54 attribute cards into the 9 categories, placing a specified number of attribute cards into each category. For the results of this test to be valid, it is important to place the exact number of attribute cards called for in each category. See the diagram below taking special note of the number of attribute cards required for each category.

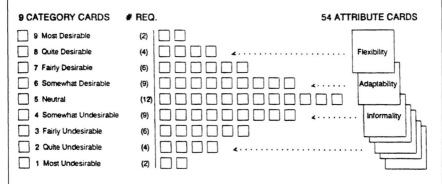

The easiest way to take this test is to first sort the 54 attribute cards into three preliminary stacks – those statements seen as desirable on one side, undesirable on the other, and the remaining attribute cards in the middle. No attention need be paid to the number of cards in each stack at this point. Once this initial sort has been completed, the attribute cards can then be further divided into the proper proportions as indicated on the category cards (as shown in the diagram above).

When you have finished your sort, please complete the information card and carefully stack the cards in the following order:

First, your information card on top, then below it the category 9 card and respective attribute cards, then the category 8 card and respective attribute cards, and so on to the category 1 card and respective attribute cards. Then place two rubber bands securely around the full deck at right angles.

As you begin your sort, please read each attribute card and ask yourself: *How desirable to my organization's culture is this attribute?*

Thank you very much for your cooperation in this study.

FIGURE 5.2   Organizational Culture Profile (OCP)

at least twice as large a sample as the number of value statements (in our case this would be $2 \times 54 = 108$, versus the 156 total we achieved) and a "loading" factor of preferably 0.5 or greater within the actual program (Harman, 1967; Chinese Culture Connection, 1987; Hair *et al.*, 1992). A factor analysis with varimax rotation identified interrelationships among the 54 value statements, and seven distinct factors were generated. Based on the groupings of the individual value statements, we chose names for each factor that reflect the overriding content of the grouping. For example, three value statements that grouped together were "Fairness," "Respect of person's rights," and "Being people oriented." We felt that "fairness" was an appropriate term to describe this grouping. The seven factors were used as dimensions to describe the culture at H-P. This procedure reduced and summarized the 54 variables without losing any valuable information, thus allowing for an accurate interpretation of the data set. A listing of these seven factors is shown in TABLE 5.2.

TABLE 5.2   H-P generated factors

Factor	Title	OCP item	Loading	% of variance explained
1	Carefulness	Being careful	0.70	13.4
		Being calm	0.69	
		Being precise	0.63	
		Fitting in	0.59	
		Taking initiative	−0.52	
		Being innovative	−0.53	
2	Flexibility	Flexible	0.73	8.8
		Adaptability	0.70	
		Being highly organized	−0.54	
		Willingness to experiment	0.51	
3	Fairness	Fairness	0.82	6.1
		Respect of person's rights	0.75	
		Being people oriented	0.52	
4	Clear philosophy	Having a clear guiding philosophy	0.73	5.4
		Working long hours	−0.59	
		Being demanding	−0.52	
5	Informality	Informal	0.85	4.0
		Being easy-going	0.58	
		High expectations for performance	−0.57	
6	Citizenship	Being socially responsible	0.58	3.8
		Emphasize single culture	0.54	
		Being innovative	−0.53	
7	Collaboration	Being competitive	−0.68	3.6
		Working in collaboration	0.62	
		Sharing information	0.59	

In order to demonstrate the methodology of calculating a division's cultural score, we present below a step-by-step example of how one dimension (Fairness) was calculated for one division:

- Step 1: Each of the five managers in Division A was given a score by averaging their response to the three value statements "Fairness," "Respect of person's rights," and "Being people oriented."
- Step 2: The five scores from step 1 were then averaged and this number represents Division A's deliberate culture on the Fairness dimension.

To evaluate the differences between the deliberate and the emergent culture within each of the four divisions for the seven factors, we employed a *t*-test method to determine any significant difference at the 95% level.

The deliberate versus deliberate and emergent versus emergent cultures among the divisions were tested using the Analysis of Variance (ANOVA), once again at the 95% level of significance.

We used a more qualitative technique to assess how the intended culture ("The H-P Way") compares to the deliberate culture. We did this by judgmentally comparing the values from *The H-P Way* document to the factors generated by our study.

RESULTS

DELIBERATE VERSUS EMERGENT

Our first examination consisted of comparing the *t*-test data to determine if there was a significant difference between the deliberate and emergent cultures among the divisions by factor (TABLE 5.3).

We can see that (in each division and on each dimension), there is an overall statistically significant difference at the 95% level between the deliberate and emergent. This indicates that non-management employees are generally perceiving a different culture actually existing at H-P than managers are trying to establish. This suggests that the deliberate culture is distinct from the emergent culture in each of these divisions.

DELIBERATE VERSUS DELIBERATE

Next, ANOVA was utilized to determine whether the deliberate cultures were the same among the divisions. TABLE 5.3 also shows the results of these

TABLE 5.3   *t*-test and ANOVA results

(a)   Sample size

Division	Mid-level managers	Non-managers	Total
A	5	60	65
B	10	27	37
C	12	16	28
D	10	16	26
Grand total	37	119	156

(b)   *t*-test

Division	1	2	3	4	5	6	7
A	SIG	SIG	SIG	SIG	SIG	SIG	SIG
B	SIG	N.S.	SIG	N.S.	SIG	SIG	N.S.
C	SIG	SIG	SIG	SIG	SIG	N.S.	N.S.
D	SIG	N.S.	SIG	SIG	N.S.	N.S.	SIG

(c)   ANOVA

Division	1	2	3	4	5	6	7
I. Deliberate							
A	3.51	6.16	6.37	6.75	4.14	3.90	5.50
B	3.33	6.38	6.83	6.33	4.47	3.77	5.43
C	3.51	6.04	6.19	6.31	3.72	3.69	5.47
D	3.73	6.10	6.13	7.57	4.23	4.20	5.60
Average	3.52	6.17	6.38	6.74	4.14	3.89	5.50
F	N.S.	N.S.	N.S.	N.S.	N.S.	N.S.	N.S.
II. Emergent							
A	5.11	5.25	5.33	4.97	5.26	4.66	4.72
B	4.49	5.95	5.80	5.85	4.85	4.27	5.35
C	4.82	4.97	5.10	4.40	4.50	4.63	5.06
D	4.86	5.45	5.58	5.94	4.42	4.44	4.54
Average	4.82	5.41	5.45	5.29	4.76	4.50	4.92
F	SIG	SIG	N.S.	SIG	SIG	N.S.	N.S.

SIG, statistically significant difference; N.S., no statistically significant difference.

computations. As can be seen, ANOVA results indicate that there is indeed a single, deliberate culture that does not vary between divisions (the *F* statistic does not show a statistically significant difference at the 95% level). This allows us to conclude that the deliberate culture in the four divisions are similar.

EMERGENT VERSUS EMERGENT

We also utilized ANOVA to determine whether the emergent cultures were the same among the divisions. TABLE 5.3 shows that four of the seven factors do show a statistically significant difference at the 95% level. This means that some or all of the following four factors are not as important in one division as they may be in another: carefulness, flexibility, clear philosophy, and informality. This finding allows us to conclude that the emergent cultures do show differences among themselves.

INTENDED VERSUS DELIBERATE

Our last examination of the H-P data was done to determine if there is a difference between the intended culture (as detailed in the document entitled *The H-P Way*) and the deliberate ("desired") culture. As mentioned previously, this analysis is qualitative. Because we did not administer the OCP to the most senior executives at H-P, we elected to use *The H-P Way* document as an indicator of the intended culture. We feel that our intuitive process (though obviously limited) is a good starting point for further research. Listed below is our suggested relationship between "The H-P Way" values and the seven H-P generated factors.

Factors	"H-P Way" value
1 Carefulness	Focus on achievement and contribution
2 Flexibility	Flexibility and innovation
3 Fairness	Trust and respect for individuals
4 Clear philosophy	The entire "H-P Way"
6 Citizenship	Conduct business with integrity
7 Collaboration	Achieve objectives through teamwork

Only factor 5 (informality) does not have a clear association with any of the "H-P Way" values. However, as David Packard discusses in his book, this is another important characteristic of H-P (Packard, 1995, p. 159).

In summary, the H-P generated factors appear to bear a resemblance to the "H-P Way" as outlined in the company document.

DISCUSSION AND CONCLUSION

We have argued that because of the strength and quality of the culture at H-P, culture dictates strategy. We further proposed that, like strategy, culture exists at different levels in an organization—intended, deliberate, and emergent. In each of the four divisions, there were significant deviations between the deliberate and emergent cultures. Our results confirm a consistency in the formal (deliberate) culture as represented by managers in four divisions, and that this deliberate culture does seem to reflect the intended culture of "The H-P Way"—a phrase which suggests an organization characterized by a formal articulation (and socialization process) of its philosophy and culture. In addition, there were significant differences between the emergent cultures of the divisions.

We noted that each division operates in a different industry. One school of thought proposes several expectations about a company operating in multiple industry environments. Such a firm would either develop strong and different subcultures (rather than a single, dominant culture) or perform poorly in those industries where the cultures are not aligned with industry demands (Gordon, 1985, 1991; Gordon & DiTomaso, 1992; Kowalczyk, 1996). Because H-P has generally been acknowledged as having had outstanding economic performance throughout the past few decades, our study concludes that the firm has allowed emergent cultures to develop that are appropriate to the industries within which the divisions operate (Barney, 1986; Mintzberg, 1989; Kotter & Heskett, 1992; Collins & Porras, 1994).

Although this study provided a substantial amount of rich and valuable data, which has led to several potentially revealing insights, it is bounded by the fact that it is a study of only one organization. Further, while recognizing that some factor analysis procedures do allow a sample size as small as ours (i.e. 2 × the number of variables), other procedures recommend 5–10 × the number of variables. Since H-P does display such a unique and ubiquitous culture (in addition to having a long record of successful economic performance), this study may be a useful starting point in providing a framework for the study of other high performance companies.

In conclusion, because achieving competitive advantage is at least partially capability based, it is important to extend the study of strategy to critical capabilities and resources such as culture. We have argued that at H-P culture drives strategy. Our results suggest that culture exists at the deliberate and emergent levels (as does strategy) and, at H-P, the cultures fit the industry requirements. We have also qualitatively examined a document outlining "The H-P Way" and we conclude that it is consistent with our empirical findings.

These findings can prove quite revealing to a company hoping to emulate H-P's success. It appears that when senior managers make a conscious and determined effort not only to establish but actually to instill what they hope to be the dominant culture, such culture does indeed initially take root within the next level of the organization (i.e. mid-level management).

However, as this intended culture is further disseminated by mid-level managers to the non-management level, numerous factors can act upon it to significantly change it from the initial creation. Senior management needs to be aware that such a change may actually be to the benefit of the organization and that organization's competitive advantage. This culture differential should not necessarily be dissuaded nor otherwise discouraged without further study and analysis by the organization. Indeed, it might be concluded that such a cultural difference should actually be *encouraged* within an innovative organization.

REFERENCES

Allaire, Y. & Firsirotu, M.E. (1984). Theories of organizational culture. *Organization Studies*, **5**(3), 193–226.

Barney, J.B. (1986). Organizational culture: can it be a source of sustained competitive advantage? *Academy of Management Review*, **11**(3), 656–665.

Barney, J.B. (1991). Firm resources and sustained competitive advantage. *Journal of Management*, **17**(1), 99–120.

Barney, J.B. (1997). *Gaining and Sustaining Competitive Advantage*. Reading, MA: Addison-Wesley.

Block, J. (1978). *The Q-Sort Method in Personality Assessment and Psychiatric Research*. Palo Alto, CA: Consulting Psychologist Press.

Boyd, B.K., Carroll, W.O. & Dess, G.G. (1995). Determining the strategic value of firm reputation: a resource-based view. Presented at the 15th Annual Conference of the Strategic Management Society, Mexico City, 15–18 October 1995.

Chinese Culture Connection (1987). Chinese values and the search for culture-free dimensions of culture. *Journal of Cross-Cultural Psychology*, **18**(2), 143–164.

Collins, J. & Porras, J. (1994). *Built to Last*. New York: HarperBusiness.

Gordon, G.G. (1985). The relationship of corporate culture to industry sector and corporate performance. In R.H. Kilmann, M.J. Saxton, R. Serpa & Associates (eds) *Gaining Control of the Corporate Culture*. San Francisco, CA: Jossey-Bass, pp. 103–125.

Gordon, G.G. (1991). Industry determinants of organizational culture. *Academy of Management Review*, **16**, 396–415.

Gordon, G.G. & DiTomaso, N. (1992). Predicting corporate performance from organizational culture. *Journal of Management Studies*, **29**(6): 783–798.

Green, S. (1988). Strategy, organizational culture and symbolism. *Long Range Planning*, **21**(4), 121–129.

Hair, J.F., Anderson, R.E., Tatham, R.L. & Black, W.C. (1992). *Multivariate Data Analysis with Readings*. New York: Macmillan.

Hamel, G. & Prahalad, C.K. (1989). Strategic intent. *Harvard Business Review*, **67**(3), 63–76.

Harman, H.H. (1967). *Modern Factor Analysis*. Chicago, IL: University of Chicago Press.

Hay Group (1995). *Targeted Culture Modeling: An Innovative Approach to Reengineering Your Work Culture*. Jersey City, NJ: The Hay Group.

Hewlett-Packard (1989). *The H-P Way*. Palo Alto, CA: Hewlett-Packard.

Kotter, J.P. & Heskett, J.L. (1992). *Corporate Culture and Performance*. New York: Free Press.

Kowalczyk, S. (1996). An exploratory study of the relationship between perceived environmental dynamism and organizational culture, presented at the Western Academy of Management Meeting, Banff, Alberta, Canada, March 1996.

Meek, V.L. (1988). Organizational culture: origins and weaknesses. *Organization Studies*, **9**(4), 453–473.

Mintzberg, H. (1975). The manager's job: folklore and fact. *Harvard Business Review*, **53**(4), 49–61.

Mintzberg, H. (1978). Patterns in strategy formation. *Management Science*, **24**(9), 934–948.

Mintzberg, H. (1989). *Mintzberg on Management*. New York: Free Press.

Mintzberg, H. (1994a). The fall and rise of strategic planning. *Harvard Business Review*, **72**(1), 107–114.

Mintzberg, H. (1994b). *The Rise and Fall of Strategic Planning*. New York: Free Press.

Mintzberg, H. & McHugh, A. (1985). Strategy formation in an adhocracy. *Administrative Science Quarterly*, June, 160–197.

O'Reilly, C.A. III, Chatman, J.A. & Caldwell, D.F. (1991). People and organizational culture: a Q-sort approach to assessing person–organization fit. *Academy of Management Journal*, **341**, 487–516.

Packard, D. (1995). *The H-P Way*. New York: HarperBusiness.

Peteraf, M.A. (1993). The cornerstones of competitive advantage: a resource-based view. *Strategic Management Journal*, **14**, 179–191.

Pfeffer, J. (1994). *Competitive Advantage through People*. Cambridge, MA: Harvard Business School Press.

Porter, M.E. (1980). *Competitive Strategy: Techniques for Analyzing Industries and Competitors*. New York: Free Press.

Prahalad, C.K. & Hamel, G. (1990). The core competence of the corporation. *Harvard Business Review*, **68**(3), 79–91.

Schwartz, H. & Davis, S.M. (1981). Matching corporate culture and business strategy. *Organizational Dynamics*, Summer, 30–48.

Stalk, G., Evans, P. & Shulman, L.E. (1992). Competing on capabilities: the new rules of corporate strategy. *Harvard Business Review*, **70**(2), 57–69.

Thompson, A.A. Jr & Strickland, A.J. III (1995). *Strategic Management*, 8th edn. Chicago, IL: Irwin.

Thompson, A.A. Jr & Strickland, A.J. III (1996). *Strategic Management*, 9th edn. Chicago, IL: Irwin.

FURTHER READING

Chatman, J.A. & Jehn, K.A. (1994). Assessing the relationship between industry characteristics and organizational culture: how different can you be? *Academy of Management Journal*, **37**(3), 555–653.

Hamel, G. (1996). Strategy as revolution. *Harvard Business Review*, **74**(4), 69–82.

Hamel, G. and Prahalad, C.K. (1989). Competing for the future. *Harvard Business Review*, **72**(4), 122–128.

Mintzberg, H. (1975). The manager's job: folklore and fact. *Harvard Business Review*, **53**(4), 49–61.

Mintzberg, H. (1990). The design school: reconsidering the basic premises of strategic management. *Strategic Management Journal*, **11**, 171–195.

Mintzberg, H. (1996). Musings on management. *Harvard Business Review*, **74**(4), 61–67.

Mintzberg, H. & Waters, J.A. (1985). Of strategies, deliberate and emergent. *Strategic Management Journal*, **6**, 257–272.

Scholz, C. (1987). Corporate culture and strategy–the problem of strategic fit. *Long Range Planning*, **20**(4), 78–87.

6

Good for Practice: An Integrated Theory of the Value of Alternative Organizational Forms

RAYMOND E. MILES, GRANT MILES, CHARLES C. SNOW

INTRODUCTION

In their critique of the transaction cost economics approach to organizational analysis, Ghoshal and Moran (1996) argued that it would be "bad for practice" if managers adopted its prescriptions. Those authors called for a positive theory of organizations whose normative implications would be both realistic and feasible. We believe that such a theory can be stated, and we offer an approach that hopefully will be "good for practice." Specifically, our theoretical framework (i) explicates the value-creating properties of each of the major organizational forms, (ii) extends the economic justification provided for older forms to current forms, and (iii) offers a language and approach for the examination of future organizational forms from an integrated economic and behavioral perspective. Following its own unique logic, each organizational form accumulates and applies know-how through operating, investment, and adaptation routines. An organizational form achieves its potential when its routines are fully developed and utilized. Managers facilitate this process by helping organization members develop the competencies they need to understand and

Strategic Flexibility: Managing in a Turbulent Environment. Edited by G. Hamel, C.K. Prahalad, H. Thomas and D. O'Neal.

apply organizational routines. Using this theoretical framework, propositions for future research on organizational forms are generated and discussed.

New organizational forms emerge as managers seek better ways of utilizing their firms' assets and capabilities. This has been the case throughout modern business history. America's first "big business," the railroads, produced the functional form of organization, the original means of organizing large commercial enterprises (Chandler, 1965). The functional organization, by introducing innovations such as professional management and line-staff authority, permitted single-business firms to operate efficiently on a large scale.

Each subsequent form of organization added a particular set of competencies that managers could use to pursue competitive strategies. The divisional organization, for example, arose in the 1920s to allow the narrowly defined companies of the time to diversify (Chandler, 1962). The matrix form of organizing, which emerged in the late 1950s and early 1960s, helped various kinds of organizations to simultaneously engage in ongoing and temporary programs or projects (Mee, 1964). In the 1970s and 1980s, the network organization proliferated, enabling the accumulation and use of multifirm assets and capabilities (Miles & Snow, 1986; Thorelli, 1986). Most recently, a futuristic organizational form that appears to facilitate continuous innovation, the cellular organization, has been identified and described (Miles & Snow, 1996).

The evolution of organizational forms has been of long-standing interest to both economists and organization theorists. In the foreword to the third edition of her classic book, *The Theory of the Growth of the Firm*, Edith Penrose (1995) succinctly traced the growing convergence across economic and organization theory concerning the concept of an organization—a concept that can encompass the single-product, owner-managed firm, the multiproduct, multinational corporation, and even the complex web of relationships in the multifirm network organization. In our view, this convergence centers around two key points of agreement: (i) organizational form is important, and (ii) each major form has its own unique advantages. To date, however, the research regarding these points has been fragmented. What is missing, we believe, is a common language and analytical approach that can be utilized across organizational forms, both new and old. Our intent, therefore, is to develop a comprehensive theoretical framework that can provide insight into the value-adding properties of all organizational forms and be used to compare the value added by different means of organizing.

AN INTEGRATED THEORY OF ORGANIZATIONAL FORM

Our theoretical framework specifies the manner in which major, well-known organizational forms contribute to the creation of economic value. In

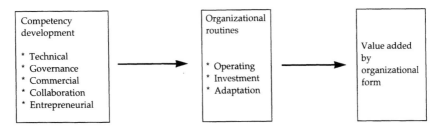

FIGURE 6.1   The value-adding process of organizing

general, each form relies on a set of organizational routines for accumulating knowledge. That know-how is then applied, both to improve current operations and to enhance future adaptability. Further, the various organizational forms differ not only in their economic value-producing mechanisms (routines), but each form requires specific knowledge-building investments to achieve its potential returns (see FIGURE 6.1).

CONCEPT OF ORGANIZATIONAL FORM

As used by Chandler (1962, 1990, 1991), Ghoshal & Moran (1996), Miles & Snow (1994), Nelson (1991), Penrose (1959), Williamson (1975), and others, the concept of organizational form includes an overall logic shaping the organization's strategy, structure, and management processes into an effective whole. Four major organizational forms have been described in sufficient detail that the ways in which they create economic value can be identified. A fifth form, evolving primarily in knowledge-intensive businesses such as professional services, offers opportunities for speculation about its value-adding potential.

Ideally, an organization encompasses only those resources and activities that can be economically utilized by means of its unique competencies. The boundary between an organization and the market is defined by both intent and outcome. Those resources which managers believe can be profitably deployed and coordinated are brought into the organization. Over time, however, only those resources whose economic value is actually enhanced by managerial know-how will remain in the organization.

Penrose (1959, p. 53) said that managerial know-how—and the ability to use it—is acquired through experience. Nelson & Winter (1982) and Nelson (1991) used the concept of routines to describe the mechanisms by which such experience-based managerial know-how is accumulated and used to coordinate the behavior of current organization members and guide the learning of new members. The ability to apply expanding knowledge to the utilization of current and future resources is the primary means by which organizations create economic value.

ORGANIZATIONAL ROUTINES

Within the organizational literature (Hannan & Freeman, 1989; March & Simon, 1958; Nelson, 1991; Nelson & Winter, 1982; Pfeffer & Salancik, 1978), at least three categories of value-producing routines have been discussed: (i) *operating routines*, which improve productivity, (2) *investment routines*, which replenish current assets and acquire new resources for expansion and/or diversification, and (iii) *adaptation routines*, which guide responses to market opportunities and direct efforts to build and apply knowledge.

Operating Routines

Most of what is accomplished by a firm on a day-to-day basis is not the result of recent planning or strategy formulation. Instead, it arises from organization members using widely understood knowledge of how and when work gets done. Such work processes, variously referred to as standard operating procedures or common practice, are stored within the organization in the form of a set of operating routines.

Operating routines are typically modified and improved over time as the organization gains experience from using them. For example, studies across various industries have identified "learning curves" reflecting the reduction of unit cost and/or product performance over time as firms refine and exploit their technological knowledge. There is increasing evidence, however, that the real value added by operating routines depends on the degree to which such routines are imperfectly imitable (Barney, 1991).

Some of the improvement in operating routines is likely to be visible and thus easily imitated by competing firms. However, other knowledge acquired and stored in operating routines is less transparent. Routines that possess causal ambiguity, and those that are embedded in key individuals or a complex social web, may be particularly valuable. Such "invisible assets" (Itami & Roehl, 1987) or "intangible resources" (Hall, 1992, 1993) are viewed as the key to sustaining a company's ability to earn above-normal returns (or rents) because they will be more difficult for competitors to copy (Barney, 1991).

Investment Routines

A second category of organizational routines is that concerned with the investment of company earnings and excess resources. Two distinct types of investment routines can be identified. The first involves decisions to renew or expand assets involved in current operations. Effectively maintaining operating routines, for example, demands the continuing reinvestment of earnings in every aspect of the firm (Chandler, 1991; Lado, Boyd & Wright, 1992). New managers must be developed, equipment replaced, new workers trained, processes upgraded, and so forth. Similarly, expansion within an existing product or service area (market penetration) may demand sophisticated investment routines. The creation of new plants or offices, the expansion of retail outlets, or the commitment to international operations all require the careful use of acquired knowledge to evaluate options.

There are times, however, when a firm may want to pursue opportunities outside its existing operations. Thus, another type of investment routine involves decisions to apply assets and resources in the pursuit of new products and markets (diversification). The value of developing sophisticated diversification routines is well documented. For example, the ability of divisionalized companies to locate and exploit new markets through the spin-off and/or acquisition of new divisions was recognized as a key capability of those firms which pioneered the divisional form (Chandler, 1962). Similarly, it has been argued that corporate executives apply their knowledge of internal capital markets through routines not unlike those of investment bankers (Teece, 1981; Williamson, 1975) and, particularly with regard to related diversification, may enjoy the benefits of holding inside information about opportunities and returns.

It should be emphasized that high value-added investment routines involve more than just the use of excess financial earnings. Just as earnings accrue over time, so too do knowledge and skills as they become routinized within current operations. Finding outlets for these excess capabilities, then, becomes an important part of the development of a firm's investment routines. Indeed, as Penrose (1959) and others have noted, it is the joint investment of earnings and acquired know-how that produces high returns for the expanding firm.

Adaptation Routines

A third set of organizational routines is that associated with adaptation—the ability to realign firm assets and resources to meet changing environmental conditions. One portion of the adaptive process concerns the use of current assets and resources. For example, the ability to put together, use, and then disband a cross-functional project team, and to do so without major disruptions or coordination costs, is not an easily learned routine. Effective adaptation routines not only gather and apply information to direct the flow of resources, but they also legitimate the process so that temporary asset and other resource shifts do not produce the costly conflicts associated with permanent power realignments.

Another important adaptive routine concerns the utilization of resources across firms, particularly as a means of responding to rapidly changing market demands (Jarillo, 1989; Piore & Sabel, 1984). The ability to quickly and efficiently relate externally to suppliers, partners, and customers, for example, is a learned routine. Improving the organization's ability to effectively operate such relational routines can minimize upstream and downstream transaction costs and/or lower coordination costs and increase returns from temporary alliances (Dyer, 1996).

Lastly, there are adaptive routines that focus on innovation. Some highly successful firms earn exceptional returns by constantly creating new products (or uses), frequently without major technological breakthroughs. Alternatively, some firms choose to focus on a steady stream of process innovations, such as applying advanced manufacturing technology to a set of standard products or services. In either case, the organization benefits by being able to sustain its own internal "Schumpeterian revolution" (Best, 1990).

Each of the three aspects of adaptation may lead to benefits for the firm. More important than any specific instance of adaptation, however, is continual improvement in the development of all three adaptation routines. In the broadest sense, routines that encourage and facilitate adaptation promote organizational learning. Accordingly, rapid resource reconfigurations such as those evidenced by "virtual" corporations (Davidow & Malone, 1992), relationship-management programs such as the Work-Out program at General Electric (Ashkenas et al, 1995), and various innovation experiments all serve to build organizing ability and lead to refinements in adaptation routines, the essence of organizational learning (Argyris & Schon, 1978; Senge, 1990). As such, maximum value arises not from any particular discovery of a new approach but from the firm learning improved methods of discovery that can be used to direct future adaptation.

SUMMARY

The three broad organizational routines just discussed—operating, investment, and adaptation—jointly serve to bring together a diverse literature on the value-adding contributions of different organizational forms. They incorporate the findings from researchers in areas such as economics, sociology, and organization theory into a common language that can be utilized across different forms. Also, the concept of organizational routine helps to clarify the managerial challenges posed by different ways of organizing. Lastly, examining the value added by organizational form through the lens of the three routines permits the determination of the unique contributions of each type of routine as well as the tradeoffs that have to be made when shifting from one organizational form to another. As noted above, each set of routines is capable of adding value to the organization. What is not yet clear, though, is how the different routines interact. Although, in a given organization, it is possible that the value produced by each set of routines is additive, it is more likely that operating, investment, and adaptation routines interact in a multiplicative fashion. For example, information about investment needs and opportunities is a normal by-product of current operations. Similarly, past experiences with investment and operating routines can be used to guide decisions regarding adaptation. Within each routine, the firm develops knowledge that is unique to its particular capabilities and circumstances. If the firm is able to generate, recognize, and apply this information across the full set of routines, it may be able to develop value above and beyond that provided by the individual routines and thereby sustain higher than normal returns on its asset utilization.

APPLICATION OF THE FRAMEWORK TO ALTERNATIVE ORGANIZATIONAL FORMS

We believe that a theoretical framework built on the above set of interactive organizational routines is useful for understanding and analyzing organizational forms. Our framework encompasses past research on traditional hierarchical forms of organizing, and it provides a means of examining the value-adding capabilities of current and emerging forms such as network and cellular organizations. In the following sections, we demonstrate this by first translating accepted thinking regarding traditional forms into the language of routines. We then use the language of routines to speculate on the ways in which newer forms may add value.

VALUE-CREATING ROUTINES IN HIERARCHICAL ORGANIZATIONS

Traditional thinking regarding the advantages and disadvantages of hierarchical forms of organizing can be easily captured within the framework of routines without altering the underlying logic. Teece (1982), for example, argued that organizational know-how could not always be fairly valued on the open market because of its tacit nature. Because of this, he suggested that a firm might do better by utilizing the divisional form of organizing and directly investing its know-how in new product or service opportunities. In the language of our framework, this involves a firm choosing to capitalize on its expertise in operating routines by also developing new investment routines to determine where and how it should diversify.

As shown in TABLE 6.1, our theoretical framework proposes that each of the major hierarchical organizational forms has the potential to produce rents by constructing and effectively using particular combinations of operating, investment, and adaptation routines that store information and capabilities not readily available to firms in an economic world governed by arm's-length relationships. The existing literature suggests some of the value-adding properties of functional and divisional forms, and these arguments are illustrated in TABLE 6.1 along with derived propositions related to the matrix form. As illustrated, the functional form adds value primarily through its operating routines; the divisional form uses operating routines plus the learned capability to utilize this know-how through value-adding related investments; and the matrix form uses both operating and investment routines but also has the potential to add value through its adaptation routines. The framework shown in TABLE 6.1 proposes that each more complex form not only incorporates the value-adding potential of the simpler form(s), but also adds its own unique emphases across its operating, investment, and adaptation routines.

In the physical world, the movement from simpler to more complex forms would be analogous to moving from a simple machine, say, a lever or a pulley, which creates a mechanical advantage, to a more complex machine, say, a block and tackle system, that may create additional advantage. There are, of course, limits to the gains achievable by simple machines, and there are limits to the value-producing potential of each organizational form. For example, a functionally organized firm will eventually reach the limits of efficiency producible by its operating routines; the divisionally organized firm will reach the limits of markets in which it can apply its know-how; and a matrix firm, while extending these limits, may become so complex in its foci that its decision-making processes are swamped. Also, as shown in TABLE 6.1, movement to a more complex form may mean giving up at least a piece of the specific gains of the simpler form.

Despite these limits, however, the value added by organizational form may, at least to some degree, persist over time. Initial returns from being the first mover to a new form that is appropriate to both the resources and industry conditions of the firm are likely to be highest as the firm gains rents similar to those earned by new product or process design. In time, though, competitors will emulate the first-mover firm and capture at least some of those rents. Nevertheless, managerial know-how, particularly the myriad requirements essential to the operation of a new form, may not be easily understood and copied. Thus, managers who are best able to understand and utilize a particular organizational form may maintain some advantage

TABLE 6.1 Value-adding potential of alternative organizational forms

| | | Organizational routines | | | | |
| | | Investment | | | Adaptation | |
Organizational form	Operating	Current assets and markets	New (related) assets markets	Flexible use of internal resources	Flexible use of external resources	Innovation in products and processes
Functional	High	High	Low	Low	Low	Medium
Divisional	Medium	Medium/high	High	Medium	Low	High/medium
Matrix	Medium/high	High/medium	Medium	Medium/high	High	Medium/high
Network	High	High	Medium	High/medium	High	High
Cellular	High	High	High	High	High	High

over their firm's competitors who are nominally employing the same type of organization.

Finally, while the successful adoption of a given organizational form provides a firm with rent-producing potential, the company sacrifices some of the value-adding potential available from other forms. That is, the M-form organization broadens the range of potential applications of its know-how, compared to the U-form, but frequently sacrifices some of the rents it might obtain by specializing its operating routines in one market. Similarly, the matrix form extends the related investment options available in the M-form to include smaller, though more numerous, new activities, but it requires a more complex set of adaptation routines, which are expensive to develop and maintain. Moreover, while the matrix form has substantial rent-producing potential from the operating routines in its stable markets, a tight managerial focus on only those routines may limit the development of necessary adaptive routines.

VALUE-CREATING ROUTINES IN NETWORK ORGANIZATIONS

An alternative, less hierarchical, approach to organizing, the network form, has emerged over the past two decades (Jarillo, 1988; Johanson & Mattsson, 1987; Miles & Snow, 1984, 1986, 1992; Powell, 1990; Thorelli, 1986). While this form of organizing has not received the same amount of research attention as the traditional forms, the language of routines is still helpful in assimilating existing knowledge and providing additional insight into the value-adding potential of the form.

A true network organizational form encompasses and refers to each of three key elements (Miles & Snow, 1994). First, it includes the individual network firm that identifies itself with, and operates primarily within, a definable set of firms at various points along an industry value chain. Second, it refers to an activated network, a currently connected group of firms whose resources are linked upstream and downstream to produce a given product or service. Third, the network organization includes the larger pool of firms which are potential (and perhaps past) partners of one another.

Application of the framework of routines proposes that all three of these elements must be included and well managed if the full rent-producing value of the form is to be captured. As proposed in TABLE 6.1, a particular network firm adds economic value in much the same way as do firms using traditional organizational forms. However, because network firms typically focus on only a segment of the industry value chain, they achieve both greater depth in their operating routines and greater facility in adapting those routines to the needs of their partners, thereby increasing the likelihood of full resource utilization (see TABLE 6.1). With regard to capital investment (replacement and/or expansion) decisions, the network firm benefits not only from its own accumulating analytical expertise, but also from information freely supplied by upstream and downstream network partners.

At the level of the activated network, value is primarily added through adaptation routines. In well-managed activated networks, each firm learns externally focused adaptation routines for achieving quick and efficient linkages to partners—routines which signal competence and responsible behavior. Network firms recognize that low transaction costs facilitate operations and returns for all partners and therefore are eager to demonstrate their own trustworthiness as well as trust in their partners. In addition, in the most advanced networks, internal and external adaptation routines may overlap as most member firms make heavy use of self-managing teams, both in the operation of their own resources and as linking mechanisms to upstream and downstream partners. The more facile network firms become in building routines for developing and utilizing teams, the greater the number of linkages the firm can manage simultaneously, and thus the more fully its resources can be utilized.

The total set of firms arrayed along the value chain from which the partners for activated networks are drawn also has organizational properties. The firms in this broader pool do not view themselves as completely independent; they identify with and feel obligations toward other current and potential network partners. Under such circumstances, innovation, often initiated by downstream partners, can become a constant process within the network. The network form is designed to allow those partners closest to the final market to make rapid changes in goods and services to meet shifting demand. In turn, the downstream firms make requests for customized outputs from upstream partners, expecting immediate responsiveness. Networks with multiple partners (active and potential) along the value chain can thus be engaged in myriad product or service innovations at any one time. These innovations provide continuous learning opportunities throughout the network and help the development of adaptation routines within the form.

In sum, TABLE 6.1 proposes that the network form has high potential to add value through the accumulation of know-how both within and across firms, each of which emphasizes a particular combination of operating, investment, and adaptation routines. Certainly, all of the value-producing potential of the network form may not accrue to every firm equally, nor even to all firms collectively. To the extent that any member firm's external adaptation routines are limited, all current and future partners suffer. Similarly, to the extent that firms dominate or are dominated by partners, neither creates or obtains the full economic value possible from their collaboration. Lastly, unless information is fully shared, total network operating efficiency is not realized. Thus, in the network organizational form, it seems likely that full value-producing potential is reached only if firms manage themselves so as to individually, jointly, and collectively utilize their assets and resources.

VALUE-CREATING POSSIBILITIES IN FUTURE ORGANIZATIONAL FORMS

The search for new ways of organizing is an ongoing process. As environments, technologies, and other factors change over time, new demands arise, which managers respond to, in part, by modifying the current arrangements of their personnel and other resources. It is our contention that having a common language and perspective for analyzing the value-adding contributions of new organizational forms will facilitate an understanding of these forms. We demonstrate this by applying the theoretical framework to an organizational form that is emerging within knowledge-based businesses.

In the most advanced network firms, as noted above, self-managing teams carry out many of the operating routines of individual firms and facilitate linkages with upstream and downstream partners. If all teams within a firm are broadly skilled and knowledgeable, any team may not only perform a wide array of tasks, but may also refer current or potential partners to that point within the firm where the most appropriate operating routines are available. Firms with such capabilities look less like traditional hierarchical pyramids and more like rotatable spheres, able to deploy resources quickly wherever they are needed (Miles & Snow, 1995). Management makes investment decisions on how broadly to train all teams for optimal resource utilization within the firm, and referral skills themselves become rent-producing routines. Thus, a rotatable, spherical organization structure maximizes the utilization of all current resources, up and down the value chain.

Self-managing teams with both technical and referral competencies are increasingly found in knowledge-based businesses such as professional services. However, in these businesses long-term, value-adding processes may have less to do with the utilization of current knowledge than they do with the continuing development and sharing of new knowledge. In such settings, there is emerging an organizational approach, perhaps even the beginnings of a new form, that is designed to maximize learning throughout an organization by building learning mechanisms into ongoing routines. In its ideal form, such an organization would exhibit little or no hierarchy and have few if any managers.

An interesting firm in this regard is Technical and Computer Graphics (TCG), located in Sydney, Australia (Mathews, 1992, 1993). The TCG Group is a multifirm network that, through sophisticated entrepreneurship and project leadership, has become not only the largest privately-owned computer service business in Australia but a model for the self-managing organization. To meet the need for continuous innovation, an organizational form with very advanced routines has evolved. For each new business venture, an initiating TCG firm first seeks to build an *external* triangular relationship involving itself, a joint-venture partner, and a principal customer. It then forms a similar *internal* relationship with one or more additional TCG firms. Having put together these external and internal alliances, the project-leader firm is the gateway through which information and resources flow for the remainder of the venture. Numerous such ventures are underway across the 13 firms at TCG at any given time.

Across the multifirm TCG network, every firm and every individual is expected to be an entrepreneur and sometimes a project leader—able to apply leading-edge operating, investment, and adaptation know-how. Although the total network staff of 200 is comparatively small, its full utilization and its external alliances give TCG enormous leverage and global reach. However, the key organizational achievement at TCG is probably not its leverage and operating routines, but is instead its unusual ability to innovate—its ability to constantly infuse the total organization with the new knowledge gained from each business venture. To describe this process, an organic rather than a mechanistic metaphor is required, and it has been suggested that TCG and other firms like it may best be described as "cellular" organizations (Miles *et al.* 1997).

Like the small firms at TCG, cells in living organisms are capable of performing all of the fundamental functions of life. They can exist on their own, but by interacting with other cells, they can produce a more complex and competent organism. Common knowledge and information are shared across the cellular firms in a manner, akin to human DNA, that reflects heredity and guides development.

In organizations like TCG, member firms and individuals are held together not by a command structure (hierarchy of authority) but by a common understanding, an articulated "constitution" that is a natural part of the stored knowledge embedded in each "cell." This knowledge describes rights and responsibilities, and it suggests general operating and adaptation routines for most internal and external interactions. New entrants to the network are guided by this common heritage, and indeed were selected largely because their "cell structure" was similar to that of the established firms. The continually evolving common heritage of cells within the larger organism is thus maintained by ongoing operations.

In TCG, for example, operating and adaptation routines provide a link between its external and internal partners. External partners bring both financial and technical resources to the project, resources valuable to TCG's continued learning. However, these resources are not just stored in the project-leader firm. Instead, TCG's innovation routines expand the learning to internal partners, who are sought not only for their skills but as a means of infusing the larger organism with information and insights from the venture.

Thus, as proposed in TABLE 6.1, potential value-producing mechanisms in the cellular organization include not only current operating routines but also the adaptation routines developed for sharing knowledge across the organization. In addition, the combination of operative and adaptation routines in the cellular organization, aided by a reliance on self-governance, give it broad ability to leverage its internal resources through external alliances. In a sense, every cell is an entrepreneurial mechanism able to invest the full complement of its own resources and those of other cells, along with the resources of external partners, in a continuing stream of new business ventures.

Summary

Application of the framework of routines to the cellular form suggests two important advances in the way that future organizational forms might add value. One avenue of value production is the diffusion of routines through-out the form, and the other is the blurring of the demarcations between routines. In the cellular organization, operating routines tend to be structured around the heavy use of self-managing teams. Because such teams carry information back and forth across firm boundaries, operating routines begin to blend into adaptation routines—and both routines are essential to the reinvestment of firm and multifirm resources. At the limit, as managerial know-how is extended throughout the organization, all routines can be performed anywhere. Such diffusion of knowledge and competence can only occur through a heavy and continuous investment in human capital.

HUMAN CAPITAL INVESTMENTS NEEDED TO ACHIEVE AN ORGANIZATIONAL FORM'S POTENTIAL VALUE

We have argued that the process by which different organizational forms create economic value is describable in terms of operating, investment, and adaptation routines. A key factor determining whether a given form's value potential is realized is the extent to which management is willing to make required investments in human capital. Such investments are necessary to create the base on which knowledge accumulates and on which value-producing routines develop. TABLE 6.2 shows five types of individual

TABLE 6.2 Human capital investment requirements of alternative organizational forms, by management level

Organizational form		Competencies			
	Technical	Governance	Commercial	Collaboration	Entrepreneurial
Functional	All	Top and middle	Top	–	–
Divisional	All	Top and middle	Top and middle	–	Top
Matrix	All	Top and middle	Top and middle	Top and middle	Top
Network	All	All	All	All	Top and middle
Cellular	All	All	All	All	All

competencies, which vary in importance from one organizational form to another. These include technical competencies applied directly in the production of the firm's goods or services, governance competencies used to direct and coordinate human resources, commercial competencies utilized in understanding and evaluating market demand and calculating resource allocation costs and benefits, collaboration competencies which build and guide relationships with customers, suppliers, and partners, and entrepreneurial competencies associated with the recognition of new market opportunities and the assembling of resources to meet them.

TABLE 6.2 also indicates the level of management where investments in the various competency types are needed to develop the value-producing routines required by each organizational form. For the functional or U-form organization, as with all of the organizational forms, technical knowledge and skills are essential to operating routines at all levels. Governance skills in the functional form, however, are primarily required only at the highest management levels, and commercial competencies are demanded only for those top-level managers who make basic product/service design and pricing decisions. The stability of the functional organization mean that transaction and entrepreneurial skills are of considerably lesser importance than in the other forms, and are usually exercised by a few top managers.

In the multiproduct or M-form organization, technical skill requirements are similar to those in the U-form. However, investments to build governance competencies must be made across a much wider range of managers because of their expected movement into leadership roles in newly created or acquired divisions. In addition, particularly at the division management level where market response decisions are being made, successful M-form organizations must provide broad commercial training.

Moving to the matrix form, governance and commercial skill requirements are widely needed, not only at the top of the functional units in the stable segment of the organization, but also among the project or regionally based units seeking to adapt to unique customer requests. Investments to develop those competencies must be made not only to allow effective operating decisions at the lowest organizational levels but also to allow resource-allocation decisions related to functional and project uses to be made at low and middle levels. Lower and middle managers must also have the knowledge, skills, and confidence to interact directly with external clients, and upper management must have invested sufficiently in competency development to be willing to risk autonomous decision making at the project level.

In the network form, requirements for investments in competencies expand again. Given the use of self-managing teams within and across firms in a network organization, governance, commercial, and collaboration competencies (along with technical competencies) are required at all levels.

Entrepreneurial skills, those taking the network member firms into new product and service areas, may still be made primarily at upper management levels.

In the cellular form, where management levels are few, we hypothesize that distinctions across competency investment requirements tend to blur. Most, if not all, organization members are expected to operate, invest, and adapt their own resources and those of the larger organization according to a continuous process of problem solving and innovation. Therefore, the competencies of all members must continue to grow if the demanding routines anticipated in this form are to develop and flourish.

It can be demonstrated that investments across all five competency sets will produce returns in less complex as well as more complex forms. For example, self-managing teams have been effectively used in U-form and M-form organizations, but they are not required by the respective logic of those forms. The effects of such "overinvestment" in competencies are not known, but one plausible hypothesis is that overinvestment will infuse older organizational forms with some of the capabilities associated with the newer forms. However, in practice, the resultant excess competence will be inhibited by the basic focus and logic of the less complex form.

IMPLICATIONS FOR RESEARCH AND PRACTICE

The theoretical framework discussed and illustrated above takes the firm and its resources, especially managerial know-how, as its focus. We propose a positive approach to the study of organizing that allows for the examination of how organizational routines can help (or hinder) the development of the value-producing capabilities of alternative organizational forms. If our framework is valid, then several implications for research and management practice are indicated.

IMPLICATIONS FOR RESEARCH

The principal research implication indicated by our theoretical framework is a test of the value-added hypothesis. That is, will firms in the same setting, and nominally employing the same organizational form, obtain returns that are predictable based on the extent to which key properties of the form—the ability to develop routines and use the stored know-how—are widely understood and exploited? To test this general hypothesis, however, will require the development of measures for both the degree of competency possessed by firm members and the emphasis placed by management on each of the routines.

A second research implication involves the examination of interactions among routines, particularly in more complex organizational forms. Both organization theory and organizational economics suggest that diversification investments made in M-form firms benefit from "insider" knowledge developed through operating in related markets. In other words, investment routines benefit from operating routines. Do similar phenomena occur in other forms? In the network, a firm's internal investment routines may be driven by knowledge gained through effective upstream and downstream interactions with other firms. In the cellular organization there may be an interaction between operating and adaptation routines such that all operations contribute toward adaptation rather than constrain it. In general, the notion of a synergistic interaction among organizational routines deserves exploration.

A final research implication is to test the overinvestment hypothesis—the efforts of some firms to develop competencies, routines, and practices that are beyond the requirements of their chosen organizational form. Does the development of practices that are not crucial to the value-adding properties of a form provide additional value, or do these practices go to waste because the firm cannot incorporate or use them? While the overinvestment research implication is perhaps the least well developed in the organiztional literature, it may be the one that derives the greatest benefit from the utilization of the theoretical framework offered here.

IMPLICATIONS FOR MANAGERS

For managers, especially those who are in a position to design or change their organizations, our framework offers three major recommendations. The first recommendation is based on the belief that the proper operation of an organization can add value to a firm. For this to occur, however, managers must be aware of the three organizational routines and potential interactions, they must diagnose the organizational form they wish to use and place proper emphasis on the routines that are critical to that form's effectiveness, and they must invest in the human capital needed to perform the routines effectively.

The second recommendation refers to firms which are considering a switch from one organizational form to another. Our framework suggests a set of benefits and costs for each form that include the need for the development of appropriate routines to capture long-term value-adding possibilities. By making explicit the competencies needed to achieve the economic benefits of the new organization, managers can determine their own readiness to make the developmental investments required to obtain the full value of the new form. At the same time, the overall focus on routines, as well as the varying importance of each type of routine to a given form, should help managers to recognize the limits of any form they choose to operate so that they do not push it beyond its capabilities.

Finally, the ability to encompass and present accumulating insights from organization theory and organizational economics in a framework anchored by recognizable strategy–structure–process configurations should facilitate teaching and learning in firms. By offering a common set of theoretical concepts, the understanding of emerging and future organizational forms can be grounded in language and ideas that are already familiar from traditional means of organizing. Thus, managers can more easily direct their efforts at developing necessary routines and communicating throughout the organization how to use them.

CONCLUSION

In response to previous calls (Ghoshal & Moran, 1996; Rumelt, Schendel & Teece, 1991), we have proposed a framework for the analysis of organizational form that is "good for practice." The theory focuses on the ways in which form adds value and identifies the routines necessary for the full development of any organizational form. We have suggested a common language independent of any particular organizational form that permits comparisons across existing forms as well as the analysis of emerging and future forms. Such an approach incorporates current knowledge of the alternative means of organizing while also offering useful insights for future research and management practice.

REFERENCES

Argyris, C. & Schon, D.A. (1978). *Organizational Learning: A Theory-in-Action Perspective*. Reading, MA: Addison-Wesley.

Ashkenas, R., Ulrich, D., Jick, T. & Kerr, S. (1995). *The Boundaryless Organization: Breaking the Chains of Organizational Structure*. San Francisco, CA: Jossey-Bass.

Barney, J.B. (1991). Firm resources and sustained competitive advantage. *Journal of Management*, **17**, 99–120.

Best, M. (1990). *The New Competition: Institutions of Industrial Restructuring*. Cambridge, MA: Harvard University Press.

Chandler, A.D. Jr (1962). *Strategy and Structure: Chapters in the History of American Industrial Enterprise*. New York: Doubleday.

Chandler, A.D. Jr (1965). *The Railroads: The Nation's First Big Business*. New York: Harcourt, Brace, & World.

Chandler, A.D. Jr (1990). *Scale and Scope: The Dynamics of Industrial Capitalism*. Cambridge, MA: Harvard University Press.

Chandler, A.D. Jr (1991). The functions of the HQ unit in the multibusiness firm. *Strategic Management Journal*, **12**, 31–50.

Davidow, W.H. & Malone, M.S. (1992). *The Virtual Corporation*. New York: HarperBusiness.

Dyer, J.H. (1996). Specialized supplier networks as a source of competitive advantage: evidence from the auto industry. *Strategic Management Journal*, **17**, 271–291.

Ghoshal, S. & Moran, P. (1996). Bad for practice: a critique of the transaction cost theory. *Academy of Management Review*, **21**(1), 13–47.

Hall, R. (1992). The strategic analysis of intangible resources. *Strategic Management Journal*, **13**, 135–144.

Hall, R. (1993). A framework linking intangible resources and capabilities to sustainable competitive advantage. *Strategic Management Journal*, **14**, 607–618.

Hannan, M. & Freeman, J. (1989). *Organizational Ecology*. Cambridge, MA: Harvard University Press.

Itami, H. & Roehl, T.W. (1987). *Mobilizing Invisible Assets*. Cambridge, MA: Harvard University Press.

Jarillo, J.C. (1988). On strategic networks. *Strategic Management Journal*, **9**, 31–41.

Jarillo, J.C. (1989). Entrepreneurship and growth: the strategic use of external resources. *Journal of Business Venturing*, **4**, 133–147.

Johanson, J. & Mattsson, L.G. (1987). Interorganizational relationships in industrial systems: a network approach compared with the transaction cost approach. *International Studies of Management and Organization*, **17**(1), 34–48.

Lado, A.A., Boyd, N.G. & Wright, P. (1992). A competency-based model of sustainable competitive advantage: toward a conceptual integration. *Journal of Management*, **18**, 77–91.

March, J.G. & Simon, H.A. (1958). *Organizations*. New York: Wiley.

Mathews, J. (1992). *TCG: Sustainable Economic Organisation through Networking*. Sydney, Australia. Industrial Relations Research Centre, The University of New South Wales.

Mathews, J. (1993). TCG R&D networks: the triangulation strategy. *Journal of Industry Studies*, **1**, 65–74.

Mee, J.F. (1964). Matrix organization. *Business Horizons*, **7**, 70–72.

Miles, R.E. & Snow, C.C. (1984). Fit, failure, and the Hall of Fame. *California Management Review*, **26**, 10–28.

Miles, R.E. & Snow, C.C. (1986). Organizations: new concepts for new forms. *California Management Review*, **28**, 62–73.

Miles, R.E. & Snow, C.C. (1992). Causes of failure in network organizations. *California Management Review*, **34**, 53–72.

Miles, R.E. & Snow, C.C. (1994). *Fit, Failure, and the Hall of Fame: How Companies Succeed or Fail*. New York: Free Press.

Miles, R.E. & Snow, C.C. (1995). The new network firm: a spherical structure based on a human investment philosophy. *Organizational Dynamics* **23**, 5–18.

Miles, R.E., Snow, C.C., Mathews, J.A., Miles, G. & Coleman, H.J. (1997). Organizing in the knowledge age: anticipation the cellular form. *Academy of Management Executive*, **11**, 7–20.

Nelson, R.R. (1991). Why do firms differ, and how does it matter? *Strategic Management Journal*, **12**, 61–74.

Nelson, R.R. & Winter, S.G. (1982). *An Evolutionary Theory of Economic Change*. Cambridge, MA: Harvard University Press.

Penrose, E.T. (1959). *A Theory of the Growth of the Firm*. New York: Wiley.

Penrose, E.T. (1995). *A Theory of the Growth of the Firm*, 3rd edn. New York: Wiley,

Pfeffer, J. & Salancik, G.R. (1978). *The External Control of Organizations*. New York: Harper & Row.

Piore, M.J. & Sabel, C.F. (1984). *The Second Industrial Divide: Prospects for Prosperity*. New York: Basic Books.

Powell, W.W. (1990). Neither market nor hierarchy: network forms of organization. In B.M. Staw & L.L. Cummings (eds) *Research in Organizational Behavior*, vol. 12. Greenwich, CT: JAI Press, pp. 295–336.

Rumelt, R.P., Schendel, D. & Teece, D.J. (1991). Strategic management and economics. *Strategic Management Journal*, **12**, 5–29.

Senge, P.M. (1990). *The Fifth Discipline: The Art and Practice of the Learning Organization*. New York: Doubleday/Currency.

Teece, D.J. (1981). The market for know-how and the efficient transfer of technology. *Annals of the Academy of Political and Social Science*, 81–96.

Teece, D.J. (1982). Towards an economic theory of the multiproduct firm. *Journal of Economic Behavior and Organization*, **3**, 39–63.

Thorelli, H.B. (1986). Networks: between markets and hierarchies. *Strategic Management Journal*, **7**, 37–52.

Williamson, O.E. (1975). *Markets and Hierarchies: Analysis and Antitrust Implications*. New York: Free Press.

Strategic Reengineering: An Internal Industry Analysis Framework

KENNETH D. PRITSKER

INTRODUCTION

This chapter introduces the concept of strategic reengineering as a process oriented framework to better manage the cross-company interrelationships in a macro-industry context. This framework includes a description of various process terms and defines a methodology to understand vertical, horizontal, and integrative process chains that create a macro-level industry. The concept of strategic reengineering is illustrated through a study of the air transportation industry, identifying the strategic opportunities associated with effectively managing horizontal and integrative value chains. The chapter concludes with a discussion of the application of strategic reengineering concepts to the formulation of corporate-, business-, and functional-level strategy.

Over the past 20 years, industries have expanded their boundaries by diversifying into new product areas, by creatively insourcing/outsourcing activities, and by entering into innovative cooperative agreements with companies from other industries. This expansion has almost blurred traditional industry boundaries by creating an economy of industries that are tightly interlinked.

As an industry's scope expands, integrative activities are developed to coordinate cross-industry interactions. In many cases, an industry's

Strategic Flexibility: Managing in a Turbulent Environment. Edited by G. Hamel, C.K. Prahalad, H. Thomas and D. O'Neal.
Copyright © 1998 John Wiley & Sons Ltd.

integrative activities are more profitable than its traditional operations because of the criticality of the functions provided and the power of coordinating these activities.

This chapter introduces strategic reengineering as a framework to understand an industry in terms of its processes and value-added chains. This internal macro-process perspective to an industry's operations creates new strategic issues to address how industries and companies will operate as a set of integrated value chains.

In this chapter, the strategic reengineering industry framework is applied to major product segments of the air transportation industry: airports, airlines, aircraft, maintenance and components. A strategic reengineering model is developed that identifies the interrelationships among the product segments. The chapter concludes with an identification of strategic process issues and a discussion of innovative strategies to strengthen a company's position in an industry.

INDUSTRY ANALYSIS ORIENTATIONS

Industry analysis typically focuses on a company's external dimensions such as its markets, customers, and competitors. Research on industry structure has investigated the influence of economic structure on competition, the advantages of strategic industry control, and the industry factors that influence profitability (Huff, 1982). Another research stream has examined how external changes such as changing customer needs, new technology, government policy, globalization and economic cycles impact a company's strategy (Hambrick, 1983). The magnitude of external changes over the past 20 years has led strategic planners to develop analytical tools that utilize external information to help create proactive strategies. As a result, strategies have tended to minimize the importance of understanding the internal industry structure.

In the 1990s, companies are experiencing major shocks from how information technology can change the internal mechanisms of an industry. Information technology is now able to link cross-company functions as well as to provide value chain linkage from raw materials to final customer usage (Upton & McAfee, 1996). This technological integration within an industry results in two phenomena. First, industry segments can be further narrowed down into individual value chains because of the ability to effectively link value chain activities (Ring & VanDeVen, 1994). Second, new industry segments are emerging with the sole purpose of integrating these specialized value chains to better serve the needs of the end consumer (Benjamin & Wignad, 1995).

The decentralization of an industry into more narrowly defined value chains has led to the emergence of new integrating industry segments. As a result, companies are aggressively competing for position in these integrating segments in order to improve the efficiencies of individual value chains and, more importantly, to gain strategic control of the industry's coordination activities (Porter, 1979).

STRATEGIC REENGINEERING: AN ACTIVITY-BASED ORIENTATION TO INDUSTRY ANALYSIS

The goal of this chapter is to characterize an internal industry structure in order to develop proactive strategies to shape an industry's technological and operational evolution. Strategic reengineering is a framework to tangibly describe the interworkings of the complex interactions between industry segments. The strategic reengineering approach groups activities into value chains and provides a method to show how those value chains interact to create our traditional industry concepts.

The foundation for this approach comes from business process reengineering's desire to establish self-contained, information-driven, value-creating organizational units based on a systematic grouping of activities. The past decade has seen the exponential growth of business process reengineering projects for all types of purposes in every kind of industry. Unfortunately, the majority of these projects have experienced implementation difficulties because they were conducted one process at a time without developing an overall context. Without a broader industry or value chain context to evaluate a process in terms of its customers, inputs, outputs, information systems, ownership and accountability, business process reengineering projects have often resulted in "turf battles" over boundaries, resources and performance responsibilities (Pritsker, 1995). Strategic reengineering establishes the context for individual processes by combining business process terminology with strategic planning frameworks to describe an industry.

An external view of an industry involves a grouping of companies into a set of sub-industries defined by products and markets. An internal industry view understands each of these products in terms of the activities necessary to produce that product. What is needed is a way to reconcile alternative viewpoints to an industry's structure (Bogner & Thomas, 1993). The strategic reengineering model brings together these two perspectives by defining internal process activities and then documenting the relationships between these activities in a broad product and market context.

Strategic reengineering industry modeling involves developing a hierarchical system to capture business processes, the value chains and the interactions between value chains to produce the end product. This hierarchical system starts with the products and product segments of a

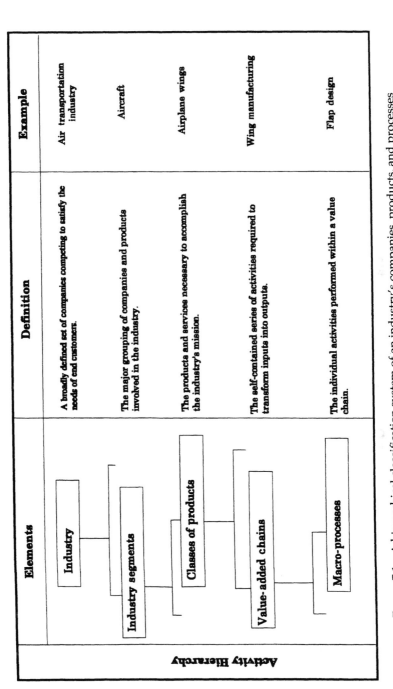

Elements	Definition	Example
Industry	A broadly defined set of companies competing to satisfy the needs of end customers.	Air transportation industry
Industry segments	The major grouping of companies and products involved in the industry.	Aircraft
Classes of products	The products and services necessary to accomplish the industry's mission.	Airplane wings
Value-added chains	The self-contained series of activities required to transform inputs into outputs.	Wing manufacturing
Macro-processes	The individual activities performed within a value chain.	Flap design

Activity Hierarchy

FIGURE 7.1   A hierarchical classification system of an industry's companies, products, and processes

of flaps, rudders, fuselage, wings, and landing gear to produce an aircraft. Each of these aircraft products has its own value chains and, when coordinated together, result in final assembly of an airplane. The second value chain type is a horizontal chain, which provides the coordination between vertical chains. An example of a horizontal chain would be airplane design, where the design activities associated with the airplane's flaps, wings, and tail are coordinated together in order to produce specified flight characteristics in an aircraft. The third value chain type is an integrative value chain, where coordination occurs across industry segments. An example of an integrative value chain would be avionics, which brings together the controls of the plane (aircraft), the flight of planes (airlines), and evaluation of the plane's performance (maintenance).

The challenge of documenting these three different scopes of value chains comes from the complex interactions between chains. Some chains are coupled, meaning the output of one chain serves as an input to another chain. A common chain interrelationship is a linked interaction, where one particular activity, such as flap design, is supportive of a vertical chain (wing manufacturing), a horizontal chain (aircraft speed controls), and an integrative chain (landing the aircraft).

Another significant modeling difficulty comes from attempting to incorporate a time element into the relationship between value chains. Modelers want to define activities as either sequential or parallel, but the reality of the air transportation industry is that many activities are performed iteratively, meaning that processes interact with each other throughout their chain of activities.

Figure 7.2 presents the different types of value chains and chain relationships. In the following section, these relationships are used to create an activity web capturing the interworkings of a broadly defined industry.

The strategic reengineering industry model captures the boundaries of each individual value chain and the interrelationships between value chains. This industry model creates an activity web by presenting a broad picture of all of the macro-processes of an industry. The activity web plots each individual value chain in three dimensions: its scope (either vertical, horizontal or integrative), its interactions (linked or coupled), and its dynamics (either parallel, sequential or iterative). The activity web is the foundation of the strategic reengineering model as its captures the operational essence of the industry and helps to identify the critical value chains.

A CASE ILLUSTRATION: THE AIR TRANSPORTATION INDUSTRY

The air transportation industry is a highly fragmented industry with complex interrelationships between its value chains. The industry

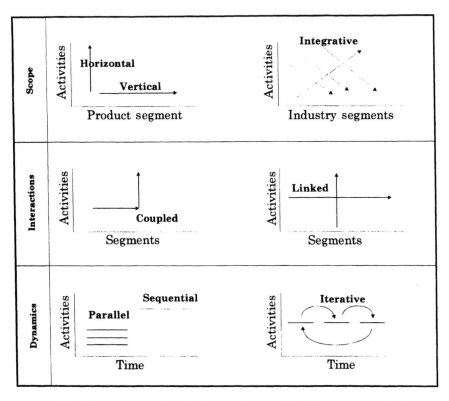

FIGURE 7.2   The types of value chains and the possible chain interrelationships

fragmentation dates back to an early anti-trust ruling that Boeing's participation in engine manufacturing and airline services was monopolistic. This ruling established the segmentation within the industry and set the tone for potentially confrontational relationships between segments.

With the deregulation of the airline industry in the 1980s, competitive forces reduced industry revenues at a time when coordination costs were soaring. In fact, it has been estimated that the industry as a whole spends 60% of all of its costs on the transferring and processing of information. The dramatic industry losses in the late 1980s and early 1990s created the need for fundamental structural changes (Dussaugo & Garrette, 1995).

Beginning in the early 1990s, the industry as a whole took the initiative to restructure its basic methods of operation. Individual companies began to improve their internal coordination mechanisms with a combination of information technology advancements, total quality management programs, business process reengineering activities, and activity-based costing systems. These initiatives in the area of process improvement set the stage for industry-wide strategic reengineering. Given the current political environment, where anti-trust enforcement is minimal and information technology can help facilitate cross-segment coordination, the air transportation industry is beginning a long journey towards evolving into a single integrated industry.

The goal of many executives in the air transportation industry is to set up an operational capability that allows the industry to operate as a series of "continuous" activities. An example of this continuous activity is the petroleum industry, which has traditionally been managed as a series of value-added chains. By structuring activities into exploration, refining, and distribution (i.e. macro-level industry value-added chains), companies have organized their purposes, people, information, and finances to create maximum value at each decentralized process step. The result is a highly flexible, highly efficient industry machine capable of responding to external demands for change. The question is, can the air transportation industry operate as efficiently as the petroleum industry?

THE RESEARCH PROJECT

A research project was launched to develop more fully the concepts of strategic reengineering and to apply those concepts to the air transportation industry. This research aimed to build a model of the industry's value-added chains in order to stimulate innovative strategies to capitalize on the industry's process restructuring. With this goal in mind, the research project had the following objectives:

1. To develop a modeling technique capable of describing the inter-workings of a broadly defined industry.
2. To test the feasibility of applying this modeling technique to a rapidly changing industry.
3. To articulate a new set of process oriented company/industry strategic issues.
4. To use the industry model to help formulate innovative strategies for process-based competitive advantage.

The research project was conducted in two phases. First, a descriptive model was created to objectively articulate each individual value chain and the various interactions between value-added chains. The second phase involved an open forum of air transportation industry company management to discuss potential applications of the model in order to: (i) evaluate the value-added chains they participated in, (ii) forecast new integrative value chains that could fundamentally change the method of intra-industry competition, and (iii) set policy on how to compete in the emerging integrated industry.

The air transportation industry has historically focused improvement activities on the vertical and horizontal value chains while accepting the inefficiencies of the current methods used to accomplish the integrative value chains. Industry profitability challenges generated interest in better understanding the cross-segment integrative activities in the industry. In today's air transportation industry, the majority of strategic initiatives are concentrating on the effectiveness of this cross-company, cross-segment coordination.

After distributing information about strategic reengineering to companies in the industry, interest in the concept led to the formulation of a Strategic Reengineering Working Group (Strategic Reengineering Institute, 1996). Forty-three companies involved in the air transportation industry were invited to participate in the working group. After a series of discussions concerning the goals and objectives of the project, fourteen companies decided to formally join the working group. The fourteen companies represented five industry segments: two airports, four component manu-facturers, two aircraft assemblers, three airlines and three airplane main-tenance companies. After agreeing to a series of information confidentiality agreements, each of these companies assigned one representative to provide product, process, organizational, and financial data. This working group had the initial mission to bring together diverse vantage points of the industry in order to construct a comprehensive operational model of the entire air transportation industry.

Twelve of the fourteen companies had already prepared a process model of their own internal activities. These individual company process models served as the starting point for the creation of the strategic reengineering industry model. Through a series of iterations over a two-month period, the individual process models were standardized in terms of the use of terminology, definitions, hierarchical classification and process boundaries. The individual segment models were then reviewed for comments by the various employees at the participating companies. After attempting to resolve disagreements on the boundaries and labels of classes of products and value chains, the working group reached consensus that the model captured the general scope and descriptions of activities in the Industry (Air Transportation Association, 1996). TABLE 7.1 shows how the five industry segments can be divided into 203 classes of products and how those classes of products can be expressed in terms of 489 value chains.

The next step of the modeling activity concentrated on specifying the various interrelationships between value chains and individual processes.

TABLE 7.1 The company–product–process hierarchy of the air transportation industry

	The air transportation industry				
	Airports	Components	Aircraft	Airlines	Maintenance
Class of products Examples of:	42 • Construction • Equipping • Systems installation	63 • Parts • Engines • Avionics	27 • Wings • Fuselage • Interiors	45 • Passenger services • Flight • Freight	26 • Diagnosis • Delivery systems • Operation control
Value chains Examples of:	76 • Facility management • Ground control • Surveillance	121 • Logistics management • Capacity planning • Manufacturing operations	63 • Model definition • Assembly • Aircraft support	137 • Fueling • Routing • Entertainment	92 • Modifications • Spares distribution • Field service

FIGURE 7.3 conceptually depicts the interrelationships between the 489 value chains that make up the industry by providing activity web plots describing each value chain as either a vertical chain (serving the particular needs of production within a product scope, e.g. wing design for an aircraft manufacturer), a horizontal chain (coordinating the interaction between chains within a segment, e.g. engine performance assessment, which ties together engine design and engine manufacturing), or an integrative chain (activities that cross traditional industry segments, e.g. airworthiness, which integrates engine performance, aircraft diagnosis, airline operation, and aircraft maintenance). Because of the complexity of the interactions of the value chains, the time dimension of these value chain interactions was not included in the presentation of the industry activity web.

After circulating the strategic reengineering industry model throughout the fourteen participating companies, the response was a combination of intense interest and curiosity as to the application of the model to setting company direction. The types of questions asked could be categorized into the following areas: (i) how do the industry's current practices map onto the model? (ii) if the profitability in the vertical chains is lower than in the horizontal chains, then what strategic leverage is gained from participating in the vertical chains? and (iii) do the integrative value chains represent several emerging internal industry segments?

An attempt was made to map the fourteen working group companies' organizational activities and performance on the strategic model. Each company went through an assessment of how many value chains it participated in within its own industry segment. For example, one airline reported competing in 100% of its segment's chains, while one of the maintenance companies found that it competed in 27% of the possible maintenance chains. The next step was to determine the number of value chains that each company participated in outside its industry segment. This assessment relied on internal employee experience to verify how the company performed certain activities outside its segment. An example of this outside involvement is the practice of airlines furnishing the interiors of newly manufactured airplanes.

Using internal financial data, an assessment was made of the revenues and costs associated with the participation both within and across segment activities. The allocation of revenues to specific segments was feasible as revenue sources are well documented. The allocation of operating costs to specific value chains was difficult without activity-based costing information, and the resulting values represented best estimates.

The data gathering and reporting mechanism used to summarize information regarding participation and profitability resulted in questions about the ability to generalize these results and the methodology used. As a result, the working group used this raw data to serve as a forum for

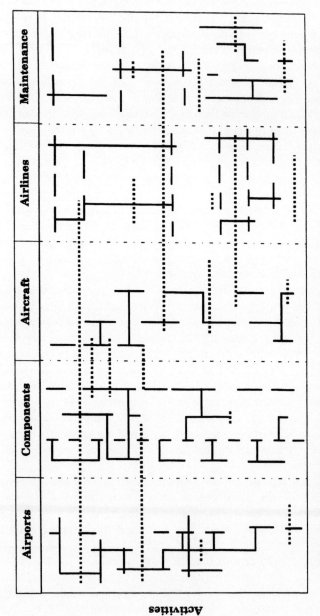

| Activities | Airports | Components | Aircraft | Airlines | Maintenance |

| **Vertical value chains:** Value created by directly providing an incremental output to a particular class of products.

— **Horizontal value chains:** Value created by providing necessary linkage between vertical chains to ensure product functionality within an industry segment.

.... **Integrative value chains:** Value created by coordinating horizontal and vertical chains across industry segments.

FIGURE 7.3   An activity web of the air transportation industry

discussion within their organizations to attempt to apply the industry model to strategic planning issues.

After distributing the activity web and the performance estimates throughout the participating companies, the majority of comments could be separated into two categories. First, there was tremendous interest in how the specification of value chains impacted current initiatives related to business process reengineering initiatives. There was a consensus that the activity web illustrated the need to view process management from a holistic perspective. This holistic viewpoint stimulated thoughts and ideas related to the purpose of individual processes and the absolute-requirement to consider process improvement projects in terms of strengthening the company's system of value chains working together to produce classes of products to meet the needs of the end customer.

The second category of comments related to top management's interest in the activity web and in the grouping of horizontal value chain across industry segments. Almost universally, managers could map their own observations, initiatives and frustrations by relating how the current industry mechanisms performed these integrative functions. The evolution of how the industry performs these integrative activities provided the most insightful comments from a strategic perspective. These comments were analyzed in detail and are categorized in the following subsections with regard to how the strategic reengineering industry model could be used to help set company and industry direction.

THE INCREASING VISIBILITY OF INTEGRATIVE CHAIN ACTIVITIES

The strategic reengineering model put into perspective how rapidly our company has expanded the scope of activities within our industry. In fact, viewing the industry model made me realize this phenomena is occurring throughout our industry.

(Director of Planning of a major airline)

Many of the comments expressed satisfaction with the efficiency of the speaker's own segment and a general level of frustration with the inefficiencies of interacting with the other segments. The labeling and graphic representation of the integrative value chains created an awareness of a company's activities to improve the efficiency of the traditional coordination mechanisms. Individual company efforts towards this goal fell into one of three categories: (i) creating specialized coordinating organizations, (ii) developing cooperative contractual agreements with adjacent value chains, or (iii) installing shared information transferring systems to directly link activities.

broadly defined industry. Each of these segments produces a "class of products" based on the characteristics of products and the industry's typical way of classifying products. The transition from a product orientation to a process orientation occurs when each class of product is viewed in terms of its unique value-added chain (Porter, 1980).

A value-added chain defines the process activities needed to produce a class of products. A review of the literature on process management identified financial, information, organizational and end-customer perspectives as being critical in establishing the boundaries of a product's value chain. The value chain's financial and information characteristics establish the skeleton of the industry modeling activity, while the customer and organizational characteristics provide the substance of the model.

First, the value chain must have a financial basis that clearly defines a beginning and an end to allow its inputs and outputs to be identified and the value created within the chain to be measured. These definitions build a foundation for activity-based costing systems and enable a design of an effective cost transferring system to quantify the economic relationships between value chains (Slywotzky, 1996). Second, the value chain's scope should be evaluated in terms of its information generated and the information required to support an industry-wide information network. This information clarity establishes the foundation for a data management system to efficiently control information within the boundaries of macro-processes and to build an information coordination system for more efficient communications across value chains (Scheer, 1992). Third, the value chain must have a clearly identified customer, typically a downstream value chain that can establish the requirements (cost, schedule, performance, quality) for the value chain's activities. The customer orientation builds a downstream production mentality that translates the desires, needs and requirements of the end customer through the value-added chain (Halal, Geranmayeh & Pourdehnad, 1993). Fourth, the value chain should be specified in such a way as to clearly establish the organizational authority needed to satisfy the process responsibilities (Quinn, 1992).

These four perspectives define the boundaries of individual value chains, which can be used to translate an industry's product orientation into a process orientation. FIGURE 7.1 summarizes this product to process transition by presenting a hierarchical classification system that defines the levels of the hierarchy. FIGURE 7.1 also provides an example of the levels of the hierarchy for the air transportation industry.

The next step of strategic industry modeling activity involves understanding the various relationships between the value chains. Value chains are designed to accomplish one of three basic purposes within the industry. First of all, vertical value chains create tangible value within a product segment. Examples of vertical value chains are the manufacturing

THE COST OF INVOLVEMENT IN INTEGRATIVE CHAIN ACTIVITIES

We probably spend 30% of all of our costs on attempting to coordinate activities with other industry segments. While these activities generate no tangible revenues, our strategic position is dependent upon them.
(General Manager of an aircraft assembler)

Almost universally, when company executives estimated the costs associated with performing the integrative chain activities, they tended to accept them as the cost of doing business. In fact, many comments were made that companies in general were spending too little on trying to gain a significant competitive advantage through improving the effectiveness of this segment integration.

THE EVOLUTION OF A COMPLEMENTARY PROCESS-ORIENTED INDUSTRY STRUCTURE OF INTEGRATIVE CHAIN ACTIVITIES

I envision the creation of several new segments in this industry to coordinate all of the cross-segment chains. Given the industry's current costs and revenues, these new coordinating segments will probably be the most influential and profitable segments in the industry.
(Manager of New Product Development for a narrowly focused maintenance company)

The strategic reengineering model identifies four major groupings of integrative chains: air traffic management, air worthiness planning and control, avionics flight systems, and aircraft support services. These four integrative chains are being developed/enhanced on a daily basis to help perform the intersegment coordination the industry requires.

Given the costs associated with this so called "red space" (the costly areas of the industry that seemingly create no revenues but absorb tremendous resources), companies are very receptive to taking aggressive steps toward improving the effectiveness of their cross-segment interactions. With the advances in information technology, communications, and data management, the industry is currently overloaded with innovative applications that fundamentally change the way the industry does business. For example, advances in the area of flight tracking, aircraft documentation, and airspace scheduling are going to redefine the cross-segment roles and responsibilities of every company in the industry.

The Competitive Battleground Over the Ownership of Integrative Chains

The industry as a whole wants and needs to see the development of these integrating chains. Our company would be more than willing to relinquish control of many of our current activities if it could obtain ownership of other coordinating activities critical to the protection of the company's core business.
(Corporate Vice President of a major engine manufacturer)

Today's air transportation industry is already seeing a new competitive battleground emerging over these integrative chains. Currently, there are significant obstacles to overcome in the evolution of these new industry segments, most importantly, the ownership of information, the assignment of revenues and costs to the traditional vertical value chains, and a fear of losing control over key aspects of a company's sphere of industry influence.

Conclusion: Strategic Reengineering as a Planning Framework

The air transportation industry provides an example of a diverse but tightly integrated operation that is experiencing the gradual evolution of new process oriented segments. FIGURE 7.4 shows the air transportation industry as a interactive product–process matrix structure. This matrix structure is the result of advances in information technology that solidify the roles and responsibilities of integrative functions that cross the industry's product segments. FIGURE 7.4 shows how these four new integrative segments of air traffic management, airworthiness planning and control, avionic flight systems, and aircraft support services support the product segments.

The fight for control of these emerging integration segments is extremely intense as companies see their revenue sources, profitability, strategic advantage, and distinctive competence all being threatened. As these integrative segments emerge, companies must plan to: (i) gain control or influence the development of those segments that influence their core business, and (ii) modify their current operations in order to effectively adapt to the new industry standards and requirements.

Given the magnitude of these structural industry changes, companies are beginning to ask a new set of questions of their strategy. With an emerging cross-segment process orientation, new corporate-, business-, and functional-level strategy issues will be raised (Porter, 1996; Varadarajan & Clark, 1994). These issues will supplement the traditional product/customer industry focus with a new set of strategic process issues. TABLE 7.2 presents an overview of the traditional strategic issues for the three levels of strategy and outlines several new process oriented strategic issues.

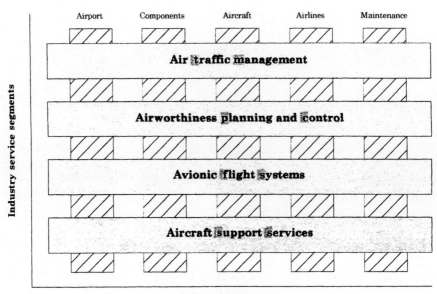

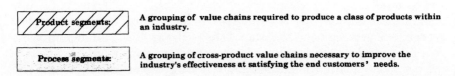

FIGURE 7.4   The product–process matrix industry structure for the air transportation industry

TABLE 7.2   Strategic process issues to supplement traditional product/market issues

Strategy	Traditional product/market issues	Supplemental process issues
Corporate level	Product portfolio Corporate partnership Internal investments	Process portfolio Strategic alliances Sphere of influence
Business level	Product positioning Distinctive competency Competitive advantage	Product customization System design System flexibility
Function level	Functional excellence Functional integration Budgetary implementation	Process effectiveness Process decentralization Balanced scorecard

CORPORATE-LEVEL STRATEGY

Strategic reengineering's ability to view industry activities as a set of interrelated processes can be used to operationalize Porter's work on the five forces of competition (Porter, 1980) from a value chain perspective. The strategic reengineering industry model offers strategic planners the opportunity to construct these five forces for competitive advantage by attempting to control key groups of value chains.

The creation of these new segments will change the dynamic relationships within an industry in terms of the functions of companies and the particular companies performing those functions. Just as outsourcing has changed industry participation of companies, the evolution of the process segments will invite companies who have developed highly specialized and highly transferable expertise in other industries (Doz, 1996). In fact, many industry experts have predicted that a company from outside the current air transportation industry will be needed to solidify the development of the integration chains because of the particular skills needed and the objectivity required to coordinate a set of existing companies with conflicting financial interests.

Strategic reengineering establishes a new set of policy alternatives to gain control of the strategic portions of the industry's activity web. As industries' integrative functions develop, corporate-level strategy will be involved with:

1. **Process portfolios:** which horizontal and integrative chains should we attempt to gain control over (and for what reason) and which horizontal and integrative chains should we encourage others to develop?
2. **Strategic alliances:** what types of cross-segment agreements would be beneficial to both parties?
3. **Sphere of influence:** how can we gain control of other processes to increase the value of our core process's output, especially through the control of information vital to downstream value chains?

BUSINESS-LEVEL STRATEGY

In an industry undergoing a strategic reengineering restructuring, business-level strategies needs to address the design of a system of value chains that can accomplish product customization with a manageable process system that is flexible enough to respond to external shocks.

Strategically reengineered processes decentralized the business strategy questions of positioning (Porter, 1980), patterns of behaviors (Miles & Snow, 1978) and strategic groups (Thomas & Venkatraman, 1988) to individually managed business units structured around a specific value chain.

In order to integrate the strategies of each of the company's value chain organizational units, business-level strategy must establish policies to direct these decentralized value chains. Specifically, a strategically reengineered company needs to view business-level issues in terms of:

1. **Product customization:** how can the company optimize the design and operation of the value chains to obtain process flexibility to customize product requests?
2. **System design:** how do we integrate the series of value chains to balance the needs for efficiency within each decentralized process organization while achieving effectiveness of the company's entire production system?
3. **System flexibility:** how do we maintain a highly efficient process structure while building in capabilities sufficiently flexible to respond to external demands for change?

FUNCTIONAL-LEVEL STRATEGY

Most companies rely on a functional organization to execute strategic decisions. The process management philosophy asks the question, "How can the Engineering Department design a product without the intimate involvement of the Sales, Manufacturing and Distribution Departments?". The answer had traditionally been to create a product–function matrix organization, a structure almost universally applied in the air transportation industry. These matrix organizations decentralize the functional organization bureaucracy, but do little to eliminate the basic functional coordination problems.

Strategic reengineering establishes a systematic set of decentralized process organizations at the intersection of the product–function matrix. All of the coordination lines of the matrix organization are now performed by specialized integrating functions (e.g. the horizontal chains) or by centralized management functions.

This new organizational approach creates a series of new internal management questions, specifically:

1. **Process effectiveness**: how can we design, manage and control a series of process oriented organizations in order to create production flexibility, economies of scope, and process standardization?
2. **Process decentralization**: how can we empower individual process managers to take their own initiative to develop methods to satisfy internal customers while meeting the minimal, yet absolute, corporate requirements?

3. **Balanced scorecard**: how can we plan and control each of these process units with a centralized management made up of human resources, information systems, customer relations, and financial evaluations?

IDEAS FOR FUTURE RESEARCH

The concept of strategic reengineering integrates the techniques of process management with the principals of strategic planning. This chapter represents an initial exploration of how strategic reengineering can be applied in a dynamic industry setting. This initial project has stimulated many ideas regarding potential advancement and applications of strategic reengineering.

One area of potential improvement is in the operationalization of processes, value chains, and value chain linkages. Currently, new management systems such as value migration, process ownership, distributive computing, and internal markets are in need of an integrating value chain framework to bring these complementary perspectives together into a unified whole. The improved clarity of value chain boundaries and interrelationships is a critical step in building a foundation for these new process management systems.

Another area for further research is the longitudinal study of the evolution of an industry's structure. The advancements in information technology have changed the basic foundation of many industries. These changes have made obsolete many previously critical functions while creating a new set of coordinating management functions. Strategic reengineering provides a framework to track the actual movements of an industry in terms of how the industry performs its processes and where economic value and financial results are created.

Strategic reengineering establishes a new set of issues for companies to contemplate when developing company direction. Each of these issues stimulates thought into the various alternative strategies to gain an advantageous position in the industry. Additional work is needed to develop a list of strategic alternatives for each of these issues and to test the performance results of the alternatives as industries begin to go through the evolutionary process of change.

ACKNOWLEDGMENTS

Many of the findings reported here were developed in a formal working group of 14 companies competing in various segments of the air transportation industry. The author expresses his appreciation to both the Strategic

Reengineering Institute and the Air Transportation Industry Working Group for their ideas and support related to the creation of this text.

Additional appreciation should be acknowledged to the Katz Graduate School of Business at the University of Pittsburgh and the Boeing Company for supporting the initial research that served as the foundation of this chapter. A special acknowledgements needs to be given to Robert Harper of the Boeing Company, whose insight into the evolution of the industry and vision of strategic implications of macro-level process management shaped the basic conclusions of this study.

REFERENCES

Air Transportation Association (1996). Industry activity hierarchy diagram. *ATA Industry Specification 2100*, Chapter 2, pp. 37–52.

Benjamin, R. & Wigand, R. (1995). Electronic markets and virtual value chains on the information superhighway. *Sloan Management Review*, Winter, 62–72.

Bogner, W. & Thomas, H. (1993). The role of competitive groups in strategy formulation: a dynamic integration of two competing models. *Journal of Management Studies*, **30**(1), 51–67.

Doz, Y.L. (1996). The evolution of cooperation in strategic alliances: initial conditions on learning processes?, *Strategic Management Journal*, **17**(2), 55–83.

Dussaugo, P. & Garrette, B. (1995). Determinants of success in international strategic alliances: evidence from the global airspace industry. *Journal of International Business Studies*, **26**(4), 505–531.

Halal, W., Geranmayeh, A. & Pourdehnad, J. (1993). *Internal Markets*. New York: Wiley.

Hambrick, D. (1983). An empirical typology of mature industrial-product environments. *Academy of Management Journal*, **26**(2), 213–230.

Huff, A. (1982). Industry influences on strategy formulation. *Strategic Management Journal*, **3**(2), 119–130.

Miles, R.E. & Snow, C.C. (1978). *Organizational Structure and Process*. New York: McGraw-Hill.

Porter, M.E. (1979). The structure within industries and companies' performance. *Review of Economics and Statistics*, **61**, 214–229.

Porter, M.E. (1980). *Competitie Strategy: Techniques for Analyzing Industries and Competitors*. New York: Free Press.

Porter, M. (1996). What is strategy? *Harvard Business Review*, November/December, 61.

Pritsker, K. (1995). Top ten reasons for reengineering failure, *Strategic Reengineering Institute Working Paper Series*, Pittsburgh, PA.

Quinn, J.B. (1992). *Intelligent Enterprise*. New York: Free Press.

Ring, D.M. & VanDeVen, A.H. (1994). Developing processes of cooperative inter-organizational relationships. *Academy of Management Review*, **19**, 90–115.

Scheer, A.W. (1992). *Architecture of Integrated Information Systems*. New York: Springer-Verlag.

Strategic Reengineering Institute (1996). Strategic reengineering: using business process reengineering concepts to redefine industry boundaries, Confidential report prepared for the ATI Strategic Reengineering Working Group, March, pp. 1–52.

Slywotzky, A.J. (1996). *Value Migration*. Boston, MA: Corporate Decisions, Inc.

Thomas, H. & Venkatraman, N. (1988). Research on strategic groups: Progress and prognosis. *Journal of Management Studies*, **25**, 537–555.

Upton, D. & McAfee, A. (1996). The real virtual factory. *Harvard Business Review*, July/August, 123–133.

Varadarajan, P.R. & Clark, T. (1994). Delineating the scope of corporate business and marketing strategy. *Journal of Business Research*, **31**, 93–105.

Changing Formal and Informal Structure to Enhance Organizational Knowledge

Tracy A. Thompson, Kathleen L. Valley

Resource-based views of the firm (Penrose, 1969; Peteraf, 1993; Rumelt, 1984; Wernerfelt, 1984) argue that imperfectly imitable resources, for example unique human resources and knowledge, are important bases for creating a stable competitive advantage. In this chapter, we investigate the attempts of one organization to enhance its knowledge competencies. We follow the organization for approximately one year, taking advantage of a natural field experiment: a reorganization from a traditional hierarchical structure to a team-based structure. Turning to the literature on knowledge creation and organizational learning, we develop propositions of the ways in which social structures influence organizational learning and the development of knowledge competencies. We use longitudinal data to examine the association between social structure, specifically levels of task-related cohesion and expressive cohesion within teams, and knowledge, operationalized as changes in productivity and product quality.

Our contribution to the literature on organizational knowledge and learning is twofold. First, by emphasizing the important role that social interaction plays in developing knowledge and offering a model of the specific roles played by task-based and expressive interaction, we add depth

Strategic Flexibility: Managing in a Turbulent Environment. Edited by G. Hamel, C.K. Prahalad, H. Thomas and D. O'Neal.
Copyright © 1998 John Wiley & Sons Ltd.

and richness to existing theories. Although we study only one organization (and therefore cannot make claims about the generation of competitive advantage), we provide a detailed look at the steps involved in building knowledge or human-based competencies. Second, we suggest and employ empirical methods that can be used to study the development of knowledge in the firm.

ORGANIZATIONAL KNOWLEDGE AND LEARNING

This section outlines the fundamental assumptions underlying our approach to studying organizational knowledge and learning. First, we follow Cook & Yanow's (1993) action-oriented view of learning, which suggests that performance of a group or organization is the best evidence of an increasing accumulation of organization and task appropriate knowledge. Second, we note that knowledge can take at least three forms: (i) cognitive knowledge in the form of mental constructs and precepts, (ii) skills, and (iii) knowledge as it is embodied in products, well defined services or artifacts (Hedlund, 1994). In this study, we focus on the latter two forms, skills and products, because they are the manifestations of knowledge most closely related to organizational effectiveness.

Third, drawing from theories of the knowledge creation process in firms we recognize that although learning first takes place in individuals' heads, if it is to affect the organization, individually-held knowledge must be transmitted to higher levels, including the small group, the organization and beyond (Simon, 1991; Weick & Ashford, 1996). As Hedlund (1994, p. 75) argues, "Posing the group as an intermediate level allows a more fine grained look at what goes on within the organization. The prominence of small groups, often temporary, in innovation and product development indicates that this is the level at which much of the knowledge transfer and learning take place."

Finally, we adopt a structuralist approach to studying the knowledge transfer and learning process in organizations. Network approaches to studying organizations assume that individuals within an organization do not operate in isolation but develop and work within an informal structure of relationships and interactions (Granovetter, 1992). The informal structure can be observed or measured by examining the interactions across members. The interactions can have various contents, e.g. task-related communication, mutually serving on committees, or going to lunch together.

An informal structure created by any given type of tie does not necessarily mirror the organization's formal structure, but the two are reciprocally influential, especially as they influence the development of knowledge. Formal organizational structure (that prescribed by the organization chart) both creates and constrains informal structure or actual interaction. In turn, the informal structure of communication and interaction both generates and constrains the development of knowledge. This process is likely recursive: the formal structure of the organization helps determine the informal structure of interaction; the informal structure of interaction drives learning; in turn, new knowledge and understandings set limits on the extent to which new formal structures are likely to be imposed.

From these assumptions, several questions emerge. First, can firms manipulate this knowledge creation process by altering formal structures in order to enhance organizational effectiveness? Can firms encourage learning and the development of knowledge competencies at the small group level? And second, if they can, what does the process look like? What role does social structure play in enabling one group to learn more than another?

CAN ORGANIZATIONS FACILITATE LEARNING?

One way organizations can encourage learning, and hence enhance organizational effectiveness, is to recombine currently held knowledge (Kogut & Zander, 1992; McGrath, MacMillan & Venkataraman, 1995). Reorganizing into teams, in essence recombining human resources, creates at least two avenues for learning. First, jobs are often modified. In this case, learning is encouraged by making people stretch into performing new tasks, or performing old tasks in new ways. Second, reorganizing into teams can stimulate learning by encouraging new transfers of knowledge from individuals to the group. The mere suggestion that the team rather than the individual is responsible for the output (and payoff) provides an incentive for the individuals within the team to spread some of their individually-held know-how to the group. Reorganization into teams does not inevitably lead to new knowledge; rather reorganization *can* enhance organizational learning *if* it fosters a realignment of the social interaction within the organization. This leads to our first proposition.

Proposition 1: Reorganization into teams will increase individual and organizational learning through a realignment of social interaction.

HOW IS KNOWLEDGE CREATED IN SMALL GROUPS?

Learning results as ideas and knowledge are transmitted from individuals to the group and applied to organizational objectives (Simon, 1991). As individuals interact with others in a newly formed group, they pass on ideas, filter the ideas of others, integrate the approaches of others into their own, and generally act as transmitters, receivers, and integrators of organizational knowledge. In this section, we argue for how different types of interaction lead to different types of learning.

Distinguishing between task-related (or instrumental interaction) and expressive interaction (Brass, 1984; Coleman, 1988), we argue that higher levels of *task-related* interaction in newly created teams will lead to higher productivity. Group performance research indicates that increased communication is a key factor influencing performance (Katz, 1982). To the extent that a shift to teams opens up new task-related conversations, new learning should result as information about how to do the job more efficiently gets transferred among members of a group.

> **Proposition 2.** Subsequent to a reorganization, higher levels of task-related interaction within a team will result in greater team efficiencies.

But the generation of knowledge sufficiently exceptional to enhance product quality involves a different process. Commitment to the group and to the organization play an important role in developing innovative and creative knowledge in product teams (Nonaka, 1996). Translated into structuralist terms, enhancing quality requires not only that the individuals within the organization communicate about their required tasks, but that they share ideas outside the scope of "normal" task-related conversations. Individuals share more information with friends than with non-friends (Berndt, 1981; Newcomb & Brady, 1982), which may be due to higher levels of contact, greater trust, and the presence of self-disclosure norms typical of close relationships (Roloff, 1987; Argyle & Henderson, 1985). Such expressive interaction generates the group commitment and trust necessary for the development of the knowledge necessary to enhance product quality.

The relationship between expressive interaction and product quality may be even more important during times of structural change. Reorganization is a time of great uncertainty to members of the organization, a time when new objectives may or may not be clear and the methods for achieving them in the newly designed organization are vague. Once expressive ties are established, organizational members may be more willing to take risks with one another and to discuss new ideas that may lead to a better product. This leads to our third proposition.

> **Proposition 3.** Subsequent to a reorganization, higher levels of expressive interaction within a team will result in higher team product quality.

STUDY BACKGROUND

Taking advantage of a natural experiment, we follow one newspaper organization as it altered its organizational routines and structures in order to manage and develop the knowledge of its core human resource, reporters in the newsroom. Literally overnight, reporters were placed into new "topic teams" which allegedly better reflected reader interests than the traditional desks or beats. Intuitively following Chandler's (1962) "structure follows strategy" logic, management hoped that shifting to a team-based production model would democratize content decisions and encourage reporters and editors to think more strategically, making them more innovative and more capable of executing the newspaper's product–market strategy.

The *Range* is owned by a large, publicly traded newspaper group (the name has been changed to provide confidentiality). Serving a major metropolitan area in the United States, the *Range*'s daily circulation is approximately 130 000, with an additional 20 000 readers on Sunday. While the newspaper faced no direct competition in the area, management was concerned with other competitive media products and the decline of readership penetration (percentage of adult population in the area that subscribes). In the year prior to the reorganization, circulation growth had not kept up with population growth.

Before the reorganization, the executive editor oversaw two assistant managing editors, who, in turn, oversaw the desks and functional departments. The newsroom had four "desks," each comprised of reporters covering an area—metropolitan news, business, features, and general assignment—plus one to three layers of desk editors (supervisors). In addition, there were functional departments—copy editing, art, and photography.

The workflow was sequential across desks and functional departments. Within a desk, the reporter received an assignment from a desk editor, wrote the story with input from the editor, and then passed it back to the editor. When the editor sent the text to the copy department, the story left the reporter and the desk, never to return. Copy editors worked in isolation from the desk as they tightened prose and added headlines. The copy department also included page designers who added graphics and photographs and formatted the article onto the page. Assistant managing editors were then responsible for getting the paper to production by the deadline. Overall, decisions at each step were made independently by whoever was controlling the story at that stage.

The reorganized newsroom is overseen by two "coordinators" who report to the executive editor. The traditional content areas have been modified to focus the reporters on the interests of local readers. Nine new "topic teams" were created. Each team was assigned a specific type of story and point of view to emphasize. For example, one team was assigned to report on jobs, employment, and work in the metropolitan area, and its charter was to focus more on consumer issues than the economy. The various desk editors have been eliminated and replaced with one supervisory layer, "topic team leaders." The functional departments still exist, but copy editing has been split into two distinct teams—presentation and editing. This reorganization also included a physical move so that the members of each team sit together in the newsroom.

Workflow has been modified to emphasize integration rather than sequential access. Reporters are more involved with the production of the story and are encouraged to work collectively with their team members and functional staff when making decisions about stories. Similarly, but to a lesser degree, functional staff are expected to make their decisions about editing and presentation in concert with reporters and team leaders. Management hoped that these organizational changes would enable reporters to "think more like publishers."

DESIGN AND DATA COLLECTION

The data presented here are part of a larger longitudinal study of organizational change. The methods involved surveying employees in the newsroom, collecting personnel data, and collecting archival data on the articles produced by the newsroom. We surveyed employees four times during the 13 months spanning August 1995 to September 1996: (i) two weeks before the organizational restructuring, which occurred in September 1995, (ii) two months after the change, (iii) seven months after the change, and (iv) one year after the change. The survey was a sociometric questionnaire that asked staff to rate their interactions with every other individual in the newsroom. Archival data on the newspaper product was taken from an electronic database maintained by the newspaper.

Although over 75 people are involved in the newsroom hierarchical structure, we used sociometric data only from members of eight of the primary topic teams, excluding those who operated solely out of satellite offices (each topic team has a color label to provide confidentiality). We excluded one topic team because it only had two people with non-overlapping shifts. The analyses included 31 reporters and 8 team leaders at time one, 29 reporters and 8 team leaders at time two, 29 reporters and 8 team leaders at time three, and 27 reporters and 7 team leaders at time four. Response rates at times one, two, three and four were 94.9%, 86.5%, 89.2% and 91.2%, respectively.

Measures

We calculated two dependent variables which measured two of Hedlund's (1994) forms of knowledge. Team productivity, which reflects knowledge in the form of skills, was calculated by taking the total number of articles produced by a team over the two-month period surrounding the survey date and dividing it by the total number of team members. This generates a productivity number that controls for team size and is comparable across teams. (Productivity figures which controlled for the total number and length of the articles in the newspaper and the size of the newspaper resulted in similar findings.)

A second variable, product quality, reflects knowledge in the form of the newspaper product itself. The switch to a team-based production model was supposed to encourage reporters to adopt a new standard of logic of journalism. This new logic, articulated in management's goals at the time of the reorganization, replaces the more insular and traditional journalistic practice of "giving the public what it *needs to know*" with "giving the public what it *wants to see*." Our measure of quality taps into the new standards that reporter teams are being asked to learn. Are the articles written *for* the reader? Do the stories grab the interest of and entertain the reader?

To generate the quality measure, we randomly selected ten articles per team that appeared on the front page of the two main sections in the newspaper (A1 and B1) over the two-month period surrounding each of the survey dates. Two teams, White and Fuchsia, had fewer than ten articles on the front page for one or more of the four time periods so we supplemented a randomly selected subset of A1/B1 pages with randomly selected articles from the appropriate main section or page for the team.

Each article was rated by four independent coders, all of whom were members of the community served by the newspaper. Coders rated each article on seven-point Likert scales in response to five questions. Principal components factor analyses revealed that responses to two of the five questions loaded onto a single factor that was stable across all four time periods: "The article is written to entertain and grab interest (7) or tell facts and disseminate information (1)"; and "The article tells the story in a way that is geared toward readers (7) or just gets the news out on the page (1)". The proportion of variance explained by this factor was 86%, 98%, 80%. and 96% for times one, two, three, and four, respectively. Because of the subjective nature of the rating task and the use of a seven-point scale, perfect agreement across coders was unlikely; coder agreement as measured by pairwise correlation coefficients on these two questions was significant in every case. To produce the final team level measure for product quality, we averaged the four coders' scorers for each article and then averaged each team's scores on the ten articles.

We obtained the independent measures of expressive and task-related interaction patterns from sociometric survey data. Respondents were provided with a list of all newsroom personnel included in the study and were asked to rate each on a seven-point scale indicating how often they talked face-to-face about task-related topics, how often they went to the other person for help, how critical the other person was to their overall productivity, and how often they relied on the other for emotional support. On all but the critical measure, a rating of seven points indicated interaction several times daily, while a rating of one indicated no interaction. For the critical measure, a rating of seven indicated that the other person was extremely critical to their overall productivity, while a rating of one indicated the other as not being at all critical. Across all time periods, the data revealed high associations between task-related interaction, helping interaction and critical work interaction (Chronbach's alpha = .97 at time one, .97 at time two, .94 at time three, and .93 at time 4). Therefore, we averaged the scores from these three measures into a single measure reflecting task-related interaction. We used the "emotional support" tie as the measure for expressive interaction.

After extracting a matrix for each team on each content tie, we calculated the average level of within-team interaction on the given tie. Within-team cohesion is the sum of the reported levels of interaction between team members divided by the total number of possible ties within the group. This measure reflects how closely tied the members of the team are to one another, where higher scores indicate more frequent interaction among members.

All of our measures are calculated at the team level for each of the four time periods. Note that the teams at time one are fictional, where the "teams" are aggregations of individuals who comprise the actual teams at time two. While the actors knew the teams to which they would later be assigned, at time one they were still working from traditional "desks".

ANALYSES AND RESULTS

We used the propositions developed above to guide our qualitative and quantitative analyses. Proposition 1 was examined by assessing the aggregate changes occurring over the four time periods. Propositions 2 and 3 were examined using qualitative analyses of the data on productivity, product quality, and social ties.

EFFECTS OF NEWSROOM RESTRUCTURING

When looking at the newsroom as a whole, TABLE 8.1 shows that productivity increased after the reorganization. The change from 25.0 articles per reporter during the two-month period at time one to 34.24 articles per reporter at

TABLE 8.1 Summary of data on team productivity and product quality

Team	Productivity[a]				Quality[b]			
	Time 1	Time 2	Time 3	Time 4	Time 1	Time 2	Time 3	Time 4
Blue	19.14	27.00	25.33	23.56	4.18	4.85	4.84	4.24
Celadon	24.12	36.40	39.57	37.17	4.36	5.28	4.11	4.16
Cream	36.63	55.60	64.60	48.65	4.83	3.96	4.69	4.16
Fuchsia	32.29	33.75	33.80	35.53	5.14	5.39	5.40	5.38
Red	20.86	25.14	24.30	24.73	4.60	3.24	3.91	4.19
Sapphire	17.38	32.75	34.60	39.85	3.36	4.16	3.81	4.21
Turquoise	26.16	32.74	32.17	31.50	3.70	4.28	3.38	4.08
White	23.38	30.50	33.50	44.20	4.04	4.25	3.68	4.83
Averages	25.00	34.24	35.98	35.69	4.28	4.43	4.26	4.41

[a]Average number of articles per reporter in a two-month period.
[b]Average article ratings, 1–7 scale.

time two is significant ($p \leq 0.01$), but none of the increases in productivity after time two are significant.

While productivity across reporters in the study increased sharply right after the reorganization and leveled off, ratings of quality in the news stories show a different pattern. Average ratings of the articles produced by reporters in the newsroom show no significant change after the reorganization.

We also assessed the changes in interaction across all reporters in the teams we studied. The average frequency of both task-related and expressive interaction across these reporters did not increase significantly after the reorganization, as revealed in the last row of TABLE 8.2. When assessing interaction at the team level, however, a slightly different pattern emerges. TABLE 8.2 shows that the average levels of within-team, task-based interaction increased significantly from time one to time two (two-tailed t-test = 4.13, $p = 0.004$) and then remained constant thereafter. The level of task-related cohesion one year after the change remained significantly higher than the level prior to the change.

Expressive interaction within teams also increased significantly from time one to time two (two-tailed t-test = 5.29, $p = 0.001$). The slight decrease at time three was not significant, but the increase in expressive cohesion between time three and time four was marginally significant (two-tailed t-test = 1.94, $p = 0.094$). As was the case with task-related interaction, the level of expressive cohesion within teams one year after the reorganization remained significantly higher than the cohesion levels prior to the reorganization (two-tailed t-test = 8.75, $p = 0.0001$).

These descriptive analyses reveal that for this organization, restructuring that involved job redesign and the creation of new teams resulted in increased productivity. Our data show that the significant increases in

TABLE 8.2   Summary of task-related and expressive cohesion data

Team	Task-related cohesion (average strength of task ties within team)				Expressive cohesion (average strength of expressive ties within team)			
	Time 1	Time 2	Time 3	Time 4	Time 1	Time 2	Time 3	Time 4
Blue	2.61	5.36	6.44	5.28	1.83	3.92	3.50	3.35
Celadon	2.95	4.58	3.72	4.30	1.85	2.85	2.40	2.76
Cream	2.55	6.17	6.22	5.28	1.50	3.25	2.83	3.17
Fuchsia	6.50	6.00	4.55	5.25	3.50	6.50	3.83	5.25
Red	1.93	4.04	3.85	4.49	1.40	2.17	3.19	3.73
Sapphire	1.67	6.00	3.89	6.17	1.50	3.50	3.67	4.83
Turquoise	3.47	5.00	4.83	4.18	2.00	2.92	2.83	3.10
White	2.96	4.67	5.42	4.86	2.19	3.25	4.00	3.50
Within team average	3.08	5.23	4.87	4.99	1.97	3.54	3.28	3.71
(s.d.)	(1.50)	(0.78)	(1.07)	(0.65)	(0.68)	(1.30)	(0.56)	(0.88)
Average across newsroom	2.00	2.04	1.93	2.05	1.58	1.72	1.68	1.81
(s.d.)	(1.30)	(1.36)	(1.32)	(1.36)	(1.03)	(1.13)	(1.20)	(1.27)

productivity occurring right after the change were sustained over time. Controlling for size of the newsroom, reporters in the newsroom were producing more articles after the change. Our data also show, however, that according to our coders' ratings, product quality did not change in the year following the reorganization.

Proposition 1 argues that reorganization increases learning through a realignment of social interaction. Our data show task-related interaction and expressive interaction to be fairly constant across time across the entire newsroom. Within-team cohesion after the reorganization is noticeably higher than the average density of ties in the newsroom overall. More importantly, the increase in cohesion among future team members at time one to actual team members at time two suggests that social interaction is realigning as a result of changes in the formal structure. Thus, Proposition 1 appears to be supported. These analyses do not, however, tell us the relationship between social interaction and learning. We turn to this question next.

THE RELATIONSHIP BETWEEN SOCIAL INTERACTION AND TEAM KNOWLEDGE

Proposition 2 asserts that task-related interaction will affect team knowledge as evidenced in production efficiencies. For productivity, we assessed the pattern of change from one time period to the next. Since we have complete productivity data for each team, statistical significance tests are unnecessary. However, to simplify the categorization of teams' productivity patterns, we considered increases or decreases greater than 20% from one time period to the next to be "significant" changes. (Twenty per cent was a natural cutoff point when the data were rank ordered.) Management had always expected reporters to work as efficiently as possible on their assignments while maintaining the quality of their reporting; thus, a comparison between productivity prior to and after the reorganization is appropriate.

Five teams revealed increases in productivity from time to time two which then leveled off through time four. Of the three remaining teams, one team, Fuchsia, had no change in productivity across all four time periods. Another team, White, showed an increase from time one to time two, no change from time two to time three, and an increase from time three to time four. The final team, Cream, showed an increase in productivity from time one to time two, no change from time two to time three, and a decrease from time three to time four.

To develop descriptions of the teams' task-related interaction patterns we used unpaired t-tests to assess the significance of the changes in the strength of the dyadic task-related relationships reported by team members. Five of the eight teams showed a significant increase in the strength of task-related ties from time one to time two (Celadon, unpaired t-test = 2.92, $p = 0.0059$; Red, unpaired t-test = 6.73, $p = 0.0000$; Sapphire, unpaired t-test = 4.82, $t = 0.0013$; Turquoise, unpaired t-test = 2.25, $p = 0.0316$; and White, unpaired t-test = 2.96, $p = 0.0056$). However, for each of these teams, none of the changes past time two was significant. Of the remaining three teams, one team, Fuchsia, had no significant changes in the strength of task-related ties within the team over the four time periods. Another team, Blue, revealed a significant increase in task-related ties from time one to time two (unpaired t-test = 6.16, $p = 0.0000$) and from time two to time three (unpaired t-test = 2.87, $p = 0.0112$) but then had a significant decrease from time three to time four (unpaired t-test = -2.99, $p = 0.0063$). The final team, Cream, had a significant increase in task-related interaction from time one to time two (unpaired t-test = 6.32, $p = 0.0002$), no changes in task-related interaction from time two to time three, and a marginally significant decrease in task-related interaction from time three to time four (unpaired t-test = -1.8, $p = 0.1017$).

TABLE 8.3 provides a summary of the association between changes in task-related interaction and changes in productivity. In six of the eight teams, the entire change pattern for task-related cohesion matches that of productivity. Using each change from one time period to the next as the unit of analysis (as opposed to the entire pattern of change), TABLE 8.3 also shows that 21 of the 24 possible changes match. Together these results provide support for

TABLE 8.3   Comparison of change patterns: productivity and task-related cohesion

	Red, Celadon, Turquoise, Sapphire	Blue	Fuchsia	Cream	White
Productivity change pattern	⇑⇒⇒	⇑⇒⇒	⇒⇒⇒	⇑⇒⇓	⇑⇒⇑
Task-related cohesion change pattern	Same	⇑⇑⇓	Same	Same	⇑⇒⇒

The symbols represent change patterns from time one to time two, time two to time three, and time three to time four.

Proposition 2. Changes in task-related interaction among team members appear to be positively related to changes in productivity. When task-related interaction increases, productivity increases; when task-related interaction levels off, productivity levels off; and when task-related interaction decreases, productivity decreases. There was no relationship between the change patterns in task-related cohesion and product quality.

As mentioned earlier, an increase in story quality was one of the major thrusts of the organizational change. Not only did management reorganize the newsroom, they also shifted the emphasis of reporting to be more local and more responsive to readers within the metropolitan market. The result was a new definition of a good news story, from one that reported facts and disseminated information to one that captured the attention and interest of the local reader. Changing from a journalistic focus to a customer focus required reporters to take on different story assignments and to learn new, more creative ways of writing. Management hoped that within-team interaction would help reporters to increase the quality of their stories, making them more appealing to readers. Unlike productivity, prior to the time of the reorganization story assignment had not explicitly focused on generating stories that would be geared toward the reader, rendering story content comparisons between time one and the later time periods inappropriate for this analysis. Thus, to assess Proposition 3, we look at patterns of change in our product quality measure and expressive cohesion between times two and four only.

Proposition 3 asserts that increases in story quality will be associated with increases in expressive cohesion. To test this, we compared changes in product quality with changes in the levels of expressive cohesion among teams. We used *t*-tests from time two to time three and time three to time four to assess the pattern of change in the quality of each team's product.

For five of the eight teams, ratings on story content showed no significant change between the time immediately following the change and one year subsequent to the change. One team, Blue, showed a marginally significant decrease in product quality from time three to time four (unpaired t-test = -1.78, $p = 0.0916$). Another team, Celadon, showed a significant decrease in product quality from time two to time three (unpaired t-test = -2.23, $p = 0.0385$). The last team, White, showed a significant increase in product quality from time three to time four (unpaired t-test = 3.19, $p = 0.0051$).

We then conducted t-tests across the same time periods to assess the patterns of change in expressive interaction for each of the teams. These analyses revealed that seven of the eight teams showed no significant changes in expressive cohesion. One team, Red, increased its expressive cohesion from time two to time three (unpaired t-test = 2.89, $p = 0.0049$), but the change from time three to time four was not significant.

These data reveal little association between product quality and expressive cohesion, providing no strong support for Proposition 3. In support of our proposition, however, the greatest positive change in reader oriented content from time two to time four (0.957, unpaired t-test = 1.94, $p = 0.0691$) was produced by Red, the only team with a significant increase in expressive cohesion during the year after the reorganization.

Understandably, we were unsatisfied with these findings. Contrary to our expectations, only two teams showed any significant increases in product quality once the teams had been formed. (White showed an increase from time three to time four and Red showed an increase from time two to time four). Furthermore, only one team showed any significant changes in expressive cohesion once the teams had been formed. These factors make inferences about the relationship between product quality and expressive interaction problematic.

When originally laying out our propositions, we reasoned that increasing levels of product quality would require trust among team members, the ability to test and question one another, and the willingness to try out new ideas as a team. We argued that increasing levels of expressive cohesion would be positively related to quality. If anything, our data show the negative side of this proposition, namely that without increases in trust over time, quality may suffer.

Our knowledge of the organization led us to question the extent to which members identified with their teams. Some of the teams experienced so much turnover during the year following the reorganization that they likely had a difficult time establishing a strong team identity. We decided to look at the association between turnover and product quality. Using archival data provided by the organization, we classified three teams as having high turnover, those with five or more incidents of entrance or exit in the year

TABLE 8.4   Comparison of change patterns: product quality
and turnover

Team	Product quality change patterns[a]		Turnover[b]
Celadon	⇓	⇒	High (8)
Blue	⇒	⇓	High (5)
Sapphire	⇒	⇒	High (6)
Red	⇒	⇒	Low (3)
Turquoise	⇒	⇒	Low (2)
Cream	⇒	⇒	Low (2)
Fuchsia	⇒	⇒	Low (2)
White	⇒	⇑	Low (1)

[a]Time two to time three and time three to time four.
[b]Time two to time four.

following the reorganization. Those with three or fewer incidents of entrance or exit we classified as having low turnover.

TABLE 8.4 shows a strong association between product quality and turnover in seven of the eight teams. Two of the three teams with falling ratings of product quality (Celadon, time two to time three, unpaired t-test $= -2.23$, $p = 0.0385$; Blue, time three to time four, unpaired t-test $= 1.78$, $p = 0.0916$) had high turnover. Of the five teams with low turnover, four had flat ratings of product quality. The team with the lowest turnover, White, showed an increase in product quality from time three to time four (unpaired t-test $= 3.19$, $p = 0.0051$). These findings suggest that turnover is negatively related to the teams' product quality.

DISCUSSION AND CONCLUSION

We began by asking whether firms can manage and grow their core knowledge competencies and, if so, what the process looks like. Our data show that after the structural reorganization, productivity in the newsroom increased while product quality, measured in ratings of how much the individual stories were geared toward the reader, stayed constant. Given that one major goal was to increase the newsroom's ability to respond to and write for the local reader, the reorganization appears to have been only partially successful. Although the average rating of how much each individual story grabbed the reader was the same one year after the reorganization than it had been prior to the change, the local reader benefited from the change in another way. Controlling for the total number and length of stories in the paper and the number of reporters in the newsroom, our productivity data show that after the reorganization the new topic teams produced more articles for inclusion in the daily paper. Thus, the newsroom was increasing the overall number of stories targeted toward local readers, replacing stories taken directly from national wire services. The change was successful in this regard.

Our second major question was to ask how knowledge competencies are developed in teams. Specifically, we focused on how newly formed teams are able to create and disseminate knowledge through interaction. We distinguished between two types of knowledge, knowledge about how to do one's current job (skills), which increases efficiency and productivity, and knowledge about how to change one's approach to the job, which results in a more reader-oriented, higher quality product. We also distinguished between two types of interaction, task-related interaction and expressive interaction.

Tying interaction types to these outcomes of knowledge, we proposed and found that new teams which are highly cohesive in task-related connections learned how to be higher producers. We also proposed a positive relationship between expressive interaction and product quality. However, our findings indicate something different. Specifically, we found little or no association between changes in expressive connections and changes in product quality. Additional analyses showed that turnover predicted changes in product quality better than expressive cohesion. High turnover has a negative impact on product quality.

The context of organizational change, specifically the development of new working groups, is a fundamental factor in these findings. Knowledge may develop in very different ways in a stable system than it does after a major reorganization. As new teams come together, task-related interaction helps members coordinate and accomplish their tasks as efficiently as possible. This effect may stabilize as the team begins to rely on accepted routines for accomplishing its objectives. As the team matures and comes to fully "know" its required tasks, the learning resulting from initially high levels of task-related interaction may be formally incorporated into the way the team meets its productivity goals and the effects of additional interaction may be minimized.

We assumed that increases in expressive ties within a newly formed team would also have a positive effect on a team's knowledge, in this case knowledge that is embodied in a more reader-oriented product. Instead we found that within-team turnover may provide an alternative or complementary explanation for differences across teams. Turnover may influence the development of knowledge in at least two ways. First, it could alter the aggregate level of task-specific knowledge in a team (e.g. if reporters new to the area replace more seasoned reporters). Second, turnover may also impede the development of group identification and trust. We suspect that movement in and out of a team destabilizes the existing social structure of the group and threatens group identity. New members must be assimilated, and departing members leave holes in the social structure of the group. Future research within organizations should attempt to examine the relationship between turnover, the skill base of team members, expressive interaction, the development of group identity and trust, and the development of knowledge.

We undertook this study to see if an organization could increase its effectiveness through changing its structure and to see what role relationships might play in the development of knowledge competencies in teams. Viewed in one light, our data could be interpreted as revealing the classic tradeoff between quantity and quality. Given that management desired increases in both, we believe that the organization's inability to improve product quality could also have stemmed from the design of the change effort, factors that affected all of the teams in this organization equally. Research examining work teams argues that team performance and learning are facilitated by including specific and measurable team goals that are linked to strategic objectives, information systems which can be used to monitor team effectiveness, a reward system that is linked to team goals, and the training and development of team leaders and members (Cohen, 1994; Hackman, 1990; Mohrman, Cohen & Mohrman Jr, 1995). Although management set a broad overall strategic direction for the newsroom, to date the teams have yet to translate that into clear performance objectives. In addition, the teams have not developed information systems to track their own performance, the organization's reward system has not been altered to encourage team incentives, and reporters have been given little training in teamwork or in how to write stories in a new and more reader-oriented way.

Despite the important role these design elements could have played in enhancing the performance of all of the teams in our study, our research does suggest the important role that social interaction and the development of new skills and relationships can play when changing structures. Creating and facilitating task-based interaction early in a team's life cycle and trying to avoid excessive turnover (or at least actively managing its negative effects on morale) can help to foster the team's development.

Finally, while we have confidence that this study provides some useful insight on the development of knowledge competencies, the assumptions and propositions suggested by our model need to be tested in future research. We observed behavior and outcomes in one organization within one industry. We encountered the difficulty of doing longitudinal analysis with only eight observations (teams) over four time periods. Finally, the specific type of teams we observed in the newsroom may not generalize well to other organizations.

Although our analyses are exploratory in nature, we have provided evidence to suggest that management can encourage learning and the development of knowledge competencies in employees by reorganizing. We have also provided support for our assertion that changes in the structure of informal interaction drive the development of knowledge competencies, and thus add to the growing understanding of how knowledge is created and disseminated in organizations.

REFERENCES

Argyle, M. & Henderson, M. (1985). The rules of relationships. In S. Duck & D. Periman (eds) *Understanding Personal Relationships: An Interdisciplinary Approach.* Beverly Hills, CA: Sage.

Berndt, T.J. (1981). Effects of friendship on prosocial intentions and behavior. *Child Development*, **52**, 636–643.

Brass, D.J. (1984). Being in the right place: a structural analysis of individual influence in an organization. *Administrative Science Quarterly*, **29**, 518–539.

Chandler, Jr, A.D. (1962). *Strategy and Structure.* Cambridge, MA: MIT Press.

Cohen, S.G. (1994). Designing effective self-managing work teams. In M.M. Beyerlein & D.A. Johnson (eds) *Advances in Interdisciplinary Studies of Work Teams: Theories of Self-Managing Work Teams*, vol. 1. Greenwich, CT: JAI Press, pp. 67–102.

Coleman, J.S. (1988). Social capital in the creation of human capital. *American Journal of Sociology*, **94-S**, S95–S120.

Cook, S.D.N. & Yanow, D. (1993). Culture and organizational learning. *Journal of Management Inquiry*, **2**, 373–390.

Granovetter, M. (1992). Problems of explanation in economic sociology. In N. Nohria & R.G. Eccles (eds) *Networks and Organizations.* Cambridge, MA: Harvard Business School Press, pp. 25–56.

Hackman, J.R. (1990). Work teams in organizations: an orienting framework. In J.R. Hackman (ed.) *Groups that Work (and those that Don't).* San Francisco, CA: Jossey-Bass, pp. 1–14.

Hedlund, G. (1994). A model of knowledge management and the N-form corporation. *Strategic Management Journal*, **15**(1), 73–90.

Katz, R. (1982). The effects of group longevity on project communication and performance. *Administrative Science Quarterly*, **27**, 81–104.

Kogut, B. & Zander, U. (1992). Knowledge of the firm and the replication of technology. *Organization Science*, **3**(3), 383–397.

McGrath, R.G., MacMillan, I.C. & Venkataraman, S. (1995). Defining and developing competence: a strategic process paradigm. *Strategic Management Journal*, **15**(4), 251–275.

Mohrman, S.A., Cohen, S.G. & Mohrman, Jr, A.M. (1995). *Designing Team-Based Organizations.* San Francisco, CA: Jossey-Bass.

Newcomb, A.F. & Brady, J.E. (1982). Mutuality in boys' friendship relations. *Child Development*, **53**, 392–395.

Nonaka, I. (1996). A dynamic theory of organizational knowledge creation. *Organization Science*, **5**(1), 14–37.

Penrose, E.T. (1959). *The Theory of the Growth of the Firm.* New York: Wiley.

Peteraf, M. (1993). The cornerstones of competitive advantage: A resource-based view. *Strategic Management Journal*, **14**, 179–192.

Roloff, M.E. (1987). Communication and reciprocity within intimate relationships. In M.E. Roloff & G.R. Miller (eds) *Interpersonal Processes.* Newbury Park, CA: Sage.

Rumelt, R.P. (1984). Towards a strategic theory of the firm. In R. Lamb (ed.) *Competitive Strategic Management*. Englewood Cliffs, NJ: Prentice Hall, pp. 556–570.

Simon, H.A. (1991). Bounded rationality and organizational learning. *Organization Science*, **2**(1), 125–134.

Teece, D. (1984). Economic analysis and strategic management. *California Management Review*, **26**, 87–110.

Weick, K.E. & Ashford, S.J. (1996). Learning in organizations, unpublished manuscript, University of Michigan.

Wernerfelt, B. (1984). A resource-based view of the firm. *Strategic Management Journal*, **5**: 171–180.

Section III

Leadership

Max DePree defines leadership as "a concept of owing certain things to the institution. It is a way of thinking about institutional heirs, a way of thinking about stewardship as contrasted with ownership" (*Leadership is an Art*, 1987, p. 10).

Jan Carlzon argues that a leader "can no longer be an isolated and autocratic decision maker. Instead, he must be a visionary, a strategist, an informer, a teacher, and an inspirer" (*Moments of Truth*, 1987, p. 5).

Chester Barnard defines leadership as "the indispensable social essence that gives common meaning to common purpose, that creates the incentive that makes other incentives effective, that infuses the subjective aspect of countless decisions with consistency in a changing environment, that inspires the personal conviction that produces the vital cohesiveness without which cooperation is impossible" (*The Functions of the Executive*, 1968 [1938], p. 283).

Philip Selznik describes leaders as "creative men . . . who know how to transform a neutral body of men into a committed polity. These men are called leaders; their profession is politics" (*Leadership in Administration*, 1984 [1957], p. 61). Contrary to popular perception, Selznik argues that "leadership is not equally necessary in all large-scale organizations, or in any one at all times, and . . . it becomes dispensable as the natural processes of institutionalism become eliminated or controlled" (1984, p. 25).

A dominant characteristic common to these descriptions of leadership is the leader's role as a multifaceted facilitator, teacher, inspirer, whose primary role involves providing a vision for the organization and coordinating the activities and resources of the organization in pursuit of that vision. This perception of leadership, though far from popular perceptions of "charismatic" leaders, on white horses, leading their charges into the fray, is, in fact, a more useful and effective form of leadership, particularly in maximizing strategic flexibility. The chapters in this section provide further insights into the complexity of leading organizations through turbulent times.

Godfrey, Whetten and Gregersen argue that firms are ill-equipped to deal with the complex decisions facing them, particularly when using a "right versus wrong" moral logic to make decisions, when the moral problems of today require a "right versus right" moral logic.

Green and Cooper consider the role of leaders in the knowledge management process: how they develop their own and others' knowledge base, and the relation between knowledge and wisdom. Drawing on religious literature, they analyze four styles of leadership: the Sage, the Visionary, the Prophet, and the Priest.

Merali and McGee describe a framework for identifying the information processes and knowledge networks involved in organizational learning and which characterize the relationships between corporate headquarters and their businesses. The authors also discuss the "scripts" that are enacted in these relationships.

O'Neal and Thomas review board roles and responsibilities, examine extant research on measuring board performance, and suggest a core set of board performance measures that can be universally applied.

Raimond argues that the traditional model of strategy, which treats the key factors in the strategic situation as objective facts that are available equally to all analysts, does not accommodate the possibility of each strategist making his or her own subjective, and possibly idiosyncratic, sense of the situation. Raimond suggests the need for a new model to cope with this cognitive perspective of strategy—a model of strategy as sense-making.

Opening Pandora's Box: Do Good Ethics Make Good Business?

PAUL C. GODFREY, DAVID A. WHETTEN,
HAL B. GREGERSEN

> There is only one social responsibility of business—to use its resources
> and engage in activities designed to increase its profits so long as it stays
> within the rules of the game. (Milton Friedman, 1970)

> Like it or not, the responsibility for ensuring a sustainable world falls
> largely on the shoulders of the world's enterprises, the economic engines
> of the future. (Stuart Hart, 1997)

> Pandora was seized with an eager curiosity to know what this jar con-
> tained; and one day she slipped off the cover and looked in. Forthwith
> there escaped a multitude of plagues for hapless man—such as gout,
> rheumatism, and colic for his body, and envy, spite, and revenge for his
> mind—and scattered themselves far and wide. Pandora hastened to
> replace the lid; but alas! the whole contents of the jar had escaped, one
> thing only excepted, which lay at the bottom, and that was hope.
> (Bullfinch, 1995)

As the world moves into a new millennium, the idea that business firms are
morally constrained to consider only how they can maximize their own
profits continues to lose currency and adherents. New ideas of corporate
social responsibility have emerged within the academy (Carroll, 1979;
Wood, 1991); these hold that firms have greater obligations to society than

Strategic Flexibility: Managing in a Turbulent Environment. Edited by G. Hamel, C.K. Prahalad,
H. Thomas and D. O'Neal.
Copyright © 1998 John Wiley & Sons Ltd.

merely profit generation. Getting beyond the profit orientation of business firms proves an arduous task, however. Social activists, business scholars, and government leaders often seek to mask conflicts between "good ethics" and "good business" by arguing that "good ethics makes good business." In this chapter, "good ethics" refers to the bundle of activities that constitute ethical firm behavior (honesty, integrity, trust, etc.) and socially responsible practices (e.g. ecological sensitivity, family-friendly work policies). By "good business" we mean those outcomes normally associated with business performance (e.g. profits, growth). Stated simply, this logic holds that morally or socially responsible behavior increases the profitability of the firm.

Our intention is not to review the logic of "good ethics makes good business" (GE/GB), but rather to show that couching appeals for moral responsibility in terms of profit potential opens Pandora's box. Such calls invite firms to consider moral dilemmas that defy traditional business logic. "Good ethics makes good business" should serve as no more than a point of entry in a firm's quest to act morally and socially responsible; indeed, a commitment to moral behavior sometimes requires that managers take actions that do not increase the profitability of their enterprises, and often involve significant personal and organizational costs. Sustainable calls for moral and social responsibility by business firms should move firms from a shallow utilitarian motivation to do good to a deeply rooted moral disposition to do good.

Fundamental to our argument is the assertion that firms are, by their history and nature, ill equipped to deal with complex decisions facing them. Specifically, we argue that firms use decision structures based in a "right versus wrong" (R/W) moral logic while the moral problems of our day require a "right versus right" (R/R) moral logic. We first elaborate the R/R nature of moral problems. We then explicate the basis of the firm's R/W decision structure. The chapter concludes with an extensive discussion of the implications of GE/GB and we sketch a brief outline of what R/R decision structures within the firm would look like.

RIGHT/RIGHT DECISION STRUCTURES AND THE MORAL FRONTIER

For the purposes of this chapter, decisions made by business firms can be divided into three broad classifications. The first class includes decisions of no moral relevance (e.g. should the colors on our corporate logo be blue or green?). We assert that this class is very small—most decisions have moral consequences. The second class of decisions includes those in which the moral issues can be classified in terms of one solution being right, the other wrong. For example, should a firm expose workers to hazardous, preventable, working conditions? Or should a firm install pollution control equipment at a substantial short-term cost? While moral—and legal—customs clearly make the first example a R/W decision, the second decision is R/W only because one of the choices is falsely portrayed. The second choice omits a full consideration of costs incurred by the firm; indeed, the work of several strategy scholars and activists (e.g. Porter & van der Linde, 1995; Shrivastava, 1995) shows that ecologically sensitive management lowers, rather than raises, the long-term operating costs of a firm. This is the logic of GE/GB—that morally "right" actions lead to increased economic profits.

A third class of moral decisions includes decisions in which competing moral claims cannot be prioritized in terms of right and wrong; rather, they exist as true right/right decisions. For example, a firm decides to locate a new plant in an offshore location. The firm could either build the plant in the port city, with the economic advantage of low transportation costs and easy access, or it could choose to co-locate its plant with a group of other plants, each of whose waste products becomes an input for another firm. Assume that locating the plant inland creates significant benefits for the local ecology but is projected to create substantial economic disadvantage for the firm over the long term. This decision, in which the competing claims of economic profit (which is a valid moral claim in its own right) and ecological sustainability cannot be prioritized into a R/W framework, is a quintessential R/R decision. Making one decision involves significant moral tradeoffs on the other dimension. In our example, either the local ecology or the firm's profitability is negatively impacted. FIGURE 9.1 illustrates the problem of R/R moral decisions.

R/R moral decisions lie along the moral frontier (see FIGURE 9.2). The moral frontier operates much like the production possibilities frontier in economic theory. A decision unit has two competing claims (goods), and

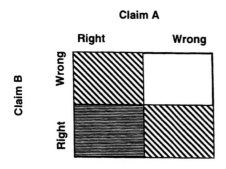
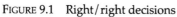

FIGURE 9.1   Right/right decisions

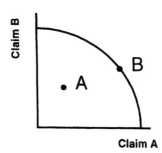

FIGURE 9.2   The moral frontier

there is a range in which performance can be improved on both dimensions (such as point A). At the frontier (point B), however, any moral choice involves a tradeoff (such as ecological sustainability versus economic profit). Thinking in terms of a moral frontier helps scholars and managers understand that calls for corporate social and moral behavior must be tailored to a firm's position on the frontier. Most firms, and most industries, lie well inside the frontier. For these firms, improvements in moral behavior increase economic profit. In fact, companies like 3M, with their active pollution control programs, move toward greater ecological responsibility and higher profits simultaneously (Shrivastava, 1995). When firms are operating below the moral frontier, R/R decisions cannot exist, and decision makers can simultaneously satisfy both moral claims. Competing moral claims can, through analysis and discourse, become complementary claims: They become at the very least R/W decisions. However, when firms operate at the frontier, no such resolution is possible. The moral frontier is not a static concept, and we describe below the forces that work to expand and contract it.

EXPANDING THE FRONTIER

Technological and social innovations work to move the frontier outward. Gladwin, Kennelly & Krause (1995) note that technological innovation represents a viable strategy for increasing the ecological carrying capacity of the planet. Advances in process technology (such as chemical production) and product technology (increasingly biodegradable components) and changes in design technology (design for disassembly) work to move the frontier outward. Technological advances prolong the point at which increasing ecological sensitivity forces real tradeoffs in economic profits. Similarly, advances in computing and communications technologies allow firms to satisfy employees' moral claims for more personal and family flexibility while still completing productive workdays.

The relentless success of capitalist enterprises also works to expand the moral frontier. As greater numbers of the world's citizens are touched by the Invisible Hand, the belief in the fundamental rightness of capitalist endeavor broadens and deepens. With capitalism's increasing acceptance as the most beneficial form of economic exchange, the moral claim that firms should be about the business of maximizing profits gains greater legitimacy. In short, the success of capitalist enterprise creates a self-sustaining force that reinforces the morality of profit seeking. Societal tolerance for profit taking moves the frontier outward as actors realize that "there is no free lunch"; economic gains incur moral costs, but the tangible economic gains exceed the intangible moral costs.

At the level of individual firms, strong economic performance moves the frontier outward. When firms enjoy high profits, large market shares, or rapid growth rates, slack organizational resources develop. In the presence of this slack, managers enjoy the "luxury of being moral"; indeed, moral behavior flourishes because the firm has discretionary resources that can be used to fund or support its moral endeavors (Carroll, 1979). The existence of slack resources allows the firm to postpone the point at which moral tradeoffs begin to occur.

CONTRACTING THE FRONTIER

At least three forces work to push the moral frontier inward, thus creating more R/R tradeoffs for firms and their decision makers. The collective weight of increasing social diversity in the business world, stakeholder theory, and the rise of the postmodern movement pushes the moral frontier back toward the origin and makes more decisions R/R in nature. Increasing diversity (and its cousin globalization) pushes the frontier inward by increasing the number of moral claims made on business firms. The cultural values of Caucasian, American males no longer sing solo at center stage; these values compete against a chorus of ethnic and national cultures and customs, all crowding for visibility and a place on the stage. With a greater number of diverse moral claimants, the risk of offending *any* claimant through *any* decision increases dramatically. Stakeholder theory is often seen as a way to balance the economic moral imperatives of the firm with the claims of other moral agents (Donaldson & Preston, 1995). If diversity gives voice to a larger number of moral claims, stakeholder theory lends those claims legitimacy. Stakeholder models often attempt to weaken the claims of shareholders by elevating the claims of other stakeholders.

Postmodernism exacerbates the managerial challenges created by stakeholder views of the firm. Postmodern philosophy rejects any claims to "meta-narratives," grand theories or models that take priority over competing views (Lyotard, 1984). While stakeholder theory legitimates the idea that several moral claimants are involved in any decision, postmodernism "levels the playing field" and argues that no claimant has *a priori* priority over other claimants. Just because the firm engages in profit-making activities does not mean that profit considerations subsume any, or all, other moral claims; moral decision making requires that every claim receive a fair hearing. Denying any claim *a priori* superiority makes every decision an R/R decision.

At the firm level, poor economic performance contracts the frontier. In the absence of sufficient slack resources, moral choices induce clear tradeoffs at a greater rate. Investing in pollution control equipment may lower long-term costs, but the firm that faces severe cash flow crises may face the tradeoff of investing in pollution control equipment or meeting payroll. In such a case, every choice the firm makes requires significant moral tradeoffs.

Kidder (1995) brings the R/R moral problem into sharper focus by highlighting four specific areas in which R/R decisions exist. R/R decisions force managers to choose between competing, and irreconcilable, moral values. Kidder presents four such cases: (i) decisions that center on the values of justice versus mercy, (ii) short-term versus long-term decisions, (iii) situations in which truth is pitted against loyalty, and (iv) individual versus community decisions. David Korten (1995) offers a fifth situation: economic growth versus ecological and/or social sustainability. The nature of these five decisions reveals the essence of R/R decisions: The moral claims each have *a priori* rightness, and choosing more of one means choosing less of the other. At the margin, being more just in a decision often means being less merciful, and choosing individual gain often results in community-wide losses.

In summary, R/R decisions exist when moral agents face moral claims that are (i) both right when considered separately; (ii) conflicting or contradictory in nature; and (iii) when the agent has an obligation to act according to both moral claims. There are no formula solutions to R/R problems; each decision is unique and each case must be considered on its own merits. Precedent becomes a dangerous element because each case may have different circumstances and thus require a different decision. Whatever the decision, the outcome forces tradeoffs between competing moral claims.

RIGHT/WRONG DECISIONS: THE LOGIC OF THE FIRM

Firms exist because they are efficient institutions for carrying out economic transactions (Smith, 1776, 1937; Williamson, 1985). Morally, the firm parlays its economic efficiency into an improved standard of living for the members of a society. Because business activity increases the prosperity of society, traditional notions of the firm granted the firm an exemption from the moral rules that govern states, churches, families, and individuals. Indeed, Adam Smith argues that the virtue of the butcher and baker lies not in their benevolence, but in their greed. Firms represent the institutional embodiment of the Hobbesian man (also known as *Homo economicus*), who is concerned with maximizing personal gain and gratification, and convinced that life is "solitary, poor, nasty, brutish, and short" (Hobbes, 1651, 1967, p. 161). Specifically, the firm has a "restless and perpetual desire of power after power, that ceaseth only in death" (Hobbes, 1651, 1967, p. 159). Hobbes postulates a world in which humans are driven solely by power (utility or profit) maximization, and use reason and rationality as a means of achieving this end. It is a view with which neoclassical microeconomics and Friedman clearly resonate.

The firm grounds itself in the moral claim, and logic, of optimization, which is an R/W decision logic. The presence of a single optimal solution (the right answer) implies the existence of suboptimal solutions (wrong answers), and the founding assumption (optimization) suggests a clear method for deciding between the two. If a firm has only limited capital to invest, it should invest in the highest net present value (NPV) project available; any other use of capital would be suboptimal. Optimization prioritizes *all* claims against the firm or its capital; there is no possibility of R/R situations. Optimization reduces competing claims to rank-ordered preferences. Discourse concerning the validity of claims is unnecessary because all such questions are answered by an appeal to the numbers. In the presence of multiple optimal solutions (a set of investments that yield the same NPV), the choice depends on the tastes and preferences of the individual decision makers, not on any obligation to choose a certain course of action. The only moral obligation imposed by the logic of optimization is that the firm must choose a solution with an NPV equal to or greater than any other choice. To act otherwise is to act immorally, in terms of the fiduciary responsibility of a firm's managers. Optimization rests as the moral foundation for private enterprise.

Historically, social institutions allowed the firm to utilize its own moral logic based on two considerations. First, private economic activity improves the general condition of society. As the existence of large-scale enterprise became a fact of life in the nineteenth century, the gains offered by private enterprise usually outweighed the losses. While the distribution of those gains may have been far less than equal, nineteenth-century America and nineteenth-century Victorian Britain saw remarkable improvements in the standard of living (Himmelfarb, 1994; Moore, 1994). Second, other strong social institutions worked to check the moral propensities of the firm. Governments took an activist role in regulating business affairs, and organized religion served as the conscience for capitalist organizations (Moore, 1994). Because of these factors, the moral logic of optimization became an acceptable, even desirable, fact of capitalistic life.

That firms should lose their moral exemption and be called upon to face R/R choices owes to their continued success. Capitalism has largely succeeded in improving the material standard of living of capitalist societies. The apparent moral success of the firm facilitates a call such as the one by Stuart Hart (1997): firms are in a unique position to foster the moral development of local and global citizens. However strong their position may be, as we have shown, the absence of fundamentally encoded R/R decision structures leaves the firm ill prepared to assume its new position.

MOVING BEYOND "GOOD ETHICS MAKES GOOD BUSINESS"

The logic of "good ethics makes good business" resonates with business practitioners largely because the logic presents moral challenges as fundamentally R/W choices; such choices are palatable to the firm, in part because the decision structure of the firm is designed to make R/W decisions. The GE/GB logic and rhetoric break down, however, when firms face moral choices of an R/R nature. Increasingly, firms face each of the five R/R tradeoffs mentioned above, be it in ecological management issues, employee relations, political lobbying, or executive compensation. When faced with these choices, GE/GB belies the inherent difficulty in making such choices. In this section, we highlight the pitfalls of GE/GB logic. We also consider how GE/GB can be a pathway for improved moral performance, and we conclude by examining how this rhetorical tool has been used in ecological management.

PITFALLS OF GE/GB

"Good ethics makes good business" creates three underlying difficulties for firms that face moral choices. First, as the notion of the moral frontier highlights, the logic of GE/GB works only for moral choices away from the frontier. To use the popular phrase, GE/GB helps managers pick the low-hanging fruit; however, it gives managers no advice or incentive to climb the tree. At the very least, GE/GB leads managers to believe that once the low-hanging fruit has been picked, the firm has met its moral obligations. Difficult but necessary moral choices may go unmade because GE/GB gives managers no rationale for moving beyond the easy moral choices. Moving toward a morally sustainable world involves making choices at the frontier (far up the tree); we need more than GE/GB to move us toward that frontier.

Secondly, GE/GB facilitates decision making inside the economics-based structure of the firm. GE/GB proposes no alternative logic for making moral decisions, and it does little to promote the moral development of capitalist enterprises or the popular image of corporate managers. R/R moral choices may involve other decision logics, such as commitment to moral obligation or the creation of community-wide benefits (although the firm may capture few to none of those benefits). Because GE/GB allows firms to make moral choices solely on individual grounds, firms have little incentive, or practice, in making decisions based on the needs of larger groups. GE/GB does little to improve managerial images, as the appeal goes to managers at the lowest level. GE/GB presumes that managers will not (or cannot) listen to a broader moral vision, thus creating a self-fulfilling prophecy.

Further, because GE/GB works within economic logic, it reinforces the primacy of the economic decision process in the firm. This strengthens, rather than provides an alternative to, the predominant metanarrative of the firm. Until managers are faced with new forms of discourse, little about the fundamental decision logic can be expected to change. By reinforcing the underlying virtue of economic profit, GE/GB may encourage managers to be even more economic in their evaluation of moral choices. Because of an ingrained belief that moral behavior leads to economic gain, at the moral frontier firms may be more likely to trade moral behavior for economic gain. The ultimate threat of GE/GB is that roles may become reversed, and that what is good for business becomes synonymous with what constitutes ethical behavior. That is, the logic of GE/GB is used improperly. This represents a truly tragic possibility.

Finally, GE/GB disturbs us because all moral virtues are now translated into economic equivalents. The aesthetic value of virtues is supplanted by their instrumental value. Under the GE/GB regime, trust is valuable not in its own right, but because it allows firms to create additional economic advantages. Ecological citizenship becomes no longer a moral obligation, but simply another way to improve shareholder wealth. Life at the moral frontier may be pragmatic, but it should never be purely instrumental. A morally sustainable society emphasizes the inherent worth of trust, ecological citizenship, honesty, integrity, and respect for others (Levinas, 1985). That virtue may be valuable is clearly acceptable; that value determines virtue is antithetical to a morally sustainable world. Calls for business to behave morally certainly improve the short-term moral landscape; however, we are concerned about the long-term condition of a society in which all virtues are traded with market values.

GE/GB AS A PATHWAY TO MORAL BEHAVIOR

While we do not believe that GE/GB is the final solution for creating a morally sustainable world, the logic can become an integral part of a larger solution. GE/GB logic applies when firms and industries operate below the moral frontier. There is abundant evidence that most firms and industries have not exhausted their opportunities for simultaneously improving moral and economic performance. Thus, because GE/GB speaks the current language of management, it becomes a powerful tool for initiating action.

Sustainable moral development focuses not only on the low-hanging fruit harvestable through GE/GB solutions, but it also helps managers focus on the entire tree—"moral behavior." Emphasizing the GB aspects of actions initiates corporate action; when activists and scholars are clear about the GE part of the equation, GE provides direction and motivation for movement. Clearly, managers are not economic ogres, interested only in the profitability of their firms. Managers have families, children, and desires for the "good life." Much of the GE/GB logic fails, in our estimation, not because it links GE with GB, but because it underemphasizes the nature and consequences of GE. The allure of good ethics must become as powerful as the allure of increased profits.

Once activists successfully show managers the entire tree, not just the low-hanging fruit, the discussion needs to shift beyond merely GE/GB to include concepts such as citizenship and moral obligation. These two virtues prepare firms for life at the frontier. Although neither concept helps resolve R/R dilemmas, each is an important building block in developing and sustaining an R/R decision structure. As long as GE/GB does not include concepts of citizenship and obligation, such calls are likely to lead to short-term, incremental gains in the moral behavior of business firms.

We highlight the positive and negative uses of GE/GB logic by examining a moral topic now popular in the strategy conversation: ecological management. Several articles in both academic and practitioner journals address the need for firms to manage with the physical environment as a key stakeholder (see *Academy of Management Review*, vol. 20, no. 4, 1995). For example, Porter & Van der Linde's (1995) *Harvard Business Review* article stands as a prime example of GE/GB. The title of the article, "Green and Competitive," gives readers the flavor of the piece. The authors argue convincingly that companies can increase their economic performance by becoming more sensitive to pollution and waste management issues, and they provide compelling case studies to document their assertions.

While the GE/GB logic invites and entices firms to begin to manage in ecologically responsible ways, authors such as David Korten (1995) and Stuart Hart (1997) take a different tack. These authors note that environmental responsibility represents only a part of the picture, and that the moral frontier is defined by sustainable development, which occurs within the carrying capacity and limits of the earth's ecosystems and social structures. Both Hart and Korten suggest that moving toward sustainable development requires a decision logic by firms in which citizenship becomes at least the equal of economic profit. At the frontier of sustainable development, many choices must be made, choices in which firms may make real sacrifices in economic profit in order to build a sustainable world (e.g. plant co-location, or being a first-mover in new technologies). For both authors, there is much more to the argument than the simple claim that improved moral performance will create increased profits.

MOVING TOWARD RIGHT/RIGHT DECISION STRUCTURES

It is beyond the scope of this chapter to fully discuss how firms can design and implement R/R decision structures for dealing with moral problems; however, we briefly outline what R/R decision structures look like. To do this, we look at other societal institutions, each of which plays a significant role in defining and regulating the moral life of a society, and each of which successfully deals with a variety of R/R choices. Because of our own tradition, and the historical origins of the modern bureaucratic firm (Weber, 1947), we base our analysis on the social structures of Western Europe and the United States. The three relevant institutions we consider are the state, the church, and the family.

THE STATE

By the term "state" we mean government at all levels. The state anchors life at the highest levels of our intersubjective experience. The modern philosophical justification for the state reverts to Thomas Hobbes (1588–1679), who argues in *Leviathan* (1651) that government derives its existence and power from the willing grant of authority by the citizenry. A rational citizenry realizes that an external authority provides an effective remedy for the problems caused by humanity's self-interest and self-gratification. The state exists because the state resolves competing, and conflicting, moral claims between individuals; indeed, the state stops the incessant "war of every man against every man" (Hobbes, 1651, 1967, p. 161). Modern theories of democratic or constitutional monarchic government rest on some form of this notion of a social contract (Melchert, 1995).

The notion of a social contract underlies the ability of the state to effectively deal with R/R decisions. Under democratic regimes, or other regimes that grant the legitimacy of fundamental rights, governments face the R/R problem of allocating limited resources among participants, each of whom has as valid a moral claim to the resource as any other. To deal with this problem, governments create structural mechanisms for sorting out the priority of moral claims on a case-by-case basis (a judiciary), or for resolving moral conflicts through discourse and general policy (a legislative body). The state presumes the *a priori* validity of moral claims and designs structures to ensure a fair, or just, allocation of resources among claimants.

THE CHURCH

By church we mean the organized sets of beliefs, and accompanying social organizations, that define, regulate, and provide overarching meaning for human life. In this sense, the church includes not only organized religions, but Western philosophy as well. We note that the church and the firm share a common societal function of production. Firms produce secular or tangible products, while churches produce sacred or intangible products. The crisis of the Reformation in Western European religion lay in sorting out competing views of the spiritual realm in the absence of a truly catholic view. The Protestant movement spawned several sects, each of which claimed equal or greater moral authority over spiritual matters than the moral authority of the Roman Catholic Church. Irreconcilable religious views were often solved by violent conflict or by political partition (Ozment, 1993).

In the seventeenth and eighteenth centuries, religious diversity found a common enemy—the rise of secular humanism. Humanists rejected the claims of a spiritual world altogether, or at least rejected the need for any institutional intermediary between individuals and God. Humanism expanded the market for spiritual solutions far beyond the choices offered by the Protestant revolution. Sects now competed for adherents not only against one another, but also against the faceless, powerful, and articulate philosophies of humanism.

The relentless rise of humanism in Western societies, culminating in Nietzsche's declaration of the death of God (1883–85), gave the church (as a collective institution) a powerful weapon in sorting out the competing claims to moral authority among the different sects. With godless humanism as the common enemy, churches could settle their differences by an ecumenicism born of a common belief in deity. Ecumenicism provides the church with a powerful mechanism for resolving the R/R claims of individual denominations: R/R claims are resolved by appealing to the larger unifying concept of the believers versus the unbelievers. Thus individual sects can accommodate competing and conflicting conceptions of God and heaven by claiming that one is better off believing than not believing.

THE FAMILY

The family represents the moral institution of private life because the family provides the primary moral socialization of the individual (Berger & Luckmann, 1967; Elkind, 1995). The morality of the Western family structure is clearly under attack, and our purpose here is to avoid, rather than join, this conversation. We note, however, that the family must deal with the competing moral claims of its members (e.g. husbands versus wives, children versus parents, child versus child). The acceptance of divorce in the Western world created a condition in which exit from the family is a viable option. With the dissolution of the family a real yet costly possibility, individual members have stronger incentives to find other ways to resolve R/R moral claims.

The latter twentieth century (from the 1960s onward) has witnessed fundamental redefinition in the roles of husband, wife, and child. Elkind (1995) describes this process as a shift from the "modern" family to the "postmodern" family. Role flexibility allows families to respond successfully to competing moral demands, both internally and externally generated. Families use role redefinition as a mechanism for resolving R/R moral dilemmas. Role definition occurs during the creation of a new family (Berger & Luckmann, 1967), and role redefinition, often accompanied by extended dialogue and discourse, presents a viable strategy for resolving moral conflicts over the life of a family.

The managerial challenge posed by this chapter lies in helping firms find the structural supports needed to effectively implement an emphasis on sound ethical practices. At the beginning of such a process, when the firm lies below the moral frontier, good ethical conduct and good business practice do not conflict. As firms approach the frontier, however, managers need to design and implement structural supports (decision systems, reward systems, structural configurations, etc.) which allow the firm to tackle the inherent paradoxes and dilemmas associated with life at the moral frontier. We submit that managers can look to the state, the church, and the family to find models of such structural supports.

The state uses formal institutional structures for resolving R/R moral dilemmas. The strength of democratic institutions lies in the power of process versus the power of content. How moral dilemmas are solved may vary over time; however, the process remains relatively constant. Firms gain R/R decision capabilities when they generate, implement, and sustain structures for handling R/R moral dilemmas. Ethics committees in hospitals, review boards, advisory panels, and other committee structures provide mechanisms for developing R/R capabilities.

Churches solve the R/R problem at the interorganizational level by establishing a set of common absolutes (e.g. it is better to be a believer than an unbeliever). The adoption by firms of absolutes such as citizenship and moral obligation to communities creates a mechanism for reframing debates between organizational units, departments, or functions. As churches have shown, finding a higher-order absolute allows a variety of moral imperatives to exist within a common structure.

Families use role flexibility to meet the multitude of R/R demands on them. This may prove the most difficult yet most successful mechanism for firms to adopt. Role flexibility in families requires the abandonment of notions of patriarchy and tradition; role flexibility at the firm level means abandoning certain notions of management and hierarchical organization. For example, employees and managers share a common fiduciary responsibility to societal stakeholders; thus there is little reason to assume that moral decision making rests only at the top of the hierarchy. This is as frightening a thought for CEOs as it is for many traditional fathers.

Pandora's box is open; few individuals believe that business firms should pursue profits when that pursuit leads to negative moral outcomes. Living in a post-Pandora world requires a fundamental new competence, one that business firms must acquire—the ability to successfully solve R/R moral decisions. We contend that calling for firms to act morally by claiming that "good ethics makes good business" does little to give firms the skills and competencies for dealing with the multitude of situations in which moral behavior may not lead to improvements in the bottom line.

REFERENCES

Berger, P. & Luckmann, T. (1967). *The Social Construction of Reality*. New York: Anchor Books.
Bulfinch, T. (1995). *Bulfinch's Mythology: The Age of Fable*. New York: Meridian Books.
Carroll, A. (1979). A three-dimensional conceptual model of corporate performance. *Academy of Management Review*, **4**, 497–505.
Donaldson, R. & Preston, L. (1995). A stakeholder theory of the corporation: concepts, evidence, and implications. *Academy of Management Review*, **20**, 65–91.
Elkind, D. (1995). *Ties that Stress*. Cambridge, MA: Harvard University Press.
Friedman, M. (1970). The social responsibility of business is to increase its profits. *New York Times Magazine*, 13 September.
Gladwin, T., Kennelly, J. & Krause, T.-S. (1995). Shifting paradigms for sustainable development: implications for management theory and research. *Academy of Management Review*, **20**, 874–907.
Hart, S. (1997). Beyond greening: strategies for a sustainable world. *Harvard Business Review*, January/February, 66–77.
Himmelfarb, G. (1994). *The De-moralization of Society*. New York: Vintage Books.
Hobbes, T. (1651, 1967). *Leviathan*. In E. Burtt (ed.) *The English Philosophers from Bacon to Mill*. New York: Modern Library (originally published 1651).
Kidder, R. (1995). *How Good People Make Tough Choices*. New York: William Morrow and Co.
Korten, D. (1995). *When Corporations Rule the World*. West Hartford, CT: Kumarian Press.
Levinas, E. (1985). *Ethics and Infinity*, translated by R. Cohen. Pittsburgh, PA: Duquesne University Press.
Lyotard, J.-F. (1984). *The Postmodern Condition*, translated by G. Bennington & B. Massumi. Minneapolis, MN: University of Minnesota Press.
Melchert, N. (1995). *The Great Conversation*, vol. II. Mountain View, CA: Mayfield.
Moore, R. (1994). *Selling God*. New York: Oxford University Press.
Nietzsche, F. (1993). *Thus Spake Zarathustra*. Buffalo: Prometheus Books (originally published 1883–85).
Ozment, S. (1993). *Protestants*. New York: Image Books.
Porter, M. & van der Linde, C. (1995). Green *and* competitive: ending the stalemate. *Harvard Business Review*, September/October, 120–138.
Shrivastava, P. (1995). Environmental technologies and competitive advantage. *Strategic Management Journal*, **16**(special issue), 183–200.
Smith, A. (1776, 1937). *The Wealth of Nations*. New York: Modern Library (originally published 1776).
Weber, M. (1947). *The Theory of Social and Economic Organization*, translated by A. Henderson & T. Parsons. New York: Macmillan.

Williamson, O. (1985). *The Economic Institutions of Capitalism.* New York: Free Press.
Wood, D. (1991). Corporate social performance revisited. *Academy of Management Review,* **16**, 691–718.

10

Sage, Visionary, Prophet and Priest: Leadership Styles of Knowledge Management and Wisdom

SEBASTIAN GREEN, PATRICE COOPER

> Those who know, seem not to know
> And those who don't pretend they do. (Tao te Ching)
>
> Knowledge . . .
> Preserved by the Christians,
> Discovered by the Realists,
> Manufactured by the Constructivists,
> Destroyed by the Postmodernists. (Kavanagh, 1996)

INTRODUCTION

New thinking in the strategic management field over the past decade has increasingly focused on knowledge and its accumulation as critical to competitiveness, organizational survival and success. Old thinking in society at large over the last two and a half millennia has focused on wisdom and knowing as critical to personal success and the survival of society. Does this old thinking have implications for new thinking? If so, it puts a very

Strategic Flexibility: Managing in a Turbulent Environment. Edited by G. Hamel, C.K. Prahalad, H. Thomas and D. O'Neal.

different spin on contemporary notions of how knowledge ought to managed and to what end.

For example, in the Tao te Ching, a Chinese text spanning 800 years, we are told that: "If the sage governs with vision then his people will not go wrong. So in his wisdom, he restrains himself ... the sage always makes sure that the people don't know what he has done, so they never want to be in control—and are never driven by ambition. He keeps them in truth acting invisibly. You see, if there is nothing to fight for there is nothing that can break the flow".

Such sentiments might not find favour in today's thrusting, macho, attention-seeking, results-oriented, business environment. But they do attest to the importance of knowledge, or more significantly wisdom, for effective leadership. Throughout history, the narrative of leadership has been peppered with accounts of wisdom and wise deeds which serve as models for other, perhaps lesser, folk. Or at least that is the case for good leaders. Bad leaders may be cunning but they are not wise, reflecting Nietzsche's argument that it is only when we fail to gain power over our creative talents and potential that we resort to that base motive of power over other people.

What type of knowledge is required for wisdom? Good judgement, understanding, compassion and right action are essential attributes of knowledge as wisdom. What is the source of such knowledge? Is it eternal or must it change to accommodate changing circumstances? This question has particular force given recent discussion in strategic management which call for a shift of emphasis to embrace transformational change (Chakravarthy & Doz, 1992). Many authors propose that to qualify as a transformation a majority of individuals must change their organizational beliefs, attitudes and assumptions (Kilmann & Covin, 1988; Coulson-Thomas, 1992) in a process termed renewal (Gouillart & Kelly, 1995). Renewal is essentially about relearning, and relearning is about creating new knowledge (Kogut & Zander, 1992). Thus the essence of transformational change is a fundamental shift in the knowledge base of the organization. Yet the concept of wisdom suggests a form of knowledge that is unchanging and universally applicable.

This, then, is the subject matter of our chapter. In it, we explore how leaders approach/develop their own knowledge and convert others to it. The metaphor of conversion leads us to explore the religious arena for examples of different conversion styles. Drawing selectively on the religious literature has the added advantage of highlighting the idiosyncratic way in which knowledge is conceptualized within the strategy literature. We argue that the latter utilizes a positivist ontology, a view of organizational knowledge as an objective, fixed, transferable commodity or resource, knowledge as content (what is known), rather than process (knowing and learning) and knowledge as impersonal, apolitical and asocial. Religious thinking tends to view knowledge in much more personal and subjective terms. Knowledge comes from within rather than from without, is as concerned with the path towards knowing as with what is known, and the question of whose knowledge becomes as important as what knowledge. This view is much more in line with a social constructivist position where "knowledge is never a matter of a lone individual learning about an external reality. Individuals interacting together impose their constructions on reality" (Douglas & Isherwood, 1978, p. 63).

First we situate our chapter within the context of the knowledge-based literature and examine the intersection between knowledge, knowledge renewal (transformation) and leadership. Second, a taxonomy of leadership styles with respect to knowledge management is constructed. Third, drawing on a religious analogy, we describe four leadership styles and suggest the different attributes pertinent to each of these ideal types with respect to knowledge creation and dissemination. The final section contrasts these styles with current conceptualizations of leadership and knowledge management.

KNOWLEDGE IN ORGANIZATIONS: AN OVERVIEW OF THE LITERATURE

The importance of knowledge for the firm's competitive advantage is now a central tenet of the strategic management paradigm (Winter, 1987; Toffler, 1990; Drucker, 1991; Nonaka, 1991; Quinn, 1992; Spender & Grant, 1996). Knowledge-based theories may be seen as an outgrowth of several streams of research. These include epistemology (Hayek, 1945; Polayni, 1962), organizational and evolutionary economics (Nelson & Winter, 1982; Winter 1987; Aoki, 1990; Demsetz, 1991), organizational learning (Levitt & March, 1988; Huber, 1991), the resource-based view of the firm (Wernerfelt, 1984; Barney, 1991; Grant, 1991), organizational capabilities and competencies (Ansoff, 1965; Prahalad & Hamel, 1990; Leonard-Barton, 1992) and innovation/new product development (Imai, Nonaka & Takeuchi, 1985; Teece 1986, Henderson & Clark, 1990; Clark & Fujimoto, 1991; Wheelright & Clark, 1992).

These research streams have come together in a number of studies which focus explicitly on strategic and managerial aspects of knowledge within firms. TABLE 10.1 provides an overview of this research under seven key research questions. Alongside each question the key concepts, processes and major contributing authors are identified.

It will readily be seen from this synopsis that a specific focus on leadership with respect to knowledge is not obvious. Our own interest in knowledge, wisdom, and who influences or negotiates knowledge and changes in knowledge cuts across all these categories but does not fit neatly

TABLE 10.1   Research on strategic and managerial aspects of knowledge

Research question	Key concepts and processes
What is knowledge?	Prahalad & Bettis, 1986; Barney, 1986; Itami, 1987; Badaracco, 1991; Lado, Boyd & Wright, 1992; Stalk, Evans & Schulman, 1992; Williams 1992
What types of knowledge exist?	Tacit versus explicit (Polayni, 1966)
	Subjective versus objective (Popper, 1972)
	Know-what versus know-how (Ryle, 1949, Revans, 1982)
	Knowledge about versus knowledge of acquaintance (James, 1950)
	Information versus know-how (Kogut & Zander, 1992)
	Articulated/articulable (Hedlund, 1994: Winter, 1987) versus non-articulable
	Verbal versus non-verbal (Corsini, 1987)
	Declarative versus procedural (Kogut & Zander, 1992)
	Automatic versus conscious, objectified, scientific (Spender, 1993, 1994)
	Embedded versus migratory (Baddaracco, 1991)
	Embedded versus embodied
	Individual versus collective (Orr, 1990), communal (Spender, 1993, 1994) or community in practice (Brown & Duguid, 1991)
	Subconcepts of knowledge: information, skill or know-how, explanation and understanding
How is knowledge acquired?	Knowledge as an outcome of learning (Cangelosi & Dill, 1965; Argyris & Schon, 1978; Argyris, 1990; Senge, 1990; Cohen & Sproull, 1991, 1996; Herriot, Levinthal & March, 1985; Nelson & Winter, 1982)
	Knowledge transfer (Bartlett & Ghoshal, 1978, 1989; Roos, Von Grogh & Yip, 1995; Almeida, 1996; Mowery, Oxley & Silverman, 1996)

Question	References
How is knowledge stored/preserved? How does a firm remember what it knows?	Organizational memory (Walsh, 1991; Huber, 1991), including: Individual memory—beliefs, structures, casual maps, assumptions, values Culture—language, stories, sagas and the grapevine (Schein, 1984) Transformations (procedures and rules) Structure (organizational roles) Ecology (workplace design) Organizational routines (Cyert & March, 1963; Nelson & Winter, 1982) or standard operating procedures (March & Simon, 1958) External archives—former employees, competitors, agencies (Walsh, 1991) Inter-organizational domains—supplier networks (Hedlund, 1994)
How is knowledge managed?	Bohn, 1994; Hedlund 1994; Von Grogh and Roos, 1996 Combinative capabilities (Kogut & Zander, 1992) Knowledge integration and application (Grant, 1993, 1996; Grant & Baden-Fuller, 1995)
What is the role of knowledge in creating sustainable competitive advantage?	Nonaka, 1991; Baddaracco, 1991; Spender, 1993; Grant, 1993; Sobol & Lei, 1994
How is knowledge transformed? How is existing knowledge changed or new knowledge created?	Nonaka, 1987, 1989, 1991; Nonaka et al., 1994; Nonaka & Takeuchi, 1995

into any one. For this we have to move to an alternative literature within the broader area of organizational change where issues of organizational learning and transformational leadership have been widely discussed. This literature presents a picture of a special type of leader which often appears during times of discontinuous change or transformation. Various words have been used to portray this kind of leadership, for example charismatic (House, 1977), transformational (Burns, 1978; Tichy & Ulrich, 1984; Bass, 1985; Bennis & Nanus, 1985; Tichy & Devanna, 1986), change-centred (Kotter, 1995), heroic (Nadler, Shaw & Walton, 1994), or the leader as steward, coach, champion or educator (Lundberg, 1996).

A review of theory and research on leadership reveals that "much of this 'new' insight on transformational type leadership repeats themes of the 1960s, although the prescriptions are often clothed in different jargon" (Yukl, 1989). Yukl suggests that the need to empower subordinates and develop a sense of ownership for what goes on in the organization reiterates the theme of power sharing, mutual trust and participative decision making emphasized by earlier theorists such as McGregor (1960), Argyris (1964) and Likert (1967). Developing human potential and activating higher-order needs in the service of the organization echoes the earlier humanistic concern for quality of work life and supportive relationships.

What has been added to these earlier perspectives is an awareness that leading change is best explained and considered in terms of the cognitive, cultural and political context and constraints in organizations (Johnson, 1990). Popularization of the idea that leadership processes are embedded in the culture of the organization, shaping it and being shaped by it (Pondy, 1978; Pfeffer, 1981; Deal & Kennedy, 1982; Schein, 1984, 1985; Sathe 1985) has directed attention to the importance of managing symbolic activities and meaning in addition to managing things. Recognition of the pivotal role of leaders in culture has direct implications for our understanding of how leaders manage knowledge.

Here we can learn from the anthropological arena, where one school of thought sees culture as systems of knowledge. To quote Ward Goodenough, "Culture consists of whatever it is one has to know or believe in order to operate in a manner acceptable to its members. Culture is not a material phenomenon; it does not consist of things, people, behaviour or emotions. It is rather an organization of these things. It is the form of things that people have in mind, their models for perceiving, relating and otherwise interpreting them" (Goodenough, 1957, p. 167).

This implies that it is not knowledge *per se* that is important, but interpretation of knowledge and the meaning afforded to it which are critical. Such interpretation is, from a social constructivist perspective, a process of negotiation between leaders (and other dominant groups) and followers. The ensuing interpretations are themselves a reflection of the prevailing culture of the organization (Calas & Smircich, 1988) and of the leader's mode of "making sense" of the current situation (Daft & Weick, 1984). The latter, as Weick (1995) suggests, may involve retrospective rationalization of past action rather than the intentional and forward-looking decisions often associated with the heroic type leaders. In short, as Smircich (1983) suggests, leadership might best be viewed as the management of meaning and the shaping of interpretations. The issue then becomes how do leaders actually go about managing these meanings, how do they construct their own knowledge base at the same time as stimulating others to learn?

To date, the strategic management literature has not focused on this area. Thus, we examine leaders as instigators of knowledge change for themselves and other members of the organization. Based on these aspects of leadership, we develop a taxonomy of leadership styles with respect to knowledge management. In the first instance, this taxonomy is derived from the observer's (emic) model rather than the actor's, i.e. leader's, (etic) perceptions of the world.

TAXONOMY OF LEADERS

REFLEXIVE AND NON-REFLEXIVE

The taxonomy hinges firstly on the different ways in which leaders themselves approach their own knowledge. Two approaches are identified. The first (lifting a postmodern theme) concerns the ability to be critical or suspicious of one's own intellectual assumptions (Lawson, 1985). This is achieved through reflexivity (Platt, 1989). Reflexive leaders turn in on themselves to question the basis of new knowledge and seek to unlearn or bypass their own accepted and often taken for granted ways of doing things. In contrast, non-reflexive leaders rely on what others have said or on experience developed in another sphere of their business life. They apply this "outside" knowledge to novel situations, trusting that what has worked elsewhere will work again irrespective of changing or different circumstances.

CONTROLLING AND EMPOWERING

The second dimension relates to the way leaders approach people in their organization. Two styles are identified from the literature on leadership. The first is termed controlling, the second empowering. The control-oriented style of leadership assumes that leaders can best get people to perform by using formal reward and punishment systems to motivate them. It emphasizes such practices as describing jobs in detail, carefully measuring job performing and handing out rewards on the basis of achievement. In the control approach employees are assumed to be in a performing role and are not asked to participate actively in organizational issues. Their actions are coordinated through rules, procedures and supervisory direction. It is typically assumed that their major interactions are the ones that they have with their supervisor, who provides them with direction and control, and administers rewards and punishments.

The empowering or involvement approach makes a very different set of assumptions about the factors that determine organizational effectiveness. Primarily, it assumes that employees can figure out the right things to do if properly informed. It also assumes that employees can be intrinsically motivated and that they are capable of a considerable amount of self-control and self-direction. Finally, it believes that employees are capable of producing important ideas about how the organization should operate.

Combining these two dimensions gives rise to four leadership styles. While we believe that these categories are discernible in many leadership domains, we find their ideal types are most clearly evinced in the religious sphere. Knowledge, and knowing, are frequently progressed by juxtaposing different frames of reference: we understand one "thing" in terms of another as in the case of metaphor or metonymy.

RELIGIOUS ANALOGY

The use of the religious analogy provides an intriguing counterpoint to the military arena from whence analogies of leadership have traditionally been lifted, Sun Tzu and Clausewitz being just two prominent examples. There is added justification for drawing on religious models. The highest form of knowledge is generally referred to as wisdom, and wisdom is a quality more generally attributed to religious leaders than to military or business ones—a point to which we return below. Not suprisingly, therefore, religious leaders have provided longer lasting role models than their business counterparts—so there ought to be something we can learn from them. Thus we have named our four categories of leadership styles in terms of religious titles: Sage, Visionary, Prophet and Priest (see FIGURE 10.1). We have sought to adumbrate their features by reference to their religious qualities in respect of their own knowledge and their impact on others' knowledge.

We have obviously been extremely selective and have resorted to what might be deemed oversimplification. The leadership styles are best viewed, therefore, as ideal types and illustrative rather than definitive of particular

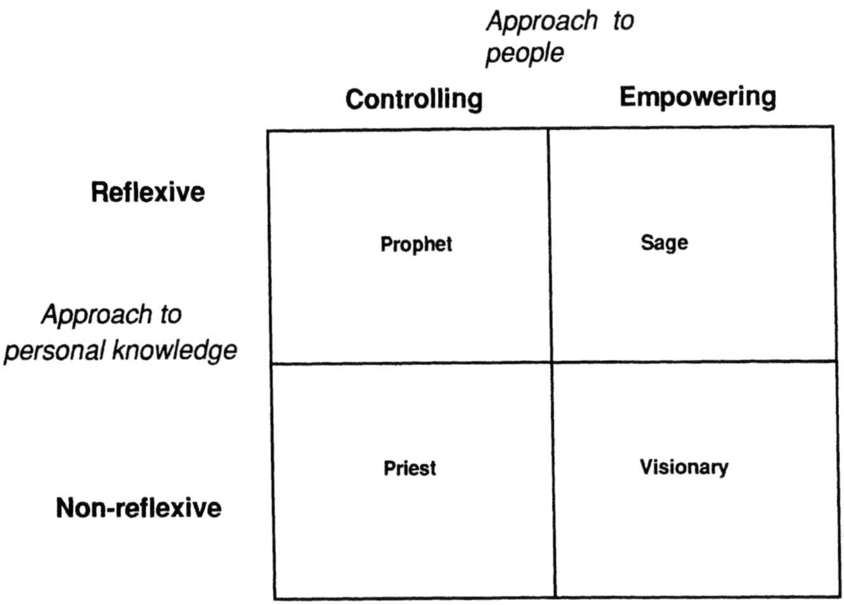

Approach to
people

Controlling   **Empowering**

Reflexive

Prophet   Sage

*Approach to
personal knowledge*

Priest   Visionary

Non-reflexive

FIGURE 10.1   Leadership styles

approaches to leadership with respect to self-knowledge and knowledge management. We refer throughout to each of the leadership styles as masculine while recognizing that many of the people throughout history who best represent these styles have in fact been women.

SAGE

In early texts, sage typically meant wise one, not just knowledgeable one. Wisdom emphasizes the link between knowledge and action, and the sage is judged to be knowledgeable only by the extent to which his actions and his words jointly elicit admiration and respect.

The sage is reflexive, looking inward to develop self-awareness—not the sudden vision of the prophet but the culmination of reflection and deep thought. The sage watches the seasons rise and fall. The sage really knows himself and thereby knows others.

The sage knows how things grow; he knows they are fed by their roots. The sage seeks to understand the principle of Ch'ang, whereby all life is nurtured by its roots. In converting people to new beliefs, it is the nourishing of people that is important. Nourishment is the best form of empowerment. The sage avoids deviousness for he knows that if he does so he will turn people against him. He avoids control, for as it is written in the Tao te Ching:

> Why is the sea the king of a hundred tributaries?
> Because everything comes down to it—so it is kingly by this name.
> So a sage that wants to rule the people must be below them.
> If he wants to be their leader, he must be behind them.
> If he has no desire to control then the people will not feel oppressed.

The sage does not confront people head on. He knows how to link with other people's energy, and thereby harness their joint endeavour to the common good. The sage's knowledge merges with, is not imposed or superimposed upon the knowledge of others. He knows, like water, how to flow round the blocks and how to find the way through without violence. It is this approach which distinguishes the sage, an attitude marked by benevolence and by compassion to others. Thus, conversion is willingly embraced; indeed, people are often not even aware of the sage's influence on them. It is the most subtle of conversions for, as already referred to in the introduction, the sage prefers invisibility; he always makes sure that the people do not know what he has done. He does not crave attention; he needs no outside confirmation of his self-worth, thus he focuses on his internal power rather than his power over others.

VISIONARY

The visionary, to state the obvious, is someone who has seen or experienced a vision, although in modern parlance the term also refers to someone who envisions the future. The word vision is one of the few religious or spiritual concepts to have successfully entered the business domain, albeit with a somewhat different usage. The religious meaning of vision is of an apparition, a sending, something foisted upon the unwary acolyte. Seeing or experiencing a vision and becoming as a consequence a visionary is essentially an unreflexive process, at least when compared to the meditation, contemplation and inward searching characteristic of the sage.

Religious vision emphasizes seeing what exists, albeit on a different plain, in the here and now, not the future. They have as their source something external to the person who sees and embraces the vision. But this external source exists in the present, not the future.

For the visionary, a critical task is to acquaint others with the substance of the vision. One does not keep a vision to oneself; it demands public promulgation. In communicating vision to others, its "beyond intellection" nature needs to be appreciated. It is not something to be treated on our earthy plane of thought, and indeed only those who have eyes to see it are likely to be able to appreciate the significance of any particular vision. Visionaries need followers, believers and faith because vision relates to the extraordinary—indeed, is counterposed to the ordinary.

Religious visions are part of the sacred, a key property of which is hierophany, whereby "something sacred shows itself to us" (Eliade, 1958, p. 7), conveying the idea that phenomenologically, people do not create sacred things. Instead sacredness manifests itself experientially as "something of a wholly different order, a reality that does not belong to our world" (Beane & Doty, 1975; Belk & Wallendorf, 1989).

Vision, as all things sacred, has conferred upon it a dignity that raises it above the ordinary or "empirical" (Pickering, 1984, p. 159). Visions are symbolic, not literal, but no less real because they are symbolic. They draw their strength by referring to something greater than what is depicted and from the ambiguity in how they are interpreted.

People are emotionally attached to all things sacred such that the visionary in propounding a new vision actively seeks change in people's commitment—not something which comes easily or can be imposed upon people. Gaining believers and followers, especially when such people need converting from an old or non-existent vision to the new one, is both a cultural process of "negotiating and tweaking meanings" and a psychological one of changing emotional attachments. And because meanings are located in people's minds, all attempts to control them can, to use Eco's phrase, at best be tentative and hazardous acts of influence. Moreover, because acceptance of new visions can challenge the authority of those who are in power, they are often resisted by the dominant religious authorities (as for example, with Saint Bernadette, who witnessed the Virgin Mary at Lourdes). Hence the visionary, like the sage, empowers others to share this faith rather than force it upon them, and to believe that his vision is real.

PROPHET

In the Old Testament, the role of the prophet is to carry the word of God to the people. The prophet is the messenger of God and the guardian of his commands. His role is given to him from without but his knowledge of how to understand it, and how and when to apply it comes from within. Once chosen or sent, his mission is to interpret the word, and give it meaning. The message might be heard from without but the knowledge of how to elaborate it in parable comes from within. The subjective experience of the message is a vital element. The awakening is just the beginning of the search for knowledge, not the end.

> Samuel grew up and God was with him. The rumour spread through the whole land that God had called him to be his prophet. God continued to reveal

himself to him and Samuel brought the word of God to the people . . . What a task for the young Samuel that God had called. For years he had guarded the ark (in the temple) and now he must guard God's word. *This was not something you could lie beside at night on a sleeping-mat like a watchdog. This was something living and yet invisible. The words God had spoken could be repeated inwardly and then told to the people* . . . So now Samuel turned from a temple boy into a wandering prophet. He went from village to village and acted as a judge when the people asked God's will. (Klink, 1967, p. 195).

The prophet is responsible for more than just upholding and spreading the word. He is not the mere mouthpiece, but the medium through which faith is articulated. His is the task of reflection on and formulation of the faith. The prophet, once chosen, looks reflexively inwards to reassess his purpose in life and to understand, embrace and articulate for the first time the command. The separate task of initiating and introducing people into the faith is the task of the priest—the distinction between interpretation of faith and induction being well recognized in many religions.

Self-purification or self-mortification distinguishes the prophet from lesser mortals and legitimates his right to be chosen to be in communion with a higher power. In many religions he becomes an incarnation of the higher power, acting as an intermediary between spirits, and so a person lifted above all others. "The prophet is a passive medium when possessed but through his ability to induce possession he is also a master of these supernatural powers" (Nadel, 1946). This contrasts with the visionary, whose encounter with the supernatural is more fleeting and less personal.

A further attribute separating the prophet from the visionary is that through his representation of and communion with the supernatural, he may not be ignored. Prophesy of the future has implications for current action—to continue in old ways is to court doom. Prophets operate through fear of what will happen if their message is not acted upon, or if their authority and divine right to provide guidance is challenged. The prophet seeks to judge and control others on the basis of his superior power and knowledge rather than empower them to find their own way or to learn for themselves. There are, of course, exceptions to this view of the prophet, as for example in Kahlil Kibran's prophet, Almustafa, who was a seeker of the silence, searching therein for "treasures found in silence that I may dispense with confidence" (Kibran, 1926). But the stereotypical relation between the prophet and his flock found in the Bible or in the Shamanism of Siberia and Northwest America involves obedience and genuflection rather than questioning, dialogue or reflection.

PRIEST

The final category of leadership style is that of the priest. Priests as religious leaders are the intermediaries between people and the higher power that people wish to address. The difference between the priest and the prophet is generally defined in terms of the source of power. A priest may supplement his ritual with a vision but basically his position depends upon learning standardized ritual beliefs and practices by becoming an apprentice and enduring a long period of formal training with older priests (Lowie, 1954, p. 161). The difference, as Evans-Pritchard wrote about the priest and prophets (shamans) of the Nuer, is that: "Whereas in the priest man speaks to God, in the prophet . . . God speaks to man" (Evans-Pritchard, 1937).

The priest is involved with education, the introduction and initiation of new generations into whichever formal religion the priest upholds. In Catholicism, for example, the priest is concerned with how faith is sustained and actively passed on from generation to generation (catechises). During his own training (another factor which distinguishes him from the prophet) and induction into the priesthood, the priest reflects upon the meaning of his and others' religious experience. Piety can only be known by discovering it oneself. Yet once he has taken his vows, then his duty is to act as a herald of the faith, leading new disciples into that faith. The knowledge which the priest is to transmit is not moulded by his interpretation of that knowledge. It is something given to be adhered to:

> The faithful were encouraged by the "Rules" to forgo all personal judgement and to obey the Church in all things. Not only were they encouraged to accept Church teachings uncritically, but they were also expected to defend them, and by no means criticise them. (Tynan, commenting on "Rules for thinking within the Church," a chapter appended to the Spiritual Exercise of St. Ignatius Loyola).

In the traditional Church there is a lack of critical thinking; there is no stimulus for it and nothing to be gained from it. As Oscar Wilde cynically but insightfully put it in *The Picture of Dorian Gray*, "A bishop keeps on saying at the age of eighty what he was told to say when he was a boy of eighteen, and as a natural consequence he always looks absolutely delightful".

Thus the priest is expected to be essentially unreflexive with respect to his knowledge of things divine. His faith (since the Council of Trent, 1545–1563) is synonymous with belief, and belief is understood as cognitive assent to doctrinal statements. In the words of Trent's catechism, "faith is an unhesitating assent to whatever the authority of our Holy Mother, the Church, teaches us to have been revealed by God".

Paralleling the priest's (required) unreflexive approach to doctrine is the approach expected of the laity to whom he administers. The *á la carte* Christian who cherry picks his way through doctrines, dogmas, precepts and teachings is not encouraged; he must still remain faithful to the message of the church. In 1865 Pope Leo XIII set out his model of the Catholic Church: "to the pastors alone is given the power of teaching, judging and ruling; the people must allow themselves to be governed, corrected and led to salvation" (quoted from Monsignor Denis O'Callaghan, 1996). This again is the language of control, very different to that of the sage.

This notion of the priest and his relation to the laity is undergoing change within the Catholic Church. The second Vatican Council (1963–1965) allowed priests to present Christian doctrine according to the needs of the times, yet adaptation is in terms of the language used to convey an essentially unchanged message of the Church. While there is a rethinking in some religions about the religious leadership role of the priest, in others traditional roles are being reaffirmed and strengthened in line with fundamentalist principles.

Discussion and Conclusions

Our description above of the four leadership styles puts an entirely different slant on the importance of knowledge and the dominant role of leaders in its construction to that generally found within the strategic management paradigm. The latter views knowledge as an objective resource, a wasting and disembodied asset to be manipulated and rendered inimitable, and subjugated to the achievement of superior firm performance. Economics and materialism are placed at the epicentre of knowledge creation and they serve as the criteria for assessing whether knowledge is useful and valuable. Where a personal and subjective dimension to knowledge is acknowledged, as in the case of tacit knowledge, the interest is in objectifying it, mining this knowledge and processing it for instrumental ends: "Residing in individual and social relationships in the firm, this knowledge is seen as tacit" (Polayni, 1962) and "the only possible way to reveal and transfer this knowledge is to establish a closer and more interactive relationship with the one possessing it" (Aadne, Von Grogh & Roos, 1996, p. 12).

The first difference noticeable from the religious domain is that leaders are afforded a significant role in the knowledge management process. They are responsible for articulating, legitimating, interpreting, and initiating others into whatever knowledge is deemed appropriate for self, societal and spiritual development—there being no necessary conflict between any of these levels of achievement. We return to this theme once we have considered the nature of appropriate knowledge.

Knowledge of things within the religious domain is differentiated from knowing or wisdom. Benjamin Hoff, in the delightful book *the Tao of Pooh* (1989), eloquently encapsulates this alternative perspective:

> The masters of life know the Way, for they listen to the voice within them, the voice of Wisdom and simplicity, the voice that reasons beyond Cleverness and knows beyond Knowledge. That voice is not just the power and property of a few, but has been given to everyone.

Wisdom is not an attribute that has been stressed in the strategic management literature, perhaps because to link wisdom with business seems at best inappropriate and at worse pretentious. Yet a consideration of wisdom and how a wise one operates is, to say the least, instructive when it comes to considering the role of leaders in knowledge acquisition and dissemination.

We have seen, for example, that the sage is wise and "knows beyond knowledge" such that his Knowledge (with a capital K to signify its equivalence to wisdom), and to a lesser extent that of the visionary and prophet, has an altogether different ring from the type of knowledge (with a little k) that we generally accord supremacy within the business arena. It is a Knowledge which is eternal rather than contingent, which is to be shared, nurtured and respected, not selfishly hoarded and discarded with the newest and latest management panacea. Such Knowledge is essentially processual in that it relates to knowing rather than knowledge, knowing how to acquire knowledge and disseminate it to others and how to convert knowledge into action. It has an internal, self-referential rather than external representational aspect, even in those non-reflexive categories we have described above. Only in the case of the priest, is knowledge a doctrine distinguished more by its static ritual articulation than by its personal, creative, dynamic and living social construction. And even with the priest, the ends to which Knowledge is put expands the intended set of beneficiaries from the selective few to the betterment of all (at least all who choose to "believe").

Such a perspective of Knowledge pricks the halo accorded to competitive advantage, and provides moral support for the increasing trend within the strategy arena to a focus on collaboration, relationships, cooperation and a stakeholder perspective. It affirms the necessity for social responsibility and the new academy of business to temper an exclusive concern with overtly selfish ends. It also raises the question as to whether transformation is really required for if one knows, really Knows, then one does not need to change this knowledge, merely apply it to a different set of circumstances. Only for those uninitiated into this superior form of existence is transformation or conversion required.

Thus, initiation rather than transformation becomes the key imperative with Knowledge accumulation. Who is responsible for such initiation? In the religious arena this is the clear responsibility of the leader. While Knowledge is there for everyone's benefit (for, as Hoff pointed out, it is no one's power or property), it is the leader who provides a role model for knowing and who catalyses others to follow the path. In stark comparison, the treatment of knowledge within strategic management has relatively little to say about leadership—a recent book on managing knowledge (Von Grogh & Roos, 1996) does not even feature leadership as an index item.

The model of leadership and of knowledge from the religious domain fits in with the view of leaders as coaches, supporters and role models rather than leaders as planners or directors. It questions the merits of that style of leadership which operates through fiat and control, for the priest and the prophet are altogether less appealing than the sage and the visionary. And even with the priest and prophet, the legitimacy is provided by reference to belief and faith rather than the exercise of raw power. It suggests that the notion of the all-powerful chief executive within the dominant coalition who can exert more influence than others through his right to control people's decisions, careers and resources is at best illusory and at worst highly dysfunctional. It suggests an unobtrusive, subtle, hands-off, patient form of leadership quite different to the current model of proactive, decisive, action-oriented, rush-in-and-sort-the-troops-out, heroic style of leadership favoured by popular management writing.

A further insight afforded by the religious domain is that being a visionary requires having a very special type of knowledge, knowledge of the divine. To have such knowledge means to be chosen: trying to conjure one up smacks of inauthenticity and sham, bringing sore knees rather than hoped for cargo. Yet virtually every article on how to do strategic management focuses on the need for a vision to set the overall direction of the organization. Generally, vision in the business domain refers to a picture of the future that is realizable through constancy of effort and dedication to the cause. Some writers see the development of vision as the product of strategic thinking—whether it be crafted or planned rationally by those in the know.

These meanings of something futuristic, of something crafted/planned, diverge from the religious meaning. No meaning is inviolate to circumstances, the hijacking of meanings being quite legitimate within a postmodern world. But there is an important sense in which the original meaning of vision ironically brings the concept down to earth. While not all will believe in the authenticity of a divinely inspired vision, the actualization of what it portends is not contingent on human effort aimed at bringing it to fruition. If you believe in the vision, you accept that it depicts what is already occurring. This contrasts with business conceptions, which typically equate vision with dreams (as in Martin Luther King's "I have a dream") of a future, hoped-for position in a competitive milieu—typically market or technological leadership. Yet as Freud and others tell us, the basis of dreams is wish fulfilment, not a strong basis upon which to face reality, whatever that might be.

There is an obvious danger of carrying any analogy too far. Yet the import of this chapter that despite the very great differences between business and religious domains, there is learning in comparing and contrasting the two. Empirical research is required to assess when and in what circumstances particular styles of leadership and knowledge management are appropriate. But while it is possible that Sages, Visionaries, Prophets and Priests can learn from strategists, it is probable that strategists have much to learn from them. Therein lies Knowledge, imitable, but none the less valuable as a consequence.

REFERENCES

Aadane, J., Von Grogh, G. & Roos, J. (1996). Representationism: the traditional approach to cooperative strategies. In G. Von Krogh & J. Roos (eds) *Managing Knowledge: Perspectives on Co-operation and Competition*. London: Sage, pp. 9–32.

Almeida, P. (1996). Knowledge sourcing by foreign multinationals: patent citation analysis in the US semiconductor industry. *Strategic Management Journal*, **17**(special issue), 155–165.

Ansoff, I. (1965). *Corporate Strategy*. Harmondsworth: Penguin.

Aoki, M. (1990). Toward an economic model of the Japanese firm. *Journal of Economics*, **28**, 1–27.

Argyris, C. (1964). *Integrating the Individual and the Organisation*. New York: Wiley.

Argyris, C. (1990). *Overcoming Organisational Defenses: Facilitating Organisational Learning*. Needham, MA: Allyn and Bacon.

Argyris, C. & Schon, D.A. (1978). *Organisational Learning*. Reading, MA: Addison-Wesley.

Badaracco, J.L. (1991). *The Knowledge Link*. Boston, MA: Harvard Business School Press.

Barney, J.B. (1986). Strategic factor markets: expectations, luck and business strategy. *Management Science*, **21**, 1231–1241.

Barney, J.B. (1991). Firm resources and sustained competitive advantage. *Journal of Management*, **17**(1), 99–120.

Bartlett, C.A. & Ghoshal, S. (1978). Managing across borders: new organizational responses. *Sloan Management Review*, **11**, 791–800.

Bartlett, C.A. & Ghoshal, S. (1989). *Managing Across Borders: The Transnational Solution*. Boston, MA: Harvard Business School Press.

Bass, B.M. (1985). *Leadership and Performance beyond Expectations*. New York: Free Press.

Beane, W. & Dory, W. (eds) (1975). Myths, Rites and Symbols: *A Mircea Cliade Reader*, **1**, New York, Harper.

Belk, S.J.R. & Wallendorf, M. (1988). A naturalistic inquiry into buyer and seller behaviour at a swap meet. *Journal of Consumer Research*, 449–470.

Bennis, W. & Nanus, B. (1985). *Leaders: The Strategies for Taking Charge*. Harper. New York: Harper & Row.

Bohn, R.E. (1994). Measuring and managing technological knowledge. *Sloan Management Review*, Fall, 61–72.

Brown, J.S. & Duguid, P. (1991). Organisational learning and communities-of-practice: toward a unified view of working, learning and innovation. *Organisation Science*, **2**, 40–57.

Burns, J.M. (1978). *Leadership*. New York: Harper & Row.

Calas, M.B. & Smircich, L. (1988). Reading leadership as a form of cultural analysis. In J.G. Hunt, D.M. Hosking, C.A. Schriesheim & R. Stewart (eds) *Leaders and Managers: An International Perspective on Managerial Behavioural and Leadership*. New York: Pergamon Press, pp. 163–178.

Cangelosi, V.E. & Dill, W.R. (1965). Organisational learning: observations towards a theory. *Administrative Science Quarterly*, **10**, 175–203.

Chakravarthy, B.S. & Doz, Y. (1992). Strategy process research: focusing on corporate self-renewal. *Strategic Management Journal*, **13**, 5–14.

Clark, K.B. & Fujimoto, T. (1991). *Product Development Performance*. Boston, MA: Harvard Business School Press.

Cohen, M.D. & Sproull, L.S. (1991). Editors' Introduction. *Organisation Science*, **2**(1), 1–3.

Cohen, M.D. & Sproull, L.S. (eds) (1996). *Organisational Learning*. Thousand Oaks, CA: Sage.

Corsini, R. (1987). *Concise Encyclopaedia of Psychology*. New York: Wiley.

Coulson-Thomas, C. (1992). *Transforming the Company: Bridging the Gap between Management Myth and Corporate Reality*. London: Kogan Page.

Cyert, R.M. & March, J.G. (1963). *A Behavioural Theory of the Firm*. Englewood Cliffs, NJ: Prentice Hall.

Daft, R.L. & Weick, K.E. (1984). Toward a model of organizations as interpretation systems. *Academy of Management Review*, **9**(2), 284–295.

Deal, T.E. & Kennedy, A.A. (1982). *Corporate Culture: The Rites and Rituals of Corporate Life*. Reading, MA: Addison-Wesley.

Demsetz, H. (1991). The theory of the firm revisited. In O.E. Williamson & S.G. Winter (eds) *The Nature of the Firm*. New York: Oxford University Press, pp. 159–178.

Douglas, M. & Isherwood, B. (1978). *The World of Goods*. London: Routeledge and Kegan Paul.

Drucker, P. (1991). The new productivity challenge. *Harvard Business Review*, November/December, 69–79.

Eliade, M. (1958). *Images and Symbols: Studies in Religious Symbolism*, translated by P. Mairet. Paris: Sheed and Ward.

Evans-Pritchard, E.E. (1937). The notion of witchcraft explains unfortunate events. In *Witchcraft, Oracles and Magic among the Azande*. Oxford: Clarendon Press, Part 1, Chapter 4.

Goodenough, W.H. (1957). Cultural anthropology and linguistics. In P. Garvin (ed.) *Report of the Seventh Annual Round Table Meeting on Linguistics and Language Study*. Washington, DC: Georgetown University.

Gouillart, F.J. & Kelly, J. (1995). *Transforming the Organisation*. New York: McGraw-Hill.

Grant, R.M. (1991). The resource based theory of competitive advantage: implications for strategy formulation. *California Management Review*, **33**(3), 114–135.

Grant, R.M. (1993). Organisational capabilities within a knowledge-based view of the firm, presented at the Academy of Management Conference, Atlanta, Georgia.

Grant, R.M. (1996). Toward a knowledge-based theory of the firm. *Strategic Management Journal*, **17**(special issue), 109–122.

Grant, R.M. & Baden-Fuller, C. (1995). A knowledge based theory of inter-firm collaboration, Academy of Management Best Paper Proceedings, pp. 17–21.

Hayek, F.A. (1945). The use of knowledge in society. *American Economic Review*, 35(4), 519–530.

Hedlund, G. (1994). A model of knowledge management and the N-form corporation. *Strategic Management Journal*, 15, 73–90.

Henderson, R. & Clark, K. (1990). Architectural innovation: the reconfiguration of technologies and the failure of established firms. *Administrative Science Quarterly*, 35, 9–31.

Herriot, S.R., Levinthal, D. & March, J.G. (1985). Learning from experience in organisations. *American Economic Review*, 75, 298–302.

Hoff, B. (1989). *The Tao of Pooh*. London: Mandarin.

House, R.J. (1977). A 1976 theory of charismatic leadership. In J.G. Hunt and L.L. Larson (eds) *Leadership: The Cutting Edge*. Chicago, IL: Illinois University Press, pp. 189–207.

Huber, G.P. (1991). Organisational learning: the contributing processes and the literatures. *Organisation Science*, 2(1), 88–115.

Imai, K.I., Nonaka, I. & Takeuchi, H. (1985). Managing the new product development process: how Japanese companies learn and unlearn. In K.B. Clark, R.H. Hayes & C. Lorenz (eds) *The Uneasy Alliance: Managing the Productivity and Technology Dilemma*. Boston, MA: Harvard Business School Press, pp. 337–381.

Itami, H. (1987). *Mobilizing Invisible Assets*. Cambridge, MA: Harvard University Press.

James, W. (1950). *The Principles of Psychology*, vols I and II. New York: Dover.

Johnson, G. (1990). Managing strategic change: the role of symbolic action. *British Journal of Management*, 1, 183–200.

Kavanagh, (1996). Aliens in hyperspace. *Working Paper Series*, Department of Management and Marketing, UCC.

Kibran, K. (1926). *The Prophet*. Harmondsworth: Penguin.

Kilmann, R.H. & Covin, T.J. (1988). *Corporate Transformation: Revitalising Organisations for a Competitive World*. San Francisco, CA: Jossey-Bass.

Klink, J.L. and Klaasse, P. (1967). *Bible for Children with Songs and Plays*. Philadelphia, PA, Westminister Press.

Kogut, B. & Zander, U. (1992). Knowledge of the firm, combinative capabilities, and the replication of new technology. *Organization Science*, 3, 383–396.

Kotter, J.P. (1995). Leading change: why transformation efforts fail. *Harvard Business Review*, March/April, 59–68.

Kwok, M., Palmer, M. & Ramsey, J. (1993). *The Tao te Ching*. Dorset: Element

Lado, A.A., Boyd, N.G. & Wright, P. (1992). A competency-based model of sustainable competitive advantage: toward a conceptual integration. *Journal of Management*, 18, 77–91.

Lawson, H. (1985). *Reflexivity, the Post Modern Predicament*. London: Hutchinson.

Leonard-Barton, D. (1992). Core capabilities and core rigidities: a paradox in managing new product development. *Strategic Management Journal*, 13, 111–125.

Levitt, B. & March, J.G. (1988). Organisational learning. *Annual Review of Sociology*, 14, 319–340.

Likert, R. (1967). *The Human Organization: Its Management and Value*. New York: McGraw-Hill.

Lowie, R.H. (1954). Shamans and priests among the plains indians. In *Indians of the Plains*. New York: McGraw-Hill.

March, J.G. & Simon, H.A. (1958). *Organizations*. New York: Wiley.

McGregor, D. (1960). *The Human Side of Enterprise*. New York: McGraw-Hill.

Mowery, D.C., Oxley, J.E. & Silverman, B.S. (1996). Strategic alliances and interfirm knowledge transfer. *Strategic Management Journal*, **17**(special issue), 77–91.

Nadel, S.F. (1946). A study of shamanism in the Nuba mountains. *Journal of the Royal Anthropological Institute*, 25–37.

Nadler, D., Shaw, R. & Walton, A. (1994). *Discontinuous Change: Leading Organisational Transformation*. San Francisco, CA: Jossey-Bass.

Nelson, R.R. & Winter, S.G. (1982). *An Evolutionary Theory of Economic Change*. Cambridge, MA: Harvard University Press.

Nonaka, I. (1987). Managing the firm as an information creation process, working paper, Institute of Business Research, Hitotsubashi University.

Nonaka, I. (1989). *Organising innovation as a knowledge creation process: a suggested paradigm for self-renewing organisations*, mimeo, Walter A Haas School of Business, University of California.

Nonaka, I. (1991). The knowledge creating company. *Harvard Business Review*, November/December, 96–104.

Nonaka, I., Byosiere, P., Borucki, C. & Konno, N. (1994). Organisational knowledge creation theory: a first comprehensive *test. International Business Review*, special issue, 337–353.

Nonaka, I. & Takeuchi, H. (1995). *The Knowledge Creating Company*. New York: Oxford University Press.

Orr, J.E. (1990). Sharing knowledge, celebrating identity: community memory in a service culture. In D.S. Middleton & D. Edwards (eds) *Collective Remembering*. Newbury Park, CA: Sage, pp. 168–189.

Pfeffer, J. (1981). *Power in Organisations*. Marshfield, MA: Pitman.

Pickering, W.S.F. (1984). *Durkheim's Sociology of Religion: Themes and Theories*, London, Routledge & Kegan Paul.

Platt, R. (1989). Reflexivity, recursion and social life: Elements for a post-modern sociology. *Sociological Review*, **37**(4), 636–667.

Polayni, M. (1962). *Personal Knowledge*. Chicago, IL: University of Chicago Press.

Polayni, M. (1966). *The Tacit Dimension*. New York: Anchor Day.

Pondy, L.R. (1978). Leadership is a language game. In M.M. McCall & M.M. Lombardo (eds) *Leadership: Where Else Can We Go?* Durham, NC: Duke University Press.

Popper, K. (1972). *Objective Knowledge*. Oxford: Oxford University Press.

Prahalad, C.K. & Bettis, R.A. (1986). The dominant logic: a new linkage between diversity and performance. *Strategic Management Journal*, **7**(6), 485–501.

Prahalad, C.K. & Hamel, G. (1990). The core competence of the corporation. *Harvard Business Review*, **68**(3), 79–91.

Quinn, J.B. (1992). *Intelligent Enterprise: A Knowledge and Service Based Paradigm for Industry*. New York: Free Press.

Revans, R.W. (1982). *The Origins and Growth of Action Learning*. London: Chartwell.

Roos, J., Von Grogh, G. & Yip, G. (1995). An epistemology of globalising firms. *International Business Review*, **3**(4), 395–424.

Ryle, G. (1949). *The Concept of Mind*. London: Hutchinson.

Sathe, V. (1985). How to decipher and change corporate culture. In R.H. Kilman, M.J. Saxton, R. Serpa & Associates (eds) *Gaining Control of Corporate Culture*. San Francisco, CA: Jossey-Bass. pp. 230–261.

Schein, E.H. (1984). Coming to a new awareness of organisational culture. *Sloan Management Review*, **25**, 3–16.

Schein, E.H. (1985). *Organisational Culture and Leadership*. San Francisco, CA: Jossey-Bass.

Senge, P. (1990). *The Fifth Discipline: The Art and Practice of the Learning Organisation.* New York: Doubleday.

Sobol, M.G. & Lei, D. (1994). Environment, manufacturing technology and embedded knowledge. *International Journal of Human Factors in Manufacturing,* **4**(2), 167–189.

Smircich, L. (1983). Concepts of culture and organisational analysis. *Administrative Science Quarterly,* **28**, 339–358.

Spender, J.C. (1993). Competitive advantage from tacit knowledge? Unpackaging the concept and its strategic implication. In B. Moingeon & A. Edmondson (eds) *Organisational Learning and Competitive Advantage.* London: Sage, pp. 56–74.

Spender, J.C. (1994). Knowing, managing and learning: a dynamic managerial epistemology *Management Learning,* **25**(3), 387–412.

Spender, J.C. & Grant, R. (1996). Knowledge and the firm: overview. *Strategic Management Journal,* **17**(special issue), pp. 5–11.

Stalk, G., Evans, P. & Schulman, L.E. (1992). Competing on capabilities: the new rules of corporate strategy. *Harvard Business Review,* March April, 57–69.

Teece, D.J. (1986). Profiting from technological innovation. *Research Policy,* **15**, 286–305.

Tichy, N.M. & Devanna, M. (1986). The transformational leader. *Training and Development Journal,* July, 27–32.

Tichy, N.M. & Ulrich, D. (1984). Revitalising organisations: the leadership role. In *Managing Organisational Transitions.* Homewood, IL: Richard Irwin.

Toffler, A. (1990). *Powershift: Knowledge, Wealth and Violence at the Edge of the 21st Century.* New York: Bantam Books.

Von Grogh, G. & Roos, J. (1996). *Managing Knowledge: Perspectives on Cooperation and Competition.* London: Sage.

Walsh, J.P. (1991). Organisational memory. *Academy of Management Review,* **16**(1), 57–91.

Weick, K.E. (1995). *Sensemaking in Organisations.* Thousand Oaks, CA: Sage.

Wernerfelt, B. (1984). A resource based view of the firm. *Strategic Management Journal,* **5**, 171–180.

Wheelright, S. & Clark, K. (1992). *Revolutionizing New Product Development.* New York: Free Press.

Williams, J.R. (1992). How sustainable is your advantage? *California Management Review,* **34**, 29–51.

Winter, S.G. (1987). Knowledge and competence as strategic assets. In D. Teece (ed.) *The Competitive Challenge.* Cambridge, MA: Ballinger.

Yukl, G. (1989). Managerial leadership: a review of theory and research. *Journal of Management,* **15**(2), 251–289.

11

Information Competences and Knowledge Creation at the Corporate Centre

YASMIN MERALI, JOHN MCGEE

INTRODUCTION

The role of headquarters is important in the transformation of the corporation and other kinds of change programmes. This chapter is concerned with the information processes and knowledge networks that underpin organizational learning and characterize distinctive relationships between headquarters and their businesses in a dynamic competitive context.

We introduce "scripts", describe a framework for identifying the underlying "scripts" that are enacted in distinctive headquarters–business relationships and characterize the information profiles underpinning each type of enactment. In the discussion that follows we position this work in the context of existing literature on headquarters–subsidiary relationships in MNCs and show how the framework can be used to develop an understanding of the information processes and knowledge networks that underpin the corporate learning in a dynamic context.

THE ROLE OF HEADQUARTERS

Over the past two decades there has been a growth of interest in the changing structure, style and role of corporate headquarters. Much of this

Strategic Flexibility: Managing in a Turbulent Environment. Edited by G. Hamel, C.K. Prahalad, H. Thomas and D. O'Neal.

interest is focused on the value creation potential of the headquarters (Goold & Campbell, 1991). The value added by the activities of the headquarters is referred to as the "parenting advantage" associated with the existence of the headquarters. As evidenced by the literature on successful headquarters styles (Goold, Campbell & Alexander, 1994), the value creation potential of the headquarters is typically realized through the activities of:

- portfolio design and development,
- (holistic) planning and resource exploitation,
- facilitation of cross-fertilization between divisions/businesses, and
- environmental sensemaking.

The way that the headquarters relates to each business and its role in coordinating collaboration across businesses is an important determinant of headquarters success. There are two interrelated strands of work which are particularly useful for enabling us to better understand patterns of successful headquarters behaviours. The first strand is concerned with the understanding of headquarters behaviours and characteristics as they relate to the external strategic domain with regard to portfolio design, acquisition and globalization strategies (e.g. Bartlett & Ghoshal, 1987; Prahalad & Doz, 1987). The second strand focuses on the headquarters–business relationships and is concerned with characterizing the types of relationships that exist and understanding how various headquarters–business interactions work (e.g. Ghoshal & Nohria, 1989, 1993). Both these strands are important in addressing the question of how the headquarters can add value. The central management imperative in this context is about obtaining the optimal value-creating arrangement, where:

- there is effective utilization of resources and competences (local and central) for sustained viability and competitive success, and
- resources and competences (business and corporate) are developed and utilized effectively to achieve a desired and feasible balance between the individual interests of the constituent businesses and the corporate interest in total value creation.

What constitutes value creation for a particular headquarters is a perception, which is a product of the operative corporate mental map. In this context, the mental map that the headquarters has of its corporate and external environment can be thought of as deriving principally from four information domains:

1. **The strategic domain:** this is made up of perceptions about how the strategic landscape looks. These perceptions are based on information about:
   - what other, competing parents are up to,

- what the overall corporate positioning is in terms of performance benchmarks and corporate image (as reflected in the opinions of key external observers such as the city, shareholders and so on), and
- what constitutes value in the parenting context.

2. **The business domain:** this is made up of perceptions about individual businesses regarding:
   - the nature of the competitive environment for each business,
   - the resources required for competitive positioning by each business in its competitive context,
   - the resource base that exists within each business, and
   - the performance of each business.

3. **The organizational domain:** this is made up of perceptions about:
   - the formal structural arrangements (e.g. centralization, decentralization), and
   - both the formal and informal processes that exist for communication, coordination and control through the organization.

4. **The competence domain:** this is made up of perceptions about:
   - the value of the competence base that exists in each of the businesses, and
   - how the overall corporate competence pool looks.

HEADQUARTERS COGNITIVE COMPETENCES AND VALUE CREATION

The cognitive part of the value creation exercise is concerned with figuring out how the collective corporate competence and resource base can be developed and leveraged most effectively given the extant strategic and business contexts. In order to be effective in this respect, it is essential that the operative mental map is congruent with the contemporaneous extant environment. This requires the headquarters staff to engage in a continuous cycle of knowledge acquisition and learning in order to:

- develop a comprehensive knowledge base on which to base action, and
- create an organizational environment (structures and relationships) that is conducive to the effective development and exploitation of corporate-wide resources and competences.

In dynamic external environments (of the type faced by businesses in fast-moving competitive industries or those operating in complex and uncertain national environments) it becomes essential that both the business and the headquarters are capable of sustaining high rates of learning in order to act appropriately in the changing external context.

HEADQUARTERS–BUSINESS RELATIONSHIPS

The relationship between the headquarters and the business both shapes and is shaped by the mental map of the business context that is held by the centre. As defined earlier, this map is based on headquarters' perceptions regarding the complexity of the business context, the resource and competence base of the business and its potential for adding value through collaboration with other businesses. These perceptions are based on the information that is acquired by the headquarters via three routes:

- directly from the external environment (external performance benchmarks),
- from other businesses operating in a similar context, and
- through the agency of the business itself (via the relationship).

When the last of these routes is a significant one the business acts as the information gatekeeper. As the information gatekeeper it is instrumental in shaping its headquarters' perceptions about it. This affects the way in which the headquarters deals with the business through the relationship.

HEADQUARTERS ARCHETYPES

In trying to understand the enactment of the headquarters–business relationship with regard to mutual perceptions and shared learning, it is useful to characterize the roles that are played by the two participants in the relationship. Each distinctive headquarters–business relationship is mediated through, and evidenced by, its transactions. The transactions are influenced by the perceptions of the business of itself in relation to the headquarters and the perceptions of the headquarters of itself in relation to the business. These perceptions are analogous to the so-called *scripts* referred to by adherents of transaction analysis (Berne, 1961).

> An individual's script is an internal conceptual structure containing a set of rules and norms and a highly cross-linked set of data about self, the world and interactions between the two. The script acts as a filtering mechanism for fresh data: nothing is accepted into a script unless it can be made to fit with what already exists. The script evolves over time as new information is incorporated, and socialization modifications occur as a result of its involvement in meaningful relationships. The nature of this evolution (e.g. in terms of what can or cannot be incorporated into the script) is itself determined by, and is characteristic of, the existing script.

The framework we propose uses the concept of scripts to describe the perceptions and norms underpinning the behaviour displayed respectively by the headquarters and the business as evidenced by the enactment of the relationship. It is suggested here that while both are developing their capabilities and knowledge over time, the respective roles that the headquarters and the business adopt *within the context of the relationship* will continue to conform to the established script.

The relationship is a key component of the headquarters' knowledge acquisition structure: it acts as a significant filter for what enters the headquarters' knowledge base. Whether formalized or not, the knowledge base of the headquarters is an inherent structural component of the script. Also implicit within the context of the headquarters' script is a perception of the channel of communication: within the script, each headquarters–business relationship has a "band width" and "integrity rating" associated with its value as an information conduit for the headquarters' knowledge acquisition activity. In our framework (FIGURE 11.1) we use two dimensions for distinguishing headquarters scripts:

1. Management focus: this is a dimension whose extreme poles are defined as *capability focus* and *product focus*. A *capability focus* exists when management engagement and concern is focused predominantly on the

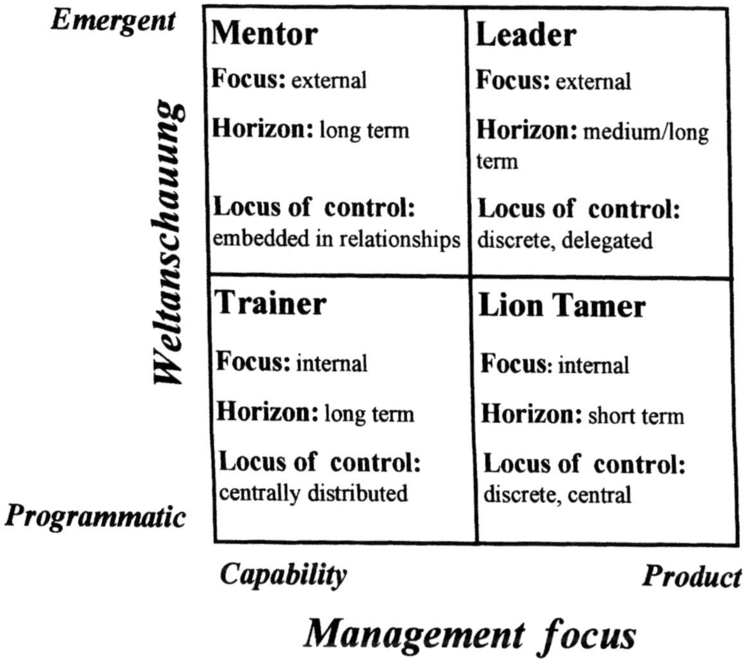

	Capability	**Product**
Emergent	**Mentor** **Focus:** external **Horizon:** long term **Locus of control:** embedded in relationships	**Leader** **Focus:** external **Horizon:** medium/long term **Locus of control:** discrete, delegated
Programmatic	**Trainer** **Focus:** internal **Horizon:** long term **Locus of control:** centrally distributed	**Lion Tamer** **Focus:** internal **Horizon:** short term **Locus of control:** discrete, central

Weltanschauung

Management focus

FIGURE 11.1   The four archetypes: outlook and locus of control

capabilities and competences of the business. A *product focus* exists when management engagement and concern is focused predominantly on the product/output of the business.

2. The *weltanschauung* (world-outlook), implicit in the script for the enactment of the relationship: this is a dimension whose extreme poles are defined as *programmatic* and *emergent*. A *programmatic weltanschauung* exists when the relationship is acted out in a fashion predicated on a mindset where the world is largely "planned for", and actions and behaviours are designed to deliver explicit outcomes. An *emergent weltanschauung* exists when the relationship is acted out in a dynamic mode predicated on a mindset where the world is viewed as uncertain, "shapable" and "shaping".

This framework uses these two variables to define different headquarters *archetypes*. It must be emphasized that the four quadrants defined by the extremes of these variables represent "pure" archetypes—the extreme ends of a continuum. We call these archetypes the *Lion Tamer*, the *Trainer*, the *Leader* and the *Mentor*. These "pure" types amount to caricatures, each one operating exclusively within a single paradigm. In reality the context of the corporation is far more complex; nonetheless, the archetypes represent useful analogues to help our understanding of the enactment of headquarters scripts. In reality there are few successful "pure" types, but centres can usually locate "native quadrants" in which their behaviour is more congruent.

The matrix showing the operating and competence characteristics associated with each archetype is given in FIGURE 11.2 and summarized below.

The Lion Tamer

The *Lion Tamer* is internally focused, and concerned almost exclusively with short-term output measures for the business. *Lion Tamers* tend to adopt a programmatic style of management where the locus of control is unashamedly centralized, with linear communications. They excel at efficiency oriented resource management. The communication channel is typically a vertical command-and-control conduit, and there are no resources allocated to horizontal coordination between businesses. This style encourages the individual business to develop a conformance orientation and a very strong regulation competence, reflected in good housekeeping and strong hygiene. Companies like Hanson have many of the attributes that characterize this archetype.

The Trainer

The *Trainer* also tends to be internally focused, but is concerned with the development of specific competences over the long term. The locus of

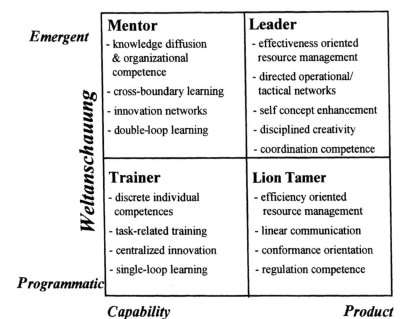

FIGURE 11.2   The four archetypes: competence characteristics

control is centrally distributed, according to a programmatic mindset. *Trainers* have a very deep commitment to training and development of the businesses in keeping with the centrally determined blueprint. In other words, they are very good at equipping individual businesses to do what they do well and to engage in continuous improvement. As we will see later, the culture here is conducive to programmed, incremental learning, with innovations being of a centrally led, programmatic nature. Companies like Unilever, Procter & Gamble and many fast moving consumer goods companies display characteristics of this archetype.

The Leader

The *Leader* has an external focus and is concerned with outputs and performance measures over the medium/long term. *Leaders* excel at efficacy oriented resource management, and are concerned with issues of flexibility and responsiveness in relation to the threats and opportunities that they perceive in the external environment. They operate via directed operational/ tactical networks, oriented towards achieving specific performance targets (e.g. exploiting economies of scale and scope). The locus of control is centrally decentralized, being formally proscribed and delegated by the centre to discrete business entities. The business culture is one of focused achievement and disciplined creativity. This style encourages the individual businesses to continually enhance their self-concept (via recognized achievement) and to develop a very strong coordination competence. Companies like Shell and ABB show many of the characteristics of this archetype.

The Mentor

The *Mentor* has an external focus and is concerned with the development of organizational capabilities over the long term. The business portfolio environment of the *Mentor* is typically complex in terms of products, which are linked through the leveraging of common capabilities. The emphasis is on knowledge diffusion and the development of *organizational* capabilities. Accordingly, the *Mentor* will commit significant resources to facilitate coordination across businesses to enable cross-boundary learning and innovation networks. The locus of control is diffuse and tends to be embedded in relationships. As shown later in this chapter, this provides an environment that is conducive to the diffusion of tacit knowledge through collaborative mechanisms. Like the *Leader*, the *Mentor* is enacting the relationship in an emergent mode. However, in the case of the *Leader*, the dominant set of emergent perceptions shaping business activity are those of the headquarters in relation to performance in the external environment, but for the *Mentor* activity is shaped dynamically by the emergent perceptions of both the actors. Companies like Canon show many of the characteristics of this archetype.

The four archetypes operate within quite distinctive paradigms. If we analyse the archetypes using Burrell & Morgan's (1979) scheme (which defines paradigms along objective–subjective and regulation–radical change dimensions) it becomes apparent that each one sits very comfortably within a single dominant paradigm (FIGURE 11.3).

The *Lion Tamer* sits comfortably within the *functionalist* paradigm and has a predominantly objectivist view of the world coupled with a need to maintain stability. The *Trainer* has a more subjectivist viewpoint and is concerned with standardization, so it sits comfortably in the *interpretivist* quadrant. The *Leader*, like the *Lion Tamer*, has an objectivist viewpoint but has a very strong concern for the radical change of structural realities and so it sits squarely in the *radical structuralist* quadrant. And finally the *Mentor* has a subjectivist viewpoint and is concerned with radically changing

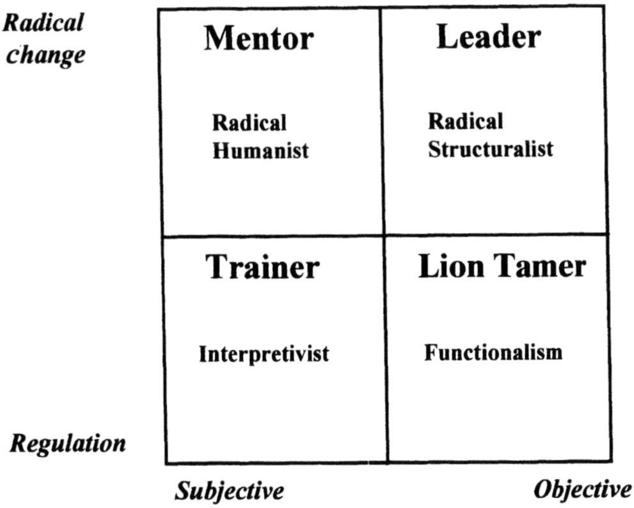

Radical *change*	**Mentor** **Radical Humanist**	**Leader** **Radical Structuralist**
	Trainer **Interpretivist**	**Lion Tamer** **Functionalism**
Regulation		
	Subjective	*Objective*

FIGURE 11.3   The four archetypes: native paradigms (after Burrell & Morgan, 1979)

intersubjective realities and can be classified quite neatly as a *radical humanist*.

INFORMATION AND ARCHETYPES

TABLE 11.1 provides a schematic representation of the types of information that underpin and characterize the enactment of each archetype.

TABLE 11.1   Information characteristics of the archetypes

Archetype	Shared model	Feedback information	Dominant control instrument	Communications system
Lion Tamer	Operational efficiency	Efficiency data	Preset internal targets	Formal, linear
Leader	Economic performance	Performance figures	External performance targets	Formal, hierarchically integrated
Trainer	Competence matrix	Discrete task-related competence measures	Formal standards and protocols	Formal functional / process integration
Mentor	Transformational capability	Progress and positioning indicators	Empowerment	Formal and informal information networking

The shared model for a given archetype characterizes the dominant headquarters perception about what constitutes the ultimate set of values that all meaningful endeavour is designed to satisfy (i.e. the ultimate "pay off" towards which the script is directed).

The feedback information characteristic for a given archetype is the type of information used by the headquarters to monitor what is happening within the business context. This is the information that is used to assess the congruence between the business' endeavours and the headquarters' perception of the shared model.

The dominant control instrument characterizes the means (or instruments) employed by the headquarters to shape the business' endeavours

The communication system characteristics for each archetype will reflect the communications infrastructures that are necessary for the enactment of each archetype.

The Lion Tamer, with its focus on operational efficiency, will employ systems that provide financial data about the business, and evaluate individual output against preset internal targets, using financial reward mechanisms to reinforce "appropriate" business behaviour. The communication infrastructure is characterized by formal protocols for linear communication through functional hierarchies.

The Leader, with its focus on economic performance through process efficacy, will employ systems that provide performance figures about the business and evaluate individual business performance against external benchmarks, using "best practice" transfer mechanisms to implant "appropriate" business behaviour. The communication structure is predominantly formal in style, characterized by vertical control channels with transverse integration linkages (or networks) between businesses for purposes of tactical and operational coordination.

The Trainer, with its focus on internal effectiveness based on business competence, will employ discrete, function/task-related competence measures to monitor business performance, using formal standards and protocols to orchestrate the development of specific competences in individual businesses so that these map on to the headquarters' blueprint of the corporate competence matrix in a complementary fashion alongside the other businesses in the portfolio. The communications structure will tend to reflect the matrix structure with formal function/process integration.

The Mentor, with its focus on developing capabilities that can both generate and survive discontinuities in the competitive and strategic contexts, will employ progress and positioning indicators to assess the nature and value of the capabilities being developed by the individual businesses and to learn about the mode in which these capabilities are leveraged by the businesses. The *Mentor* is concerned with aspects of effective organizational learning, and it perceives the headquarters–

business relationship as one within which a learning partnership exists. Accordingly, it reinforces "appropriate" business behaviour through continued empowerment of the business within the relationship context. The communications structure is an organic one, characterized by a fusion of formal and informal communications (and relationship) networks linking the individual business with each other and with the headquarters.

There is currently a high level of expectation that information technology (IT) will enable organizations to radically transform what they do and the way they do it (Hammer, 1990; Scott Morton, 1991). Communications technology and database technology coupled with multimedia capabilities enable both intra-organizational and inter-organizational access to rich, shared data. This capability is an important one for underpinning the formalized process integration and information dissemination activities at the different levels described for each archetype. The implementation of inter-organizational information systems provides some very important capabilities in the context of organizational networking and collaboration (Scott Morton, 1991). It also supports collaborative activity among individuals across time and space divides: for example, video conferencing enables "meetings" to be held between groups of individuals who are physically located at different ends of the world; teleworking is becoming a significant mode of operation for knowledge workers, and the Internet is widely perceived as a global "information highway". These capabilities herald the potential for the "virtualization" of organizations by developing "virtual structures" of individuals and groups engaged in collective productive activity from physically disparate locations. This "virtualization" phenomenon will relax some of the structural and practical constraints associated with the physical organization of coordinated activity. An interesting challenge for corporations that are concerned with developing information and knowledge networks that support organizational learning (e.g. organizations aspiring to the *Mentor* archetype in our framework) will be to integrate the electronically mediated structures with the informal, physical interpersonal communication needs that are important in establishing shared values and common cause.

LEARNING CHARACTERISTICS OF THE ARCHETYPES

This section characterizes learning in terms of:

- the type of learning predominant in each archetype (using Ashby's (1940) concepts of single-loop and double-loop learning in the context of Argyris & Schon's (1978) model of organizational learning), and
- the relative strengths of the archetypes in managing mechanisms for organizational learning (based on Boisot's (1987) work).

ADAPTIVE AND GENERATIVE LEARNING CHARACTERISTICS OF THE ARCHETYPES

In order to understand what type of learning is happening in each of the archetypes it is useful to look at the relationship between the *espoused theory* of the organization and the *theory-in-use* for the different archetypes. The *espoused theory* defines the norms that organizational endeavour is supposed to conform to. The *theory-in-use* encapsulates what actually goes on in the organizational context: it is implicit in the strategies, norms and assumptions that govern the actual patterns of task performance. In single-loop learning, changes and improvements are directed towards conforming to the *espoused theory*, so that all learning is adaptive (geared towards "doing what you do better") and serves to maintain the *status quo* of the espoused theory. In double-loop learning, on the other hand, the learning that results from changes in the *theory-in-use* is fed back into the model of the *espoused theory*, and can result in its modification. In other words, double-loop learning challenges the espoused norms and is generative (about "doing something *different*" or "*being* something different").

The *Lion Tamer* is committed to the maintenance of the *status quo*, and is not actively engaged in promoting learning in the businesses.

The *Trainer*, with its commitment to the promotion of centrally determined, programmatic, incremental learning, is predominantly engaged in single-loop learning of the adaptive type.

The *Leader* is focused on process issues and has a strength in adaptive learning. However, it has a strong external focus and encourages "bounded innovation" at the business level to "inform" the espoused theory. In this sense, the *Leader* shows a certain predisposition to shift towards the generative learning mode.

The *Mentor* is concerned with championing generative learning. Double-loop learning is promoted through the provision of contexts within which cross-boundary discourse and the process of organizational enquiry can be situated, and the requisite variety (Ashby, 1956) of models can be generated to spawn innovative ways of leveraging organizational core competences.

KNOWLEDGE MANAGEMENT CHARACTERISTICS OF THE ARCHETYPES

The four archetypes have distinctive characteristics associated with their role in promoting knowledge dissemination and learning across the corporate context. In the discussion that follows we highlight some of the distinctive features of the four archetypes in this context. We employ a simplified version of Boisot's model for organizational learning (Boisot,

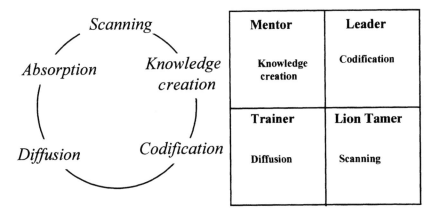

FIGURE 11.4   The model for organizational learning (after Boisot, 1987) and distinctive archetype characteristics

1987) to illustrate the relative strengths of each archetype in orchestrating the corporate learning process (FIGURE 11.4).

We use the notion of "phases" from Boisot's cycle to define archetype learning characteristics in the following context:

- *Scanning* is concerned with obtaining information to develop a map of the organizational and external environment—so it involves developing a map of "what is" within that environment and identifying any problems or opportunities that are presented by the environment.
- *Knowledge creation* is concerned with "know-how" and insights that are obtained from dealing with or solving a perceived opportunity or problem. The knowledge at this stage ("new knowledge") will be confined to the knowledge base of the "solver(s)", and is likely to be tacit knowledge.
- *Codification* is concerned with codifying the knowledge so that it can be communicated to those outside the solver(s). The codification may consist of verbal articulation of what is known by the solver, or it may be manifest in the demonstration of a procedure or action by the solver(s). The knowledge at this stage is explicit.
- *Diffusion* is concerned with communicating and spreading the codified "new knowledge" through the organization. Successful diffusion results in the incorporation of the "new knowledge" into the regular patterns of task performance of those outside the solver(s).
- *Absorption* occurs when the "new knowledge" has become so incorporated into organizational recipes and routines that it is an implicit part of "how things are done around here". In other words the status of

what started out as "new knowledge" has changed from being tacit *individual* knowledge to becoming part of the tacit *organizational* knowledge base.

Of the four archetypes, the *Lion Tamer* is the least engaged in promoting corporate organizational learning. Its learning competence is almost exclusively associated with the *scanning* phase of the learning cycle. It establishes the extant environmental and business states and bases its decisions on well-established formal criteria. Its communication process is concerned with the dispatching of performance targets to its businesses so that they *know what* to deliver.

The *Leader* is interested in replicating the most efficacious and efficient formulae for process execution across the businesses. Its distinctive learning competence is associated with the *codification* phase of the learning cycle. Its strength is in orchestrating the efficient replication of good ideas that are generated at the business level, and it does not engage actively with the knowledge creation processes that may be going on in individual businesses. When business performance indicators reflect superior process management at any location, the *Leader* is good at codifying the superior process features underlying that performance so that these can be replicated elsewhere in the organization. In other words, those businesses required to update their process execution *know what* to do. Although the distinctive capability of the *Leader* is in *codification*, to be effective in leveraging this capability the successful *Leader* will have supporting competence in *scanning, knowledge creation* and *diffusion*. It has a moderate competence for *absorption* as it acts predominantly through explicitly directed structure and process change.

The *Trainer* is interested in enabling individual businesses to fulfil their roles effectively, and it actively engages in transferring task/function-related competences or *know-how* across businesses. The *Trainer's* distinctive competence is associated with the *diffusion* phase of the learning cycle, using training programmes to move knowledge from the domain of the "classroom" into the domain of the workplace. As outlined earlier, the *Trainer* operates within a programmatic *weltanschauung,* and the associated learning tends to be adaptive rather than generative. Although the distinctive capability of the *Trainer* is in *diffusion,* to be effective in leveraging this capability the successful *Trainer* will have adequate supporting competence in the other four phases.

The *Mentor* is concerned with developing capabilities (*know-how*) across the businesses and it is particularly engaged with issues of organizational learning, knowledge creation and innovation. The *Mentor's* distinctive competence lies in actively managing the *knowledge creation* phase of the learning cycle. The *Mentor* creates an organizational structure and climate conducive to engagement in the types of activities associated with organizational learning. Cross-business, cross-functional, multidisciplinary teams and projects are used to enable cross-fertilization of ideas and to generate the requisite variety that is needed for the spawning of new ideas (for example Canon has a corporate R&D function and uses dynamic task forces made up from a variety of divisions to tackle particular projects). With respect to the other stages of the learning cycle, the climate created by the *Mentor* is designed to promote high rates of cycle completion (i.e. to accelerate the movement of knowledge from the *tacit individual domain* to the *tacit organizational domain* and also to increase the frequency of cycle execution (i.e. to continually encourage innovation). In this context it is important for the *Mentor* to develop a high level of competence in *all* phases of the cycle.

DISCUSSION

The framework that we described in the previous section defines the four different headquarters archetypes ("pure" types) using the two variables, management focus and *weltanschauung*, for the enactment of the headquarters–business relationship. The contingencies of dynamic contexts demand more complex behavioural capabilities of the headquarters than can be explained by the simplistic dichotomous patterns embodied by the "pure" types. In this section we review our framework of archetypes in the more complex contexts of multi-business and multinational corporations.

In the discussion that follows we show how the framework can be used to develop an understanding of the information processes and knowledge networks that underpin the corporate learning in a dynamic context. Finally, we position this work in the context of existing literature on headquarters–subsidiary relationships in MNCs, and highlight some interesting issues to address through future longitudinal studies in this domain.

MULTI-MODE OPERATION

As described earlier, each headquarters–business relationship is distinctive. In order to be effective in each of its relationships with individual businesses, the headquarters must have the capability to switch modes of engagement between relationships across the businesses (to cater for the heterogeneity of business contexts) and to adopt the most appropriate archetype for each relationship context. Within any specific relationship the headquarters must have the capability to position itself in the appropriate part of the continuum for each dimension of the archetype framework. This means that within a multi-business or multinational corporation, head-quarters staff must have the competence to enact a variety of relationships grounded in different archetypes. This view concurs with literature on MNCs (for example, Prahalad & Doz 1987; Ghoshal & Nohria, 1989, 1993), which indicates that successful headquarters operate in a fashion that optimizes the fit with individual subsidiary contexts.

The difficult positioning question arises when the headquarters is engaged in coordinating complex activities that entail collaboration between the businesses. The work on MNC coordination and control mechanisms (Prahalad & Doz 1987; Ghoshal & Nohria, 1989, 1993) provides structures for determining conditions of fit which are useful to explore in relation to our framework and are discussed below.

A different positioning challenge arises when the headquarters finds itself situated squarely within a given quadrant of our framework and decides to migrate across the framework to reposition itself in a different quadrant. Such a migration would require a change in the fundamental perceptions underpinning the headquarters' self-script, resulting in changes in its primary focus, values, aspirations, behaviours, structures, attitudes and relationship scripts. We need to develop our framework further in order to articulate candidate strategies for such migrations

COORDINATION MECHANISMS

The literature on headquarters–subsidiary coordination indicates that simple contexts require relatively simple coordination mechanisms (Martinez & Jarillo, 1989). In their review of coordination mechanisms, Martinez & Jarillo (1989) provide the schema of coordination mechanisms shown in TABLE 11.2, and they point out that the subtler, less formalized modes are more costly than the structural and formal mechanisms.

It is clear that in our framework the quadrants do vary significantly in the coordination competence that is required for enactment of the different scripts. For example, the *Lion Tamer*, with its strong adherence to the functionalist paradigm and its formal hierarchical structure, has simpler requirements than any of the others. The *Leader* has a more complex mode of operation than the *Lion Tamer*—it is engaged in managing multiple linkages across different businesses, and is focused on performing effectively against changing external criteria, and so it requires sophisticated coordination capabilities. On the other hand the *Leader* is less complex than the *Mentor*, because the *Mentor* is concerned with more uncertain futures (with its long-term focus and its concern with issues of innovation and transformation) and uses informal mechanisms extensively, while the *Leader* tends to work within bounded rationality and through formal mechanisms. The

TABLE 11.2   Common coordination mechanisms (Martinez & Jarillo, 1989)

Structural and formal mechanisms

1. Departmentalization or grouping of organizational units, shaping the formal structure
2. Centralization or decentralization of decision making through the hierarchy of formal authority
3. Formalization and standardization: written policies, rules, job description and standard procedures, through instruments such as manuals, charts, etc.
4. Planning: strategic planning, budgeting, functional plans, scheduling, etc.
5. Put and behavior control: financial performance, technical reports, sales and marketing data, etc., and direct supervision

Other mechanisms, more informal and subtle
6. Lateral or cross-departmental relations: direct managerial contact, temporary or permanent teams, task forces, committees, integrators, and integrative departments.
7. Informal communication: personal contacts among managers, management trips, meetings, conferences, transfer of managers, etc.
8. Socialization: building an organizational culture of known and shared strategic objectives and values by training, transfer of managers, career path management, measurement and reward systems, etc.

coordination competence required by the *Trainer* is simpler than that required by the *Leader*: the *Trainer* needs a degree of coordination suitable for disseminating training standards across the businesses, but it does not have the same pressures for dynamic process integration as the *Leader*.

PATH DEPENDENCY AND COMPETENCE BUNDLES

While we do not postulate a path dependency in terms of migrating around our framework, there is a "progression" in terms of the complexity of coordination mechanisms and competence repertoires of the different archetypes. The *Lion Tamer* is the most "primitive" form in this context, with the *Trainer* and *Leader* assuming an intermediate position and the *Mentor* being the most "advanced". Taking a resource based view (Peteraf, 1993; Wernerfelt, 1984) of the four archetypes, it is likely that the value creating potential of the headquarters is a function of its *co-specialized* resource and competence "bundles" (rather than being simply a function of individual competences). The relative complexity of the competence bundle associated with each archetype is directly related to the complexity of behaviour of the archetype. The *Lion Tamer* is the least complex of the four, while the *Mentor* has the most complex competence bundle. Many of the competences associated with the simpler forms are still relevant (if relatively less important) in the context of the more complex archetypes, it is just that they are incorporated into a more complex competence bundle. For example, to function effectively, all four archetypes need to have the good house-keeping, hygiene and scanning competences associated with the *Lion Tamer*, while the *Mentor's* competence bundle also includes the coordination and codification competence that characterizes the *Leader*.

OPTIMAL DESIGN FOR COORDINATION

The optimal position for a particular headquarters on our framework of archetypes involves balancing the needs of the individual business against the corporate interest in total value creation.

As we have seen, the more complex archetypes in our model incorporate the more complex coordination mechanisms. The literature consistently highlights the fact that the more complex the coordination mechanisms, the greater the cost associated with it. According to this literature the decision of where to position the headquarters in terms of adopting effective coordination mechanisms depends on achieving an acceptable fit between the complexity of what one needs to achieve in the business context and the cost of providing particular coordination mechanisms (Martinez & Jarillo, 1989).

These ideas are evident in the stream of work on international business environments (Prahalad & Doz, 1987) and the implications for headquarters–subsidiary relations (Ghoshal & Nohria, 1989, 1993). Prahalad & Doz (1987) employ their responsiveness/integration matrix to characterize headquarters–subsidiary relationships in areas where the complexity of the business context demands local responsiveness which has to be balanced against the need for global integration. They suggest the need for local responsiveness of the subsidiaries and the requirement for global integration by the corporation to be evaluated and managed through differentiated headquarters–subsidiary relationships.

Ghoshal & Nohria (1989) define individual headquarters–subsidiary relations in terms of their relative degree of centralization, formalization and normative integration (these features are all compatible with components of our archetype characterization). They see, for example, the transnational as requiring "integrated variety" form of organization where headquarters plays a key role in coordinating variety and promoting learning. In their conception, as in ours, headquarters can play a variety of roles, ranging from simple uniform controlling and checking to complex coordination and knowledge management.

LEARNING AND KNOWLEDGE NETWORKS

In dynamic, uncertain contexts, there is a great emphasis on the importance of learning, innovation and knowledge creation (Nonaka & Takeuchi, 1995). In practice, the adaptive learning mode is embraced and implemented widely, and is orchestrated from the centre in many documented cases. The management challenge is to create capabilities for generative learning (of the type articulated by Hamel & Prahalad, 1994; Senge, 1990). This trend is most evident in the literature on MNCs, where the twin needs for local responsiveness and global coordination legitimise the role of the headquarters as the corporate level orchestrator of the performance delivered by the local businesses. This literature underlines the importance of learning and innovation in global competitiveness. Recent literature on MNCs also indicates that more sophisticated styles are emerging in the context of global competitiveness, and that corporate level mental maps need to accommodate generative change, as businesses continue to learn about new market and national contexts. For example, Bartlett & Ghoshal (1987) suggest that there is a trend towards the transnational form of organization where companies need to develop competence in global competitiveness, multinational flexibility and worldwide learning simultaneously. Organizations appear to be moving from reliance on formal information and strategic planning systems to more informal and flexible systems based on interpersonal communications and relationships (Bartlett & Ghoshal. 1995; Roth & Nigh, 1992). This literature highlights a shift from hierarchy, rules, procedures and formal goal setting to devices such as liaison roles, staff transfers, the use of integrating roles/departments and socialization into a common managerial culture. This shift is particularly significant in the context of organizational learning as it provides many of the ingredients that are considered to be important in the composition of a climate that is conducive to information sharing and the diffusion of knowledge and expertise from individual or localized domains into the wider corporate resource pool.

In the context of our framework, the success of the headquarters in promoting generative corporate learning is predicated on:

- its openness and ability to learn from the external and corporate environment, and
- its ability to promote learning across the business.

A schematic representation of the learning activity is provided in FIGURE 11.5, and the requisite headquarters competences are outlined over the page.

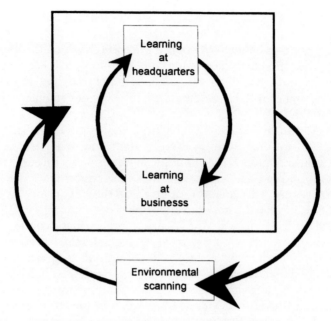

FIGURE 11.5   The headquarters and learning

In order to learn from its context the headquarters needs to have the requisite competence base required to:

- modify its self-script: this involves the revision of purpose, behaviour and appropriateness values.
- update its mental map in a dynamic fashion: this involves dynamic acquisition and internalization of knowledge about the things that we identified earlier as components of the mental map.
- develop appropriate business relationship scripts: this involves the provision of appropriate structure/formalization/normative context (Ghoshal & Nohria, 1989) to establish the knowledge acquisition mechanism through which the businesses can update the headquarters' mental map.
- establish mechanisms for acquiring external information directly from the environment and through inter-organizational networks.

Primarily the headquarters promotes learning across the business by creating the right conditions for learning to happen. In order to do this it needs to:

- decide where collaborative value creation potential lies among businesses: this is done on the basis of the headquarters' mental map.

- orchestrate/facilitate appropriate linkage development: this is done via the coordinated enactment of the appropriate headquarters–business relationships. In the context of our framework these relationships encompass structure, information flows, formal and informal communication systems, shared values, behavioural and processual norms, and formal and normative control mechanisms.

CONCLUSION

This chapter describes four archetypes of the headquarters–business relationship using *capability–product* and *programmatic–emergent* as the principal dimensions for differentiation. These archetypes are discussed in terms of the types of information that characterize their enactment, and their learning and knowledge management characteristics.

The issue of headquarters styles is not new. The archetype framework enhances earlier writings that have concentrated on organizational fit with environmental complexity by adding distinctive elements of learning and knowledge management. The archetypes are defined by types of information processes and knowledge networks that underpin organizational learning and characterize distinctive relationships between headquarters and their businesses. The framework can be used to identify the overall pattern of headquarters–business relationship scripts and to evaluate them.

Successful parenting requires continuous learning by the corporate centre and its businesses. In dynamic contexts changes in headquarters *weltanschauung*, capabilities and aspirations will involve migration within the framework. Where migration across the framework is explicitly planned (for example, when the role of the headquarters is re-evaluated, or when "transformation" initiatives are designed), the *process* of migration is a continuous one of movement through a continuum of states, rather than a discrete step change. Management values, information, communication and relationship infrastructures need modification and development to *maintain* an existence in a new mode. Establishing an appropriate "soft systems" infrastructure is critical and complex: establishing the logic of the enabling technological infrastructure is consequent, and relatively straightforward (Merali, 1997). There is a danger that migration from the "primitive" to the more complex quadrants will lead to loss of capabilities associated with the start quadrant as management focus switches to capabilities associated with the new quadrant: care must be taken to ensure that desirable capabilities are retained and assimilated into the competence base of the "new being".

The corporate characteristics typified by our *Mentor* quadrant are identical with those advocated by popular management rhetoric as the most desirable for all organizations in all situations. However, in complex dynamic environments few "pure" types exist, and it is possible (and even desirable) for mixed modes of operation to co-exist in a single corporation. Our framework helps managers to evaluate their existing headquarters scripts and enables them to determine a desirable future situation. It is not normative in any way.

ACKNOWLEDGEMENTS

We thank Neil Frearson for his comments and suggestions on earlier drafts and for his contributions and guidance regarding the use of scripts in our framework.

REFERENCES

Argyris, C. & Schon, D.A. (1978). *Organisational Learning*. Reading, MA: Addison-Wesley.

Ashby, W.R. (1940). Adaptiveness and equilibrium. *Journal of Mental Science*, **86**, 478–483.

Ashby, W.R. (1956). Self-regulation and requisite variety. In *Introduction to Cybernetics*. Chichester: Wiley.

Bartlett, C.A. & Ghoshal, S. (1987). Managing across borders: new organizational responses. *Sloan Management Review*, **29**(1), 43–53.

Bartlett, C.A. & Ghoshal, S. (1995). Changing the role of top management: from systems to people. *Harvard Business Review*, **73**(3), 132–142.

Berne, E. (1961). *Transactional Analysis in Psychotherapy*. New York: Grove Press.

Boisot, M. (1987). *Information and Organisations: The Manager as Anthropologist*. London: Fontana/Collins.

Burrell, G. & Morgan, G. (1979). *Sociological Paradigms and Organisational Analysis*. London: Heinmann.

Ghoshal, S. & Nohria, N. (1989). Internal differentiation within multinational corporations. *Strategic Management Journal*, **10**(4), 323–338.

Ghoshal, S. & Nohria, N. (1993). Horses for courses: organizational forms for multinational corporations. *Sloan Management Review*, **34**(2), 23–35.

Goold, M. & Campbell, A. (1991). *Corporate Strategy and Parenting Skills*. London: Ashridge Strategic Management Centre.

Goold, M., Campbell, A. & Alexander, M. (1994). *Corporate-Level Strategy*. New York: Wiley.

Hamel, G. & Prahalad, C.K. (1994). *Competing for the Future*. Boston, MA: Harvard Business School Press.

Hammer, M. (1990). Reengineering work: don't automate, obliterate. *Harvard Business Review*, **90**(4), 104–112.

Martinez, J.I. & Jarillo, J.C. (1989). The evolution of research on coordination mechanisms in multinational corporations. *Journal of International Business Studies*, Fall, 489–514.

Merali, Y. (1997). Information, systems and *Dasein*. In F.A. Stowell *et al.* (eds) *Systems for Sustainability: People, Organizations and Environments* New York: Plenum Press, pp. 259–600.

Nonaka, I. & Takeuchi, H. (1995). *The Knowledge-Creating Company*. New York: Oxford University Press.

Prahalad, C.K. & Doz, Y.L. (1987). *The Multinational Mission: Balancing Local Demands and Global Vision*. New York: Free Press.

Peteraf, M.A. (1993). The cornerstones of competitive advantage: a resource-based view. *Strategic Management Journal*, **14**, 179–191.

Roth, K. & Nigh, D. (1992). The effectiveness of HQ/subsidiary relationships: the role of coordination, control and conflict. *Journal of Business Research*, **25**, 277–301.

Scott Morton, M.S. (1991). *The Corporation of the 1990s*. New York: Oxford University Press.

Senge, P.M. (1990). *The Fifth Discipline*. New York: Doubleday/Century.

Wernerfelt, B. (1984). A resource-based view of the firm. *Strategic Management Journal*, **5**, 171–180.

12

Evaluating Board Performance

DON O'NEAL, HOWARD THOMAS

INTRODUCTION

Can the executives of a corporation be trusted to operate the firm in the best interests of its owners? This has long been a primary concern of shareholders, bolstered by Berle & Means' (1932) assertion that wide dispersion of ownership gives managers more control than owners. Monks & Minow (1991) assure us that the gap between ownership and control may now be of even greater concern than it was then.

A board of directors is, in effect, hired by the owners to oversee the management of the firm—to ensure that management operates the firm in the best interests of its owners, rather than in management's self-interest. The board's role generally includes responsibility for control (e.g. hiring, monitoring, and replacing top management), service (e.g. advising/counseling top management), and strategy (e.g. reviewing, ratifying, and evaluating the effectiveness of corporate strategies) (Mace, 1971, Andrews, 1987).

How effective are boards in discharging these responsibilities? How is board performance measured? Who evaluates board performance? Answers to these questions can provide important clues to the role boards play in corporate successes and failures.

How is board performance assessed? Assessment of board performance most often seems based on how well top management actions and decisions are aligned with owners' interests. Perhaps it is more accurate to say that

Strategic Flexibility: Managing in a Turbulent Environment. Edited by G. Hamel, C.K. Prahalad, H. Thomas and D. O'Neal.
Copyright © 1998 John Wiley & Sons Ltd.

board performance is seldom an issue until management actions result in corporate performance that fails to meet owners' expectations. In other words, board performance is usually not an issue until *company* performance falls below shareholder expectations and investors do not see the board as being sufficiently responsive.

Why is poor board performance discussed so often, but good performance rarely? Actually, this is consistent with the way individual performance is often evaluated—criticism when expectations are not met, but silence when they are. The reason may lie in the common perception that individuals (and boards) are compensated for performing certain tasks to certain standards and, so long as performance meets these expectations, further comment is not necessary. On the other hand, feedback is essential when these standards are not met, so that performance can be improved.

In the case of boards this may not be the complete explanation. Board performance is seldom evaluated except in the context of corporate performance—particularly negative corporate performance. When a company does poorly its board is held responsible. On the other hand, when a company does well, its board is rarely praised. In other words, we associate negative corporate outcomes with boards, but commending them for positive corporate outcomes is unusual. Perhaps this speaks to the challenge of outcome-based performance evaluation—the difficulty in determining to what extent an outcome is influenced by a particular individual, group, or action.

Lack of objective evaluation of board performance may be due, at least in part, to lack of specific responsibilities or expectations against which board performance can be judged. In short, many (perhaps most) boards have neither a process for evaluating board performance, nor any specified measures of performance. This is illustrated by directors' responses to a survey of board processes (O'Neal, 1995), in which 60 CEOs and corporate directors, representing 36 US companies in 23 industries, participated. Together, these directors represent firms ranging in size from $10 million to $17 billion in gross sales, including 14 listed in the Fortune 500. Questions relating to board performance included:

How is board performance most often evaluated?

> The most frequent response was "informally or *ad hoc*," followed closely by "not at all." Formal methods of evaluation, both verbal and written, were ranked so low as to appear virtually non-existent.

Who is most often involved in evaluating board performance?

> "Chairman" was, by far, the most frequent answer, followed by "Full board," then "Board committee." At the bottom of the rankings were "Owners/stockholders" and "Institutional Investors."

What criteria are most often used by the board to measure board performance?

"Profitability" and "Creation of shareholder value" tied for the most frequently-used criteria, followed, in order, by:

- Open discussion of problems
- Succession planning
- Corporate growth
- Performance against strategic objectives
- Vision/strategic direction
- Compensation planning
- Stakeholder concerns
- Capital structure (debt/equity)
- Dividend policy
- Corporate restructuring (downsizing, acquisitions)
- Market share

Responses to this survey are consistent with studies of boards in other countries. In interviews with directors from eight countries (Canada, Finland, France, Germany, Great Britain, The Netherlands, Switzerland, and Venezuela), Demb & Neubauer found that "fully two-thirds (66%) said . . . that the performance of the board was not evaluated. In many cases, it was clear that our question raised the point for the first time" (1992, p. 162).

In short, it appears that formal evaluation of boards, whatever their nationality, may be more the exception than the rule, and whatever evaluation *is* done appears to be most often by the chairman or the directors—in effect, boards evaluating their own performance. In addition, the most popular measures of board performance actually assess *company* performance—at best, an indirect measure of board performance.

In response to the question, "To whom is the board most responsible?", the near-unanimous first choice was "Owners/shareholders," leaving little doubt that directors see that their primary responsibility is to the firm's owners (O'Neal, 1995). This is reinforced by their emphasis on which board performance criteria are most important—those that are most important to the firm's owners. Yet, when it comes to *who* evaluates board performance, the owners are far down the list. This inconsistency, although related to some degree to lack of an effective process for soliciting feedback from a widespread set of shareholders, is perhaps due more to lack of a consistent method for evaluating board performance and the absence of agreed-upon measures against which to measure competence. This may be mitigated, to some extent, by the increasing percentage of share ownership currently concentrated in mutual, insurance, and pension funds, which should make it easier to agree on more universal processes for evaluating board performance.

So, although the board is hired to select, advise, and monitor the firm's top managers, there is little evidence of any process for evaluating how effectively these responsibilities are discharged. Extrapolating board performance from company performance—the most common method—is, at best, an indirect measure, and is often too slow to be sufficiently responsive for today's increasingly turbulent competitive environment. This absence of an effective process for evaluating board performance is likely due to: (i) inadequate definition of board responsibilities, and (ii) lack of specific criteria against which performance can be measured.

The purposes of this study are, therefore, to: (i) review board roles and responsibilities, (ii) examine extant research on measuring board performance, and (iii) suggest a core set of board performance measures that can be universally applied, regardless of company, industry, or nationality.

BOARD ROLES AND RESPONSIBILITIES

The primary responsibility of the board is to serve as a governance structure safeguard between the firm and owners of equity (shareholders), as well as between the firm and its management (Williamson, 1985). There is general agreement that the three most important roles of the board are to: (i) monitor and control top management, (ii) offer advice and counsel, and (iii) evaluate corporate strategy (Mace, 1971; Andrews, 1987). This is reinforced by responses to a recent survey of corporate directors (O'Neal & Thomas, 1995), which portrays, as the board's most important responsibilities, those associated with control (e.g. maximizing shareholder wealth, CEO succession planning, evaluating management performance, and determining management compensation). Responsibilities associated with service (e.g. advising and counseling, selecting new directors, protecting and enhancing the firm's reputation), and with strategy (e.g. formulating and ratifying corporate strategy, safeguarding stakeholder interests, buffering top management), although considered important, were clearly secondary to the board's responsibility to monitor and control top management.

As individuals, and as groups, the responsibilities we are assigned become the bases of our compensation (Scheer, 1971; Berg, 1976; Sherman, Bohlander & Snell, 1996). Justification of ongoing compensation is based on continuing to meet assigned responsibilities. Periodic performance evaluation is necessary to confirm that responsibilities continue to be effectively discharged.

Board performance can, therefore, be evaluated by: (i) clearly specifying board responsibilities, (ii) determining specific measures of performance for each responsibility, (iii) conducting periodic evaluations to determine how effectively each responsibility is being executed, and (iv) taking action to improve performance where it falls below specified levels. Essential to this process is the establishment of criteria and methods for measuring board performance.

MEASURING BOARD PERFORMANCE

Over the years numerous researchers and business practitioners have discussed and written about board performance, from a wide variety of perspectives. Of those, we will use as examples three that have not only examined the topic comprehensively but have also suggested questions to be asked/answered in assessing board performance.

Parker (1979) suggests seven sets of questions to be used by a chair to test the effectiveness of his or her own board, and to determine what can be done to improve it (Box 12.1).

More recent, and more universal, is Demb & Neubauer's (1992) study of directors in eight different countries, which groups the elements of board performance under: (i) the board's role, (ii) its working style, and (iii) the directors themselves (Box 12.2).

Most recent, and most comprehensive, is GOOD PRACTICE FOR DIRECTORS: STANDARDS FOR THE BOARD (1995), published by the Institute of Directors (London). Based on a study involving several hundred UK directors, this research suggests a set of board tasks and indicators of good practice, categorized by: (i) vision, mission and values, (ii) strategy and structure, (iii) delegation to management, and (iv) responsibility to shareholders and other interested parties Box 12.3.

The genesis of these studies—all three are of European origin—suggests two questions: "Are the results of these studies applicable to US boards?" and "Are there no similar studies of US boards?" As will be demonstrated in the next section, the answer to the first question is "Yes." Not only are they consistent with the roles and responsibilities of US boards, but the suggested questions are quite relevant to measuring their performance.

The answer to the second question is also "Yes." There have been a number of studies of US boards, with respect to performance. However, as shown in TABLE 12.1, the majority have examined the relationships between boards and various aspects of corporate performance—most often corporate financial performance (Kerr & Bettis, 1987; Zahra & Pearce, 1989; Walsh & Seward, 1990; Zajac, 1990; Judge & Zeithaml, 1992). A few have addressed more specific outcomes, such as: how interlocking directorships (i.e. multiple board membership) impact corporate performance (Burt, 1983; Davis, 1991), the relationship between CEO duality (i.e. the CEO is chair of

---

BOX 12.1

1. Has the board recently (or indeed ever) devoted significant time and serious thought to the company's longer-term objectives and to the strategic options open to it for achieving them?

If so, have these deliberations resulted in a board consensus or decision on its future objectives and strategies, and have these been put in writing?

2. Has the board consciously thought about and reached formal conclusions on what is sometimes referrred to as its basic "corporate philosophy"—i.e. its value system, its ethical and social responsibilities, its desired "image" and so forth?

If so, have these conclusions been codified or embodied in explicit statements of policy—e.g. in respect of terms of employment, etc.? Does the company have formal procedures for recording and promulgating major board decisions as policy guidelines for down-the-line managers?

3. Does the board periodically review the organizational structure of the company, and consider how this may have to change in the future? Does it review and approve all senior appointments as a matter of course?

4. Does the board routinely receive all the information it needs to ensure that it is in effective control of the company and its management?

Have there been any "unpleasant surprises"—e.g. unfavourable results or unforseen crises—that could be attributed to lack of timely or accurate information?

5. Does the board routinely require the managing director to present his annual plans and budgets for their review and approval?

Does the board regularly monitor the performance of the managing director and his immediate subordinate managers in terms of actual results achieved against agreed plans and budgets?

6. When the board is required to take major decisions on questions of future objectives, strategies, policies, major investments, senior appointments, etc., does it have adequate time and knowledge to make these decisions soundly—rather than finding itself overtaken by events and, in effect, obliged to rubber stamp decisions already taken or commitments already made?

7. If you accept the premise that it is for directors to direct and for managers to manage, what proportion of the board's time and attention *as a board* is devoted to the kinds of issues raised in the foregoing six questions, and how much to immediate issues of day-to-day *management*?

A simple analysis of board agendas and minutes for the last 12 months or so will quickly give you a rough answer to this question.

Box 12.2

"Board's role" involves:
  board's mission/purpose
  division of responsibilities—board/management
  board involvement
    which activities
    what priorities
"Working style" includes:
  board size/structure/committees/meeting schedule
  information flow
    management → board
    board → management
  board culture/environment
"Directors" addresses:
  committee composition—insiders/outsiders
  director orientation
  nomination/selection/performance evaluation/tenure

TABLE 12.1   Board influence on corporate performance

Study	Board dimension	Corporate Performance
Burt (1983)	Board interlocks	Reduced profit, uncertainty
Kerr & Bettis (1987)	CEO compensation	Financial (stock performance)
Kosnik (1987)	Board effectiveness	Greenmail payments
Zahra & Pearce (1989)	Board structure, efficiency	Financial (ROE, EPS, DPS, RDA, stock)
Zajac (1990)	CEO selection, compensation	Financial (ROA)
Davis (1991)	Board interlocks	Poison pill amendments
Rechner & Dalton (1991)	CEO duality	Financial (ROE, ROI, profit margin)
Judge & Zeithaml (1992)	Board involvement	Financial (ROA)

the board) and corporate performance (Rechner & Dalton, 1991), and how boards respond to "greenmail" attempts (Kosnik, 1987). All of these studies examine the perceived corporate outcomes of specific board actions or processes. But they *do not* address *board* performance *per se*.

Andrews addresses board performance by offering a set of questions designed to survey "a board's opinion of itself" (1979, p.56). But, intended for use in interviews with individual directors (conducted by a corporate staff member), his questions seem designed more to solicit directors'

Box 12.3

1. **Corporate vision, mission and values:**
   How effective is the board in helping to determine the company's vision/mission?
   Does the board help determine the values to be promoted throughout the company?
   How effective is the board in reviewing company objectives to make sure that they are consistent with the:
   > company vision/mission?
   > company values?
   > needs of shareholders and other stakeholders?

   How well does the board help determine, support and enforce company policies?

2. **Corporate strategy and structure:**
   Does the board review and evaluate present and future opportunities, threats and risks in the external environment; and current and future strengths, weaknesses and risks relating to the company?
   Does the board help:
   > determine corporate and financial strategic alternatives?
   > review and select those to be pursued?
   > decide the resources, contingency plans and means to support them?

   Are business strategies and plans for different parts of the company determined and regularly reviewed by the board?
   Does the board ensure that the company's organizational structure and capabilities are appropriate for implementing its chosen strategies?

3. **Board/management relationship/responsibilities:**
   Does the board have performance measures to monitor how well the firm's strategy, policies, and legal and fiduciary responsibilities are being carried out?
   Does the board ensure that internal control procedures provide reliable and valid information for monitoring operations and performance?
   Does the board clearly delegate authority to management and regularly review management's effectiveness?
   Does the board ensure that senior management's successes and failures are communicated to them, and ensure that proper rewards, sanctions and training are implemented?

4. **Board responsibility to shareholders/stakeholders:**
   Does the board take into account the legitimate interests of shareholders and other organizations, groups and individuals (stakeholders) who have an interest in the achievement of company objectives?
   Does the board monitor relations with shareholders and other interested parties by the prescription, use and evaluation of appropriate information?
   Does the board ensure that communications with shareholders and other interested parties and the general public are effective?
   Does the board, where appropriate, promote the goodwill and support of shareholders and other relevant interested parties?

opinions and recommendations for how the board could become more effective, than to actually measure board performance. Although responses to Andrews' questions would, no doubt, be useful in determining what might be appropriate measures of board performance, they do not, in themselves, appear sufficient to effectively measure board performance.

CORE MEASURES OF PERFORMANCE

Although corporate performance may have once been an effective measure of board performance—and may still be the ultimate measure—the lag-time between board actions and corporate outcomes is likely to be of such duration that corrective action is not sufficiently timely for today's more dynamic competitive environment. Competitive responsiveness requires prompt and direct feedback. This can be enhanced by measuring board performance directly, rather than indirectly, using measures that may also prove to be effective predictors of corporate performance. Although studies which directly address how board performance should be measured (Parker, 1979; Demb & Neubauer, 1992; Institute of Directors, 1995) are not inconsistent in their recommendations of board performance measures, neither are they in total agreement as to what the specific responsibilities of a board of directors should be. TABLE 12.2 compares these three studies with what is surely one of the most widely heralded sets of board responsibilities yet offered—the General Motors Board of Directors Corporate Governance Guidelines (1994).

Although all four studies offer their perspectives of what should be a board's responsibilities, along with questions that address to what extent they are being carried out, none provides specific measures against which a board's performance of those responsibilities can be measured. A board's performance, like the performance of the firm it governs, can only be effectively evaluated when its actions and their outcomes can be measured against specific predetermined expectations of what the board *should* do (i.e. board objectives). As shown in FIGURE 12.1, this requires: (i) clearly-defined board responsibilities, (ii) setting specific board objectives, both short- and long-term, based on board responsibilities, (iii) determining measurable criteria for each objective, and (iv) evaluating actual board performance—to what extent the board did or did not achieve its objectives.

The purpose of board performance evaluation is twofold: (i) to determine in what areas the board is discharging its responsibilities effectively, and (ii) to provide feedback so board performance can be improved in areas where expectations are not being met. This requires setting *measurable* objectives for each board responsibility. Measurable means defining precisely *what* is to be accomplished (e.g. how much, of what activity, and to what quality

TABLE 12.2 Board responsibilities

Board responsibilities	Parker (1979)	Demb & Neubauer (1992)	Institute of Directors (1995)	General Motors (1994)
Corporate mission, philosophy				
Vision/mission	X		X	
Philosophy (values, ethical/social responsibility, image)	X			
Corporate objectives/strategy/structure				
Objectives	X		X	
Strategy	X		X	
Structure	X			
Succession (selecting key people)			X	X
Board/management relationships				
Division of responsibilities		X		X
Monitoring management	X		X	
Controlling management	X		X	
Advising/counseling management				
Evaluating management performance			X	X
Evaluating resources/capabilities			X	
Information—timeliness/accuracy	X	X	X	X
Board decision making	X		X	
Management development				X
Board boundary-spanning				
Stakeholder relationships (stakeholder interests, communication, goodwill/support)			X	X
Evaluating opportunities/threats			X	
Board structure				
Director selection		X		X
Composition		X		X
Performance evaluation		X		X
Tenure		X		X

standards) *by when*. Measurement criteria will, of course, vary from one board to another, depending on the board's defined responsibilities and its firm's unique circumstances.

CONCLUSIONS AND IMPLICATIONS

If, in executing its responsibilities of control, service, and strategy, the board of directors does, in fact, influence corporate performance, then effective evaluation of board performance is at least as important as evaluation of the CEO and the top management team. Yet, it seems that measuring board

FIGURE 12.1   Board evaluation process

performance is not a common practice, at least for a broad cross-section of boards. This may be a major contributing factor in those corporate situations in which boards appear to have been asleep at the switch while it was widely perceived that their firms were deeply in trouble (e.g. IBM, General Motors, American Express, DEC, Eastman Kodak).

Why does this happen? On the one hand, CEO and director hubris may be a strong influence, as suggested by Monks & Minow (1991). On the other hand, surveys of directors suggest that the directors themselves see (and may deplore) this lack of board responsibility and accountability (Demb & Neubauer, 1992; O'Neal, 1995). Lacking an effective mechanism to call the board into account, representatives of large investor groups (e.g. pension funds, insurance funds, mutual funds) have begun taking it upon themselves to become actively involved in providing feedback to the boards of companies that are perceived as underperformers. Initially ignored by the CEOs they approached, these investor-activists soon learned that publishing lists of the worst performers would quickly bring pressure on both the board and the CEO. This "default" measure of board performance may offer a powerful incentive for boards to become more actively involved in initiating processes for having their performance evaluated in a more constructive, effective, and timely manner.

Toward that end, Boulton offers suggestions for helping to develop boards "into effective operating units" (1983, p. 94), describing five areas of board development:

1. Defining the board's role, including:
   - assuring continuity within the corporation,
   - selecting key executives,
   - monitoring their performance.
2. Establishing a working (boardroom) climate that will:
   - encourage director participation,
   - allow participation in the early stages of the decision-making process.

3. Providing directors with information:
   - the right kind of information,
   - in the right format,
   - without overloading a director's ability to review and understand it.
4. Selecting committed and competent directors, who will:
   - work well with the board,
   - speak up,
   - question decisions,
   - provide an appropriate balance of experience and expertise.
5. Structuring the board:
   - developing board committees to effectively carry out board responsibilities, including legal matters, financial matters, corporate objectives and policies, corporate strategies and business, personnel and organizational information, external and environmental matters, and *ad hoc* committees for special problems.

Effective measurement of board performance must begin with clearly specified board responsibilities and objectives, described in measurable terms, and quantified (e.g. what actions are required, in what quantity, and by when?). Board responsibilities and objectives must then be broken down into implementable tasks and actions, and assigned, as appropriate, to the full board, board committees, and individual directors. Once assigned, effectiveness of task performance must be measured against specific objectives, and reinforced (when performance meets or exceeds expectations) or corrected (when below expectations). In either case, timely, objective, and ongoing feedback is the key to board effectiveness—learning quickly when performance is successful, and even more quickly when it needs improvement, and how to improve.

How might this feedback be provided? We can begin with measurable objectives, based on specific board responsibilities. Although what these responsibilities should be depends on whom you ask (Blair, 1950; Mattar, 1985; Waldo, 1985; Houle, 1989; Carver, 1990; Conference Board, 1994; Lorsch, 1995; Pound, 1995), they should be based on the particular firm and its circumstances, and the role its board intends to fulfill. Once measurable objectives have been set, the board's performance, based on how effectively it has achieved these objectives, can be analyzed in a number of ways. For example, FIGURE 12.2 shows a board "report card" which includes a representative list of board objectives, and a system for evaluating performance against each objective. Evaluation is, in this example, directed toward demonstrating in which areas board performance is markedly superior, where it is good, where it needs improvement, and where it is totally unacceptable. A report of this sort is designed to drive board improvement, rather than simply critique board performance. The objectives shown are

Board objectives	PERFORMANCE*			
	0	1	2	3

<u>Corporate mission, philosophy</u>
  Vision/mission
  Philosophy
  (values, ethical/social
    responsibility, image)				

<u>Corporate objectives/strategy/</u>
<u>structure</u>
  Objectives
  Strategy
  Structure
  Succession (selecting key people)				

<u>Board/management relationships</u>
  Division of responsibilities
  Monitoring management
  Controlling management
  Advising/counseling management
  Evaluating management performance
  Evaluating resources/capabilities
  Information – timeliness/accuracy
  Board decision making
  Management development				

<u>Board boundary-spanning</u>
  Stakeholder relationships
  (stakeholder interests,
    communication, goodwill/support
  Evaluating opportunities/threats				

<u>Board structure</u>
  Director selection
  Composition
  Performance evaluation
  Tenure				

```
* Performance measures: 0 = unacceptable
                        1 = needs improvement
                        2 = good
                        3 = superior
```

FIGURE 12.2   Board performance evaluation

not, in themselves, specific enough to be measured. They are categories, each requiring a backup document listing the specific, measurable objectives that have been set, and describing how the board's actual performance compares with each objective. Although examples of specific, measurable criteria have been addressed by only a few researchers (Louden, 1975;

Mueller, 1982; Houle, 1989), they will be as company-specific as are board objectives. For example, specific board objectives in the category of "evaluating management performance" might include setting annual short- and long-term performance objectives for the CEO, formally evaluating CEO performance against those objectives and providing feedback on a quarterly basis, and making specific recommendations for how performance can or should be improved and by when.

At the level of the individual director, evaluating board performance may be as straightforward as evaluating the performance of any other individual in the organization. At the committee and board levels it is likely to be more complex, considering the challenges of measuring team performance, particularly where some of the responsibilities are not easily quantified or measured. But still, performance of any type can be measured, if there is a genuine desire and effort to do so.

This leads naturally to a final question, "Who should be responsible for measuring board performance?" Although there is no consensus answer, perhaps we should begin by rephrasing the question to "who *does* measure board performance?", or "who *will* measure board performance?". The answer to either of these questions is likely to be "anyone who is negatively affected by the firm's performance," which may be a good guide to determining appropriate measures of performance. If a board can deliberately cultivate a sensitivity to its firm's stakeholders—who they are and what each stakeholder group expects of the firm—then the most effective evaluation of board performance may come from the board itself.

Regardless of who measures board performance, or by what criteria, it seems that most boards, and their firms, would find it easier and more effective to be the primary force in assuring that their performance is evaluated in a timely and effective manner. Better, by far, than waiting for feedback from irate stakeholders, in response to a corporate crisis.

REFERENCES

Andrews, K.R. (1979). Appraising director and board performance against rising standards of competence and responsibility. *Harvard Business Review*, May/June, 46–56.

Andrews, K.R. (1987). *The Concept of Corporate Strategy*. Homewood, IL: Irwin.

Berg, J.G. (1976). *Managing Compensation*. New York: AMACOM.

Berle, A. & Means, G.C. (1932). *The Modern Corporation and Private Property*. New York: Macmillan.

Blair, W.T. (1950). Appraising the board of directors. *Harvard Business Review*, January, 101–113.

Boulton, W.R. (1983). Effective board development: five areas for concern. *Journal of Business Strategy*, 3(4), 94–100.

Burt, R.S. (1983). *Corporate Profits and Cooptation*. New York: Academic Press.

Carver, J. (1990). *Boards that Make a Difference*. San Francisco, CA: Jossey-Bass.

The Conference Board (1994). *Corporate boards: improving and evaluating performance*, report number 1081–94-RR.

Davis, G.F. (1991). Agents without principles? The spread of the poison pill through the intercorporate network. *Administrative Science Quarterly*, **36**, 583–613.

Demb, A. & Neubauer, F.-F. (1992). *The Corporate Board*. New York: Oxford University Press.

General Motors (1994). *Corporate Governance Guidelines*.

Houle, C.O. (1989). *Governing Boards: Their Nature and Nurture*. San Francisco, CA: Jossey-Bass.

Institute of Directors (1995). *Good Practice for Directors: Standards for the Board*. London: Institute of Directors

Judge, W.Q. & Zeithaml, C.P. (1992). Institutional and strategic choice perspectives on board involvement in the strategic decision process. *Academy of Management Journal*, **35**(4), 766–794.

Kerr, J. & Bettis, R. A. (1987). Boards of directors, top management compensation, and shareholder returns. *Academy of Management Journal*, **30**(4), 645–664.

Kosnik, R.D. (1987). Greenmail: a study of board performance in corporate governance. *Administrative Science Quarterly*, **32**, 163–185.

Lorsch, J. (1995). Empowering the board. *Harvard Business Review*, January/February 107–117.

Louden, J.K. (1975). *The Effective Director in Action*. New York: AMACOM.

Mace, M.L. (1971). *Directors: Myth and Reality*. Cambridge, MA: Harvard Business School Classics.

Mattar, E.P., III (ed.) (1985). *Handbook for Corporate Directors*. New York: McGraw-Hill.

Monks, R. & Minow, N. (1991). The director's new clothes (or the myth of corporate accountability). *Journal of Applied Corporate Finance*, **4**(3), 78–84.

Mueller, R.K. (1982). *Board Score: How to Judge Board Worthiness*, Lexington, MA: Lexington Books.

O'Neal, D.E. (1995). *Director networks and director selection: keys to the strategic role of the board of directors*, dissertation thesis, Urbana-Champaign, Illinois: University of Illinois.

O'Neal, D.E. & Thomas, H. (1995). Director networks/director selection: the board's strategic role. *European Management Journal*, **13**(1).

Parker, H. (1990). *Letters to a New Chairman*. London: Director Publications.

Pound, J. (1995). The promise of the governed corporation. *Harvard Business Review*, March/April, 89–98.

Rechner, P.L. & Dalton, D.R. (1991). The impact of CEO as board chairperson on corporate performance: evidence vs. rhetoric, *Academy of Management Executive*, III, 2, 141–143.

Sherman, A.W., Jr, Bohlander, G.W. & Snell, S. (1996). *Managing Human Resources*. Cincinnati, OH: South-Western College Publishing.

Scheer, W.E. (1971). *The Personnel Director's Handbook*. Chicago, IL: Dartnell.

Waldo, C.N. (1985). *Boards of Directors: Their Changing Roles, Structure, and Information Needs*. Westport, CT: Quorum Books.

Walsh, J.P. & Seward, J.K. (1990). On the efficiency of internal and external corporate control mechanisms, *Academy of Management Review*, **15**(3), 421–458.

Williamson, O.E. (1985). *The Economic Institutions of Capitalism*. New York: Free Press.

Zajac, E.J. (1990). CEO selection, succession, compensation and firm performance: a theoretical integration and empirical analysis. *Strategic Management Journal*, **11**, 217–230.

Zahra, S.A. & Pearce, J.A. II (1989). Boards of directors and corporate financial performance: a review and integrative model. *Journal of Management*, **15**(2), 291–334.

13

Where Do Strategic Ideas Come From?

PAUL RAIMOND

INTRODUCTION

Much traditional strategy theory has treated strategic ideas as though they arose from the proper analysis of the market environment and the company. The solution was to be found in the analysis of the situation. The key elements of the situation were treated as though they were objective facts, known and obvious to all impartial observers.

Recently research from a cognitive perspective has suggested a different view. Strategists competing in the same market may have radically different mental models of how that market works. A strategic group of firms may share a mental model of the market which includes only those competitors, customers and distributors with whom they have always been most comfortable. Their model renders them blind to many potential dangers in their environment. Two or more stakeholders may have entirely different understandings or mental models of the situation which they have jointly to manage. Consequently they are unable to agree on any solution to their problem.

What model of strategy could explain these studies? The traditional model, which treats the key factors in the strategic situation—competitors, market trends, customers, critical success factors—as objective facts available equally to all analysts does not accommodate the possibility of each strategist making his or her own subjective and possibly idiosyncratic sense

Strategic Flexibility: Managing in a Turbulent Environment. Edited by G. Hamel, C.K. Prahalad, H. Thomas and D. O'Neal.

of the situation. To cope with the studies of strategy from the cognitive perspective we may need a model of strategy as sense-making.

Strategic management is not developing alone in this direction. Parallel developments are apparent elsewhere in the social sciences, as for example in psychology and neuropsychology.

A case, the Morgan Motor Company Ltd, subject of a BBC-TV film, is discussed from the point of view of strategy as sense-making. It has much to tell us about how strategy is made.

In particular, the model of strategy as sense-making affords insights into the question of where strategic ideas come from, and how to increase the richness, variety and originality of strategic ideas.

WHERE DO STRATEGIC IDEAS COME FROM?

Traditional theories of strategy making leave us with a puzzle. The puzzle is: where do strategic ideas come from? Traditional theory provides many techniques for analysing the market environment and the company with the purpose of arriving at an understanding of the situation, the problem to be solved. Once we have several strategy alternatives for dealing with the problem or opportunity, then traditional strategy theory is again helpful in enabling us to analyse the alternatives so as to select the best. But traditional theory has relatively little to offer on the crucial stage, which is the creation of ideas for new, novel and original strategy alternatives. We are far better equipped with techniques for analysing situations once they exist and proposals once they have been suggested than with techniques for inventing, imagining and creating new ideas.

This is not an ideal situation. There would be no problem if companies always had far more brilliant new creative ideas than they could possibly use. If such a happy state were the norm, then it would be reasonable to direct the greater part of our attention to finding better analytical devices to help us choose between them. It seems, however, that this is not generally the case. Companies do not mostly suffer from having so many good strategic ideas that their problem is choosing between them. Marketing departments are not customarily burdened with having far too many good new product ideas, every one of which is sure to make excellent profits if only it were the one chosen. More often the search is on to find just one really good idea. At a societal level we are not overburdened with an excess of good, workable ideas for solving the problems of Northern Ireland, African famines, or getting the European Union to work. There might be some benefits in knowing where strategic ideas come from, and how to get more of them and better.

TRADITIONAL STRATEGY THEORY

A large part of strategy theorising has been concerned with developing better tools of analysis. So we have financial analysis, investment appraisal, multicriteriate analysis, statistical analysis, and so on. We have fewer tools for generating new useful ideas. We have devoted less time to discovering how to do that.

Implicit in much (but not all) strategy theory is an assumption that all the elements of the strategic situation exist "out there", as objective factors, independent of us as observers, available for analysis equally to all researchers. The size of the market, the names of the competitors, the identity of the customers are unquestioned facts, as real and undeniable as this book. This is reality, so we must all see it the same way.

Strategic ideas, from this point of view, are a matter of finding the correct solution, or at least the best solution, to the problem situation. Just as the elements of the situation are "out there" to be analysed, so too the answer is out there to be found. The role of the strategist is rather like that of Sherlock Holmes. By painstaking careful analysis of all the available evidence, together with the application of scientific logic, the answer will be found. There is likely to be one right answer, and perhaps one or two second-best alternatives.

There may be a touch of caricature here to make the point. But consider a foundation technique such as SWOT analysis, familiar to most strategists. As delineated in the books of many strategists such as Ansoff (1965) and Argenti (1980), the elements of SWOT are as follows.

1. Objectives. There is no debate about what objectives are. The objective of the corporation is profit maximization so as to maximize returns to shareholders.
2. Analyse the strengths and weaknesses of the company. Objectively. Analytically.
3. Analyse the opportunities and threats in the external environment. Objectively. Factually. Analytically.
4. Strategy. The inevitable result of good technique and precise analysis.

Most strategy practitioners would doubtless say that they do not rely overmuch on SWOT analysis, although it is in most practitioners' toolkit. But SWOT used in this fashion does exemplify an approach to strategy which still pervades much of what we do. It is a view of strategy as the rigorous analysis of external fact, objectively observable by all analysts.

SOME STUDIES SUGGEST A DIFFERENT VIEW

A number of recent studies of particular markets and cases when taken together suggest a different view. Markets may not only be objective phenomena equally visible to all observers, a fact out there in the external world, rather like stars in the sky. Studies from a cognitive perspective have shown us cases where a strategist's understanding of the market is an outcome of an interaction between the market and the strategist observing it. Participants are seen to select some competitors as worthy of their attention and exclude others, to select some customers as being "their sort of customers" and to exclude others. In this way they build a mental model of their market and their place in it. This selective sense-making has potential strength and inherent weakness. It allows the firm to focus on target customers and precise market segments. Intelligence gathering and strategic awareness can be directed to those competitors and market trends that are believed to be most relevant or threatening. The inherent weakness is that much is excluded which may prove significant later. Information systems that monitor the factors which were of prime relevance when the system was designed may be blind to new threats not foreseen by the information system designer. Some of the major British shirt manufacturers were continuously well informed of the activities of all their British competitors. They paid no attention to imports of shirts from the former colonies. Gentlemen throughout the British Empire had always sent home to England for their shirts. That tradition and mindset went unquestioned, just as one would not ask a chap if he was a gentleman. Just not done. Shirts designated "empire made" were assumed to be inferior, not at all the sort of thing a gentleman buys. That attitude and the dismissive term "empire made" lasted longer than the Empire. In the fullness of time, when shirts made in the Far East could match British quality at only one third of the landed cost, imports began to capture market share in Britain. But it was not the market that the traditional British shirtmakers were watching. Traditional British shirtmakers, like Tootal, sold their shirts through traditional British gentlemen's outfitters such as Dunn & Company and Hepworths. In such traditional retailers the "empire made" imports were not seen. The imports were going into boutiques and department stores, and so were the customers in increasing numbers. It took a long time for the traditional British shirt makers to notice what was happening, longer still to admit that it was worthy of notice, still longer to respond. Tootal and many of its compatriots have ceased to make shirts. Adapting was not easy. Many of the British shirt makers were locked into their old model of the market in several ways: by culture and tradition, by political stance, by past capital investment, and by personnel and top management. The companies and the trade association had lobbied long and hard for protection of British industry and jobs against imports. They could hardly do an about-face and close Lancashire factories and import shirts. Their balance sheets showed the bulk of net worth locked up in manufacturing plant, mostly in Lancashire. It would be no easy matter to write off those assets as worthless or unsaleable if production was moved overseas. Staff, including those who made the strategic decisions, had been selected and bred for their expertise in traditional British cloth and shirt making. The dynasties intermarried so as to keep an eye on each other. As one shirt company director remarked of the EEC anti-cartel legislation, "You don't need cartels if your families have always married within the industry". Those traditional skills and upbringing soon became less relevant in the radically changed market. More relevant were fluency in Cantonese and skill in international finance. The old mental model had been carried through into all aspects of the business, making it difficult to recognize the significance of unexpected events, difficult to respond. The new entrants to the market were able to bypass the traditional long-established strengths of the English shirt makers by inventing a new definition of the shirt market in the UK.

Reger's 1990 study of Chicago bankers showed that the key features of a market may not be equally obvious to all the players in that market. Reger interviewed a large number of the key strategists in the Chicago banking market. She checked to ensure that they did indeed identify each other as the competitors in that market. She then asked them what were the key dimensions of competition in that market. Her expectation was that most strategists would agree on most key factors. There were good reasons for this expectation. The strategists had been competing in that market for a long time, on average 18 years. They knew each other and met often. Besides, much marketing and strategy theory tends to imply that the market is a fact, an objective phenomenon "out there". But the bankers did not agree on most of the key dimensions of competition. They each had their own model of how the market worked and what was important.

These two examples suggest that, at least in these cases, players in a market do not automatically share the same mental model of their market. The model is not the market. The map is not the territory. Each player looks at the totality of the environment and selects what he or she considers to be relevant, linking the selected bits together to form a working model. In total the Chicago bankers identified over 300 issues as key dimensions of competition. Each banker selected only a few. The old assumption implicit in so many marketing texts and lectures, that the market is a certain size, with identifiable characteristics and players, known to all, an objectively observable phenomenon, a given fact, is open to question. The players in a market may not all have the same mental model of the market. If they do, it may be worth asking why. For a new competitor, a potential entrant, it may be worth asking, if they are all looking at the market in the same way, how can I create a different perspective which allows me to destabilize the market and capture some customers? In a sense, markets are mindsets.

The study of the Scottish knitwear industry by Porac, Thomas & Baden-Fuller (1989) shows a community of manufacturers creating a shared mental model of a market which includes only the like-minded and excludes all others. There are many manufacturers of pullovers throughout the world but the Scottish group considers only those that reside in the Scottish Border country and make products like theirs. There may be many millions of people throughout the world but the Scottish group is concerned only with those customers who traditionally buy its sweaters through its type of retailers. On competitors they say "The majority of our competitors are either within our own group, or within our own town". On customers their view is that "We are not interested in anybody other than the top 2% in any country".

It is open to question whether this mental model is healthy in the long term for the Scottish firms. They have focused on a target group of customers and segmented the market, both practices widely recommended in marketing and strategy theory (e.g. Porter, 1980). But their mental model seems to make them blind to any threat or change coming from outside the traditional cosy world of familiar business associates. Contacts with the market are through retail shop owners who are already their customers. The contact occurs through the manufacturers' agents. The agents are selected because their non-knitwear products are compatible with the Scottish manufacturers' image. The agents talk only to shops that sell only these traditional image products to customers who also fit the image. If the market is destabilized it may be a long time before they notice. To an outside observer it seems that the Scottish knitwear manufacturers have much in common with the late lamented English shirt makers, and are reminiscent of Janis's work on Groupthink (1982). Porac, Thomas & Baden-Fuller (1989) observe that "Through processes of induction, problem-solving, and reasoning, decision-makers construct a mental model of the competitive environment which consists minimally of two types of beliefs: beliefs about the identity of the firm, its competitors, suppliers and customers, and causal beliefs about what it takes to compete successfully within the environment which has been identified". Those beliefs and the mental model of which they are important components may dangerously restrict the firm's sensitivity to signals from the environment, from that part of the environment not included within the model. In the Scottish case the model seems to be blind or at least inattentive to any competitor not resident in Hawick, any potential customer who is not already one of their traditional customers.

The model is also likely to inhibit creativity by greatly reducing the range of problems considered, the range of informational inputs, and the range of options generated and contemplated. Strategic ideas are an output of prevailing mental models and are limited by them.

The market that the Scottish manufacturers compete in is not, as defined in much literature, an objective fact whose nature and components are equally obvious to all. Rather it is a market which they have selected and defined for themselves, and may in part have imagined. Even within the strategic group of Scottish knitwear manufacturers within Hawick the players do not all share exactly the same mental model of their market. As Porac, Thomas & Baden-Fuller observe, "To speak of the mental model of Scottish knitwear manufacturers is a bit problematic since variations exist from firm to firm in how managers conceptualise the details of the competitive environment".

The notion that the definition of a strategic situation may be as much a creation of the mind of the strategist as it is an objective fact is turned to powerful use by Mitroff & Emshoff (1979), and Mason & Mitroff (1981). Their central thesis is that two or more parties to a decision may disagree on the best strategy to adopt because, perhaps unknown to them, each side has a different set of underlying assumptions about the situation. Those underlying sets of assumptions are what we have here been referring to as opposing mental models of the situation. A dispute at the level of strategy can, according to these authors only be resolved by working back to the underlying assumptions, or mental models, which are also in opposition, albeit unsurfaced. Their remedy is to generate a mutually acceptable fresh set of assumptions from which a new, shared strategy can then be derived:

> An ill-structured problem is one for which various strategies for providing a possible solution rest on assumptions that are in sharp conflict with one another. With this kind of situation, the primary purposes of the methodology are as follows:
> (A) to help surface for explicit examination the underlying assumptions that analysts often bring with them to a problem situation
> (B) to compare and evaluate systematically the assumptions of different analysts
> (C) to examine the relationship between underlying assumptions and the resultant policies which are derived and dependent upon them, and
> (D) to attempt to formulate new, novel, and originally unforeseen policies on previously unexamined and unforeseen assumptions. (Mitroff and Emshoff, 1979)

The Strategic Assumption Surfacing methodology is used by Mitroff and colleagues primarily as a problem solving device, particularly where there is disagreement between stakeholders. It also has rich potential to enrich strategic creativity. When a company, or indeed an individual, considers that it has an insufficient range of strategic ideas for coping with a situation, one solution is to work back to the underlying model of the situation, which

Mitroff and colleagues call the set of assumptions. Experiment with other ways of seeing the situation, other models, which in turn give rise to "new, novel, and originally unforeseen" ideas for strategic solutions. An example of a satellite television company illustrates the method. The company was competing on programmes. If our programmes are better than the competitors' we win the viewing figures battle and attract more advertisers. All competitors were competing in the same way, head-to-head. How else might we think about our business? Could we define our business in some other way, with different competitors, different customers, being a different sort of business ourselves? Note, please, that we are not proposing to change the business. We change only the way we think about the business, the mental model which we hold of the business situation. Suppose instead we see our company as being in the business of delivering a particular set of desirable target customers to the advertisers. If that is our brief, how might we do that? That change of model gives rise to new ideas. We succeed by getting to know the target customers' buying habits. We might for example form a link with a credit card company for better data on customers' buying preferences. That new idea does not arise when we only define ourselves as a broadcaster of TV programmes. Having two ways of defining ourselves gives us more than twice as many strategy and new product ideas. It breaks us out of our convergent, increasingly narrow, thinking.

ELEMENTS OF A MODEL OF STRATEGY AS SENSE-MAKING

These and many other studies from a cognitive perspective indicate a need for a new model of strategy, in effect a new way of making sense of what strategy is and how it works. One such model would be to view strategy as a process of sense-making. Its key features might be as follows.

The aim of strategy making is to make sense of the strategic situation so as to create effective ways of dealing with it.

There is benefit in viewing the strategic situation from a multiplicity of perspectives or models since these give more insights, fuller understanding and greater variety of strategic ideas for dealing with the situation.

The model of the strategic situation is a product of the interaction between the strategists and the situation. It is neither wholly "out there" nor "in here", but both.

The model of strategy as sense-making is not intended to exclude traditional and objectivist models of strategy but to complement them. Objectivist models focus attention on rational analysis of objective data. The sense-making model draws attention to the way that the strategists are constructing the situation, to the possibilities of alternative perspectives, and the effects and benefits of employing various perspectives.

TABLE 13.1   The traditional approach to strategy and the sense-making approach compared

	SWOT model of strategy	Sense-making
Objectives	Known Not in question Rational, economic	Created by the people managing the company
Competitors	Known Objective fact Not in question	Identified/selected by the company from among many possibilities
Market structure and configuration	A fact, universally recognized akin to a map of physical terrain	Company makes its own sense of the market situation. Can actively pursue a fresh approach to a market so as to destabilize it in the company's favour
Strategy	A logical outcome of the SWOT analysis Choice from among few options	Subject to creative invention by the company Wide range of choices Range of choice limited not solely by market facts but also by company's ability to change its models

The strategist selects from among a near-infinite universe of sensations those elements which seem to him or her to be important, and creates from them an explanatory model of the strategic situation.

The choice of elements, the relationships between them, and the explanatory mental model of the strategic situation are as much a product of the strategist as they are of the objective data.

The strategies which result are designed to cope with the situation as portrayed in the strategist's mental model, rather than with any objective, external world, if such could be said to exist in the absence of any observers.

The contrast between the traditional approach to strategy based on the rational analysis of objective data, here exemplified by SWOT analysis, and the sense-making model of strategy is shown in TABLE 13.1.

PARALLEL DEVELOPMENTS IN SOCIAL SCIENCES

There have been comparable developments apparent in various fields of the social sciences concerning the way we think, how we obtain and structure knowledge, how we know and make sense of the world. These developments are noticeable, for example, in psychology. Behaviourism was the dominant paradigm up to the 1970s, and still has its supporters. In recent years a greater influence has been gained by the information processing model. That in turn may be further extended by the sense-making or natural selection model associated with Edelman and others.

Behaviourism, also known as stimulus–response theory, sought to understand a person or an animal by observing its behaviour. What went on inside the mind of the subject was not observable by an outsider, therefore it could not be studied. Behaviourism studies events in the outside world; a stimulus is applied to the organism; it reacts. Stimulus and reactions are events in the outside world, visible to the impartial observer, which makes them valid for scientific study. Rosch (1992) describes behaviourism as follows.

> [FIGURE 13.1] is a diagram of the behaviourist world-view. The first arrow, the stimulus, is something that the experimenter does to the organism (human or animal); it is in the external world, observable by everyone. The second arrow is what the organism does after the stimulus, also something observable by everyone. The square between the two arrows is the mind, considered as a blackbox, a box that is not publicly observable and hence not subject to scientific investigation, hence unnecessary to talk about. For the strict behaviourists, the biological organism was also in the black box. So psychologists could be completely objective; they need only chart the relationships between stimuli and responses.

Some of the early work on strategy in the 1960s and 1970s bore some resemblance to the behaviourist school of thought. Most attention in strategic planning was directed to analysing the external environment. Little attention was given to the internal processes and politics which might go on within the firm. The firm was assumed to be rational economic in its behaviour, seeking to maximize profits, measured as returns to shareholders. The internal workings of the firm were not observable or measureable by outsiders. There was in any case nothing to study; the firm

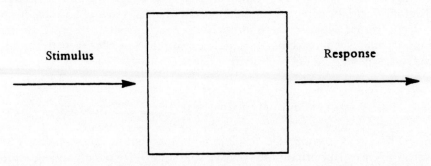

FIGURE 13.1 The stimulus–response model. *Source*: Rosch (1992). Reprinted by permission

was assumed to behave logically, rationally, economically, in pursuit of known economic objectives. It was more important to study events in the outside world, sometimes called the real world. External events, such as demand trends, economic growth rates and competitor positioning, were objective facts observable to all, and measureable.

The information processing model takes the view that when the information or stimulus comes into the brain of the organism it has to be processed in order that the appropriate response can be made:

> [FIGURE 13.2] is a typical representation that might be found in any text book of what mind looks like in present information-processing psychology.
>
> It is still a box with input and output but now inside you have smaller boxes, inside of which there are yet smaller boxes. The ideal is to be able to take the mind as a whole that shows intelligence and explain it in terms of parts, or mechanisms that are progressively less intelligent, more mechanical than the whole. It is an information processing view, because it represents the flow of something called information from the external world into the senses and, mediated by attention, into the very short term, short term and long term memories, thence to be used in solving problems and making decisions, finally resulting in behaviour again in the external world. Information also flows back through the system, for example, knowledge and expectations from a long term memory influence attention and the information that will enter the senses.
>
> The form of the chart is that of a computer model. (Rosch, 1992)

Edelman's ideas on how the mind works reject the analogy with the computer, passive recipient of inputs for processing. Instead, the mind is

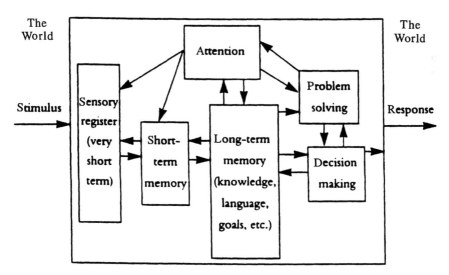

FIGURE 13.2   The information processing model. *Source*: Rosch (1992). Reprinted by permission

considered to be active; actively going out into the world, making its own sense of what it sees around it, selecting from among the myriad and near-infinite variety of sense impressions all around. Edelman likens the process of sense making to film making:

> When one looks at a film it looks very tidy. But if you look at the process there's an awful lot of stuff on the cutting room floor. What an artist does is take an awful lot of circumstances even under a rather vague idea and then as the idea begins to build put the pieces together and construct them leaving a lot of debris on the cutting room floor, selecting against and selecting for. The director has an idea and that gets fitted. (Edelman, 1995)

Verschure (1995) makes the same point: "The world does not contain neatly organised bits and pieces of information that await to be picked up by the brain. It is more a chaos that needs to be structured by the brain".

This view, as presented by Edelman, Verschure and others, has much in common with the sense-making approach to management of Karl Weick:

> Most map/territory discussions imply passive actors facing an intractable, material world which they register imperfectly and categorize crudely. Managerial life is often different, involving proactive people who enact, manipulate, influence, create or construct territories that realize their maps. (Weick, 1990)

The present exploration into how we make sense of our world, how we gain insights and information and act upon them, is of central importance in many areas of human science, in neuropsychology, psychology, epistemology, as much as in strategic management, knowledge management and organizational learning. Similar models and viewpoints reappear in the several branches of science, though sometimes under different names.

IMPLICATIONS OF A SENSE-MAKING MODEL OF STRATEGY

From the near-infinite variety of data contained in the universe, the strategist selects those facts, figures and impressions that seem relevant to the present question. That question may be: what should be our strategy in this market for the next five years? Should we enter the European market? Or similar examples. The selection is influenced by the strategist's prior experience, existing mindset and predisposition. The strategist is seeking a recognizable pattern or model which relates the relevant elements so that he or she can understand the situation and work with it. The model tends to be self-sealing in that new data are selected in accordance with what the model deems to be relevant, and interpreted through the model. Thus the model is not easily changed. In a changing environment a model which does not change may become dangerous for the strategist and his or her company.

The model of strategy as sense-making directs researchers' attention to the ways in which strategists create models and project them on to the environment. The quality of the models and the process of sense-making then become significant issues in strategy research.

THE IMPLICATIONS OF A SENSE-MAKING MODEL FOR STRATEGIC IDEAS

In a model of strategy as sense-making, strategic ideas are the outcome of the strategist's mental model of the situation. New strategic ideas do not arise solely from further analysis of external data but by the strategist's reflecting upon that data. Enlightenment comes to the prepared mind, and poring over the data may be an essential part of that preparation. The mind also has a part to play in the act of creation, which produces a new idea.

Seeing the strategic situation in only one way, imagining it to be reality rather than a personal, partial model of reality, limits the production of strategic ideas to those which fit the mental model. Learning to view the strategic situation through two or more perspectives, or mental models, increases the variety, range, richness and creativity of the strategic ideas generated to deal with the situation.

There is, however, a paradox. The additional variety of strategic ideas which an additional mental model of the situation could offer only become available if the additional mental model can be accepted alongside the strategist's original mental model. Two sets of strategic ideas are only available if the strategist is able to accommodate two mental models of the same situation. But, as we have previously seen, the original mental model tends to be self-sealing, selecting only those data that fit the model and interpreting them in keeping with that model. The Morgan Motor Co. Ltd case which follows contains just such a situation, where two sets of people have two entirely different understandings of the Morgan company's situation and consequently two opposing sets of strategic ideas for dealing with it.

MORGAN MOTOR COMPANY LTD

The Morgan case is well known in British business schools. The written case is widely used. There is also a BBC TV film of the company. For the television film, Sir John Harvey-Jones, ex-chairman of ICI, was sent in to advise the family management.

The Morgan Company is run by Peter Morgan, son of the founder, and Charles Morgan, son of Peter.

The company makes traditional sports cars by hand. The company has always been profitable. The waiting list for the cars is variously estimated at six years or eight years. One dealer who received 12 cars in one year for a waiting list of 460 confirmed orders reckons he has a 40-year waiting list.

It soon emerges that there are two completely different ways of understanding the situation. Peter and Charles Morgan see Morgan as a continuing success, still making cars, still making profits, after 80 years, a family firm successful in the third generation. Sir John Harvey-Jones sees Morgan as a disaster waiting to happen: "If they don't do something soon, and I pray they will do something, this will all disappear".

The two groups disagree radically on everything: pricing, investment, profits, production methods, marketing, staffing, strategy. The two groups appear to have two completely different understandings or mental models of the company's strategic situation. Both models are internally consistent. The Morgans' views on staffing are consistent with their views on marketing, pricing and objectives. Sir John Harvey-Jones's views on marketing and pricing are consistent with his views on staffing, investment, objectives, and strategy for Morgan, though they differ in every respect from the Morgans' views. Each person can give a logical justification for his view on each element of strategy and tactics because for him all the elements are causally related in his own mental model of the total situation. He makes sense of the total situation rather than of separate bits in isolation. As Sir John observes, "there is such fear that changing anything will destroy the magic". Charles declares, "we don't want to change anything really because people love the car just as it is".

The mental model is not easily changed. Harvey-Jones cites the eight-year waiting list as proof that Morgan has a problem. But in Peter and Charles's model the waiting list is not a problem. "We call the waiting list 'popularity peaks'. Hopefully they stay there". The models seem to be self-sealing, each element within a particular model being causally related to every other element, each new piece of information being interpreted or being selected to be ignored through the model. In this case neither side is willing to listen to the other. Neither side is willing to explore the other's view or give credence to it. The stance is: I'm right, you are wrong. It is a dialogue of the deaf, which becomes mutual condemnation.

Once the opposing sides have embraced their particular view as an article of faith one can easily see how and why they have difficulty breaking out of it. But there remains the interesting question of why they see the situation so differently. They are all looking at the same universe of facts. There is, for example, a long waiting list. But there is no agreement on the significance of that waiting list. The case and film material do not allow us to reach hard and fast conclusions on the genesis of their different mental models but there are some clues that may be suggestive. For each of the opposing sides the model of the company seems to be derived from a more fundamental model or set of beliefs about how companies in general are supposed to work. That more fundamental model seems to be heavily influenced by the person's previous experiences elsewhere. Sir John believes that Morgan should maximize profits and reinvest while it has the opportunity. His approach is consistent with a general view of companies as investment opportunities. For him the economic system works best by directing investment resources to those firms that offer the best opportunities for maximizing returns to investment. That approach is entirely consistent with his previous experience as chairman of a very large group of companies, where head office acts as a central bank reinvesting profits and resources into those business units which promise the best yields. Peter and Charles Morgan seem to see Morgan more as a family trust. Sir John described it as "a bloody museum ... It's not a business". Peter and Charles seem determined to carry on the tradition of the founder H.F.S. Morgan in every possible way.

CONCLUSION

A view of strategy as sense-making adds an additional perspective to the way we think about the process of making strategy. It is not a replacement for an objectivist view but a complement. Competitors do exist out there in the outside world, as objective analysts have always told us they do. But the choice of whom we will compete against and how is more a subjective choice of the strategist. A company chooses to put together a particular configuration of selected customers, selected competitors, preferred dimensions of competition and its own designed offerings emphasizing certain characteristics. This configuration is the enactment of its mental model, as Weick (1990, 1995) described it. The company may choose to compete in exactly the same way as existing competitors in so far as it can, perhaps because it has no other ideas. Or it can adopt a different approach, destabilizing the market, as Polaroid did with cameras, Sony did with cassette players, Direct Line did with motor insurance, Daewoo is attempting to do with automobiles, and the satellite television company did by playing with the idea of seeing itself as in the business of delivering selected customers to advertisers, not just as delivering TV programmes to viewers. The market is not solely "out there" as objective fact, nor solely "in here" as creative imagination. It is the interplay of both. The sculptor Michelangelo is reported to have said that he could see an angel caught within the block of marble. His task as sculptor was to set it free. If that angel were wholly objective fact "out there" in the block of marble, any competent sculptor could have released precisely the same angel. If the angel were entirely "in

here" a creation of Michelangelo's self-sufficient imagination, he would
have had no need of the marble.

The mental model may be conscious or unconscious. By raising it to
consciousness we may be better able to see the limitations it places on us in
terms of problem solving and the creation of strategic ideas. We may then be
able to experiment consciously with different mental models, different ways
of understanding situations leading to different and novel ways of tackling
them. Unconscious mental models make us their prisoners. Being unconscious of our dominant mental model, we project it on to our world and
believe it to be reality. As Assagioli (1974, 1991) observed, "What we identify
with dominates us. What we can disidentify from, we can dominate".

How do we put this into practice in making strategy for a company?

REVIEW YOUR STRATEGY

The present strategy is the outcome of an implicit mental model of the
competitive world. The strategy is at best only as good as that model. Often
that model is so deeply buried in the thinking, in the traditions and culture
of the company that people are no longer aware of it. It exerts a guiding
influence over the company's actions and predetermines what strategic
options are considered and which are unthinkable. But as long as the
company remains unconscious of its implicit mental model it has difficulty
in breaking out of the straitjacket on its strategic thinking. It is difficult to
update and change the assumptions and mental models that underlie our
world view if they remain inaccessible and unconscious. The first step is to
make explicit the assumptions and mental model on which the present
strategy is based. The strategy is the company's chosen way of dealing with
the situation portrayed in its model of reality. What is that model?
Questions which help to reveal the model include the following:

1. The present strategy will only be successful as long as certain key
   conditions continue to exist. What are those conditions?
2. Vulnerabilities. If you were to read in the financial press next month that
   the company had gone out of business, what do you suppose would have
   been the four most likely causes?
3. What is the justification of the present strategy?

REVIEW YOUR SEVERAL OPERATING SYSTEMS

Implicit in the selection and training of staff are assumptions about the kind
of world in which the company will be operating in the future. What world

are we assuming? Similarly, the company information system, market intelligence system, the information selected for reporting to the board of directors are based on a mental model of the world which says what is important information. Without such a model the selection of the information would make no sense. So what is the implied model? Note that this exercise often has a secondary benefit when it reveals that some of the subsystems and the strategic thinking are not operating on the same world view. The main purpose of the exercise is, however, to clarify further the mental model which guides the company's sense-making and strategic thinking.

REVIEW THE MENTAL MODEL

Review the mental model implicit in the company's current strategy and operating systems. Is it robust? Does it need revising? Updating? What are the cardinal assumptions on which it depends? There may be some surprises here. Notice that when Arie de Geus conducted a similar exercise as Strategic Planning Director of Shell they found that the implicit assumptions which they were making could not exist outside of a fairy story.

PLAY WITH DIFFERENT WAYS OF SEEING THE WORLD

There are several ways of doing this. One is to imagine a change in the relationship between key players, as for example between the oil majors and the companies that construct oil platforms, a move from an adversarial relationship to partnering. What would such a world be like? Would we wish to make it happen? Should we be prepared for the possibility of it happening? A second valuable exercise is to change one key variable. For example some oil companies set out to think the unthinkable and imagine what the world would be like if the oil price trebled. The companies that had done that particular piece of strategic thinking and thought through their responses were much better prepared when the oil price hike actually happened than those who had not given it a thought.

Scenario planning in essence consists of imagining two or three different but likely states of the world at a given future date and asks how robust is the company's strategy and readiness for each of these scenarios. A further way to enhance strategic creativity is to treat the present way that the market is structured as being simply a temporary phenomenon that happens to suit the entrenched competitors. Then the question is: how could we change the structure of the market so as to destabilize the market in our favour? That is what Direct Line did in UK Motor insurance, what the satellite television company did in its field, and what Macdonalds did in the restaurant business.

All of this can be done as a strategic thinking and creativity review in the safety of the boardroom, though it is better done at a resort hotel or somewhere similar away from routine pressures and routine thinking. The process is similar to the "thought experiments" which formed the basis of most of Einstein's creative thinking.

REDESIGN ALL THE OPERATING SYSTEMS

A new world view, a new strategy and a new set of key assumptions may well imply changes in the type and people we will need, in the information which will in future be significant, in the performance measures that we will monitor and reward. The new model requires to be operationalized. Stop a while. Leave the ideas alone to be mulled over at leisure, as it were off-line. As yet we have done nothing to change the company. Changing the company is the last thing we do. First we do our strategic thinking.

REFERENCES

Ansoff, I. (1965). *Corporate Strategy*. New York: McGraw-Hill.
Argenti, J. (1980). *Practical Corporate Planning*. London: Unwin.
Assagioli, R. (1974). *The Act of Will*. Harmondsworth: Penguin
Assagioli, R. (1991). *Transpersonal Development*. London: Crucible.
Edelman, G. (1995). *The Man Who Made Up His Mind*. BBC TV programme.
Janis, I. (1982). *Groupthink*. Boston, MA: Houghton Mifflin.
Mason, R. & Mitroff, I. (1981). *Challenging Strategic Planning Assumptions*. Chichester: Wiley.
Mitroff, I. & Emshoff, J. (1979). On strategic assumption-making. A dialectical approach to policy and planning. *Academy of Management Review*, **4**(1).
Porac, J., Thomas, H. & Baden-Fuller, C. (1989). Competitive groups as cognitive communities. The case of Scottish knitwear manufacturers. *Journal of Management Studies*, **26**(4).
Porter, M. (1980). *Competitive Strategy. Techniques for Analysing Industries and Competitors*. New York: Free Press.
Reger, R. (1990). Managerial thought structures and competitive positioning. In A. Huff (ed.) *Mapping Strategic Thought*. Chichester: Wiley.
Rosch, E. (1992). Cognitive psychology. In J. Hayward & F. Varela (eds) *Gentle Bridges. Conversations with the Dalai Lama on the Sciences of Mind*. Boston, MA: Shambala.
Verschure, P. (1995). *The Man Who Made Up His Mind*. BBC TV programme.
Weick, K. (1990). Cartographic myths in organisations. In A. Huff (ed.) *Mapping Strategic Thought*. Chichester: Wiley.
Weick, K. (1995). *Sensemaking in Organisations*. New York: Sage.

FURTHER READING

Boden, M. (1994). *Dimensions of Creativity*. Cambridge, MA: MIT Press.

Brooks, G. (1995). Defining market boundaries. *Strategic Management Journal*, **16**.

Dutton, J., Fahey, L & Narayanan, V. (1983). Toward understanding strategic issue diagnosis. *Strategic Management Journal*, **4**(4).

Edelman, G. (1994). *Bright Air, Brilliant Fire. On the Matter of the Mind.* Harmondsworth: Penguin.

Gardiner, H. (1993). *Creating Minds. An Anatomy of Creativity.* New York: Basic Books.

Holyoak, K. & Thagard, P. (1995). *Mental Leaps. Analogy in Creative Thought.* Cambridge, MA: MIT Press.

Kelly, G. (1955). *A Theory of Personality. The Psychology of Personal Constructs.* New York: W.W. Norton.

Meindl, J., Stubbart, C. & Porac, J. (1996). *Cognition Within and Between Organisations.* New York: Sage.

Porac, J. & Thomas, H. (1994). Cognitive categorization and subjective rivalry among retailers in a small city. *Journal of Applied Psychology*, **79**, 1.

Raimond, P. (1996). Two styles of foresight. Are we predicting the future or inventing it? *Long Range Planning*, **29**(2).

Sacks, O. (1995). *An Anthropologist on Mars*. London: Picador.

Yates, B. (1983). *The Decline and Fall of the American Automobile Industry.* Empire Books.

Zajac, E. & Bazerman, M. (1991). Blind spots in industry and competitor analysis. Implications of (mis)perceptions for strategic decisions. *Academy of Management Review*, **16**.

Section IV

Partnership

In "Hybrid arrangements as strategic alliances: theoretical issues in organizational combinations" (*Academy of Management Review*, **14**(2), 1989), Bryan Borys and David Jemison define hybrid organizational arrangements as those "in which two or more sovereign organizations combine to pursue common interests" (p. 234). Borys and Jemison discuss five major forms of hybrid organization—acquisitions, mergers, joint ventures, license agreements and supplier arrangements—and emphasize their importance as alternative ways for firms to expand their capabilities, enter new product markets, deal with resource constraints and develop internationally. The chapters in this section add new dimensions to that perspective.

Dyer, Cho and Chu study more than 400 relationships between automakers and their suppliers, in the US, Japan and Korea, to examine the extent to which automakers manage their suppliers as partners or at arms-length. Results show that US firms have traditionally managed all suppliers at arms-length, Korean firms have managed all suppliers as partners, and Japanese firms have utilized both types of relationships.

Floyd, Lubatkin, Nunes and Heppner compare managerial knowledge structures of French and German middle managers, and find differences sufficient to suggest that collaborations between firms in these two countries face significant challenges.

14

Strategic Supplier Segmentation: A Model for Managing Suppliers in the 21st Century

JEFFREY H. DYER, DONG SUNG CHO, WUJIN CHU

INTRODUCTION

During the past decade we have seen an increased emphasis on alliances, networks, and supply chain management as vehicles through which firms can achieve competitive advantage. Indeed, the typical industrial firm spends more than one half of every sales dollar on purchased products—and this percentage has been increasing with recent moves towards downsizing and outsourcing (US Bureau of Census, 1985; Bresnen & Fowler, 1994). Consequently, supply chain management and purchasing performance is increasingly recognized as an important determinant of a firm's competitiveness. Two widely differing supplier management models have emerged from both practice as well as academic research on the issue of how to optimally manage suppliers. The traditional view, or the *arms-length model* of supplier management, advocates minimizing dependence on suppliers and maximizing bargaining power. Michael Porter (1980, p. 123) describes this view of supplier management as follows:

> In purchasing, then, the goal is to find mechanisms to offset or surmount these sources of suppliers' power ... Purchases of an item can be spread among alternate suppliers in such a way as to improve the firm's bargaining power.

This chapter was first published in 1998 in the *California Management Review*, **40**(2), and is reproduced here, in shortened form, by permission of The Regents of the University of California.

The key implication of this model for purchasing strategy is for buyers to deliberately keep suppliers at "arms-length" and to avoid any form of commitment. The arms-length model was widely accepted as the most effective way to manage supplier relationships in the United States until the success of Japanese firms, which did not use this model, forced a re-evaluation of the model's basic tenets.

In contrast to the arms-length model, the success of Japanese firms has often been attributed to close supplier relationships, or a *partner model* of supplier management (Cusumano, 1985; Womack *et al.*, 1990; Dyer & Ouchi, 1993; Nishiguchi, 1994). Various studies suggest that, compared to arms-length relationships, Japanese-style partnerships result in superior performance because partnering firms: (i) share more information and are better at coordinating interdependent tasks (Fruin, 1992; Clark & Fujimoto, 1991; Womack *et al.*, 1990; Nishiguchi, 1994), and (ii) invest in relation-specific assets which lower costs, improve quality, and speed product development (Asanuma, 1989; Dyer, 1996a). However, while Japanese-style partnerships have economic benefits, some researchers have found that these types of relationships are costly to set up and maintain, and may reduce a customer's ability to switch away from inefficient suppliers (Helper, 1991; Sako, 1992).

The practical application of these two models can be found in the automotive industry, where General Motors has historically used an arms-length model while Toyota has employed a partner model. It has been well documented that, particularly during the much publicized reign of Jose Ignacio Lopez de Arriortua, General Motors attempted to generate cost savings by fostering vigorous supplier competition and maintaining arms-length relationships. Dr Lopez pushed suppliers to reduce prices by renegotiating contracts and opening up parts to competitive bidding—sometimes going through more than five rounds of bidding. Although critics argue that the long-term negative effects of this strategy are yet to be felt, Lopez is credited with saving GM roughly $3.0–4.0 billion as a result of these tough supplier management practices (*Business Week*, August 8, 1994).

In contrast, Toyota (and more recently Chrysler in the United States) has developed long-term partnerships with suppliers who are given implicit guarantees on future business. In return, suppliers make relation-specific investments to enhance their productivity in the Toyota relationship.[1] Past studies indicate that these relation-specific site, physical, and human asset investments reduce inventories, improve quality, and speed product development (Asanuma, 1989; Dyer, 1996a).

Of course, the key question facing purchasing executives is: which model of supplier management is superior? Many firms in considering a model for supplier management tend to dichotomize this issue, choosing either the arms-length model or the partnership model. For example, US automakers have historically relied primarily on the arms-length model of supplier management, whereas Japanese automakers are believed to have exclusively relied on a partner model (though, as we will show, this is not an entirely accurate perception). Our research on 453 supplier–automaker relationships in the US, Japan, and Korea suggests that firms should think more strategically about supplier management, and perhaps should not have a "one size fits all" strategy for supplier management (see the appendix for a brief discription of the study). Instead, each supplier should be analyzed strategically to determine the extent to which the supplier's product contributes to the core competence and competitive advantage of the buying firm. As we shall show, a company's ability to strategically segment suppliers in such a way as to realize the benefits of both the arms-length as well as the partner models may be the key to future competitive advantage in supply chain management. In this chapter we lay out a framework to assist managers in deciding whether to manage a particular supplier in an arms-length or partnership fashion. To illustrate the advantages of supplier segmentation, it is useful to examine the supplier management practices of US, Japanese, and Korean automakers.

SUPPLIER–AUTOMAKER RELATIONSHIPS IN THE UNITED STATES

Previous studies suggest that arms-length supplier relationships differ from supplier partnerships on a number of key dimensions, including length of contract, continuity of relationship, degree of information sharing, relation-specific investments, and levels of trust (Helper, 1991; Dyer & Ouchi, 1993). Data from a sample of arms-length supplier relationships (as selected by US automakers) are shown in TABLE 14.1. As predicted, these relationships are characterized by short-term contracts, frequent rebidding, low levels of information sharing, low levels of relation-specific investments, and low levels of trust.

However, an intriguing finding emerged when we asked US automakers to select a sample of supplier relationships that were partnerships or "most like a *keiretsu* relationship." Data from the "partner" sample are also provided in TABLE 14.1. What is particularly important to note is that the partner relationships do not differ significantly from the arms-length relationships. The US automakers' most partner-like supplier relationships are also characterized by frequent rebidding, low levels of information sharing, low levels of relation-specific investments, and low levels of trust. These findings suggest that US automakers' relationships with partners were not significantly different than their relationships with arms-length suppliers. The only real (statistically significant) difference between arms-length suppliers and partners was the length of the contract awarded to the part-

TABLE 14.1   Supplier–automaker relationships in the United States

General characteristics	"Arms-length" suppliers (N = 46)	"Partner" suppliers (N = 46)
Annual sales	$428 MM	$373 MM
Percentage of sales to automaker	33.5%	33.9%
Relation-specific assets		
Distance between plants (miles)	589	413
Percentage of capital equipment that is not redeployable	15.4%	17.7%
Annual "person-days" of face-to-face contact	1169	1385
Number of guest engineers	0.45	0.47
Information sharing/assistance		
Extent to which supplier shares confidential information[a]	3.1	3.3
Extent to which supplier shares detailed cost data[a]	4.5	4.3
Extent to which automaker assists supplier with cost reduction[a]	2.1	1.9
Extent to which automaker assists supplier with quality[a]	2.9	3.1
Trust/contracts		
Extent to which supplier trusts automaker to be fair[a]	4.2	4.7
Extent to which supplier expects unfair treatment if automaker has the chance[a]	4.2	3.6
Average contract duration (years)	2.4	4.7[b]

[a]Supplier response on a 1–7 Likert scale; 1 = Not at all, 7 = To a very great extent.
[b]Significantly different from arms-length sample ($p < 0.05$).

ners. Partner suppliers received contracts of much longer duration (4.7 years versus 2.4 years). In effect, the partner suppliers were simply those higher performing suppliers who were more likely to re-win business and receive long-term contracts because they were better at meeting automaker expectations. US automakers have historically managed all suppliers in an arms-length fashion–partners are not really treated much differently than arms-length relationships. By way of comparison, let us examine the case of Japan.

SUPPLIER–AUTOMAKER RELATIONSHIPS IN JAPAN

Of course, by now it is well known that Japanese automakers have networks of *keiretsu* suppliers with whom they have close (and most US managers believe exclusive) relationships. Many studies of supplier–assembler relationships in Japan give the impression that all suppliers are part of the *keiretsu*. For example, in the automobile industry one hears about the "Toyota Group" or the "Nissan Group." However, this perception is inaccurate. Although it is true that most Japanese suppliers work closely with their customers, affiliated suppliers (*kankei kaisha*) definitely fall into the *keiretsu* category, while independent suppliers (*dokuritsu kaisha*) do not. To understand how purchasing executives at one Japanese automaker thought about supplier management, our conversation with the purchasing general manager at a Japanese automaker is illustrative. In response to the questions, "do you think about your suppliers differently?" and "do you interact with suppliers differently?", the purchasing general manager proceeded to draw a set of concentric circles (see FIGURE 14.1). After doing so, he explained that there were roughly 30–35 suppliers that fit into the innermost ring. These were suppliers that were subsidiaries (*kogaisha*) or affiliated suppliers (*kankei kaisha*) of the automaker. In Japan, these companies would definitely be considered as *keiretsu* companies. The automaker holds an equity stake in these companies (greater than 20%) and typically transfers personnel to work at these companies on a part or full time basis. The automaker has a subsidiaries department that works with these companies on such matters as long-term strategic plans, capital investments and capacity planning, finance, and personnel transfers. These are in fact the automaker's set of closest suppliers. Not surprisingly, these suppliers produce high value components that tend to be highly customized to the automaker's particular models.

In the second concentric ring, the purchasing manager identified roughly 90 suppliers (including the 35 subsidiary suppliers) who were members of one of the automaker's supplier associations. Members of this supplier association were those suppliers who were making customized inputs. It included some independent suppliers (like Yazaki, a wire harness supplier, and Zexcel, a supplier of air conditioners) with whom the automaker had to work closely due to a high degree of component customization and a high degree of interdependence. In some cases the automaker held a small equity stake (typically less than 10%) in the independent supplier and on occasion the automaker would transfer personnel to work at these suppliers. In short, this group of suppliers included the inner *keiretsu* group of suppliers as well as a few independent firms that provided competition for the *keiretsu* suppliers. Not all suppliers were allowed to join this association, primarily because the nature of the information exchanged was often proprietary and the automaker needed to coordinate closely with these suppliers.[2]

Finally, the outer ring represented a second supplier association which was open to all first tier suppliers. The suppliers in this association (who were not allowed to participate in activities of the first supplier association or subsidiaries department) tended to make more standardized or

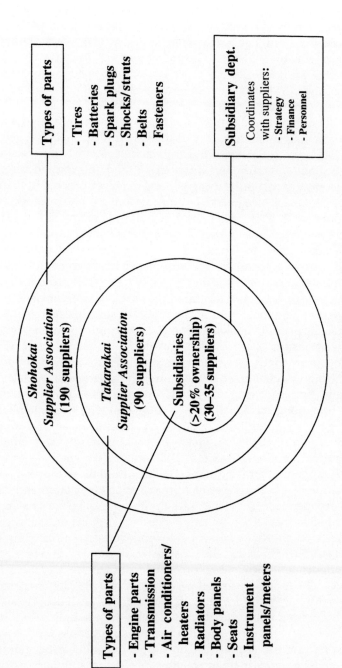

FIGURE 14.1   Strategic supplier management

commodity-like parts such as tires, fasteners, batteries, belts, spark plugs, etc.—parts that were not customized to a particular customer's model. Consequently, it was not so important for the supplier and automaker to coordinate closely on design, development, and manufacturing activities.

Although our interviews with Japanese executives suggested that automakers had somewhat different relationships with *kankei kaisha* than with *dokuritsu kaisha*, we wanted to verify these differences empirically. Consequently, we conducted the same supplier–automaker analysis in Japan that had done in the United States. We asked Toyota and Nissan for a sample of their most independent or arms-length suppliers, as well as a sample of their closest partnerships. We compared these two groups using the same measures as in the United States. Interestingly, the findings were quite different than what we found in the United States (see TABLE 14.2). The

TABLE 14.2   Supplier–automaker relationships in Japan

General characteristics	"Arms-length" suppliers (N = 48)	"Partner" suppliers (N = 45)
Annual sales	$1400 MM	$935 MM
Percentage of sales to automaker	18.9%	60%[b]
Relation-specific assets		
Distance between plants (miles)	125	41[b]
Percentage of capital equipment that is not redeployable	13.2%	30.6%[b]
Annual "person-days" of face-to-face contact	3181	7270[b]
Number of guest engineers	2.3	7.2[b]
Information sharing/assistance		
Extent to which supplier shares confidential information[a]	5.3	6.2[b]
Extent to which supplier shares detailed cost data[a]	4.3	5.9[b]
Extent to which automaker assists supplier with cost reduction[a]	2.6	4.2[b]
Extent to which automaker assists supplier with quality[a]	3.0	4.4[b]
Trust/contracts		
Extent to which supplier trusts automaker to be fair[a]	6.0	6.3
Extent to which supplier expects unfair treatment if automaker has the chance[a]	1.6	1.6
Average contract duration (years)	3.0	3.0

[a]Supplier response on a 1–7 Likert scale; 1 = Not at all, 7 = To a very great extent.
[b]Significantly different from arms-length sample ($p < 0.05$).

data indicate that while there were some similarities between the arms-length and partner suppliers (i.e. both groups of suppliers reported high levels of trust), there were also significant differences. Although all Japanese suppliers reported high levels of information sharing, face-to-face contact, trust, and "re-win" rates (compared to the US sample), the partners shared more information with the automaker, had twice as much face-to-face contact and twice the number of co-located engineers, and received greater assistance from the automaker. The partners also made significantly greater investments in relation-specific assets (e.g. partner supplier plants were, on average, 80 miles closer to the automaker). The differences between arms-length and partner suppliers were much greater in Japan than in the United States.

These data raise an important question. Why do Japanese automakers distinguish between independent and affiliated suppliers and why do they manage these relationships differently?[3] Furthermore, why do we find differences in the way automakers manage supplier relationships in Japan, but not in the United States? Before fully exploring the answers to these questions, we turn to the case of Korea.

SUPPLIER–AUTOMAKER RELATIONSHIPS IN KOREA

Korea has been a late entrant into the auto industry with automakers Hyundai, Kia, and Daewoo attempting to catch up with their US and Japanese competitors. These late entrants have had the opportunity to see different supplier management models being practised by their Japanese and US competitors. Thus, we were interested to see if Korean supplier relationships followed the US model or the Japanese model. To study this issue, we studied a sample of *chaebol* (partner) suppliers in Korea and compared these relationships with a sample of non-*chaebol* relationships.

Generally speaking, the Korean model of supplier management follows the Japanese model in that it is characterized by a close relationship between the automaker and the supplier, with high levels of interaction between the two parties (TABLE 14.3). Korean suppliers and automakers typically have exclusive relationships, with 72% of all suppliers supplying to only one automaker (Oh, 1995). The relationships tend to be characterized by substantial face-to-face contact and the automaker may transfer personnel to the supplier's organization. TABLE 14.3 shows that suppliers have also made specialized capital investments that are specifically tailored to the current automaker.

Korean automakers also provide assistance to their suppliers in the areas of quality, cost reduction, factory layout, and inventory management. Not surprisingly, there is much information sharing between the supplier and

TABLE 14.3   Supplier–automaker relationships in Korea

General characteristics	"Arms-length" suppliers (N = 202)	"Partner" suppliers (N = 15)
Annual sales	$29.5 MM	$37.7 MM
Percentage of sales to automaker	49.6%	81.9%[b]
Relation-specific assets		
Distance between plants (miles)	78	87
Percentage of capital equipment that is not redeployable	39%	53%[b]
Annual "person-days" of face-to-face contact	1072	4886
Number of guest engineers	0.61	0.73
Information sharing/assistance		
Extent to which supplier shares confidential information[a]	4.9	5.0
Extent to which supplier shares detailed cost data[a]	5.6	4.4
Extent to which automaker assists supplier with cost reduction[a]	3.3	3.4
Extent to which automaker assists supplier with quality[a]	3.8	4.3
Trust/contracts		
Extent to which supplier trusts automaker to be fair[a]	4.9	5.0
Extent to which supplier expects unfair treatment if automaker has the chance[a]	3.8	4.9
Average contract duration (years)	3.0	3.0

[a]Supplier response on a 1–7 Likert scale; 1 = Not at all, 7 = To a very great extent.
[b]Significantly different from arms-length sample ($p < 0.05$).

the automaker. First-tier Korean suppliers tend to be small and unsophisticated compared to their Japanese counterparts. As a result, providing assistance to suppliers is a virtual necessity for the Korean automakers' own survival.

The formal duration of the typical legal contract is 3 years but most contracts are renewed automatically. In fact the average length of the continuing relationship is 12½ years, with a third of all first-tier suppliers enjoying a continuing relationship with the automaker since the founding of the automaker (Chung, 1995). However, despite the fact that suppliers are highly dedicated to a particular automaker, the level of trust between the supplier and the automaker is significantly lower than what we find in Japan. Surprisingly, trust levels are comparable to US levels.

Although the Korean model of supplier management closely follows the Japanese model in many respects, beyond the issue of trust there is another important difference: we do not find strategic supplier segmentation. All suppliers are managed in a similar manner. Consequently, the level of relation-specific investments, information sharing, assistance, and trust is not significantly different between *chaebol* and non-*chaebol* suppliers (TABLE 14.3).

Although the strategic implications of these country differences, rather than an analysis of why these differences have emerged in each country, is the primary focus of this chapter, a brief comment on institutional and cultural factors that may have led to these differences is warranted. For example, US industry has long been characterized by a strong dependence on "market forces" to achieve efficiency. Organization theory, as developed in the US, supports the notion that firms lose power when they increase their dependency on outside suppliers (Emerson, 1962; Pfeffer & Salancik, 1978). Further, a Western legal philosophy which allows for the substitution of a specific relationship with a legal relationship, along with values of independence and autonomy, has contributed to arms-length contracting (Peterson & Shimada, 1978). By comparison, Japanese and Korean firms do not feel comfortable substituting a contract for a relationship and prefer to avoid any procedure that will involve a third party (Smith, 1983). Moreover, some claim that Japanese cultural norms and values as well as institutionalized practices such as interfirm employee transfers (*shukko*) result in a high level of "goodwill trust" in Japan, which translates into cooperative interfirm relationships (Dore, 1983; Sako, 1991). However, trust in Japanese relationships is described as varying depending on the nature of the relationship (e.g. family and kin are trusted more than classmates or individuals from a common hometown, who are more trusted than non-classmates and individuals from a different region of the country). Overall, the Japanese and Korean economies have been influenced to a much greater extent by government and social networks compared to the United States. Reliance on market forces have a tendency of leading to "spot equity," resulting in arms-length relationships while social networks strive for "serial equity," resulting in more long-term relationships (Ouchi, 1984). Although, like their Japanese counterparts, Korean suppliers enjoy a long-term relationship with their automaker customers, the relationship is characterized by lower levels of trust. One reason for this is the Korean government's policy of nurturing large conglomerates (*chaebols*) and its failure to set up laws and regulations to protect small-to-medium sized businesses in their dealings with the powerful *chaebols*. As a result, many small businesses have been at a relative disadvantage in trading with the *chaebols*, which have been in a position to dictate the terms of trading agreements and the relationship in general. This has led to lower levels of inter-firm trust in Korea.

Although national differences in supplier management styles are clearly present today, if we look at this phenomenon dynamically, we can see that supplier management styles in the three countries are more similar today than they were 10 years ago (Helper & Sako, 1995; Cusumano & Takeishi, 1991). Indeed, we see a convergence of supplier management styles in the three countries towards a mixture of partnerships and arms-length re-lationships. Namely, there are firms such as Chrysler in the US who are making much greater use of the partnership model than they have previously. Moreover, in Japan firms like Honda and Mitsubishi have introduced the arms-length model to a greater extent than their more traditional Japanese counterparts (e.g. Toyota and Nissan). These changes seem to indicate that management practices, though influenced by the institutions of the home countries, are not necessarily culture-bound.

STRATEGIC SUPPLIER SEGMENTATION

What are the implications of these three different approaches to managing supplier relationships? To answer that question, we must first examine the strengths and weaknesses of each approach to supplier management. In FIGURE 14.2 we summarize the strengths and weaknesses of each approach to supplier management. The population of suppliers used by each automaker is represented by a circular sphere (for simplicity, we ignore the small set of suppliers that sell to automakers in each country). The extent to which the circle overlaps another automaker's circle indicates the extent to which the two automakers share suppliers. In the United States, Chrysler, GM, and Ford have maintained non-exclusive (arms-length) arrangements with suppliers. Consequently, they share a common set of suppliers. As a result, many suppliers have been able to grow to sizable scale. Furthermore, suppliers can learn from working with multiple customers. However, by attempting to maintain multiple sources of supply and a high degree of relative bargaining power, US automakers have also restricted, to some ex-tent, the size and scale of suppliers. Thus, suppliers are smaller on average, than first-tier Japanese suppliers to Toyota and Nissan (see TABLES 14.1 and 14.2). Furthermore, due to low levels of trust, suppliers' investments in relation-specific assets are low relative to Korean and Japanese suppliers.

Korean automakers are on the other extreme. Rather than share all suppliers (through arms-length relationships) Korean automakers demand a high degree of loyalty from suppliers. As one Korean supplier executive commented, "[Our customer] would unsheathe the swords if we tried to supply to other Korean automakers" (interview, July 1, 1994). As a result, suppliers make relation-specific investments and coordinate their activities closely with their primary automaker customer. Thus, Korean automakers

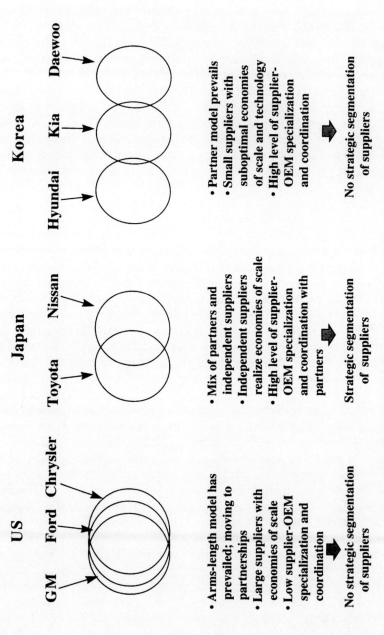

US

GM   Ford   Chrysler

• **Arms-length model has prevailed; moving to partnerships**
• **Large suppliers with economies of scale**
• **Low supplier-OEM specialization and coordination**

No strategic segmentation of suppliers

Japan

Toyota   Nissan

• **Mix of partners and independent suppliers**
• **Independent suppliers realize economies of scale**
• **High level of supplier-OEM specialization and coordination with partners**

Strategic segmentation of suppliers

Korea

Hyundai   Kia   Daewoo

• **Partner model prevails**
• **Small suppliers with suboptimal economies of scale and technology**
• **High level of supplier-OEM specialization and coordination**

No strategic segmentation of suppliers

FIGURE 14.2   Characteristics of supplier management (US, Japan, and Korea)

enjoy the benefits of dedicated, specialized suppliers. Furthermore, investments made by one automaker to develop its suppliers do not spill over to competitors. However, these practices also keep suppliers small, thereby resulting in suboptimal economies of scale. Moreover, because suppliers only work primarily with one customer, they do not have opportunities to learn from multiple customers. Consequently, this impedes the suppliers' abilities to learn and upgrade their technological capabilities.

The Japanese automakers in our study (Nissan and Toyota) were the most effective at strategically segmenting suppliers to realize the benefits of both the arms-length and partner models.[4] Independent Japanese suppliers such as Bridgestone (tires) and Mitsuboshi Belting Co. (belts, hoses) realized economies of scale by selling their relatively standardized products to all automakers. Moreover, these suppliers made fewer investments in assets dedicated to a particular automaker. Automakers provided less direct assistance to these suppliers, in large part because the benefits of assistance to the supplier would easily spill over to competitors. In contrast, affiliated suppliers like Nippondenso and Calsonic made substantial investments in relation-specific assets and coordinated activities closely with automakers through frequent face-to-face interactions. Toyota and Nissan provided significantly more assistance to affiliated suppliers to help them lower production costs, improve quality, and minimize inventories. Toyota and Nissan had greater incentives to assist these suppliers since their own success is inextricably tied to the success of these particular suppliers.

Furthermore, we found that this segmentation of suppliers extended through the value chain, to first- and second-tier suppliers. For example, Nippondenso also segments its suppliers and provides differential assistance to suppliers depending on the nature of the component and relationship. Not all suppliers are allowed to join the Nippondenso supplier association, but rather only those suppliers that meet specific size, dependency, and performance criteria (i.e. suppliers must sell at least $10 million per year to Nippondenso and have 30% of their total sales to Nippondenso). Consequently, Nippondenso focuses its assistance on the 69 suppliers in its supplier association while other suppliers must work their way into the association or somehow demonstrate that their contribution is worthy of Nippondenso assistance and resources. Thus, by replicating this pattern down through the supply chain, Toyota's entire production network realizes the benefits of strategic supplier segmentation.

To achieve the advantages of both the arms-length and partner models, our research suggests that suppliers should be analyzed strategically and then segmented into two groups: one group of suppliers that provide necessary, but non-strategic inputs, and another group that provides strategic inputs. By "strategic" we mean those high value inputs that may be useful in differentiating the buying firm's product. In the Japanese auto industry, these are transmission and engine parts, air conditioners, body and instrument panels, etc.—inputs provided by Japanese affiliated suppliers. These parts are customized to the model and help differentiate the model from competitor offerings. Non-strategic parts, which are typically provided by independent suppliers, are those parts such as belts, tires, batteries, etc. that are not customized and do not differentiate the model. Our research suggests that these two groups of suppliers should be managed differently in order to optimize purchasing strategy.

DURABLE ARMS-LENGTH RELATIONSHIPS

For inputs that are necessary, but non-strategic, firms should employ *durable arms-length (quasi-market) relationships*. Non-strategic inputs tend to differ from strategic inputs along two key dimensions: (i) asset specificity or the need for relation-specific investments, and (ii) component value added. Non-strategic inputs are those which are standardized and stand-alone— meaning that there is a low degree of supplier–buyer interdependence and the need for coordination is low. Consequently, there is little need for investments in relation-specific assets. In addition, the value added by non-strategic components is likely to be relatively lower than for strategic inputs. Thus, they have less ability to influence the cost/value of the final product.

Of course, the phrase *durable arms-length relationships* seems paradoxical since arms-length relationships suggest short-term, rather than long-term, trading expectations. However, the traditional notion of arms-length relationships—buyers frequently rotating purchases across multiple supplier sources while employing short-term contracts—is no longer an economically sensible approach in most industries. There are three primary reasons that the traditional arms-length model is no longer valid:

1. The administrative or transaction costs associated with managing a large number of vendors typically outweigh the benefits. In fact, some studies have found that in some instances the administrative and inventory holding costs associated with procurement actually outweigh the unit costs (Hannaford, 1983). Surprising as it may seem, firms may spend more money negotiating and processing an order than they do on the item itself. To illustrate, GM has traditionally employed roughly 8–10 times more people in procurement than Toyota due to the high cost of managing a large supplier base.
2. Dividing purchases across multiple suppliers reduces the ability of suppliers to achieve significant economies of scale (Dyer & Ouchi, 1993). Furthermore, it is not clear that a buying firm has more relative bargaining power simply by having more alternative sources of supply.

Buyer bargaining power may increase as much (or perhaps more) by increasing purchases from a single supplier, thereby making that particular supplier more dependent on the buyer. As Chrysler purchasing chief Tom Stallkamp observed in describing Chrysler's move towards supplier partnerships, "We have found that the more we buy from a particular supplier, the more responsive the supplier is to our needs" (interview, December 1, 1995).

3. Vigorous competition can be achieved with two or three suppliers as long as the suppliers are equally competent and managed skillfully (McMillan, 1990; Dyer & Ouchi, 1993). Buying firms do not need a large number of suppliers in order to maintain vigorous supplier competition. For example, vigorous competition exists in the commercial aircraft industry between Boeing, McDonnell Douglas, and Airbus even though there are only three suppliers of aircraft (Vayle & Yoffie, 1991). Similarly, Toyota maintains effective competition between just two suppliers by adjusting volume between the suppliers based on their performance.

In terms of actually managing suppliers, the durable arms-length model differs from the traditional arms-length model in the following respects. First, initial supplier selection requires some *capabilities benchmarking* to determine which suppliers have the potential for the lowest costs over the long term. Then, two or three suppliers can be selected to be long-term suppliers. The traditional arms-length model simply opens up the bidding to all suppliers without regard for their capabilities or the costs of working with and managing a large supplier set.

Second, the supplier and buyer make some dedicated investments in interfirm coordination mechanisms, such as order entry systems, electronic data exchange, and logistics systems which will get the product to the buyer where and when the buyer needs it.

Finally, the supplier is assured of future business as long as prices are competitive. Relatively frequent *price benchmarking* is necessary to maintain vigorous price competition between the two suppliers. For example, the buyer may create some automatic reorder dates (e.g. once a year) at which time suppliers must rebid for business. Bidding and reordering can also be carried out electronically according to pre-announced criteria so that procurement administrative costs can be kept to a minimum. The frequent price benchmarking (bids) keeps suppliers on their toes—they know they must continually offer low prices. However, they are willing to make the necessary investments in coordination mechanisms and logistics/ distribution processes because they have a long-term commitment for at least some business.

In summary, this quasi-market approach is superior to the traditional arms-length approach because it: (i) minimizes procurement (transaction) costs, (ii) allows suppliers to maximize economies of scale, which is critical in standardized, commodity-like products, and (iii) maintains vigorous competition. Buyers may also reopen the business to all bidders at longer time intervals (e.g. every five years), to ensure that their long-term suppliers still have the lowest costs and best capabilities. The price benchmarking (and open bidding) intervals should be shorter the more commodity-like the product and the greater the environmental and technological uncertainty regarding the factors which influence the cost structure of suppliers (i.e. the more frequently suppliers' production costs are likely to change). Since durable arms-length suppliers provide inputs which do not differentiate the buyer's product, the key is to secure these inputs at low cost both in terms of unit price and administrative cost.

Strategic Partnerships

Strategic partnerships (*quasi-hierarchies*) are necessary when supplying firms provide strategic inputs—inputs which are typically high value added and play an important role in differentiating the buyer's final product. Generally speaking, these inputs are not subject to industry standards and may benefit from customization due to multiple interaction effects with other components in the final product. Because of the potential benefits of customization (e.g. higher quality, or new features) strategic inputs require a high degree of coordination between supplier and buyer. Thus, strategic partnerships require multiple function-to-function interfaces between supplier and buyer. For example, a strategic supplier's design engineers must coordinate with buyer design engineers to ensure flawless product fit/smooth interfaces. The buyer's sales organization must share marketing information with the supplier's sales and product development functions to ensure that the supplier clearly understands the final customer's needs and the role of their component in the overall product strategy. Buyer manufacturing engineers must coordinate with supplier engineers to ensure that the supplier's product can be easily assembled at the buyer's plant. Not surprisingly, relation-specific investments are necessary in order for the supplying firm to coordinate effectively with the buying firm and customize the component. These include investments in dedicated plant and equipment, dedicated personnel, and tailored manufacturing processes. It is not unusual for an affiliated supplier in Japan to have plants tailored and solely dedicated to the "parent" company customer.

Due to multiple functional interfaces and relation-specific investments, organizational boundaries between supplier and buyer begin to blur. The partners' destinies become tightly intertwined. Furthermore, the incentive compatibility of the partners is high because each party has made co-specialized investments which are of little value outside of the relationship.

Thus, each party has strong incentives to help the other as much as possible. This explains why Toyota and Nissan provide such high levels of assistance to their affiliated suppliers—because their own success is highly dependent on the success of their affiliated suppliers. Thus, creating interfirm knowledge-sharing routines which transfer know-how and technology to suppliers is important because it is critical that their affiliated suppliers have world class capabilities. Similarly, because the success of strategic suppliers is tied closely to the success of the buying firm, strategic suppliers must be dedicated to helping the buying firm create competitive advantage in the final product market. This means that partner suppliers must be willing to exert efforts at innovation and quality and be responsive in ways that go beyond the explicit requirements of the contract.

In terms of managing strategic partnerships, the buying firm must be effective at: (i) capabilities benchmarking to ensure that the best possible partners are chosen, (ii) developing trust so that partners will be willing to make relation-specific investments and share information, and (iii) creating interfirm knowledge-sharing routines to effectively coordinate activities and optimize inter-firm learning. For a comparison of the durable arms-length relationship model and the strategic partnership model, see TABLE 14.4.

We should also note that strategic partnerships tend to be preferred (i) in complex-product industries[5] where the demands of complexity increase the value of effective inter-firm coordination, (ii) during a long-term economic expansion when scarcity of resources may be a problem, and (iii) when long-term value creation (through quality, new technologies, etc.) is the goal. In contrast, durable arms-length relationships may be more desirable (i) in simple-product industries or industries with high levels of standardization of components, (ii) in declining industries where suppliers have chronic excess capacity due to exit barriers and high fixed costs, and (iii) when short-term cost reduction is the primary goal. However, vacillating between arms-length relationships and partnerships is unlikely to be a successful strategy given the long-term commitment and relation-specific investments required for strategic partnerships to be successful. Buyers that violate partnership agreements will develop a reputation for behaving opportunistically and thus will have great difficulty in convincing suppliers to make the investments necessary for strategic partnerships to work effectively.

CONCLUSION

As global competition has increased during the past decade, executives have been under tremendous pressure to make their organizations as "lean" and efficient as possible. To meet the challenges of the new competition, executives have been encouraged to downsize their organizations, focus on

TABLE 14.4   Contrasting durable arms-length relationships with strategic partnerships

	Durable arms-length relationships (quasi-markets)	Strategic partnerships (quasi-hierarchies)
Product / input characteristics	Commodity / standardized products Open architecture products Stand-alone (no or few interaction effects with other inputs) Low degree of supplier–buyer interdependence Low value inputs	Customized, non-standard products Closed architecture products Multiple interaction effects with other inputs High degree of supplier–buyer interdependence High value inputs
Supplier management practices	Single functional interface (i.e. sales to purchasing) Price benchmarking Minimal assistance (minimal investment in interfirm knowledge-sharing routines) Supplier performance can be easily contracted for ex ante Contractual safeguards are sufficient to enforce agreements	Multiple functional interfaces (i.e. engineering to engineering, manufacturing to manufacturing) Capabilities benchmarking Substantial assistance (substantial investments in interfirm knowledge-sharing routines) Supplier performance on non-contractibles (i.e. innovation, quality, responsiveness) is important Self-enforcing agreements are necessary for optimal performance (i.e. trust, stock ownership, etc.)

their "core competencies," and outsource all other "non-core" activities. Due to this trend towards outsourcing, effective supplier management has become increasingly important to a firm's overall competitiveness. Our research indicates that rather than employ a "one size fits all" strategy for procurement, firms should think strategically about supply chain management. To optimize purchasing effectiveness, executives should strategically segment their suppliers into strategic partners and durable arms-length suppliers in order to allocate different levels of resources to each group. Since resources are a scarce commodity in any company, they should be allocated mainly to suppliers who fall into the partner category. Strategic partners are those suppliers that provide inputs that are typically of high value and play an important role in differentiating the buyer's final product. The buyer should maintain high levels of communication with these suppliers, provide managerial assistance, exchange personnel, make relation-specific investments, and make every effort to ensure that these suppliers are world class in terms of their overall capabilities.

On the other hand, buyers do not need to allocate significant resources to manage and work with durable arms-length suppliers. Durable arms-length suppliers are those that provide non-strategic inputs (e.g. standardized inputs that do not help differentiate the buyer's final product). As a result, durable arms-length suppliers do not need the same degree of attention or resources as strategic partners. Durable arms-length relationships will tend to be characterized by less face-to-face communication, less assistance, fewer relation-specific investments, and frequent price benchmarking relative to strategic partnerships. However, like strategic partnerships, long-term (enduring) relationships are fostered in order to minimize the administrative costs of procurement and to allow suppliers to realize economies of scale in production. For these suppliers, the buyer should attempt to minimize total procurement costs, which includes both unit price and administrative costs.

Our research on supplier–automaker relationships in the US, Japan, and Korea indicates that relationships in the US (as of 1992) have been characterized by arms-length relationships,[6] while those of Korea have been characterized by partnership (although it is important to note that partner (*keiretsu*) suppliers in Japan have closer automaker relationships based on virtually all criteria when compared to partner (*chaebol*) suppliers in Korea). We also found that automakers in the US and Korea have tended to manage their suppliers in a uniform way. Consequently, US automakers have not realized the benefits associated with supplier partnerships, while Korean automakers have not enjoyed the benefits associated with the arms-length model. Of the automakers in our sample, only Toyota and Nissan had realized the benefits of both the partner and arms-length models by strategically segmenting their suppliers. Many previous studies have suggested that the Japanese model of supplier management has been a major source of differential advantage for Japanese automakers. Our research shows that strategic supplier segmentation is one of the reasons for this differential advantage.

ACKNOWLEDGEMENT

The authors would like to thank the Sloan Foundation and the International Motor Vehicle Program at MIT for generously supporting this research.

APPENDIX

The sample consisted of three US (General Motors, Ford, Chrysler), two Japanese (Toyota, Nissan), and three Korean (Hyundai, Daewoo, Kia) automakers and a sample of their suppliers. Each automaker's purchasing department selected a representative sample of suppliers, which included both partners (i.e. *keiretsu/chaebol* suppliers) and non-partner (i.e. independent) suppliers. US automakers were asked to identify suppliers they felt were "most like a *keiretsu*" relationship. We interviewed sales and engineering vice-presidents at 70 suppliers (30 US, 20 Japanese, 20 Korean), during which the survey was developed and pretested. To minimize key-informant bias and follow the general recommendation to use the most knowledgeable informant (Kumar, Stern & Anderson, 1993), we asked the purchasing managers at each automaker to identify the supplier executive who was most responsible for managing the day-to-day relationship. This person was typically the supplier's sales vice-president, sales account manager, or in some cases, the president. The final survey was then sent to the key supplier informant identified by the automaker. Key informants had been employed at their respective organizations for an average of 16 years and thus had a long history of working with the automaker. Usable responses were obtained from 135 US (66% response rate), 101 Japanese (68% response rate) and 217 Korean (55% response rate) suppliers. The data collection was done between 1992 and 1994. The US and Japanese data were collected in 1992, reflecting data for 1991, and the Korean data were collected in 1994, reflecting data for 1993.

NOTES

1. Transaction or relation-specific investments are assets that are uniquely tailored to a particular exchange relationship and which have low salvage value outside of

the relationship. Williamson (1985) identified site, physical, human, and dedicated assets as four distinct types of transaction-specific investments.

2. We should note, however, that due to US pressure on Japanese automakers to open their markets and eliminate supplier exclusivity, the automaker has combined the two supplier associations into a single association.

3. Asanuma (1989) and Kamath & Liker (1994) have also noted that Japanese firms think about and manage different groups of suppliers somewhat differently; however, no previous studies have compared "partners" with "non-partners," nor have they been comparative with other countries.

4. However, while Toyota and Nissan were more likely to segment suppliers than their US and Korean counterparts, they did not realize the full benefits of the arms-length model due to an over-reliance on partnerships. This may explain why Nobeoka (1995) found that higher performing Japanese automakers were more likely to use more suppliers for a given component.

5. Complex products are defined as products/systems comprised of a large number of interdependent components, functions, and process steps (see Clark & Fujimoto, 1991, pp. 9–10).

6. However, we should note that supplier management practices at Chrysler have recently changed significantly in the direction of the partner model (Kamath & Liker, 1994; Dyer, 1996b).

REFERENCES

Asanuma, B. (1989). Manufacturer–supplier relationships in Japan and the concept of relation-specific skill. *Journal of the Japanese and International Economies*, **3**, 1–30.

Bresnen, M. & Fowler, C. (1994). The organizational correlates and consequences of subcontracting: evidence from a survey of South Wales businesses. *Journal of Management Studies*, **31**(6), 847–864.

Business Week (1994). Hardball is still GM's game. 8 August, 26–27.

Chung, J.-T. (1995). A study on the performances by configurations of assembler–supplier relationships in Korean auto industry, MA thesis, College of Business Administration, Seoul National University, Seoul, Korea.

Clark, K.B. & Fujimoto, T. (1991). *Product Development Performance*. Boston, MA: Harvard Business School Press.

Cusumano, M.A. (1985). *The Japanese Automobile Industry: Technology and Management at Nissan and Toyota*. Cambridge, MA: Harvard University: The Council on East Asian Studies.

Cusumano, M.A. & Takeishi, A. (1991). Supplier relations and management: a survey of Japanese, Japanese-transplant, and US auto plants. *Strategic Management Journal*, **12**, 563–588.

Dore, R. (1983). Goodwill and the spirit of market capitalism. *British Journal of Sociology*, **34**(4).

Dyer, J.H. & Ouchi, W.G. (1993). Japanese style business partnerships: giving companies a competitive edge. *Sloan Management Review*, **35**(1), 51–63.

Dyer, J.H. (1996a). Specialized supplier networks as a source of competitive advantage: evidence from the auto industry. *Strategic Management Journal*, **17**(4), 271–292.

Dyer, J.H. (1996b). How Chrysler created an American keiretsu. *Harvard Business Review*, July August, 42–56.

Emerson, R.M. (1962). Power-dependence relations. *American Sociological Review*, **27**, 31–40.

Fruin, W.M. (1992). *The Japanese Enterprise System*. New York: Oxford University Press.

Hannaford, W.J. (1983). *Systems Selling: A Marketing Guide for Wholesaler-Distributors*. Washington, DC: Distribution Research & Education Foundation.

Helper, S. (1991). How much has really changed between US automakers and their suppliers. *Sloan Management Review*, Summer.

Helper, S. & Sako, M. (1995). Supplier relations in Japan and the United States: Are they converging? *Sloan Management Review*, Spring, 77–84.

Kamath, R.R. & Liker, J.K. (1994). A second look at Japanese product development. *Harvard Business Review*, November/December, 154–170.

Kumar, N., Stern, L.W. & Anderson, J.C. (1993). Conducting interorganizational research using key informants. *Academy of Management Journal*, **36**(9), 1633–1651.

McMillan, J. (1990). Managing suppliers: incentive systems in the Japanese and US industry. *California Management Review*, Summer, 47–58.

Nishiguchi, T. (1994). *Strategic Industrial Sourcing*. New York: Oxford University Press.

Nobeoka, K. (1995). Benefits of quasi-market strategy within the assembler–supplier network: a case study in the Japanese automobile industry, discussion paper series no. 54, RIEB, Kobe University.

Oh, K.C. (1995). An international comparison of product development and supply systems in the automobile industry, research report 364, Korea Institute for Industrial Economics and Trade, Seoul, Korea.

Ouchi, W.G. (1984). *The M-Form Society*. New York: Avon Books.

Peterson, R. & Shimada, J.Y. (1978). Sources of Management problems in Japanese–American joint ventures. *Academy of Management Review*, October, 796–804.

Pfeffer, J. & Salancik, G. (1978). *The External Control of Organizations*. New York: Harper & Row.

Porter, M.E. (1980). *Competitive Strategy*. New York: Free Press.

Sako, M. (1991). The role of "trust" in Japanese buyer–supplier relationships. *Ricerche Economiche*, **XLV**(2–3), 449–474.

Sako, M. (1992). *Prices, Quality, and Trust*. Cambridge: Cambridge University Press.

Smith, R.J. (1983). *Japanese Society: Tradition, Self and the Social Order*. Cambridge: Cambridge University Press.

US Bureau of Census (1985). *Annual Survey of Manufacturers*. Washington, DC: US Government Printing Office.

Vayle, E.J. & Yoffie, D.B. (1991). *Collision Course in Commercial Aircraft: Boeing–Airbus–McDonnell Douglas — 1991 (A)*. Cambridge, MA: Harvard Business School Press.

Williamson, O.E. (1985). *The Economic Institutions of Capitalism*. New York: Free Press.

Womack, J.P., Jones, D.T. & Roos, D. (1990). *The Machine that Changed the World*. New York: Harper.

15

An Investigation of the Knowledge Structures of French and German Managers

STEVEN FLOYD, MICHAEL LUBATKIN, PANCHO NUNES, KARSTEN HEPPNER

INTRODUCTION

Is there a European style of management? Have managerial practices of the various European nations converged to some worldwide norms? Or do certain managerial practices within a nation persist, and come to represent a nation's "administrative heritage?" Will such differences in Europeans' perceptions about what it means to be a manager and how to organize interfere with attempts to form collaborative, inter-firm alliances across national borders? In this study, we explore the differences in the managerial knowledge structures of French and German middle managers to begin to answer these questions.

Mintzberg's (1973) work has become central to what is known today in the comparative management literature as the "universalist hypothesis." He argued that managers' jobs are remarkably similar from one setting to another and that the work of managers can therefore be usefully described by a common set of behaviors and attitudes. That is, at some basic level, people in organizations act and think similarly regardless of their

Strategic Flexibility: Managing in a Turbulent Environment. Edited by G. Hamel, C.K. Prahalad, H. Thomas and D. O'Neal.
Copyright © 1998 John Wiley & Sons Ltd.

nationality, and these similarities can be the basis for a generic theory of management. Support for the universalist hypothesis and its corollary, the "convergence hypothesis" is also found in the works of some organization theorists (Chandler, 1986) comparative labor economists (Dunlap *et al.*, 1975), and political scientists (Montgomery, 1986). The convergence hypothesis views a nation's level of industrialization as a key contingency factor; i.e. as a nation becomes more industrialized, its managers will naturally mimic or converge to some worldwide set of best practices, regardless of their home nation's culture. In contrast, the "divergence" hypothesis maintains that nations matter; that managerial work within a nation will partially reflect the culture and institutional routines of that nation, such that the variations in administrative heritages across nations will exceed the variation within nations (Calori *et al.*, 1997; Ghoshal & Bartlett, 1990).

This study extends past research efforts by comparing the knowledge structures of managers from the two leading nations in the push towards the consolidation of the European Union, i.e. French and German managers. Knowledge structures are particularly relevant in testing the two competing administrative hypotheses in general, and in the heritages of the German and French managers in specific, because both nations have been lead advocates of European consolidation. That is, faced with declining regulations and trade impediments, rising R&D costs, shortening product life cycles, growing barriers to market entry and an increasing need for global-scale economies, many politicians, economists and managers from France and Germany have been trying, in the words of Bartlett & Ghoshal (1995, p. 368), to "shift away from the all encompassing obsession with preemptive competition to a broader view of building competitive advantage through selective and often simultaneous reliance on both collaboration and competition." Thus, the central question in this study is whether there exists a common approach to organization and management between these two countries that would facilitate mutual understanding and integrative work efforts.

As a conceptual framework, we adapt Cohen & Levinthal's (1990) model of inter-organizational learning. Their three-dimensional concept "absorptive capacity" provides a basis to define the dimensions on which the knowledge structures of the French and German managers are to be compared. Absorptive capacity represents a useful way to understand the factors governing the potential for different organizations to collaborate and learn from one another. And, as a practical matter, inter-organizational learning—the exchange of knowledge about products, markets, "best practices," etc.—becomes the *raison d'être* for cross-border alliances. In short, this study will attempt to draw inferences about the collaborative potential of French and German managers by measuring the differences in perceptions of what they do (the technology of management), how they do it (underlying beliefs about management and organization), and why they do it (dominant commercial logics).

A NATIONALLY BOUND THEORY OF ADMINISTRATIVE HERITAGE

The premise that administrative heritage exists at the national level, and that beliefs about management and organization are associated with that heritage, can be deduced from the literature of organizational culture. Just as organizational culture is viewed as an outcome of a learning process, shaped by the shared history and experiences of an organization's members (Schein, 1985), so too is administrative heritage. For example, Aldrich, McKelvey & Ulrich (1984) assert that a firm learns from its experiences to repeat those behaviors that have previously led to favorable outcomes. They refer to this learning as "selective survivability of experiments in organizational design." Similarly, Nonaka (1994) describes organizational knowledge creation as an ongoing process by which managers converge or agree upon a limited set of administrative practices that have proved successful. According to his model, however, organizational practices are also judged by standards that "transcend factual or pragmatic considerations," such as value premises. Both views suggest the emergence of a set of important beliefs about management and organization that members of an organization share in common.

Organizational culture represents members' more universal beliefs about "how things ought to be" (Schein, 1985), while administrative heritage addresses members' more particular beliefs of "how things ought to be done" (Bjur & Zommorrodian, 1986). Moreover, the culture of an organization influences the characteristics of its heritage by prescribing the bounds of acceptable administrative inferences and practices. Indeed, some view the administrative practices that make up a firm's heritage as tangible, surface manifestations of an organizational culture (Denison, 1990, p. 32). Finally, the directionality of the influence can go both ways. For example, by changing some administrative practices, a firm can transform its members' "ought to be" beliefs about, among other things, risk-taking, cooperation, and autonomy (Schein, 1985).

Making the inferential leap from the level of organizational culture to administrative heritage at the national level, however, requires the assumption that "national culture" is a meaningful concept and that it is associated with the management of organizations. Underlying this assumption are two important issues for this study: one related to theory building— the link between national culture and administrative heritage—and the other methodological. With respect to theory, we can turn to two streams of work. First, there is a rich cross-cultural literature that views culture as having a nationally bound component (Adler, 1983; Hofstede, 1993, 1980). For example, Hofstede (1980) found that national culture explained 50% of the differences in managers' attitudes, beliefs and values, and therefore referred to the phenomenon as a "collective mental programming." Within the context of Nonaka's (1994) model, it seems reasonable to assert that national culture will significantly influence the value premises and normative standards that managers utilize when judging administrative practices. Further, Laurent (1983) found evidence that organization culture and firm-specific administrative heritage do not moderate or reduce the influence of national culture. He observed managers from the US and nine European countries, and found that national culture differences were at least as pronounced among managers working within the same multi-national firm as among managers working for firms from their native lands.

Secondly, there is a stream of work that suggests that the social and political institutions of a nation both shape, and are shaped by, the nation's culture (Chandler, 1990; Redding, 1994; Whitley, 1992). This helps to explain how institutions within a nation develop a distinct set of enduring routines that legitimizes certain ways of organizing and at the same time sets them apart from the accepted routines of other nations. Some theorists have drawn a linkage between these national routines and a firm's administrative practices by viewing institutions as the societal context in which a firm's practices develop (DiMaggio & Powell, 1983; Sorge & Maurice, 1990). As such, legitimized institutional routines that endure within a nation are both expressions of the nation's culture (or, value premises) *and* predictors of its firms' administrative heritage.

As to the methodological issue, the challenge is that no nation is likely to have a single, well-defined national culture. Indeed, it must be granted that cultural diversity exists within as well as between nations, particularly in relatively young countries like Germany, where immigration has recently accelerated. Still, numerous empirical studies have utilized nation-state as a measure for national culture (Adler, 1983), and many have found empirical support for this level of analysis (Very *et al.*, 1997). This is not to say that every manager in a nation has all the characteristics assigned to that culture, but rather that managers from the same nation, in a collective sense, will differ from those of another nation. Given, therefore, that national culture is a meaningful level of analysis, and that there is a convergence of institutional routines within nations, then the administrative heritages of firms from two nations will differ to the extent that their national cultures also differ.

We draw upon insight from cross-cultural studies and recent evidence from institutional investigations to develop predictions about the administrative heritages of two specific nations, France and Germany. Other nations could have been selected, but, as mentioned, these two nations have been the primary advocates of European consolidation. Also, there is enough accumulated data about these two cultures and their respective institutions to allow us to make some rough generalizations about their respective administrative heritages. Finally, the extant literature makes a compelling, albeit not always empirical, case that the values and practices of German and French firms are predictably different. Accordingly, if statistical tests for differences in managerial perceptions across nations are significant, we feel comfortable in ascribing such differences to the effects of national administrative heritage.

We will detail these differences, for they will serve as the basis of our study's national-bound administrative heritage hypotheses. Before doing so, however, it is necessary to define what we mean by administrative heritage because, to date, there has been little consensus as to how to operationalize the concept. Some define it in terms of planning (Hart, 1992), organizing (Bartlett & Ghoshal, 1995), or controlling activities (Gupta & Govindarajan, 1991). Field researchers focus on how managers allocate their time across various activities (Mintzberg, 1973), while cognitive researchers try to uncover the meaning that managers ascribe to their activities (Nonaka, 1994). Grounded theory researchers try to describe the underlying processes associated with managerial work (Burgleman, 1983).

While consistent with many of these, our definition of administrative heritage focuses on elements of organization and management that are related to the potential for inter-organizational learning. Cohen & Levinthal define absorptive capacity as a firm's ability to "recognize" the value of new, external knowledge, assimilate it, and apply it to commercial ends (Cohen & Levinthal, 1990, p. 128). This definition succinctly captures the steps involved in the interfirm learning process. First, for information to be successfully exchanged (i.e. absorbed), at least one of the participants involved in the exchange must be familiar enough with the "know-whats," or the other's technical knowledge, to appreciate the value embedded within it. For example, a theory in physics only has meaning to someone who already has enough background in that science to "talk the same language." Second, one of the partners must also understand the "know-hows," the other's routines or problem solving behaviors, to appreciate the thought processes underlying the other's knowledge. The firm must not only be able to recite the theory, but also understand how it was derived. Third, a partner must appreciate the "know-whys," the other's vision or dominant commercial logic underlying the knowledge base. The firm should not only be able to understand the derivation of a theory, but also how it can be applied to solve practical problems.

The determinants of absorptive capacity are essentially equivalent to the dimensions of managerial knowledge structures in that the former is nothing more than a special case of the latter. Put differently, for collaboration to occur between managers from two different nations, the capacity for successful knowledge transfer must be present. Accordingly, we adopted these three dimensions in attempting to capture the aspects of management and organization that would be related to absorptive capacity.

CULTURAL DIFFERENCES AND ADMINISTRATIVE HERITAGE

Based on the work of Hofstede (1980) and others, there is a strong consensus that the French, as a culture, express a higher acceptance of *power distance* than the Germans. Power distance refers to the degree to which power differences are deemed acceptable by society. A high acceptance of power difference reflects a societal belief that there "should be" a well-defined order in which everyone has a rightful place. For example, Laurent (1983) found that French managers view organizations as a formal pyramid of differentiated levels of power. The managerial ranks represent an elite social group, or *cadre*, to which one belongs as a result of attending the proper schools and in which one remains "forever."

In contrast, formal German organizations rely less on the use of hierarchical authority than do the French, and there is little expectation that managers should motivate and control workers. Instead, management is viewed as part of every German's job. Distinctions between managerial and worker classes in German organizations are minimized by the fact that "Germans simply do not have a very strong concept of management" as a unique social grouping (Lawrence, 1994). Like the "working class" employee, the president of a German firm is likely to have worked as an apprentice, and the managers' ascent up the hierarchy is far more likely to come from hard work and superior technical knowledge than from attendance in elite schools. Indeed, the German system of industrial democracy insures that workers are very much involved in management.

The French have also been shown to have a greater need for *uncertainty avoidance* than the Germans, i.e. they less willingly accept ambiguity and risk, although this difference is not as pronounced as the difference in power distance. Hofstede (1980) found the French scoring moderately high, while the Germans scored in the middle of the 53 nations studied. Perret (1982) found French managers to be preoccupied with absolute accuracy for all control indicators. Consistent with this, Broussard & Maurice (1974) found that the French have more rules, more staff and more departmentalization than the Germans. The French firm also relied much more on bureaucratic as opposed to face-to-face coordination than the German firm (Sorge & Warner, 1978). Schneider (1985) found that the French place a high premium on work rules, even at the expense of entrepreneurial behaviors. Rules are important in Germany, too, but the German system of rules is much less about work instructions and much more about assuring that everyone is treated fairly. German workers are expected to solve technical problems on their own, without direction from staff or management (Kieser, 1994).

The linkage of power distance and uncertainty avoidance with administrative heritage can be inferred from the works of Punnet & Ricks (1992) and Hofstede (1980). Both posit that firms from high power distance, high uncertainty avoidance nations will rely on centralized planning and controlling systems, such that power and influence reside at the hierarchical top. In these nations, centralization tends to be viewed by all members of an organization as the way "things ought to be done" because power, privilege, and respect are naturally ascribed to those at the top. Centralization also tends to be viewed by top managers as necessary to gain control over uncertainties; they would rather not delegate the responsibility for key business decisions, nor do the subordinate managers expect that they would. It follows from the cross-cultural literature that French managers, because of their higher need for power distance and uncertainty avoidance, will rely more on formal authority than will German managers.

Supporting evidence comes from the institutional literature: those who have compared the social and political institutions in these two countries find that decentralization appears to be a more legitimate means of control among German institutions while centralized routines have endured among French institutions. Large, integrated industrial organizations developed early in the twentieth century in France, while Germany continued to rely on a loose system of guilds and middlemen to coordinate production (Lawrence, 1994). Although the guilds became increasingly dependent on the merchants to market their products and to define quality, otherwise they were run as autonomous businesses. The Germans' tradition of craft work and guilds leaves them with very little appreciation for the importance of planning or strategy (Lawrence, 1994), much less the need to centralize such activity. In France, however, the tradition of centralization is deeply embedded. As Calori *et al.* (1997) point out, the belief in a strong, centralized administrative philosophy is part of the French "heritage." It was reflected in the way that King Louis XIV (1661–1715) ruled the French empire; in the ideologies of the "Jacobins" who inspired the French revolution (1783–1799); in the state government of Napoleon I (1804–1815); and in the way that the French managed their colonial empire. It is even evident in the philosophies of Descartes (*Le Discours de la Methode*, 1637) and Compte (*Cours de Philosophie Positive*, 1850), who developed the principle of the "hierarchy of knowledge," a principle that to this day has had a profound effect on the style of pedagogy used at French schools. At the firm level, the French attitude toward centralized planning is best exemplified by the work of Henri Fayol (1918), whom many consider the founder of business planning.

Finally, the French appear to have approximately the same needs for *individualism* but lower levels of *aggressiveness* than do the Germans (Hofstede, 1980). Individualism, and its opposite, collectivism, refer to the degree to which the society emphasizes the role of the individual versus the group. Aggressiveness, and its opposite, nurturing, refer to the degree to which a society prefers the stereotypical masculine values of competitiveness, assertiveness, and ambition, as opposed to a more nurturing, caring-for-others set of values. Tying these values to socialization controls, Punnet & Ricks (1992) and Hofstede (1980) posit that in more aggressive nations such as Germany, firms will rely more on formal incentives, which encourage individuals to compete, while in more nurturing nations such as France, firms will emphasize more informal, social controls, which value and preserve social relationships. And, in comparison to the French, who are well known for their emphasis on relationship building as a part of doing business, the German's are well known for formality in their business interactions. This tendency also results in fully specified work relationships and very weak informal systems within German organizations. In Germany, there are no "grey areas" (Lawrence, 1994).

In summary, the cross-cultural literature finds that the French show higher acceptance for power distance and uncertainty avoidance than the Germans. The evidence also suggests that French institutions have legitimated a set of administrative routines (centralized authority, bureaucratic planning, control) that are fully consistent with these cultural preferences. German institutions have had a similar effect on managerial preferences, but different institutional arrangements have led to somewhat opposite inclinations in their administrative practice (decentralization of authority, avoidance of bureaucratic work controls). Interestingly, the importance of maintaining warm interpersonal relationships in France has a humanizing effect on their work organizations, making centralized authority and bureaucratic controls more tolerable (Calori *et al.*, 1997). Greater distribution of authority and less bureaucracy in German organizations, on the other hand, has likely increased opportunities for other forms of intrinsic satisfaction (e.g. autonomy), thereby reducing the need for the softening effect of informal social relationships.

IMPACT OF NATIONAL DIFFERENCES ON COLLABORATIVE POTENTIAL

TABLE 15.1 summarizes how cultural differences between France and Germany are expected to affect the three dimensions of administrative heritage associated with managerial knowledge structures. As the table shows, the effects of differences in power distance, uncertainty avoidance,

TABLE 15.1 Cultural differences and administrative heritage in France and Germany

Culture	Dimensions of administrative heritage		
	"Know-whats"	"Know-hows"	"Know-whys"
Power distance	French managers seen as a professional "cadre" versus German managers seen as workers who excelled at doing the work	French reliance on hierarchy/authority versus German reliance on decentralization/autonomy	French emphasis on differentiation/superior position versus German emphasis on quality/efficiency
Uncertainty avoidance	French managers seen as controllers of work flow versus German managers seen as teachers of technical skills	French reliance on bureaucratic staff versus German reliance on individuals' knowledge of work	French emphasis on planning as a centralized activity versus German emphasis on planning as part of operations
Aggressiveness	French managers seen as social leaders versus German managers seen as task leaders	French reliance on informal social system to accomplish work versus German reliance on the formal definition of work relationships	French emphasis on social identifications at work versus German emphasis on identification with the work itself

and aggressiveness suggest differences in how managers in Germany and France perceive what managers do ("know-whats"), how work is organized ("know-hows"), and the commercial logic behind work organizations ("know-whys"). In order to clarify these expected differences, the table may appear to overstate the magnitude of such differences, in some ways putting German and French management at opposite ends of theoretical continua (centralization–decentralization, formality–informality, controllers–teachers, planning–operations). It is not our intention to posit sharp, absolute distinctions, but rather, to capture the relative differences or tendencies in how the French and Germans perceive these aspects of their administrative heritage.

As the table shows, greater acceptance of power distance in France is expected to show up in a sharper notion of management as a separate and more elite profession than in Germany. In addition, because uncertainty avoidance tends to be higher in France, we expect that French managers will perceive themselves first and foremost as controllers of the work flow. The German tradition of craft work, however, should reduce the role of management in controlling the work of others, and in the tradition of apprenticeship; German managers are more likely to see themselves more as teachers. Coupled with a more technical orientation, higher levels of aggressiveness are expected to increase German managers' perceptions of management as task leadership. The value that French managers place on warm relationships, on the other hand, is likely to increase their perception that management has an important social dimension.

More acceptance for power distance and higher levels of uncertainty avoidance are likely to affect French managers' beliefs about how organizations ought to be managed. In the French mind, the key principles underlying how one manages rest on centralized decision making, formal authority and bureaucratic controls. Taken together, these are the key characteristics of the mechanistic form, or what Mintzberg refers to as the machine bureaucracy (Mintzberg, 1973). Lower on both power distance and uncertainty avoidance, Germans' beliefs about organization are more like those of the traditional guild, where coordination relies on the technical knowledge of workers themselves. In modern organizational theory, this configuration is comparable to the professional form (Morgan, 1989), where workers are given relatively more autonomy in applying their knowledge to the task. Rather than being forced to conform to process or outcome standards defined by staff members, workers are more likely to create their own standards and coordinate their activities face-to-face. More personal coordination of work does not necessarily lead to the development of strong interpersonal ties, however. It is the French who are more likely to see work organization as comprised of networks of informal relationships.

Consistent with their organizational ideology and their tendency to value general knowledge over technical skill, the French are likely to see the dominant logic of economic enterprise as an important point of focus and centralized control. Germans, on the other hand, value technical knowledge more and are thus much more likely to think about economic logic in terms of operational efficiency and technical quality. Taking Porter's (1980) framework as a guide to our speculation on this point, if the French are less operationally and technically oriented, then they may be more market and differentiation oriented. Put differently, the focus of French strategists is on achieving differentiated market position. The French also appear to perceive social relationships at work as an end in themselves, and hence social identification may be a fundamental part of the enterprise logic in France. Germans, on the other hand, would appear more likely to identify with the work product itself.

METHODOLOGY

RESEARCH DESIGN

Although previous research provides many clues about how institutional and cultural differences may affect the way managers in the two countries perceive managerial and organizational processes, the theory is far from definitive. As we have already observed, the links we have drawn are no more than tendencies at this point, and it is impossible to discern with any certainty the extent to which causal mechanisms are at work. Indeed, the measures we developed to assess managers' perceptions are themselves grounded in institutional forces, and the relationships identified may in part be a function of the interconnectedness of historical circumstances or third-variable causation. However, research in applied areas cannot always await definitive theory.

This study was thus designed to be exploratory, rather than confirmatory, utilizing existing theory on inter-organizational collaboration as a conceptual framework. With this intent as a launching pad, the research design explores expected relationships as a basis for building new theory. To some, the use of a questionnaire in a theory-building study may seem problematic, but our approach is entirely consistent with the discussion of inductive theory-building. Indeed, a data collection procedure based on questionnaires offers the advantages of anonymity and large numbers, and is well suited for studies where the goal is to measure managerial perceptions.

It is important to emphasize that perceptions—in addition to "objective reality"—are a critical factor in assessing the potential for inter-organizational collaboration. Whether or not managers' perceptions accurately reflect their organizational setting or, for that matter, their own behavior, perceptions are crucial in the way they approach learning. For example, even if a particular German organization *in fact* has a strong informal organization (contrary to its administrative heritage), a manager in the organization who believes informality to be unimportant will have difficulty learning from a French organization where managers believe that informal relationships are central. In short, perceptions are the basis of belief, and accepting new beliefs is the process of learning.

DATA COLLECTION

We obtained the cooperation of two highly respected business schools (Ecole Supérior de Commerce de Lyon and Universitat zu Köln). Using a list of recent participants in their programs, a questionnaire containing the study's key constructs was mailed to 545 and 481 French and German managers, respectively. Management professors at the cooperating institutions also translated the original English version of the survey into French and German. Then, to minimize differences in meaning across settings, the surveys were retranslated into English and compared with the original version.

We received 370 responses, 169 from French managers after two mailings, or an overall response rate of 31% (21% after first mailing), and 101 from German managers after one mailing, or, like the first mailing to the French managers, a 21% response rate. We think that these response rates are reasonably good given the number of constructs contained in the questionnaire and its eight-page length.

MEASURES

In developing survey measures for the three dimensions of collaborative potential, we had two goals in mind. First, it was important that the measures were true to the dimensions of absorptive capacity as articulated by Cohen & Levinthal (1990). Second, given the exploratory character of this research, our preference was to include the largest number of items for each dimension that was consistent with a questionnaire of reasonable length. Therefore, each of the three sets of items analyzed in this study was adopted from previously developed instruments with as little modification as possible. The "know-whats" or managerial skill items were taken from a questionnaire developed by Vengroff, Magrondi & Montgomery (1987). Because we were not assessing matched pairs of organizations directly for their absorptive capacity, it was impossible to measure specific technologies;

instead we measured managers, perceptions about how the generic technology of management was used within their organization, based on Montgomery's (1986) definitions of managerial work. Coming from the discipline of public administration, Montgomery was interested in identifying all the skills that might be required by a manager to perform his or her administrative duties. He developed this list with the financial assistance of the US Agency of International Development, a critical incident method, and 40 research assistants. Each assistant observed at least one manager at his or her place of employment for between five and ten days. The assistant kept a diary of all the tasks that the manager did which were deemed either to be of special importance or that required at least one hour to complete. In all, a list of 3055 events was compiled, which was inductively classified by Montgomery and his research team into 44 skill requirements. Montgomery (1986) then converted each content valid skill requirement into a questionnaire item using a 5-point Likert scale based on how frequently each skill is required by the managerial job, and then provided partial validation of this list in Vengroff, Belhaj & Ndiaye (1991).

The "know-hows," or 35 items assessing organizational values, beliefs and norms, were taken from definitions of organizational culture by Very *et al.* (1997), Hofstede (1980), Bond (1987), and Denison (1990). This part of the survey was intended to assess the principles underlying the more observable managerial activities. More specifically, each manager was asked to respond on a 5-point Likert scale, in terms of each item's perceived importance in how an organization "ought to be." Finally, the "know-whys," or 19 items measuring dominant commercial logics, were taken from an operationalization of Porter's (1980) competitive strategy model. These measures have been used in many previous studies, and they have been shown to offer a generic, economic rationale for firm conduct at the business-unit level (Segev, 1989).

RESULTS AND DISCUSSION

The focus of this study is to test the validities of the two competing hypotheses about managerial work; i.e. universalist and divergence, by determining what areas of managerial knowledge, if any, differentiate French and German managers. To do so, we wanted first to control for any differences in our data that might be driven by factors extraneous to the two national administrative heritages. We therefore established measures for three possible covariates: industry sector, size, and hierarchical level. We measured industry sector according to whether the primary business of the organization was to provide a service or to manufacture a product. We measured size as the total number of employees in the organization. Like industry sector, prior research suggests that size may be an important determinant of managerial perceptions, organizational structure, and firm strategy. Finally, we measured hierarchical level (lower, lower-middle, upper-middle, top management) for each respondent because this could also affect managerial perceptions.

We then used a series of three stepwise logistic regression analyses, entering the set of the three covariate measures in a hierarchical manner, to identify which items from each of the three dimensions of managerial knowledge were the best differentiators between French and German managers. This non-parametric procedure is not reductionist as is factor analysis, and therefore well suited for exploratory investigations. Specifically, the stepwise logistic regressions produce a "map" of the most salient differences on each of the three dimensions ("know-whats," know-hows," "know-whys"), while removing items from the analysis whose association with the dependent variable (i.e. French or German) is not significant ($p < 0.10$). Finally, we examined these differences for consistency with the expectations in TABLE 15.1.

As TABLE 15.2 shows, fewer than half of the items in each dimensions remain (20 of 42 "know-whats," 13 of 35 "know-hows," 3 of 19 "know-whys") as a result of the analysis, yet the accuracy with which respondents are correctly classified by the equations are 90.6, 86.0 and 73.7%, respectively, and all highly significant ($p < 0.001$). Although they are not statistical estimates of parameters in the population of all French and German managers, these percentages do suggest that there are systematic differences in the perceptions of our respondents, with each of the three dimensions of managerial knowledge structures, even after controlling in a hierarchical manner for industry sector, size, and hierarchical level. Thus, we find strong statistical evidence to reject the universalist hypothesis and its corollary hypothesis about convergence.

Further, the overall pattern shown by the signs of the regression coefficients (negative sign predicts France, positive sign predicts Germany) aligns with the expectations in TABLE 15.1. For example, TABLE 15.3 (i) summarizes differences that appear in the "know-whats." Items under the French column appear as expected to reflect greater acceptance of power distance, higher uncertainty avoidance, and lower aggressiveness. That is, these factors seem to foster perceptions on the part of the French that managers should rely more on bureaucratic controls, centralization, and an emphasis on community relationships. Also as expected. German perceptions (controlling for their level in the hierarchy) anticipate a wider distribution of decision-making authority, on the other hand, as indicated by higher responses to items like analyzing policy options, determining priorities, negotiating with representatives of other organizations, and considering organizational direction in the light of economic trends. It also appears that Germans focus more on operational resources and the application of rules in management while the French see management more in terms of bureaucratic and financial controls.

TABLE 15.3 (ii) summarizes the differences in the "know-hows" of managerial knowledge. Once again as expected, the French appear to believe more than Germans that organizations should narrow salary gaps, provide life-time job security, and contribute to the cultural enrichment of employees. Such egalitarian attitudes have been linked to the preservation of social harmony and are thus consistent with lower levels of aggressiveness among the French. In addition, higher levels of uncertainty avoidance are consistent with the French perception that organizations should use bureaucratic controls, such as clear measures of performance, to monitor individual behavior and limit risk taking to the managerial ranks. Consistent with lower power distance values, however, the German managers in this sample believe more than French managers that organizations should delegate decision making authority to the lowest possible levels and allow managers to adopt their own unique approach to work.

Finally, TABLE 15.3 (iii) summarizes the differences in the dominant commercial logic, or "know-whys" of managerial knowledge. The tradition of guilds and greater emphasis on the technical side of management shows clearly in the German belief in using the latest technology and focusing on special market needs. The French item which shows up in this category— compensating employees at above-average levels—is generally associated with a differentiation or market-oriented strategy.

There are also items in TABLE 15.3 that cannot be explained in terms of cultural differences and items that are contrary to the expectations outlined earlier. The latter include the German sample's apparent preference for bending the rules to achieve organizational objectives ("know-whats"), the French emphasis on arguing with upper managers over resource constraints ("know-whats"), and the German belief in giving attention to employees' personal problems ("know-hows"). Thus, our findings are not entirely consistent with the predicted comparisons of managerial knowledge in France and Germany. However, these inconsistencies with out expectations may themselves be interesting, because they suggest not a possible revision in how we think about the French and Germans, but rather in how they think about themselves. Recall that our questionnaire was intended to capture perceptions of reality and not some objective truth. The fact that the German managers indicated that they frequently "bent the rules to achieve organizational objectives," does not necessarily mean that the Germans actually "bend the rules" more than the French, and, indeed, the opposite may be true. "Frequently" is a relative concept, scaled by the eyes of the beholder. As such, what may be perceived as frequent to a German manager on this item of rule-bending might be perceived as infrequent to the French.

TABLE 15.2 Logistic regression results

Variable	"Know-whats"	"Know-hows"	"Know-whys"
Controls			
Industry sector	−1.073	−0.772	−0.886**
Organization size	0.578*	0.707**	0.833***
Level in hierarchy	1.837*	0.754*	0.450
Managerial activities			
Setting goals for an organization or unit	−0.898*		
Coping with unexpected conditions/events	−1.124**		
Analyzing policy options	1.154**		
Becoming involved with local social activities	1.757***		
Determining priorities in assigned tasks	0.831*		
Writing clear/concise official reports	−1.067**		
Conveying organizational goals to the outside world	−1.244**		
Applying detailed rules/regulations	0.773*		
Handling monetary resources to stay within project costs	−0.757*		
Negotiating with representatives of other organizations	1.493***		
Managing resources efficiently	0.856*		
Analyzing data	−0.6451		
Bending the rules to achieve organizational objectives	0.921**		
Developing good relationships with the local community	−1.583***		
Organizing resources/services to minimize operating costs	1.783***		
Arguing with upper managers over resource constraints	−1.373***		
Keeping accurate financial transactions records	−1.318***		
Being listened to/followed by subordinates	−0.976**		
Dealing with politicians at local/regional/national level	1.578**		
Considering organizational directions in light of economic trends	1.151**		

Organizational values/beliefs/norms			
Contributing to the cultural enrichment of employees		-0.931**	
Using clear measures to judge individual performance		-0.723*	
Increasing ethnic/racial diversity in the workforce		0.643**	
Being responsive to concerns of local community		0.644*	
Challenging people to give their best effort		-1.315**	
Narrowing gap between lowest/highest salary levels		-0.924**	
Providing life-time job security for all employees		-0.722**	
Delegating decision-making authority to lowest possible levels		1.291***	
Allowing a manager to adopt his/her own unique approach to the job		1.075**	
Allowing managers to take risks		-1.303***	
Encouraging competition among individuals		0.639*	
Communicating how each person's work contributes to overall objectives		-0.994**	
Giving attention to employees' personal problems		1.040**	
Dominant commercial logic			
Using the latest technology			0.664**
Compensating employees at above-average levels			-0.821***
Focusing on special market needs			0.552**
Constant	-8.348**	1.612	-4.533***
Chi-square	167.91	106.45	29.456
	(p < 0.000)	(p < 0.000)	(p < 0.000)
Percentage correctly classified	90.63%	85.99%	73.71%
DF	20	13	3

N = 270 (France = 169; Germany = 101).
DV: 0 = France; 1 = Germany.

TABLE 15.3 Contrasting perceptions of French and German managers

French perceptions	German perceptions
(i) Know-whats (logistic regression correctly classified 91% of cases): managerial skills	
Setting goals for organization or unit	Analyzing policy options
Coping with unexpected conditions/events	Determining priorities in assigned tasks
Writing clear/concise official reports	Applying detailed rules/regulations
Handling monetary resources to stay within project costs	Negotiating with representatives of other organizations
Developing good relationships with local community	Managing resources efficiently
Keeping accurate financial transactions records	Organizing resources/services to minimize operating costs
Being listened to/followed by subordinates	Dealing with politicians at the local/regional/national level
Arguing with upper managers over resource constraints	Considering organization direction in light of economic trends
	Bending rules to achieve organizational objectives
(ii) Know-hows (logistic regression correctly classified 86% of cases): "ought to be"s	
Contributing to cultural enrichment of employees	Increasing ethnic/racial diversity in workforce
Providing life-time job security for all employees	Being responsive to concerns of local community
Communicating how each person's work contributes to overall objectives	Delegating decision-making authority to lowest levels
	Allow a manager to adopt his/her own unique approach to the job
Using clear measures to judge individual performance	Encouraging competition among individuals
Challenging people to give best effort	Giving attention to employees' personal problems
Narrowing gap between lowest/highest salary levels	
(iii) Know-whys (logistic regression correctly classified 74% of cases): commercial logics	
Compensate employees at above-average levels	Using latest technology
	Focusing on special market needs

The purpose of this research, however, was not to build a comparative model of objective reality. Rather, it was to compare the perceptions that French and German managers hold about their own knowledge structures, and to see whether any of these were traceable to differences in national culture or institutional heritage. The fact that such differences do appear suggests that inter-organizational collaborations, such as commercial joint ventures, between the two countries are likely to face significant challenges along at least three dimensions. These challenges are made more acute because they seem to be traceable to deeply rooted historically dependent predispositions about which managers may be only dimly aware. Of course, given the scope of this study, we can only infer that these perceptual differences actually translate into collaborative impediments. This unexplored issue represents fertile directions for future investigations, particularly with the expanding number of strategic alliances now being completed by firms from the two countries.

REFERENCES

Adler, N.J. (1983). Cross-cultural management research: the ostrich and the trend. *Academy of Management Review*, 8(2), 226–232.

Aldrich, H., McKelvey, W. & Ulrich, D. (1984). Design strategy from the population ecology perspective. *Journal of Management*, 10, 67–86.

Bartlett, C.A. & Ghoshal, S. (1995). *Transnational Management: Texts, Cases and Readings in Cross-Border Management*. Homewood, IL: Irwin.

Bond, M. (1987). Chinese values and the search for culture-free dimensions of culture. *Journal of Cross-Cultural Psychology*, 18(2), 143–164.

Bjur, W. & Zommorrodian, A. (1986). Towards indigenous theories of administration: an international perspective. *International Review of Administration Science*, 52, 397–420.

Broussard, M. & Maurice, M. (1974). Existe-t-il un modele universel des structures d'organization. *Sociologie du Travail*, XVI(4).

Burgleman, R. (1983). A model of the interaction of strategic behavior, corporate context, and the concept of strategy. *Academy of Management Review*, 8, 61–70.

Calori, R., Lubatkin, M., Very, P. & Veiga, J. (1997). Modelling the origins of nationally-bound administrative heritages: a historical institutional analysis of French and British firms. *Organization Science*, 8(6), 681–696.

Chandler, A. (1986). The evolution of modern global competition. In M. Porter (ed.) *Competition in Global Industries*. Boston, MA: Harvard Business School Press.

Chandler, A.D. (1990). *Scale and Scope, the Dynamics of Industrial Capitalism*. Cambridge, MA: Belknap Press.

Cohen, W. & Levinthal, D. (1990). Absorptive capacity: a new perspective on learning and innovation. *Administrative Science Quarterly*, 35, 128–152.

Denison, D. (1990). *Corporate Culture and Organizational Effectiveness*. New York: Free Press.

Di Maggio, P.J. & Powell, W.W. (1983). The iron cage revisited: institutional isomorphism and collective rationality in organizational fields. *American Sociological Review*, 48, 147–160.

298 *An Investigation of the Knowledge Structures of French and German Managers*

Dunlap, J., Harbison, F., Kerr, C. & Meyers, C. (1975). *Industrialism and Industrial Man Reconsidered*. Princeton, NJ: Inter-University Study of Human Resources.

Fayol, H. (1918). *Administration Industrielle et Générale*. Paris: Dunod.

Ghoshal, S. & Bartlett, C. (1990). The multinational corporation as an inter-organizational network. *Academy of Management Review*, **15**(4), 603–625.

Gupta, A. & Govindarajan, V. (1991). Knowledge flows and the structure of control within multinational corporations. *Academy of Management Review*, **16**(4), 768–792.

Hart, S. (1992). An integrative framework for strategy-making process. *Academy of Management Review*, **17**(2), 327–351.

Hofstede, G. (1993). Cultural constraints in management theories. *Academy of Management Executive*, **7**(1), 81–94.

Hofstede, G. (1980). Motivation, leadership and organization: do American theories apply abroad? *Organizational Dynamics*, **9**(1), 42–63.

Kieser, A. (1994). Why organization theory needs historical analyses—and how this should be performed. *Organization Science*, **5**(4), 608–620.

Laurent, A. (1983). The cultural diversity of western conceptions of management. *International Studies of Management and Organizations*, **13**(1/2), 75–96.

Lawrence, P. (1994). German management: at the interface between eastern and western Europe. In R. Calori & P. DeWoot (eds) *A European Management Model: Beyond Diversity*. London: Prentice Hall.

Mintzberg, H. (1973). *Managerial Work*. New York: Harper & Row.

Montgomery, J. (1986). Levels of managerial leadership in southern Africa. *Journal of Developing Areas*, **21**, 15–30.

Morgan, G. (1989). *Creative Organization Theory*, Newbury Park, CA: Sage.

Nonaka, I. (1994). A dynamic theory of organizational knowledge creation. *Organization Science*, **5**(1), 14–37.

Perret, M.S. (1982). The impact of cultural differences on budgeting, unpublished PhD dissertation, University of Western Ontario.

Porter, M. (1980). *Competitive Strategy*. New York: Free Press.

Punnet, B. & Ricks, D. (1992). *International Business*, Boston, MA: PWS-Kent.

Redding, S.G. (1994). Comparative management theory: jungle, zoo or fossil bed? *Organizational Studies*, **15**(3), 323–359.

Schein, E.H. (1985). *Organizational Culture and Leadership: A Dynamic View*. San Francisco, CA: Jossey-Bass.

Schneider, S.C. (1985). Strategy formulation: the impact of national culture: the case of France, presented at the Northeast regional meeting of the Academy of International Business, March, Boston, MA.

Segev, E. (1989). A systematic comparative analysis and synthesis of two business level strategic typologies. *Strategic Management Journal*, **10**(5), 487–505.

Sorge, A. & Maurice, M. (1990). The societal effect in strategies and competitiveness of machine tool manufacturers in France and West Germany. *International Journal of Human Resource Management*, **1**(2), 141–172.

Sorge A. & Warner, M. (1978). Manufacturing organization and work roles in Great Britain and West Germany, discussion paper of the International Institute of Management, Berlin.

Vengroff, R., Magrondji, J. & Montgomery, J. (1987). *Country training plan: Central African Republic, NASPAA country training plan design team report prepared for the Agency for International Development*, California Polytechnic University, Ponoma.

Vengroff, R., Belhaj, M. & Ndiaye, M. (1991). The nature of managerial work in the public sector: an African perspective. *Public Administration and Development*, **11**, 95–110.

Very, P., Lubatkin, M., Calori, R. & Veiga, J. (1997). Relative standing and the performance of recently acquired European firms. *Strategic Management Journal*, **18**(8), 593–615.

Whitley, R. (1992). *European Business Systems, Firms and Markets in their National Contexts*. London: Sage.

Competence

Kenneth Andrews was among the early proponents of what he referred to as distinctive competence: "The distinctive competence of an organization is more than what it can do; it is what it can do particularly well" (*The Concept of Corporate Strategy*, 1987 [1971], p. 47). Andrews suggested that firms should "identify the skills that underlie whatever success has been achieved" (1987, p. 48), and "find or create a competence that is truly distinctive." (1987, p. 48).

The fact that "The core competence of the corporation" (C.K. Prahalad and Gary Hamel, *Harvard Business Review*, May/June, 1990) has become one of the most-requested *Harvard Business Review* articles ever printed may attest to the continued and, indeed, increasing perception of the importance of this concept. Prahalad and Hamel define core competencies as "the collective learning in the organization, ... harmonizing streams of technology, ... the organization of work and the delivery of value" (1990, p. 82), and suggest that developing core competencies is the key to competitiveness. The chapters in this section lend credence to the critical nature of firms' competences.

Arguing that the competence concept has more to offer than the resource-based view, Durand develops a renewed model of competence, in which competence describes a firm's capability to combine, bundle and integrate resources into products and services.

Garvis and Bogner propose a decision model, based on dynamic competence theory, for use by MNCs in determining optimal organization form. The authors argue that learning benefits and costs arising from development and dispersement of firm competencies better explain organizational structure decisions than do transaction-cost and knowledge-based models.

McGrath empirically tests the idea that idiosyncratic competitive advantage, represented by rent potential, is a consequence of emerging competence, and of a firm's innovativeness in differentiating itself from its competitors through efficiency, distinctive value, or customer relationships.

Volberda and Baden-Fuller suggest that all organizations face a paradox between renewal and preservation, and identify four mechanisms by which multi-unit firms accumulate and dissipate new skills and capabilities to match firm-level distinctive competences with industry-level sources of competitive advantage. These mechanisms are selection, hierarchy, time, and networks.

Chapter 16 Revisiting Key Dimensions of Competence
Thomas Durand

Chapter 17 Structure Decisions and the Multinational Enterprise: A Dynamic Competence Perspective
Dennis M. Garvis, William C. Bogner

Chapter 18 Discovering Strategy: Competitive Advantage from Idiosyncratic Experimentation
Rita Gunther McGrath

Chapter 19 Strategic Renewal and Competence Building: Four Dynamic Mechanisms
Henk W. Volberda, Charles Baden-Fuller

16

The Alchemy of Competence

Thomas Durand

In medieval times, alchemists were seeking to turn base metals into gold. Today managers and firms seek to turn resources and assets into profit. A new form of alchemy is needed in the organization. Let's call it competence.

INTRODUCTION

The resource-based theory of the firm arose after the work of Penrose (1959) and was developed by Wernerfelt (1984), Rumelt (1984), Barney (1986), Collis (1991), Amit & Schoemaker (1993), Grant (1996) and several other contributions. This model very rightly pointed out that the firm's performance is not just the result of the external environment in the competitive game (Porter's five forces, external positioning etc.); the firm's performance also varies according to the resources tapped and leveraged by the organization to satisfy clients' needs in the marketplace.

Interestingly enough, the resource-based view of the firm did not really raise any interest among practitioners until Prahalad & Hamel (1990) published their core competence piece, as Wernefelt (1995) suggests.

This clearly stressed that a unique combination of core competencies can indeed generate a truly competitive advantage. In addition, Prahalad & Hamel (1990) suggested a re-think of strategy in terms of competence rather than for organizational strategic business units (SBUs). The resource-based view led to a knowledge-based perspective (Conner & Prahalad, 1996;

Strategic Flexibility: Managing in a Turbulent Environment. Edited by G. Hamel, C.K. Prahalad, H. Thomas and D. O'Neal.
Copyright © 1998 John Wiley & Sons Ltd.

Kogut & Zander, 1996). More recently an attempt was made to build a theory of competence-based strategy. The term competence is meant here to enlarge the concept of resource while building on the resource-based perspective.

Prahalad & Hamel's (1990) core competencies led to Hamel & Heene (1994) and Sanchez, Heene & Thomas (1996), as well as to the Heene & Sanchez (1997) and Sanchez & Heene (1997) volumes.

One of the key intents of this chapter is to discuss why we think that the competence concept has something more to offer than the resource-based view, bringing into the picture the "organizational alchemy" that is necessary to properly leverage the resources and assets at hand.

In any case, the line of reasoning behind the resource/competence-based view of the firm remains essentially as follows: the firm taps sources of resources and assets and combines these into products and services for the clients through *ad hoc* management processes taking place within the organization. We choose to use the generic word competence to describe these capabilities to combine, bundle and integrate resources into products and services.

Some of these competencies are distinctive enough to be labelled core competencies, i.e. leveraging specific sets of capabilities and assets which give the firm a potentially significant and sustainable competitive advantage over its competitors.

In Prahalad and Hamel's terminology, to be "core" the competencies have to meet three criteria: (i) offer real benefits to customers, (ii) be difficult to imitate and (iii) provide access to a variety of markets.

The heart of the matter has precisely to do with the uniqueness of the various recombinations of core competencies that the firm may achieve in designing, manufacturing and distributing products and services to customers in the marketplace. A higher-level resource bundling process is thus at work to create an offer that will be attractive to and valued by the clients.

FIGURE 16.1 illustrates McGee's (1995) symbolic representation of the argument. The figure also shows the dynamic learning loops taking place within the firm as well as between the firm and its competitive environment.

One should immediately note, however, how vague and fuzzy the concepts of resource and competence used in most of the management literature remain. Either the competence concept is nothing else but the standard resource concept and the resource-based theory stands as a self-sufficient relevant framework, or there is something more to the competence idea—and this is our opinion—and we should clarify in what sense. This is our objective in this chapter. We feel that the management literature has not paid enough attention to the issue of properly defining competence. Only recently have some contributions started to offer clearer and more

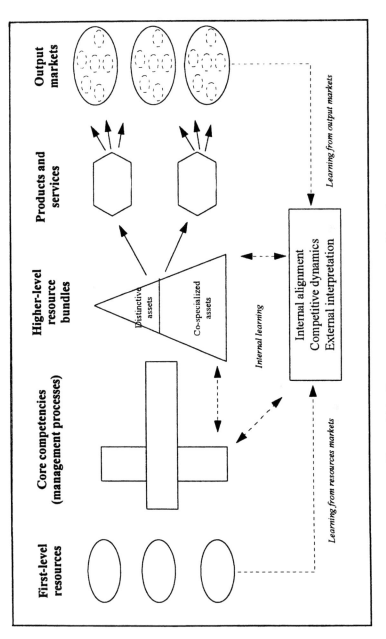

FIGURE 16.1 Resources, competences and learning

precise definitions of terms and concepts (e.g. Sanchez, Heene & Thomas, 1996). Nevertheless, it seems to us that the available decompositions of competence into subcategories and sub-elements still deserve much attention.

We strongly believe that in order to be meaningful, a theory needs to be based on a solid, carefully enunciated set of definitions and classifications. This to us is a prerequisite to consistency and articulation of the emerging theory, as well as to its empirical testing. If the concepts used relate to no clear real managerial element, no subsequent empirical work can take place.

This chapter aims at developing a renewed model of competence by reviewing the classical distinctions and characterization made in the literature around the various terms associated with the competence-based theory of the firm. The chapter is thus mostly conceptual in its form and scope. We chose to illustrate its content using a set of graphical representations and brief textual metaphors, shown in italics.

The next section is devoted to a brief survey and discussion of the many dimensions of competence identified in the management literature. Two concrete typologies of competence are discussed as a way to clarify what the content and scope of the discussion really are. The following section deals with the issue of competence creation and building as well as the theme of learning, and the fourth section then presents our model, a revised view on competence using the "knowledge"/"know-how"/"attitudes" referential system stemming from research in education. This paradigm is used to discuss further key additional concepts such as the idea of vision in strategy, the coordinated deployment function, Sanchez's (1996) "know-what"/ know-why", the specificities of competence dynamics for each one of the three main dimensions of this model of competence, and the interactions among these three dimensions. A brief summary concludes the chapter.

The following two sections are thus designed as building blocks, which are to be used in a reconstruction of a model of competence in the fourth section.

DIMENSIONS OF COMPETENCE

The literature recognizes many different distinctions around the concept of competence. Some of these relate more specifically to knowledge, others to resources or assets. We choose here to list them as if they were all suggested and applied to competencies, in the broad, generic sense of the word. Only later will it be possible to limit and specify the concept of competence more clearly.

CLASSICAL DISTINCTIONS

The *tacit/articulated* distinction has frequently been recognized as important. Organizational learning and technology are known to be at least partly tacit, i.e. embedded in the routines and informal processes of the organization.

This distinction can actually be challenged if one adopts the perspective of Von Grogh and Roos (1995) based on the auto-poeisis concept. They, indeed, suggest that knowledge (and, more generally, competence) can only be transmitted, recognized and thus evaluated through interaction. Therefore, the cognitive limits of both the speaker and the listener (the enunciation, the languaging, the attention paid, the message received and understood given the existing knowledge base of the listener, etc.) will unavoidingly lead to a distorted recognition of the knowledge. In that sense, knowledge is thus necessarily tacit, at least to a certain extent. Similarly the *individual/collective* duality of competence remains as one of the main espistemic challenges of management. Schneider & Angelmar (1993) and Durand, Mounoud & Ramanantsoa (1996) clearly make this point.

Hedlund & Nonaka (1992) actually combine these two dimensions to discuss the comparative dynamics of knowledge management in the Japanese versus the Western firm (see FIGURE 16.2). They identify several key processes, including articulation versus internalization as well as appropriation versus extension of knowledge. It should be noted that they suggest that a good way of protecting competence may actually be to have the individual members of an organization keep it as tacit as possible. This is indeed embeddedness.

The *cognitive* versus *behavioral* dimension of competence has been paid less attention—in our opinion, not as much as it should have been. Competence-based theory seems to have been more preoccupied with cognitive capabilities like knowledge, skills, patents or technologies than with individual or group behaviour, culture or identity of an organization. However, we argue that certain firms may benefit from their corporate identity acting as an engine for change, while in other cases the existing culture may represent a significant inertia, hindering adaptation and creative strategic moves (Durand, 1997). This has to do with the issue of unlearning, which is discussed in the next section. The lack of recognition of behavioral and cultural aspects may have to do with the uncoupling that occurred between strategic management and the human resources field, where behavior and identity are known to be essential.

The *positive/negative* duality suggests that competence may not only be positive as an asset but also negative in the form of a burden. When a firm suffers from a capability, this should be regarded as incompetence. Some argue that one should not try to qualify and evaluate competence as positive

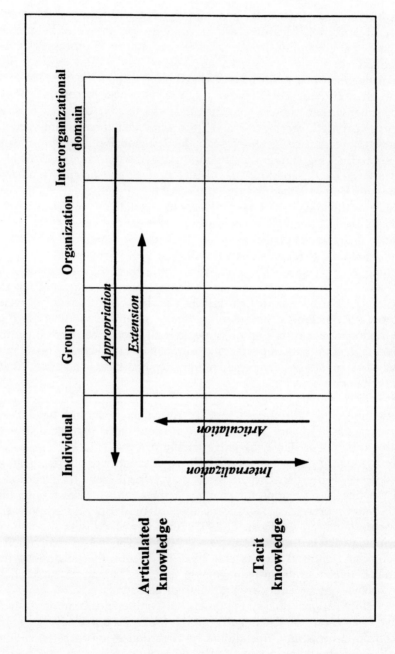

FIGURE 16.2 Knowledge categories and transformation processes

or negative. We insist that the competence-based theory needs to assess the value of the firm's portfolio of competence.

More classically found is the *tangible/intangible* distinction. Indeed, in the broad sense of the competence-based theory, tangible assets such as equipment, buildings, products, etc., and intangible assets like brandnames, serve as ingredients in the firm's competence base, while more intangible elements such as organizational processes or culture contribute to the "organizational alchemy" of competence.

An interesting point is made by Sanchez, Heene & Thomas (1996), as they very rightly suggest the addition of a *coordinated deployment function* to the *assets and resources* categories.

"A football team is more than a set of skilled players; a dish is more than a set of ingredients." (Durand, 1997).

Management is precisely about organizing processes to make it happen, leveraging assets and resources, and building new capabilities.

We suggest that the essence of competence is to be looked for in this intangible "organizational alchemy", which cannot easily be imitated. Porter (1996) indeed argues that any tangible resource can be identified, described and thus imitated, if not acquired. The imitability criteria put forward by Prahalad & Hamel requires intangibility, and there is difficulty in explaining how it works. This is where, we think, we need to look for the real content of competence.

There is another interesting debate about the real nature of competence. Can a firm, performing well on some markets because of specific core competencies, be called competent for some other markets that it has never tried to enter but where the same competencies could be valorized? This actually related to two possible distinctions: the *intended* versus *contingent* and *demonstrated* versus *potential* dualities.

As Barney puts it, is it being competent to be lucky?

"Think of a farmer in Texas buying a piece of land to raise his cattle and finding oil there. Would you say that he built a competitive advantage? No; but he is lucky enough to tap a source of economic rent".

In Barney's view, the rent may not have been created or tapped intentionally and may be purely contingent, while the competitive advantage comes from an intended, proactive strategy. This relates to the goal attainment and intention criteria put forward by Sanchez & Heene (1997). We would challenge this view. We feel that the bottom line remains the firm's performance, wherever it originally came from. Luck may have played a role or not; an asset or a capability, if exploited, makes the firm more competent than those who do not hold this element of competence. If the farmer does not exploit the oil source, he ignores his asset and has no rent. If he does, he benefits from a lucky move and indeed performs better economically and financially than his neighbouring farmer with no oil. In our view, contingency may thus be part of the competence game. This actually relates to the path dependence concept of industrial economics (Dosi, Teece & Winter, 1991). History clearly matters as experience shapes up competence which was built through various learnings mechanisms along the way. Luck may thus have played a significant role in the historical competence building.

Along similar lines but with a slightly different perspective, one may distinguish the set of *demonstrated* capabilities from those that are *potential* or latent. Is your firm really competent if it holds core competencies, which you claim could be used to develop new products/services for markets totally new to your firm? There is often more than a giant step from potentiality to reality. Could your firm be regarded as equally competent as a company already fully established on these new markets with resources and capabilities already bundled into effective products and services? Obviously not.

Electric utilities have a real potential in telecoms. Indeed, both businesses may be seen as a matter of cables and distribution. Yet those that have not yet entered the telecom market are certainly not as competent as existing telecom operators.

TWO EXAMPLES OF COMPETENCE CLASSIFICATIONS

All in all, these many distinctions encountered throughout the literature help characterize what competence is about. We shall call upon some of them in our reconstruction in the fourth section. As a first attempt, we actually used them as segmentation tools to suggest a preliminary typology of competence (Durand, 1997). This is shown in TABLE 16.1. We also compare this classification to the categories of Sanchez, Heene & Thomas (1996), as shown in FIGURE 16.3. For further discussion, see Durand (1996).

We believe that these classifications have at least one merit: they help root a theoretical discussion into the ground of reality and thus may contribute to keeping any further theorizing exercise from drifting too far away from meaningful managerial concerns.

A key point should be stressed here: a clear distinction is made between (i) the assets and resources of the firm and (ii) individual and organizational capabilities, knowledge, processes, routines and culture. In other words, on one hand there are ingredients—tangible and intangible—which can be

TABLE 16.1   Preliminary typology of competence

Competence	Examples
Stand-alone assets: tangible and intangible	Equipment, buildings, products, softwares, brandnames
Cognitive capabilities: individual and collective, explicit and tacit	Knowledge, know-how skills, technologies, patents
Organizational processes and routines: related to the coordinated deployment of Sanchez, Heene & Thomas (1996)	Coordinating mechanisms in the organization, combining individual actions into collective functioning
Organizational structure: may facilitate or hinder the ability of a firm to adapt to certain changes	The structural design of the organization and its linkages to the environment (suppliers, clients, etc.)
Identity: may facilitate or hinder the ability of a firm to adapt to certain changes	Behavioural and cultural characteristics of the firm Shared values, beliefs, rites and taboos are symptoms of the identity

acquired and exchanged with basically no need for human resource transfers. These may be called non-social assets and resources. On the other hand, there is what we regard as the "organizational alchemy", i.e. intangible, difficult-to-buy and difficult-to-imitate capabilities. These clearly relate to the "integrated coordinated deployment of resources and assets" suggested by Sanchez, Heene & Thomas (1996). In short, they view competence as management processes in the organization. We shall use this point as a building block of our model, extending this idea to include other elements as discussed below.

Note in passing that, in their classification, "operations" seem to be left apart. We feel this may be misleading. We suggest considering operations as management processes which indeed contribute to the overall set of processes performing the coordinated deployment of assets and capabilities. This is clearly what total quality management (TQM) has repeatedly claimed over the past 15 years.

At the same time as we suggest the inclusion of operations (and operational processes) into the idea of coordinated deployment, we feel that it is relevant to extend this coordinated deployment function to strategy and culture as well.

Indeed, internal strategic alignment, or policy deployment in TQM terminology, precisely aims at sharing a strategic overall vision within the firm and bringing it down to clear and meaningful orientations for each and every member of the organization.

This relates to the polarization of particles in physics, e.g. photons in a laser beam.

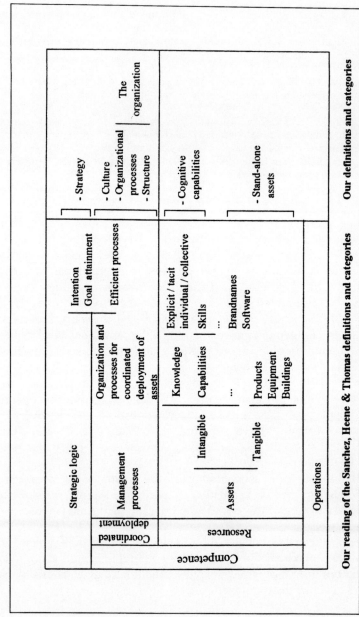

FIGURE 16.3   Compared definitions and categories

In this sense, strategic vision when shared throughout the layers of the firm contributes to the coordinated deployment of assets and capabilities, including the energy and commitment of the human resources. We shall come back to this later, when discussing will and motivation as key elements of competence.

Also note that this point may be extended even further to include the identity or the culture as a cement or a glue holding the organization together and thus is an element of what we chose to call the "organizational alchemy" of competence.

LEARNING, COMPETENCE BUILDING AND LEVERAGING

Interestingly enough, the literature has paid much more attention to learning, i.e. the flux, than to competence, i.e. the cumulated stock. We believe that this results from the difficulty of grasping competence ("*I know that I don't know; I don't know what I know, etc..*") while it is apparently easier to study learning mechanisms.

LEARNING

The literature classically identifies various forms of learning. Arrow (1962) and Atkinson & Stiglitz (1969) pointed to *learning by doing* as action empirically helps to build up know-how and knowledge. In turn, Rosenberg (1972) described as *learning by using* the learning process which takes place when a client uses a new product and/or service, thus building up knowledge and know-how about using it. This idea was extended through *learning by interacting* (Von Hippel, 1976; Lundvall, 1988), where the user–designer interaction again helps to build up capabilities and thus improvement in both the product itself and how to use it. Many other forms of learning mechanisms may be mentioned here. Among these, we insist on two which will prove useful in building our model. First comes *learning by learning*. The process of learning helps build an ability to learn and learn again.

> Teachers indeed know that the role of education is as much helping individuals learn how to learn as providing them with knowledge. The content of what is learnt may not be as important as the process of helping students to build a capability to learn more later by themselves.

Second, we insist on the paradox of *learning by unlearning* (Durand, 1992). This is an essential point as, too often, individuals as well as organizations are stuck with routines and habits which put them in a difficult situation when change is needed. Bettis & Prahalad (1995) also emphasize this aspect. Paradoxically one may argue that the most difficult part of learning for experienced people is to unlearn what is now becoming obsolete and a factor of inertia. This is particularly true for the behavioral and cultural side of competence.

> The painful transition of Central and East European economies offers a good example of this. Another example is given by the many difficulties encountered by public utilities in their adaptation to deregulation.

Another classical perspective on learning relates to the *formal* teaching and training part versus what one may call the *companionship* approach. Typically, articulated knowledge can be taught and learnt in the class room. Conversely, tacit know-how, by nature, cannot be transferred formally and needs some form of "do it with me" or "observe and imitate" as a mechanism relevant for competence transfer. This in part relates to the *learning by doing* mentioned above.

There is an additional important aspect of learning which will be needed in our model. Piaget (1970) clearly showed that children learn not only through formal teaching but also and simultaneously through sensory information stemming from action. Children thus build knowledge and know-how at the same time. In turn this means that (i) formal teaching and (ii) action are two sides of the same coin. This is also pointed out by Senge (1990). We shall extend this idea further in the fourth section, applying it to interaction and attitudes as well.

STAGES OF COMPETENCE

An additional and important element of competence building needs to be brought in before our attempt to integrate these different ingredients into a model. We suggested (Durand, 1992) that knowledge builds up as information is integrated and assimilated into frameworks which ensure coherence and structure to the accumulated knowledge base. Yet information is not just data. Information is data that has been acknowledged, sieved, transformed and adapted to fit into the pre-existing structure of knowledge. The psychology literature suggests that individuals tend to reject data that do not fit their previous knowledge while they overemphasize data that reinforce their existing understanding and beliefs (Hogarth, 1980; Barnes, 1984; Schwenck, 1984, 1988; Stubbart, 1989). One may thus consider that data need to be enacted before they reach the status of information, which can then be integrated as an element of knowledge.

At the other end of the spectrum, expertise should be regarded as much higher a step than knowledge. Not only does expertise relate to a significantly more advanced level of competence, it also requires an integrated combination of knowledge and know-how, thus assuming a "state-of-the-art" ability to understand, explain and even act within the domain of competence. In a way expertise transcends competence, through both (i) a quantum leap in the level of competence and (ii) a recombination and merger of various elements of competence (e.g. knowledge and know-how).

In other words, as Durand (1992) suggested, there is a sequence of stages from data and information, to knowledge and expertise as shown below:

In the next section, we extend this to other forms of competence than just knowledge (namely know-how and attitudes).

This is also suggested in a way by FIGURE 16.4. A list of terms is presented. These have already been used in this chapter, but we now specify in what sense they relate to competence. More specifically, one should note that this list tends to mix two significantly different forms of competence, namely knowledge (as information) and know-how (as skill or capabilities). This reinforces the need to differentiate among at least two scales of increasing competence. At the same time, the list helps to better specify different

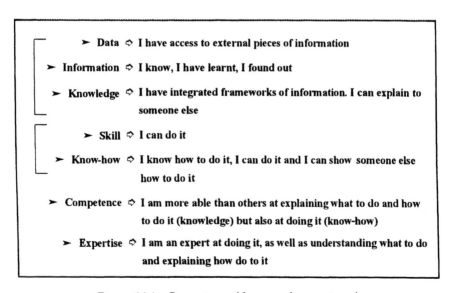

FIGURE 16.4   Competence (degrees of competence)

degrees of competence, e.g. data, information, knowledge and expertise. This list, once adapted, will constitute another building block of our reconstruction in the next section.

A CONTINUUM OF COMPETENCE LEVERAGING AND BUILDING

The emerging competence-based theory pays a lot of attention to the question of competence building and leveraging. We suggested that there is more of a continuum than an opposition between these two aspects of the management of a competence portfolio (Durand, 1997). FIGURE 16.5 illustrates this point. As it stretches to adapt to new market requirements, the firm may "pivot" around existing competencies, among which are core competencies, thus leveraging its existing set of distinctive capabilities and assets, and in turn "reinforcing" them. It may also have to build new competencies, either from internal sources within the organization (thanks to a "synergistic fit" with other profit centres) or from the outside ("networking access") on an inter-organizational mode as discussed by Hedlund & Nonaka (1992). "Adaptability" refers to the ability of some companies to keep a permanent ability to learn, unlearn and relearn again. This in turn relates to Teece & Pisano's (1994) idea of "dynamic capabilities".

Along similar lines, although from a different angle, it is also possible to identify degrees in the difficulty encountered by the firm adapting its

	Accessing competence			
	Holding		**Accessing**	
	Same competence required	*Competence held elsewhere*	*Inter-organizational competence*	*Learning capability*
	Reinforcement	*Synergistic fit*	*Networking access*	*Adaptability*
Leveraging	++++ Full leveraging	+++ Internal leveraging	++ External leveraging	+ Leveraging the learning capability
Building		and adaptation +	absorption and rebuilding ++	and competence building +++
	Static access to competence		*Dynamic access to competence*	

FIGURE 16.5   A continuum of competence leveraging and building

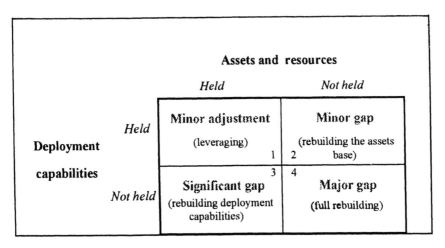

FIGURE 16.6   Preliminary typology of competence gaps

portfolio of competence when faced with change. Durand & Guerra-Vieira (1997) suggest strategies to bridge the "competence gap". FIGURE 16.6 illustrates this idea as it distinguishes the resource and asset gap versus the "organizational alchemy" or coordinated deployment gap. We suggest that it is significantly more difficult for the firm to build new competence than to access resources and assets. As was already discussed, Prahalad & Hamel's (1990) imitability criteria leads to the idea that assets and resources may be identified and accessed while complex human and behavioral aspects of the organization may be more difficult not only to imitate but also to manage and transform. Competence in a precise, specific sense should indeed be searched as the basis of this "organizational alchemy". This is exactly what we are after.

Most of the points discussed in this and the previous section are now going to be integrated and in a way extended into a revised presentation of the dimensions of competence that we see as relevant for theory development. This is the focus of the next section.

RECONSTRUCTING A COMPETENCE REFERENTIAL

THREE GENERIC FORMS OF COMPETENCE: KNOWLEDGE, KNOW-HOW AND ATTITUDES

We suggest borrowing from research on education the three key dimensions of individual learning: knowledge, know-how and attitudes, following

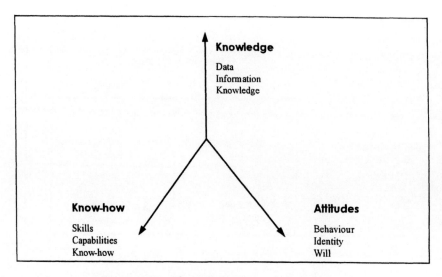

FIGURE 16.7   Three dimensions of competence

Pestalozzi (1994), who referred to "head, hand and heart" (see FIGURE 16.7). Given the specific concern of this chapter, we need to specify:

• what is meant by each of these categories of competence,
• the dynamic accumulation of competence through learning mechanisms,
• the interactions among these three interdependent dimensions,
• how managerial levers can affect and leverage this potential of competence described by these three dimensions.

Knowledge corresponds to the structured sets of assimilated information which make it possible to understand the world, obviously with partial and somewhat contradictory interpretations. Knowledge thus encompasses the access to data, and the ability to enact them into acceptable information and integrate them into pre-existing schemes, which obviously evolve along the way.

Know-how relates to the ability to act in a concrete way according to predefined objectives or processes. Know-how does not exclude knowledge but does not necessitate a full understanding of why the skills and capabilities, when put to operations, actually work. Know-how thus relates in part to empiricism and tacitness.

Attitudes are too often neglected in the resource-based view as well as in the competence-based theory of the firm. This may be due to the traditional lack of interest of economists in behavioural and social aspects. We believe that behaviour but even more so identity and will (determination) are essential parts of the capability of an individual or an organization to achieve anything. This is a matter of choice in defining concepts. We argue that a dedicated organization, eager to succeed, is more competent than a demoralized, passive one with exactly the same knowledge and know-how.

These three dimensions will be the generic axes of our competence referential.

As an illustration, while the profile of competence of a historian should clearly be positioned close to the knowledge axis, the engineer would be placed further down the know-how dimension while the politician would be expected to be closer to the attitudes axis.

These are obviously caricatures. Note, for example, that the engineer not only deals with empirical know-how but also attempts to introduce as much knowledge into his practice as possible. This is exactly the difference between techniques (empirically-based with little understanding of why it works) and technology (more science-based with clear explanations for why it works, thus making it possible to extend the technology to other applications much more easily and quickly). Ansoff (1986) pointed out very rightly that technical skills are difficult to extend as they are empirically built, mostly tacit, context-specific and locally embedded, while the acceleration in technological development comes from the scientific base, which increasingly helps technological diffusion and extension.

Also note that the knowledge side of the competence space shown in FIGURE 16.7 is characterized by articulated forms of competence, while the know-how/attitudes dimensions embed more tacitness.

We further propose extending this referential to collective learnings as well. This is naturally a risky shift, which would need to be discussed at length as it requires a paradigmatic shift. This will not be done here. Some discussion of this matter may however be found in Durand, Mounoud & Ramanantsoa (1996), who advocate for interactionism and the theory of social representations (Moscovici, 1988). They see it as a way out of the internal contradiction of managerial/organizational cognition, i.e. the trap of the so-called organizational mind.

ENRICHING THE REFERENTIAL

One may then further enrich the picture by introducing some of the elements discussed in the previous sections see FIGURE 16.8. The "attitudes" category is itself a composite dimension, as we suggest that it combines the behavioural dimension (know-how-to-behave), the culture or identity of the

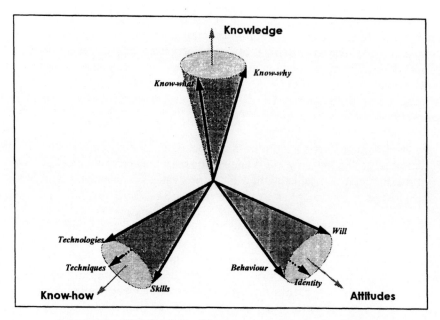

FIGURE 16.8   Enriching the three basic categories of competence

organization and the idea of will, i.e. determination and commitment. These are clearly distinct items, which should be recognized as such.

As an illustration of the importance of organizational behaviour and its links to competence and performance, Hambrick (1989) discusses how team behavior at top management level can lead to two polar extremes, fragmentation and groupthink. Both situations are shown to be inefficient, thus reinforcing the idea that collective behavior may be an element of competence or incompetence.

Similarly, the "know-how" axis is also a composite dimension. It clearly relates to skills, individual and collective processual capabilities, as well as technologies. As discussed above, technologies are at least in part understood and modelled. They are more than just empirical techniques. They thus lean in part towards the knowledge dimension, while techniques lean the other way.

Now turning to the knowledge axis, it should be noted that the "know-what/know-why/know-how" distinction put forward by Sanchez (1996) is dealt with only in part by the referential presented since only know-how appears as one of the three generic axes. The know-what/know-why turn out to be two different variants or subcategories of knowledge. Know-what is in a sense hinting in the direction of know-how, through a flavor of intuition, without the cognitive explanation that the "know-why" has to offer.

The "know-why" is actually twofold. On one hand it stands for the expertise of the knowledgeable, who can explain to a skilled worker why their "know-how" works and how to modify and improve the corresponding skill.

On the other hand, the "know-why" also includes a strategic understanding of why it is relevant to choose whatever strategic path the "know-what" suggests. The strategic dimension of the second type of know-why is far reaching.

We therefore suggest that the "know-why" clearly relates to strategy and strategic vision, and constitutes a very important aspect of the competence of the organization.

MANAGERIAL LEVERS AND THE COMPETENCE BASE

The three basic dimensions of our referential of competence, together with the subdimensions that we just added, help understand key aspects of the competence base. Yet one should recognize that management is not necessarily capable of acting upon these dimensions.

Standard managerial levers are of a different nature:

- *Strategizing* (strategic thinking leading to a strategic vision, a strategic logic thus relating to the "know-why", strategy deployment and strategic decision making). This relates to the knowledge (know-what and know-why) dimension.
- *Organizing* (the organizational structure as well as management processes). This relates more to the "know-how" dimension.
- Motivating (i.e. setting up incentives but also coaching, encouraging positive thinking and behaviour, promoting dedication and will). This relates to the "attitudes" dimension.

FIGURE 16.9 illustrates the respective positioning of each of these three main managerial levers for action.

The strategic vision includes the idea of a goal set up for the whole organization and shareable, if not shared, thus leaning slightly towards the attitudes, will and commitment dimensions. This is even more so for strategic deployment, which clearly means deploying the strategic vision for each subpart and every member of the organization.

Motivation fits in between these strategic dimensions and the attitudes. Motivation clearly combines an intent, a far-reaching goal and a positive, proactive attitude made up of will, determination and commitment. More than ever, motivation should be regarded as a key element of competence. Human resource managers are obviously well aware of this, as are line

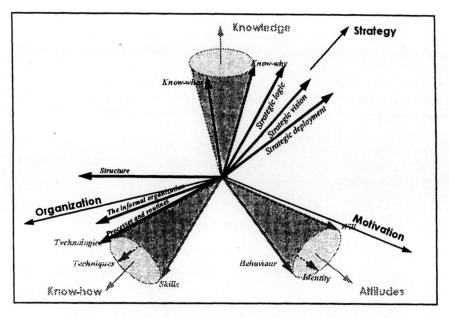

FIGURE 16.9   Enriching the three basic categories of competence

managers. And so are sports coaches. This is indeed a key element of team building and managing. How come, then, most of the literature on competence-based theory simply ignores this key aspect? Do management researchers forget what management is all about?

The organization with its two basics dimensions, the organizational structure and the management processes, is also shown in FIGURE 16.9. One may also add to this the informal organization. The organizational structure falls more on the articulated side of the referential, while the informal organizational and most of the processes are closer to the know-how axis. Management processes relate to the collective capabilities of the firm, thus including the technologies. Note that processes may be regarded as twofold. On one hand stand the organizational processes set up and explicitly monitored by management; on the other are the routines which were generated historically by the organization, possibly from a distorted appropriation of some management processes, long forgotten. Routines in that sense may be regarded as informal processes. They therefore tend to be more deeply rooted and embedded in the organization. In that sense, the informal organization and the routines also relate to the behavioral and cultural dimensions of attitudes, thus leaning towards this axis.

This specific positioning of the standard managerial levers (strategizing, organizing and motivating) with respect to the proposed key dimensions of competence in our model thus raises the issue of the interaction between managerial tasks and competence building and leveraging. The links are obviously not so direct, but nevertheless exist. How could management operate on the same wavelength (according to the same dimensions) as the competence base in order to better build and leverage competence? This issue is essential and should be paid more attention in future research.

ENLARGING THE CONTENT OF COORDINATED DEPLOYMENT

This in turn leads to the idea that the heart of the concept of competence, the "organizational alchemy", as we call it, which has to do with the co-ordinated deployment of resources and assets, should be enlarged beyond management processes. Indeed, while Sanchez, Heene & Thomas (1996) actually associate their coordinated deployment function to the management processes only, we argue that this idea should be significantly extended to the cultural identity, the strategic vision and the organizational structure. We argue that the identity (the shared values, rites, taboos and beliefs) operate as a cement holding the organizational pieces together at least as efficiently as any other coordinating and integrating mechanism.

We further argue that a shared vision also contributes to the coordinated deployment of strategy, channeling people's energy, motivation and commitment. Finally, we suggest that the organizational structure is also a key element of the same coordinated deployment of assets and capabilities.

In other words, we suggest reviewing and enlarging the content of the coordinated deployment concept in order to encompass four elements: the management processes, the identity, the strategic vision and the structure. This is shown in FIGURE 16.10. In so doing, we clearly relate to Strategor's (1988) *tetrahedron* of strategic management.

THE DYNAMICS OF COMPETENCE BUILDING

This framework can also be enriched with the theme of competence building. In a way, competence is a stock accumulated as a result of an ongoing flux of learning, reinforcing and enlarging the competence base of the organization.

The "data → information → knowledge → expertise" sequence described earlier can now be extended and adapted to the two other axes of the referential, i.e. the two other generic forms of competence, as shown in TABLE 16.2.

This illustrates the parallelism that prevails in the way learning mechanisms operate for each dimensions of the referential. Know-how is

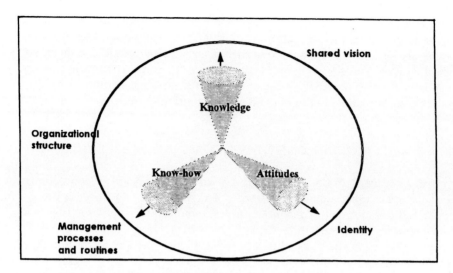

FIGURE 16.10   Coordinated deployment

TABLE 16.2   Parallel learning processes and stages

Knowledge	Know-how	Attitudes
Data reception	Action	Interaction
Information	Skills and capabilities	Behaviour, culture, will
Knowledge	Know-how	Attitudes
Expertise	Expertise	Expertise

built through action, which shapes skills and techniques. Similarly, attitudes are shaped through interaction when individuals conform to group or organizational behaviour, adopt the same cultural values and share the same basic commitments.

Expertise requires one step further. As discussed, expertise needs some form of quantum leap in competence together with a merger of the three generic dimensions of competence. FIGURE 16.11 illustrates this idea graphically, detailing the learning processes at hand.

Four interesting comments may be made on this matter:

1. The pre-existing stock of competence (the existing skills, knowledge base and identity) significantly affects the learning capabilities. It may operate as a booster to build up competence fast. It may also transform itself into a source of bias and inertia, hindering any real new learning. As discussed earlier, history indeed matters. The "installed base" counts.

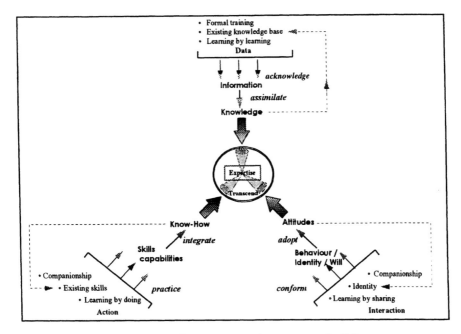

FIGURE 16.11   The dynamics of competence building

This is shown graphically in FIGURE 16.11. For each axis, the dotted arrows loop back on the pre-existing competence base, which in turn influences new learnings. The result of learning is not just a function of the learning process. It also depends upon the pre-existing base of competence.

2. If knowledge building stems from exposure to external data enacted as information and integrated into frameworks, know-how is built through action and companionship while attitudes are shaped through interaction in companionship.

3. It is action (taking place in the form of the various learning mechanisms described here) which transforms the potential competence, not yet demonstrated, into reality. Through the dynamics of competence building and learning, what one could possibly do becomes what one can actually do.

4. As discussed earlier, the expertise combines the three generic forms of competence identified (knowledge, know-how and attitudes) into an integrated higher-level competence. Experts understand, can explain and can even do better than others, with state-of-the-art ability. Expertise is beyond assimilation and digestion. It tends to transcend competence and merge its key generic dimensions.

THE THREE GENERIC DIMENSIONS OF COMPETENCE ARE INTERDEPENDENT

Two different aspects of interdependence may be formulated here. They are illustrated in FIGURE 16.12. First, building upon Piaget's work, we recognize with Senge (1990) that there is little real learning and knowledge building without action. Knowledge and know-how are in fact built simultaneously as learning needs action. This idea can be extrapolated and extended. We argue that learning actually takes place in organizations simultaneously for the three generic dimensions of our referential. This happens, in parallel but in an interrelated mode, through information, action and interaction.

Secondly, we suggest looking at the case of workers highly vulnerable to technical change as they built their competence around purely empirical know-how with little or no knowledge of other technologies. When the technological process, e.g. the equipment, is changed, they lose most of their competence. Without knowledge they are not in a position to adapt to the change. Know-how without knowledge is thus very vulnerable.

Again, we suggest extending this idea to the interactions among the three generic dimensions of our referential.

What would collective know-how be without appropriate group

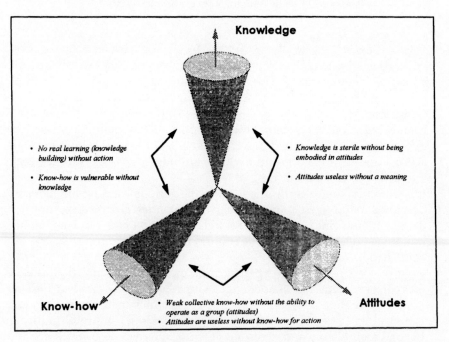

FIGURE 16.12   The three dimensions of competence are inter-dependent

attitudes, i.e. without the capability to behave as a group? Similarly, attitudes without know-how may prove useless, as much as attitudes may be meaningless without knowledge and thus understanding of the stakes and challenges at hand. Pure knowledge without relevant know-how is sterile, and knowledge without attitudes may even prove counterproductive.

In other words, information, action and interaction are three parallel and interrelated modes of learning, building up competence simultaneously. Conversely, an unbalanced competence base, leaning more towards one of the three generic dimensions of our referential, may prove inappropriate.

In this sense, the three generic dimensions of competence in our model are interdependent.

CONCLUSION

We first pointed out the lack of attention paid to clear and work-able definitions and concept specifications in the literature devoted to the resources/competence-based view of the firm. We then summarized the key distinctions encountered describing the dimensions of competence (tacit/articulated, individual/collective, cognitive/behavioural, positive/negative, tangible/intangible, intended/contingent, demonstrated/potential, assets and resources/coordinated deployment function). We have also presented and compared two examples of competence classifications, thus relating the concepts to real managerial categories. We have clearly distin-guished resources and assets from what we called "organizational alchemy", or the coordinated deployment of assets and resources, offering to keep the wordcompetence for the latter category. We further discussed different forms of learning as well as the idea of a sequence in knowledge development, before referring to the competence building/leveraging continuum.

Using these ingredients as building blocks, we then presented a revised model of competence around three generic forms (knowledge, know-how and attitudes). We stressed the importance of the latter, which is too often neglected in the literature on competence/resource-based theory. We related the know-how/know-what/know-why decomposition to the framework presented, and introduced strategy and vision as well as the organizational structure and processes in the model. This led to the idea of enlarging the content of the coordinated deployment of assets and resources, to include not only management processes but also the identity, the shared vision and organizational structure. These, we argue, are the four elements of the essence of competence.

We have also shown how managerial levers (strategizing, organizing, motivating) relate to the three generic dimensions of our model for the competence base.

We then introduced the dynamics of competence building into the model, discussing the unique status of expertise and the importance of the pre-existing competence base influencing the flow of learning. We finally suggested that the three generic dimensions of competence in our model are interdependent, reinforcing each other as learning takes place simultaneously in all directions through information, action and interaction.

Altogether, the model presented here should make it possible to address and possibly enrich most of the questions that theory building on competence-related topics has to deal with. It is intended as a framework designed to permit further theoretical development as well as simpler presentation and diffusion of the concepts towards practitioners.

REFERENCES

Amit, R. & Schoemaker, P.J. (1993). Strategic assets and organizational rent. *Strategic Management Journal*, **14**, 33–46.

Ansoff, I. (1986). Strategic management of technology. *Journal of Business Strategy*.

Arrow, K.J. (1962). The economic implications of learning by doing. *Review of Economic Studies*, **29**, 155–173.

Atkinson, A.B. & Stiglitz, J.E. (1969). A new view of technological change. *Economic Journal*, **76**, 573–578.

Barnes, J. (1984). Cognitive biases and their impact on strategic planning. *Strategic Management Journal*, **5**, 129–137.

Barney, J.B. (1986). Strategic factor markets: expectations, luck and business strategy. *Management Science*, **32**, 1231–1241.

Bettis, A.R. & Prahalad, C.K. (1995). The dominant logic: retrospective and extension. *Strategic Management Journal*, **16**, 5–14.

Collis, J. (1991). A resource-based analysis of global competition: the case of the bearing industry. *Strategic Management Journal*, **12**, 49–68.

Conner, K.C. & Prahalad, C.K. (1996). A resource-based theory of the firm: knowledge versus opportunism. *Organization Science*, **7**(5).

Dosi, G., Teece, D. & Winter, S. (1991). Toward a theory of corporate coherence. In G. Dosi, R. Gianetti & P.A. Toninelli, (eds) *Technology and the Enterprise in a Historical Perspective*. Oxford: Oxford University Press.

Durand, T. (1992). The dynamics of cognitive technological maps. In P. Lorange, J. Roos, B. Chakravarty & A. Van de Ven (eds) *Strategic Processes*. Oxford: Blackwell.

Durand, T. (1997). Strategizing innovation: competence analysis in assessing strategic change. In A. Heene & R. Sanchez (eds) *Competence-Based Strategic Management*. Chichester: Wiley.

Durand, T. & Guerra-Vieira, S. (1997). Competence-based strategies when facing innovation: but what is competence? In H. Thomas, D. O'Neal & R. Alvarado (eds) *Strategic Discovery: Competing in New Arenas*. Chichester: Wiley, pp. 79–97.

Durand, T., Mounoud, E. & Ramanantsoa, B. (1996). Uncovering strategic assumptions: understanding managers' ability to build representations. *European Management Journal*, **14**(4), 389–398.

Grant, R.M. (1996). Prospering in dynamically-competitive environments: organizational capability as knowledge integration. *Organization Science*, **7**(4).

Hamel, G. & Heene, A. (eds) (1994). *Competence-Based Competition*. Chichester: Wiley.

Hambrick, D. (1989). Putting top managers back into the Strategy picture. *Strategic Management Journal*, **10**(special issue), 5–15.

Hedlund, G. & Nonaka, I. (1992). The dynamics of knowledge. in P. Lorange, J. Roos, B. Chakravarty & A. Yan de Ven (eds) *Strategic Processes*. Oxford: Blackwell.

Heene, A. & Sanchez, R. (eds) (1997). *Competence-Based Strategic Management*. Chichester: Wiley.

Hogarth, R. (1980). *Judgement and Choice: The Psychology of Decision*. Chichester: Wiley.

Kogut, B. & Zander, U. (1996). What firms do? Coordination, identity and learning. *Organization Science*, **7**(5).

Lundvall, B.A. (1988). Innovation as an interactive process: from user–producer interaction to the national system of innovation. In C. Freeman & B.A. Lundvall (eds) *Small Countries Facing the Technical Revolution*, London: Pinter.

Marino, K.E. (1996). Developing consensus on firm competencies and capabilities. *Academy of Management Executive*, **10**(3), 40–51.

McGee, J. (1995). Presentation at the Third International Workshop on Competence-Based Competition, Ghent, November 1995.

Moscovici, S. (1988). Notes towards a description of social representations. *European Journal of Social Psychology*, **18**, 211–250.

Penrose, E. (1959). *The Theory of the Growth of the Firm*. Oxford: Blackwell.

Pestallozzi, J.H. (1994). *Mes recherches sur la marche de la nature dans l'évolution du genre humain*, traduction et édition de Michael Soëtard. Lausanne: Editions Payot (originally published 1797).

Piaget, J. (1970). *L'Epistémologie Génétique*. Paris: PUF.

Porter, M. (1996). What is strategy? *Harvard Business Review*, November/December, 61–78.

Prahalad, C.K. & Hamel, G. (1990). The core competence of the corporation. *Harvard Business Review*, **68**(3), 79–91.

Rosenberg, N. (1972). *Technology and American Economic Growth*. New York: Armouk.

Rumelt, R.P. (1984). Towards a strategic theory of the firm. In R. Lamb (ed.) *Competitive Strategic Management*, Englewood Cliffs, NJ: Prentice Hall, pp. 556–570.

Sanchez, R. (1996). Managing articulated knowledge in competence-based competition. In R. Sanchez, A. Heene & H. Thomas (eds), *Dynamics of Competence-Based Competition*. London: Elsevier.

Sanchez, R. & Heene, A. (1997). A systems view of the firm in competence-based competition. In R. Sanchez, A. Heene & H. Thomas (eds) *Dynamics of Competence-Based Competition*. London: Elsevier.

Sanchez, R., Heene, A. & Thomas H. (1996). Towards the theory and practice of competence-based competition. In R. Sanchez, A. Heene & H. Thomas (eds) *Dynamics of Competence-Based Competition*. London: Elsevier.

Senge, P. (1990). *The Fifth Discipline*. New York: Doubleday/Currency.

Strategor (1988, 1993), *Stratégie, Structure, Décision, Identité–Politique Générale d'Entreprises*, ouvrage collectif, InterEditions.

Schneider, S. & Angelmar, R. (1993). Cognition in organizational analysis: who's minding the store? *Organization Studies*, **14**, 347–374.

Schwenk, C. (1984). Cognitive simplification processes in strategic decision-making. *Strategic Management Review*, **5**, 111–128.

Schwenk, C. (1988). The cognitive perspective on strategic decision-making. *Journal of Management Studies*, **25**, 41–55.

Stubbart, C. (1989). Cognitive science: a missing link in strategic management research. *Journal of Management Review*, **10**, 724–736.

Teece, D.J. & Pisano, G. (1994). *The Dynamic Capabilities of Firms: An Introduction.* Laxenburg, Austria: International Institute for Applied Systems Analysis.

Von Grogh, G. & Roos, J. (1995). Conversation management. *European Management Journal*, **13**.

Von Hippel, E. (1976). The dominant role of users in the scientific instrument innovation process. *Research Policy*, **5**.

Wernerfelt, B. (1984). A resource-based view of the firm. *Strategic Management Journal*, **5**, 171–180.

Wernerfelt, B. (1995). The resource-based view of the firm: ten years after. *Strategic Management Journal*, **16**.

17

Structure Decisions and the Multinational Enterprise: A Dynamic Competence Perspective

DENNIS M. GARVIS, WILLIAM C. BOGNER

INTRODUCTION

The theory of the multinational enterprise (MNE) represents a major framework for international business research (Dunning, 1981, 1988, 1995). Originally proposed to explain the entry choices of American firms into foreign markets (Casson, 1987), the focus of MNE research has now shifted towards the management of well-established multinational firms and competition among multinational companies from multiple countries (Kogut 1990; Gupta & Govindarajan, 1991).

A fundamental decision faced by firms operating in foreign markets is whether the firm's advantage is most effectively pursued by using the market, the firm, or a hybrid form (Kogut & Zander, 1993). While firms cannot quickly or easily change established relationships, over time firms can alter this choice to improve firm performance. Transaction costs and knowledge-based theories of the MNE present two notable explanations of the market-hybrid-hierarchy (M-H-H) decisions made by multinational firms (Teece, 1986; Hill & Kim, 1988; Kogut & Zander, 1993; Grant & Baden-Fuller, 1995). The differing conclusions drawn from these theories, however,

Strategic Flexibility: Managing in a Turbulent Environment. Edited by G. Hamel, C.K. Prahalad, H. Thomas and D. O'Neal.
Copyright © 1998 John Wiley & Sons Ltd.

have generated significant academic debate (McFetridge, 1995; Kogut & Zander, 1995).

This chapter suggests that while both of these theories are informative, they provide static and incomplete explanations of M-H-H decisions. While these frameworks are particularly useful when considering co-specialized assets, economies of scale or scope, and similar efficiency considerations such as maintaining high operating capacity for capital investments through partial backward integration, they are less helpful when explaining decisions by firms seeking to increase returns to human skills and learning. Both transaction costs and knowledge-based theories provide explanations for the choices made in such situations, but they lack the specificity that the other decisions receive because they do not focus on the key considerations in such decisions, i.e. the building and maintaining of competencies. Accordingly, we submit that dynamic competence theory (Bogner, Thomas & McGee, 1998) offers a model of the multinational firm's M-H-H decision in these situations that is comprehensive yet parsimonious. This is not to say that issues of scale economies, vertical integration efficiencies, and protection of co-specialized assets should not be considered. They should, and where determinative they should guide the M-H-H decisions. However, the rise of global standards of living, along with increased efficiencies in communication and transportation, has created more opportunities in multi-domestic, downstream, consumer good industries. Unlike the more commodity-oriented products of global strategies, these products' profitability is less likely to be determined by such operating efficiencies. For these products and services this chapter proposes that the learning benefits and costs associated with transfers of unique knowledge and the resulting returns to firm competencies explain decisions regarding the M-H-H choice better than either transaction cost or knowledge characteristics alone.

In the model presented here we intend to focus on the factors that influence M-H-H decisions made by multinational firms seeking global advantage in the multiple foreign markets in which they already compete. To this end, this chapter places the M-H-H decision within the context of the well-established multinational firm and away from influences on initial entry into new foreign markets. In the following section we describe the key characteristics and perspectives of the transaction cost, knowledge-based, and dynamic-competence explanations of the M-H-H decision. We then make the argument for a competence- and learning-based explanation for MNE structure decisions, and model the key cost and benefit linkages in an MNE. This is followed by specific propositions about when particular choices would be made and the conditions under which they are likely to be found. Finally, the chapter sets out the limitations of the model as well as the potential for future research using the arguments presented here.

Theories of the Multinational Enterprise

MNE theories, originally proposed as an explanation of foreign direct investment in overseas production (Dunning, 1981, 1988), have evolved in recent years as a new view of multinational firms has evolved. Here the MNE is seen as a network of existing multinational operations with multi-directional advantage transfers between vertical and horizontal business units (Ghoshal & Bartlett, 1990; Kogut, 1990; Quinn, 1992). The MNE in the perspective studied here has well-established foreign operations, such that advantages are not realized merely by entering new markets, but instead gained from effectively managing activities in existing foreign markets (Kogut, 1990; Gupta & Govindarajan, 1991). Researchers have applied existing theories to explain how these M-H-H decisions are made in this context. Each offers a different perspective.

Transaction Cost Theory

The classic economic theory assumption that the market is the efficient mechanism for conducting transactions is examined under transaction cost theory (Winter, 1991). Here the combination of asset specificity with the bounded rationality and opportunism of individuals creates certain risks for the firm contracting in the market (Williamson, 1991). When governance costs of these market transactions become too high, the market fails and firms internalize transactions (Williamson, 1991). Generally then, firms face market or hierarchy choices in governing transactions. The boundaries of the firm expand to internalize transactions within the firm when the organizational costs of increased coordination and administration are lower than the transactions costs of the market (Williamson, 1991; Tallman, 1992).

Based on the internalization advantage described by Dunning, MNE researchers applied transaction cost theory to suggest that firms will internalize cross-border transactions that involve asset-specific foreign investments and self-interested parties acting with guile (Teece, 1986; Casson, 1987; Tallman, 1992). In other words, it is the high costs of negotiation, monitoring, and enforcement associated with foreign contracts between firms that cause market failure such that firms internalize transactions by using foreign subsidiaries. This approach has been expanded to include the increased use of hybrid arrangements, such as strategic alliances and joint ventures (Hennart, 1988, 1993; Parkhe, 1993).

Criticism of the transaction cost approach is considerable. Winter (1988) argues that the transaction cost explanation of the firm is misdirected because it neglects the cumulative effect of productive knowledge of the firm. Specifically, the boundaries of the firm are not determined by a singular solution to a governance problem, but instead are the cumulative effect of various solutions to technological and organizational problems. Tallman (1992) suggests that the deterministic cost minimization criteria imposed by transaction cost theory does not acknowledge the existence of firm-level managerial choices, and, therefore, transaction cost explanations render strategic factors and strategy irrelevant. More generally, transaction costs explanations only provide a threshold level of distinction between the cost effects of good and bad choices with no differentiation among those firms that choose well. Dunning (1995) recognized that the rise of alliance capitalism has not been adequately addressed within existing theoretical boundaries. Kogut & Zander (1993) and Ghoshal & Moran (1996) go so far as to contend that the opportunism assumption is unnecessary and unwarranted in explaining firm behavior. Interestingly, none of these critics highlight the absence in transaction costs of the costs and benefits of learning and knowledge integration for competitive strategies that rely on processes linked to distinctive competencies.

KNOWLEDGE-BASED THEORY

Knowledge theory addresses aspects of MNE structure not addressed by the transaction cost literature. In the knowledge-based theory, the firm is viewed as a social community in which knowledge is created and transferred (Kogut & Zander, 1993). Ongoing interactions between individuals and groups within the firm lead to the development of understandings such that knowledge may be efficiently transferred from ideas into products and services (Nonaka, 1994; Grant 1996). In this sense, the speed and efficiency of knowledge creation and transfer within the firm, and not governance costs, determine firm boundaries (Kogut & Zander, 1993; Chang, 1996).

The knowledge theory of the MNE proposes an evolutionary path of a firm in multiple foreign markets (Kogut & Zander, 1993). Specifically, tacit knowledge is more efficiently and rapidly transferred between units within the hierarchy of the firm than between firms in the market (Zander & Kogut, 1995). Hybrid arrangements are used to transfer tacit knowledge between firms that hold different knowledge bases (Grant & Baden-Fuller, 1995). Accordingly, the M-H-H decision made by the multinational firm is influenced by the tacit nature of the knowledge being transferred.

This approach is not without problems or critics. Kogut & Zander (1993) admit that although the capabilities of the recipients of knowledge transfer are important, they are not included as part of the knowledge-based calculus that determines the M-H-H form of transfer. Furthermore, like the transaction cost approach, the knowledge-based approach is marked by a strong element of determinism, dependent upon the tacit dimensions of knowledge. Transaction cost researchers contend that Kogut & Zander's framing of the transfers of tacit knowledge is no different than an internalized transaction costs relationship (McFetridge, 1995). Importantly, although firm processes are identified by Kogut & Zander, the primary focus is on categorization of knowledge types.

DYNAMIC COMPETENCE THEORY

Competence-based theories of persistent profitability represent a developing paradigm in strategic management research (Hamel, 1994; Bogner, Thomas & McGee, 1998). Competence models focus on the external competitive effects of the firm's internal idiosyncratic resources and learning processes (Bogner, Thomas & McGee, 1996). In such a view the firm's core competence has two components: skills and cognitive process (Bogaert, Martens & Van Cauwenbergh, 1994). Skills and cognitive traits combine to produce core products, which provide the basis for successful diversification and globalization (Prahalad & Hamel, 1990). As a result, in all markets a firm's competitive advantage is derived from being able to provide a mix of firm-level skills and knowledge that is superior in competition against competitors' mixes of skills and knowledge (Henderson & Cockburn, 1994). Importantly, the focus is on changes in profits, thus both revenue and cost implications of M-H-H decisions are considered.

The dynamic competence view does not see the M-H-H choice as one based on static conditions. Over time, competencies have to be sustained at their unique and distinctive levels by the process of continuous organizational learning (Bogner, Thomas & McGee, 1996). In the context of this chapter this means that effective management of the learning processes, as well as competence transfer and knowledge, will directly affect the MNE's ability to exploit its skills globally and continually. And, in turn, these firm-level capabilities will impact the M-H-H choice.

Looking at the MNE through the lens of dynamic competence theory, the firm consists of a geographically dispersed network (Ghoshal & Bartlett, 1990) of skills and knowledge flows (Gupta & Govindarajan, 1991) that have to be managed to maximize profits. To do that they have to be integrated and coordinated around the firm's core activities (Prahalad & Hamel, 1990). For the existing MNE, the advantage to having an in-country unit comes from integrating unique knowledge learned at the unit level with knowledge flows from other units in unique ways, from transferring the resulting competencies effectively across the whole organization, and from the ability to bundle local skills and knowledge with firm-wide competencies. In order for competence-based competition to be effective, a system of organizational learning tied to competence development and exploitation must be deployed throughout the organization (Bogner, Thomas & McGee, 1998).

THE LEARNING BASIS OF AN MNE STRUCTURE BUILT AROUND COMPETENCE

As was recognized at the start, some decisions can focus on economic efficiency without regard to knowledge or competitive transfer. But in all other cases, M-H-H decisions will focus on the costs and benefits of nurturing and building competence, and of levering-up those resources throughout the firm. Transaction cost and knowledge views significantly inform this understanding, but a clearer view can be developed by using those ideas in a model that focuses explicitly on learning and competence exploitation.

In a dynamic, learning MNE each in-country unit can contribute to both the maintenance and the exploitation of firm-wide competence. FIGURE 17.1 illustrates the process by which the MNE develops, nurtures, and levers-up its competencies through these linkages. The individual country units develop unique knowledge and skills through their close contact with customers, suppliers, governments, etc. (activity 1). To this end, effective top management encourages activities that will lead to new insights on the "grassroots" level. Management also recognizes that the often tacit and unique market understandings of the individual units have to be brought together if individual, country-level insights are to be turned into

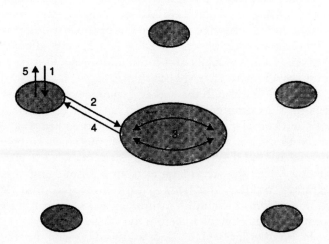

FIGURE 17.1   In-country unit's contribution to the maintenance and exploitation of firm-wide competence (see text for details)

organization-wide knowledge (activity 2). Integration processes are needed to translate insights and ideas into shared, explicit understandings that collectively can be richer than the individual contributions from the units. As a result, new, unique organization-wide knowledge is created (activity 3). It is at this point that firm-wide competence emerges. This valuable knowledge then has to be transferred to all units in the firm that can use it (activity 4). Finally, the local units have to be able to effectively exploit this unique output in their operations (activity 5).

An MNE based on competence requires both ongoing inbound and outbound communications and knowledge flows. The role of these activities in competence creation, maintenance, and exploitation is important in part because of the nature of "experimental learning" (Huber, 1991). Experimental learning is the type of learning that is done by an organization when it systematically creates new, unique knowledge. Such knowledge is important to firm competencies in two ways (Helleloid & Simonin, 1994). First, it is the basis for the establishment of new competence. Second, it is the way in which firms continue to advance their distinctive skill levels over time so as to stay ahead of learning competitors. Without its own source of unique knowledge, the information flowing through the system is not unique and the firm cannot build or sustain distinctiveness.

Experimental learning relies heavily on "front-line" individuals, whether sales, factory-floor, R&D, or any other close-to-the-market personnel. With the discretion to experiment, these people can gain a wide range of new insights. Because insight is by definition personal, the firm must provide the means by which it can become explicit and be spread throughout the firm (Nonaka, 1994; Grant, 1996). Thus, experimental learning in activity 1 creates the inputs for the integration process of activity 3, where competencies form and improve (Huber, 1991; Helleloid & Simonin, 1994).

These learning benefits are not cost-free (Kogut, 1989). Like knowledge theory, a dynamic competence view considers the costs of creating and transferring tacit knowledge into the organization (activities 1 and 2). But it also considers the cost of exploiting that knowledge through different organizational means once it becomes explicit so as to capture rents from the competence (activities 4 and 5). Like transaction cost theory, this model recognizes that firms consider the costs of protecting resources from the opportunism of other firms when making the M-H-H decision. But here the focus is particularly on competencies and the costs of sustaining and protecting those resources in each scenario. Through the lens of competence theory, the costs of creating, transferring, and protecting knowledge are all learning costs, and it is against these costs that the returns to competencies from M-H-H choices are measured.

Comparison of costs against the benefits in a dynamic competence perspective is complicated by a few considerations. First, the benefits to competence may not be completely lost when the organization does not rely on control structures for in-country activities. Competencies can be kept alive through learning activities elsewhere in the organization and pricing may allow a firm to capture some or all of the returns to its competence without downstream ownership. Thus, firms do not face a situation where the choice between hierarchy and market also means a choice between above-average or commodity returns from competence.

Second, M-H-H decisions are not easily devisable with respect to the two flows of knowledge captured in FIGURE 17.1. For example, the in-country sales personnel that bundle and exploit existing competencies (activity 5) are often simultaneously engaging in the front-line experimental learning that will drive competence improvement or even open the way for the development of wholly new competencies (activity 1). With respect to each national market, a firm generally will have to undertake all of the activities in FIGURE 17.1 if it undertakes any.

Third, the benefits from knowledge inflows accrue in all units, not just the one providing the knowledge inflow. Similarly, the benefits that any in-country unit receives from competence transfers reflects not only its own contribution, but that of all other units as well.

Dynamic competence also makes assumptions about managers. As with the other perspectives on MNEs, here managers of firms are assumed to be profit seekers. They are assumed to desire sustained above-average profitability over the long term and to specifically recognize that continually building and sustaining competencies will be the basis for that profitability. Further, it is assumed that firms recognize the role of experimental learning in underpinning sustained competencies and how such learning involves people from throughout the organization. In this light, the balancing of learning benefits and costs in a multinational firm's decisions on M-H-H structure can be understood.

CHOICES AMONG FORMS UNDER A DYNAMIC COMPETENCE VIEW

In discussing M-H-H decisions by MNEs the several constructs mentioned above have to be considered simultaneously for each choice. In setting out propositions about the choices that MNEs make, the conceptual conditions surrounding each choice are first set out. The propositions themselves are not complex; it is the focus of the variables that is important in distinguishing this perspective. The propositions are stated, and outcomes of the particular conditions that may lead firms to that choice are mentioned. The choice between using the market or exercising some form of control with either a hierarchy or a hybrid form is analyzed first. Then the tradeoff between hierarchies and hybrids when the market is not the choice is considered.

MARKET CHOICE

One way to assess the choice of the market from the dynamic competence view is to analyze the net gain that investing in the alternatives, hierarchies and hybrids, provides. The market is seen here as the least-cost alternative. Firms choose not to use the market when the added benefits of hybrid or hierarchy exceed the added costs of hybrid or hierarchy. It is a marginal decision. In a dynamic competence view the gains firms realize are driven by the ongoing learning and competence nurturing processes of FIGURE 17.1. Thus, marginal costs to the firm are those associated with establishing an effective learning system and maintaining the benefit flows therefrom. Flows of knowledge between in-country units and the firm occur in the two ways previously modeled. While these are integrated in actuality, they will be bifurcated for analyzing the criteria that drive market choice, breaking them into the inbound (activities 1 and 2) and outbound (activities 4 and 5) aspects of competence dynamics.

The inbound information flow captured by activities 1 and 2 potentially benefits all of the units in the organization by building and nurturing firm-wide competencies. Indeed, the true value of the competencies developed and nurtured in activity 3 comes from the firm's ability to spread them to many units in the organization through core products (Prahalad & Hamel, 1990). Further, the contribution to organization-wide learning and competence development (activity 3) is not just that which comes from any particular location. Thus, it can reasonably be expected that the total firm benefits of developing and nurturing a competence firm-wide will exceed the contribution of any one unit. In this situation the inbound contribution of each unit must be considered on the margin. Specifically, the marginal contribution of a particular unit to a competence level on all of the firm's competencies occurs because the unit is part of a hierarchy or hybrid structure versus the market. This is the unit's marginal benefit to the whole firm. Even if the return benefits to the contributing unit itself are limited (activities 4 and 5), if the total of the marginal returns that competence brings throughout the firm due to an in-country linkage exceeds the cost of maintaining that linkage, then the firm will choose either a hierarchy or hybrid relationship and forgo the market.

In the situation just described the total Learning Benefits of Inbound knowledge flows (LB_I) exceed the costs. This will happen when the value of the in-country unit's insights, as measured by the increased value of a competence to all units of the firm, exceeds the costs of both building and maintaining the hierarchical or hybrid linkage (including the cost of capital), as well as facilitating the learning flows. Indeed, because in this view these links are maintained to facilitate knowledge flows for competence learning, such costs are called Learning Costs (LC). Thus, when:

$$LB_I > LC \qquad (17.1)$$

firms will not choose the market.

Similarly, the marginal benefits of a competence to any particular unit's profitability through the conduct of activities 4 and 5 may greatly exceed that unit's contribution to building and maintaining the competence as distinctive. In this situation the inward flows from any particular unit that are captured by activities 1 and 2 may be of little value in sustaining or expanding the organization-wide core competencies. But if the Learning, Benefits from competencies that flow Outbound (LB_O) to that unit exceed the cost of the whole system (LC), then a non-market linkage will be maintained. Thus, when:

$$LB_O > LC \qquad (17.2)$$

firms will not choose the market.

Logically, the test will be the combination of Equations 17.1 and 17.2. The cumulative benefits from both inflows and outflows ($LB_I + LB_O$) may be greater than the associated costs (LC), even though the separate benefits of each component (LB_I, LB_O) may not be sufficient on their own. Earlier we mentioned that the inbound and outbound flows in a hierarchy or hybrid cannot be separated. A firm gets both when a non-market structure is chosen. The two benefits need to be combined in determining when non-market options will be taken.

$$(LB_I + LB_O) > LC \qquad (17.3)$$

Still, it is important to retain the first two equations. They illustrate that there are two very different aspects to the returns that dynamic competence produces firm-wide, and that even when one of the two elements on the left-hand side of Equation 17.3 goes to zero, the returns from the other flow can be sufficient to move a firm away from the market. We can now rewrite Equation 17.3 to reflect market choice:

$$(LB_I + LB_O) < LC \qquad (17.3a)$$

By choosing the market the firm is giving up the ability to use information from an in-country unit to nurture and build its competencies, as well as the ability to have that unit exploit any distinctive, firm-level knowledge in its marketplace transactions. But choosing to rely on the market does not mean that the marketplace operates perfectly, nor does not mean that the firm would gain no benefits from building and maintaining competencies in a non-market relationship. Instead, considerations regarding the benefits and costs of building and maintaining competencies with the other units of the firm must be compared. The relationships captured in the equations set out can be expressed verbally in the following propositions:

Proposition 1: Firms will choose hierarchical or hybrid structural forms when the organization-wide benefits of learning and competence transfer associated with the inflows and outflows of knowledge from an in-country unit exceed the costs associated with maintaining an in-country unit ($LB_I + LB_o > LC$).

Proposition 2: Firms will engage in market transactions, rather than hierarchical or hybrid structural forms, when the costs of learning and competence transfer associated with an in-country unit exceed organization-wide benefits of enhanced competencies ($LB_I + LB_o < LC$).

The market choice indicated by Proposition 2 would most likely occur in situations where transactions involve commodity goods and where none of the non-competence-based rationalities mentioned at the start of this Chapter exist. Commodity products by definition lack the distinctive traits that can add unique value and for which premium prices can be charged. Competencies instill just such unique traits, so their absence in end-products also suggests the absence of any potential benefits that would result from building information linkages. Similarly, markets may be chosen because commodity market information will seldom be country specific. The global market for commodities mirrors the lack of particular value that knowledge from any individual country's market would likely provide. It is not that competencies do not exist in firms in commodity industries. Indeed, many competencies may be found in the core business of firms competing in such markets. It is just that these competencies are not tied to the knowledge and insight generated in any one country or location. As such, it is less likely that the learning that improves any competence is distinctly coming from the local presence of an in-country unit. In a commodity market the full returns that an upstream competence can provide can often be realized through intermediate market prices. When summed, a threshold level of benefits from competence enhancement from an in-country presence is not reached and the market is chosen.

Market choice will be considered in situations where non-commodity goods are involved as well. These are scenarios of the costs for maintaining and controlling a hierarchy or hybrid that does not produce sufficient returns. For the MNE, considerations such as small country market size or the costs imposed by geographic dispersion are two situations that can lower benefits or impose high costs. The list of potential variables impacting decisions in Equation 17.3a are as various as the products and countries in the global marketplace. In any situation where competence exploitation is seen as the key to profitability the rules in Proposition 1 and 2 will guide the market/non-market choice.

HYBRID AND HIERARCHY CHOICE

Having distinguished situations for market choice, the focus can shift to the choice between hybrid and hierarchy. The approach taken in this chapter is to look at the hybrid and hierarchy as choices that weight the same learning concepts, but in different ways. There is more variation in the hybrid form, so the analysis will begin there.

Hybrid forms represent an ill-defined set of relationships between two entities (Borys & Jemison, 1989). Strategic alliances and joint ventures are often described as hybrid forms, although only the latter has a distinctive legal character to it. Strategic alliances are, in fact, legal contracts. As such, they are technically market transactions. However, strategists note that there is something distinctive beyond the arms-length relationship of a market contract involved here. Indeed, the terms of an alliance contract often reflect the very considerations that transaction costs suggest will cause firms to avoid contracts. Stated another way, strategic alliances are ways of attending to the problems of contingent claim contracts without having to specify *ex ante* all of the contingencies. Instead, the firms are tied in an agreement that creates meaningful interdependence and, hence, incentive for a mutually beneficial resolution of future conflicts.

It seems axiomatic that strategic alliances will be "strategic," i.e. they will be critical to the execution of a firm's strategy. In a dynamic competence view where building and sustaining competencies are the key to long-term competitive advantage, alliances gain their strategic character when they nurture or develop competencies in one or more of the alliance partners. This being said, it is quite clear that the usage of the term "strategic alliance" is much more widely spread than this description would allow. Some firms' PR departments seem to put the label on any contract, no matter how tangential to the firm's strategic goals. But when including strategic alliances with joint ventures as hybrid forms, this discussion takes the more focused view. Here for a hybrid relationship to exist each partner firm must have some degree of meaningful control over discretionary actions taken in the course of the relationship. If no such control exists for a firm, then the firm is in the same situation as if in the marketplace. And if one of the firms gains *de facto* control over all strategically meaningful decisions, then the form for that firm is essentially hierarchical.

Between the extremes just discussed there exists a wide range of hybrid options (Contractor & L'Orange, 1988; Hennart, 1993). However, in all cases the hybrid choice will be predicated on the same criteria as considered in the market choice discussion: learning benefits and costs. Only for these choices the assumption is made that the inbound or outbound information flow (or both) $((LB_I + LB_O) > LC)$ is sufficient to eliminate the market from consideration. Management's goal remains to maximize returns to competence. The firm is looking neither for the alliance or venture form that would necessarily maximize the revenue flow from learning benefits $(LB_I + LB_O)$, nor the one that will minimize the learning costs (LC). Instead, the firm seeks the organizational form that maximizes the difference between benefits and costs:

$$\max (LB_I + LB_O) - (LC) \qquad (17.4)$$

where LB_I and LB_O represent the two distinct inbound and outbound flows discussed above in the market choice section.

Building on the role given to continuous knowledge development and the protection of organizational knowledge once created, dynamic competence theory would seem to have a strong bias for the control that is given by hierarchy. This is because the same critical information flows that this model emphasizes in creating benefits in hybrids also represent one of the major threats to the protection of competence due to leakage to current or potential rivals. This potential loss of competence, albeit in the future, imposes monitoring costs in hybrids similar to those described by transaction cost theory, but beyond those found in market transactions. These are evaluated with other costs when considering any hybrid option. Among the hybrid options available, the firm is looking for the linkage that would necessarily maximize the difference between the revenue flow from learning among all of the **Hybrid** options ($LB_{IHY} + LB_{OHY}$ and this expanded range of costs of the system that allows learning in the **Hybrid** (LC_{HY}). In other words, the hybrid form that brings the largest net gain:

$$\max(LB_{IHY} + LB_{OHY}) - (LC_{HY}) \qquad (17.4a)$$

where LB_{IHY} and LB_{OHY} represent the inbound and outbound learning benefits and LC_{HY} the total costs of the hybrid.

Using some form of hybrid structure to economically take advantage of the unique knowledge of in-country units suggests both lower costs and meaningful information flows. Indeed, the major appeal of a hybrid is that the same or similar learning benefits can be available at lower cost and risk than in the hierarchical alternative. However, as with costs, both benefits of Equation 17.4a may be adversely affected by particularities of the hybrid relationship; here due to the different levels of control the hybrid options provide and their different effects on the inward and outward information transfers. Although organizations hope to learn through alliances, partners may place restrictions on the access and distribution of information created in the relationship. For example, while increased control may make it easier for one partner to transfer learned knowledge outward to other units in the organization (activity 4), it may make the other partner less willing to allow the similar outward flow of its competencies into the hybrid. Indeed, the first partner may be reluctant to transfer skills for the same reason despite its controlling interest. Hence the hybrid relationship creates a dampening effect on one of the flows critical to full competence exploitation.

Similarly, the more power a particular partner has in the alliance, the more information it should be able to extract and bring into the firm for broader use via activity 2. This higher level of control, however, will probably be accompanied by higher costs. So reducing costs (and control) increases hybrid partners' interest in restricting the unique knowledge that the hybrid generates (activity 1) to only hybrid operations (activity 5). Firms would be particularly averse to seeing distinctive knowledge generated in the hybrid being used by a partner in another setting where the firms are rivals. This may reach the point where even minority partners can constrain the potential benefits of a majority partner.

In both cases just discussed the competitive advantages of the partners in markets elsewhere (markets where competence-based advantage is the basis for persistent above-average profits) constrain the effectiveness of the hybrid in the market of interest. Even if the competence could be protected, the additional rents that they generate may have to be shared with alliance partners of the in-country units. Yet, in both cases the definition of a strategic alliance as one where each partner contributes something of *strategic* importance also creates potential payoffs beyond those achievable by any firm independently. The nature of the hybrid linkage, therefore, can distinctly impact both the learning benefits and the costs.

The Best Hybrid versus Hierarchy

In balancing the benefits and costs of competence building and distribution, the firm is not only considering the variety of hybrid options that are available, it is also considering the option of hierarchical control. As the preceding discussion intimates, there is a preference for hierarchy since the flow of learning and knowledge is maximized and protected in this option, but the costs are also likely to be the highest. If Equation 17.4a represents the best hybrid option, then it is simply a matter of comparison to the costs and benefits of the hierarchy. This may be a comparison of positive gains, or it may be a situation where hierarchy is not even profitable. (A latter situation is one in which the market would have been selected by Equation 17.3a in the absence of a viable hybrid option.) Since the former case is the only one considered here, the decision rule between **Hy**brid and **Hie**rarchy compares the best hybrid option. If the relationship is:

$$\max (LB_{IHY} + LB_{OHY}) - (LC_{HY}) > (LB_{IHI} + LB_{OHI}) - (LC_{HI}) \qquad (17.5a)$$

then the best hybrid option is chosen. But if the relationship is:

$$\max (LB_{IHY} + LB_{OHY}) - (LC_{HY}) < (LB_{IHI} + LB_{OHI}) - (LC_{HI}) \qquad (17.5b)$$

then the hierarchy is used.

All of the variables in Equations 17.5a and 17.5b may vary by firms, markets, and products. As before, isolating one variable at a time and keeping the others constant allows for analysis of conditions that may cause firms to choose one form over the other. In some conditions this analysis will favor the hybrid form. For example, there may be situations in which learning benefits actually increase, i.e. are greater, in the hybrid structure. This may occur when the in-country unit is the alliance partner and it has a distinct identity reflecting the country or product use. The imposition of structural rigidity, organizational bureaucracy, or an incompatible culture may destroy the very entrepreneurial activities (activities 1 and 5) that are so desired in experimental learning. Thus, in comparing the choice of hybrid to hierarchy we can make the following proposition:

> Proposition 3: Other thing being equal, firms will choose hybrid structural forms, rather than hierarchical forms, when learning benefits of the hybrid are greater than those offered by hierarchical control.

The same degree of independence that an entrepreneurial, in-country partner brings to experimental learning also may reflect meaningful cost savings. A major challenge for firms seeking to internally develop or acquire an in-country unit is the cost of developing and nurturing the learning linkages. Established partners may greatly cut the cost of coordinating communication among far-flung units through the use of existing inbound systems and processes, particularly where costs are shared broadly among the partners.

> Proposition 4: Other things being equal, firms will choose hybrid structural forms, rather than hierarchical forms, when learning costs of the hybrid are lower than those offered by hierarchical control.

As with the market choice analysis, we have broken out the benefit and cost flows to illustrate that both have a role that could determine choice.

However, as before, we also note that it is the net benefit that is determining whether Equation 17.5a or 17.5b applies. Thus:

> Proposition 5: Firms will choose between the alternative structural forms, hybrid or hierarchy, on the basis of maximizing the difference between the returns from learning benefits and costs.

DISCUSSION

The proposal of a dynamic competence theory of MNE structure is suggested as an improvement over the limitations of the models derived from transaction cost and knowledge-based theories on several grounds. First, this view helps capture the dynamics of competition, as established multinational firms seek returns in multiple geographic markets in which other firms also compete. In this context, it is proposed that structure decisions require comparison of benefits and costs associated with strategies seeking returns to firm-wide competencies, rather than static cost-minimization decision rules applied to transactions or knowledge transfers. Second, we have expanded the view of firm knowledge beyond categorization as tacit or articulated to encompass the role of knowledge, knowledge creation, and learning as essential components of competitive advantage. In this context, knowledge created as a result of experimental learning processes, indicated by activity 1 in our model, and by integration processes, indicated by activity 3, represents necessary sources of competencies in the multinational firm. Finally, we have identified elements of opportunism as sources of information leakage and learning costs in structure decisions. Rather than treating such factors as determinative of hierarchy decisions, however, we have suggested that such costs must be weighed in comparison to benefits represented by the alternative structural forms. If this is the concept of self-interestedness that transaction costs theorists hope to capture, then the dynamic competence model does so with more precision.

LIMITATIONS

Several limitations exist as impediments to developing the propositions stated in this chapter. Given the recent emergence of the dynamic competence view, operationalization, measurement, and testing of the fundamental constructs and suggested relationships is at the developmental stage. These problems are neither unique nor insurmountable. Indeed, they are similar to those experienced by researchers attempting to operationalize concepts such as opportunism and asset specificity in the transaction costs stream of research and knowledge tacitness in the knowledge-based stream. As the dynamic competence stream of research continues to develop, it is expected that these problems will be overcome.

MANAGERIAL IMPLICATIONS AND CONCLUSIONS

The dynamic competence view proposed here, which compares learning benefits and costs, provides a relevant framework for managers of established MNEs as well as academics. We suggest that the market-hybrid-hierarchy structure decision for multinational companies can be made by focusing cost–benefit analysis, a well-established managerial decision tool, on comparisons of learning benefits and costs under each alternative. Such comparisons, in which quantitative and qualitative costs and benefits associated with the development and maintenance of firm competencies are identified, lends itself to alternative scenario analysis. Analyses of such factors under the dynamic competence view should provide managers with insight that is more managerially relevant than transaction costs and knowledge-based views of structure decisions. This is because the dynamic competence view focuses on capturing the flows of value-adding resources, such as knowledge, as well as costs of acquiring them. Managers should realize that while the other perspectives may contribute to structure decisions, the failure to incorporate dynamic considerations limits their effectiveness.

In conclusion, we set out to offer dynamic competence theory of MNE in comparison to transaction costs and knowledge-based theories. We sought to overcome the limitations and address the weaknesses of the prior approaches in explaining the market-hybrid-hierarchy decision made by established multinational firms. We proposed that this structural decision is premised upon the maximization of returns to firm competencies, which are realized by maximizing the differences between learning benefits and costs. This perspective overcomes weaknesses in the extant literature by offering a dynamic strategic perspective that emphasizes the maximization of returns from firm processes associated with building and maintaining competencies. Future research for the dynamic competence theory of the multinational enterprise would include empirical studies as well as further theory development.

REFERENCES

Bartlett, C.A. & Ghoshal, S. (1989). *Managing across Borders: The Transnational Solution.* Cambridge, MA: Harvard University Press.

Bogaert, I., Martens, R. & Van Cauwenbergh, A. (1994). Strategy as a situational puzzle: the fit of components. In A. Heene, R. Sanchez & H. Thomas (eds) *Competence Based Competition*. Chichester: Wiley.

Bogner, W.C., Thomas, H. & McGee, J. (1998). Core competence and competitive advantage: a dynamic, theory based model. *British Journal of Management*, under second review.

Borys, B. & Jemison, D.B. (1989). Hybrid arrangements as strategic alliances; theoretical issues in organizational combinations. *Academy of Management Review*, 14, 234–249.

Casson, M. (1987). *The Firm and the Market*. Oxford: Basil Blackwell.

Chang, S.J. (1996). An evolutionary perspective on diversification and corporate restructuring: entry, exit and economic performance during 1981–1989. *Strategic Management Journal*, 17(8), 587–612.

Contractor, F.J. & L'Orange, P. (1988). Why should firms cooperate? In F.J. Contractor & P. L'Orange (eds) *Cooperative Strategies in International Business*. Lexington, MA: Lexington Books.

Dunning, J.H. (1981). *International Production and the Multinational Enterprise*. London: George Allen & Unwin.

Dunning, J.H. (1988). The eclectic paradigm of international production: a restatement and some possible extensions. *Journal of International Business Studies*, 19(1), 1–32.

Dunning, J.H. (1995). Reappraising the eclectic paradigm in an age of alliance capitalism. *Journal of International Business Studies*, 26(3), 461–491.

Ghoshal, S. & Bartlett, C. (1990). The multinational corporation as an inter-organizational network. *Academy of Management Review*, 15(4), 603–625.

Ghoshal, S., & Moran, P. (1996). Bad for practice: a critique of the transaction cost theory. *Academy of Management Review*, 21(1): 13–47.

Grant, R.M. (1996). Prospering in dynamically-competitive environments: organizational capability as knowledge integration. *Organization Science*, 7(4), 375–387.

Grant, R.M. & Baden-Fuller, (1995). A knowledge-based theory of inter-firm collaboration. Paper presented at the SMS 15th Annual International Conference, Mexico City, Mexico.

Gupta, A.K. & Govindarajan, V. (1991). Knowledge flows and the structure of control within multinational corporations. *Academy of Management Review*, 16(4), 768–792.

Hamel, G. (1994). The concept of core competence. In A. Heene, R. Sanchez & H. Thomas (eds) *Competence Based Competition*. Chichester: Wiley.

Helleloid, D. & Simonin, B. (1994) Organizational learning and a firm's core competence. In A. Heene, R. Sanchez & H. Thomas (eds) *Competence Based Competition*. Chichester: Wiley.

Henderson, R. & Cockburn, I. (1994). Measuring competence? Exploring firm effects in pharmaceutical research. *Strategic Management Journal*, 15, 63–84.

Hennart, J.F. (1988). A transaction costs theory of equity joint ventures. *Strategic Management Journal*, 91, 361–374.

Hennart, J.F. (1993). Explaining the swollen middle: why most transactions are a mix of "market" and "hierarchy." *Organization Science*, 4(4), 529–547.

Hill, C.W. & Kim, W.C. (1988). Searching for a dynamic theory of the multinational enterprise: a transaction cost model. *Strategic Management Journal*, 9, 93–104.

Huber, G. (1991). Organizational learning; the contributing processes and the literature. *Organization Science*, 2(1), 88–115.

Kogut, B. (1989). A note on global strategies. *Strategic Management Journal*, 10(4), 383–389.

Kogut, B. (1990). International sequential advantages and network flexibility. In C.A. Bartlett, Y. Doz and G. Hedlund (eds) *Managing the Global Firm.* London: Routledge.

Kogut, B. & Zander, U. (1993). Knowledge of the firm and the evolutionary theory of the multinational corporation. *Journal of International Business Studies,* **24**(4), 625–645.

Kogut, B. & Zander, U. (1995). Knowledge, market failure and the multinational enterprise: a reply. *Journal of International Business Studies,* **26**(2), 416–421.

McFetridge, D. (1995). Knowledge, market failure and the multinational enterprise: a comment. *Journal of International Business Studies,* **26**(2), 409–415.

Nonaka, I. (1994). A dynamic theory of organizational knowledge creation. *Organization Science,* **5**(1), 14–37.

Parkhe, A. (1993). Strategic alliance structuring: a game theoretic and transaction cost examination of interfirm cooperation. *Academy of Management Journal,* **36**(4), 794–829.

Prahalad, C.K. & Hamel, G. (1990). The core competence of the corporation. *Harvard Business Review,* **68**(3), 79–91.

Quinn, J.B. (1992). The intelligent enterprise: a new paradigm. *Academy of Management Executive,* **6**(4), 48–63.

Tallman, S.B. (1992). A strategic management perspective on host country structure of multinational enterprises. *Journal of Management,* **18**(3), 455–471.

Teece, D.J. (1986). Transactions cost economics and the multinational enterprise. *Journal of Economic Behavior and Organization,* **7**, 21–45.

Williamson, O.E. (1991). The logic of economic organization. In O.E. Williamson & S.G. Winter (eds) *The Nature of the Firm.* Oxford University Press: New York.

Winter, S.G. (1988). On Coase, competence and the corporation. *Journal of Law, Economics, and Organizations,* **4**, 163–180.

Winter, S.G. (1991). On Coase, competence and the corporation. In O.E. Williamson & S.G. Winter (eds) *The Nature of the Firm.* Oxford University Press: New York.

Zander, U. & Kogut, B. (1995). Knowledge, and the speed of the transfer and imitation of organizational capabilities: an empirical test. *Organization Science,* **6**(1), 76–92.

18

Discovering Strategy: Competitive Advantage from Idiosyncratic Experimentation

RITA GUNTHER MCGRATH

INTRODUCTION

Strategists in successful firms face a deep dilemma. "Stick to the knitting," they are advised, as those competences built up over time give a firm an idiosyncratic, differentiated set of advantages, which competitors will find difficult to replicate (Wernerfelt, 1984, Dierickx & Cool, 1989; Barney, 1991). At the same time, the annals of business history are replete with tales of firms who attempted to capitalize on existing positions and were blindsided. Competitive actions, environmental shifts, and the emergence of new technologies can render carefully nurtured competences obsolete overnight (Tushman & Anderson, 1986; MacMillan, 1988; D'Aveni, 1994).

Leveraging the competitive advantages of today, in other words, can lead firms to sacrifice the future. The solution, it is commonly argued, is to pursue innovations—broadly defined as forays into new technologies, new products, or new markets—on a continuous basis. Unfortunately, innovations are highly uncertain, often resulting in expensive disappointments. Outcomes are as likely to be "mistakes" as successes (Van de Ven, 1986; Block & MacMillan, 1993).

Strategic Flexibility: Managing in a Turbulent Environment. Edited by G. Hamel, C.K. Prahalad, H. Thomas and D. O'Neal.
Copyright © 1998 John Wiley & Sons Ltd.

In short, while it is widely recognized that innovation is crucial to long-term competitiveness, managing the process through which innovations become competitive advantages is still relatively opaque (Bettis & Hitt, 1995). In this chapter, I argue that while it may not be possible to exactly predict the future strategies made possible by innovation, it is possible to systematically manage their discovery.

THE NEED FOR DISCOVERY-DRIVEN EXPERIMENTATION

A key reason why innovation, as opposed to other forms of strategic action, is often advocated has to do with differentiation. Strategies which competitors can rapidly match or follow diminish differentiation, as customers perceive little difference between rivals (Lieberman & Montgomery, 1988). The likelihood of this occurring increases to the extent that few differences in resources, knowledge or experience separate competing firms. To the extent that competitors base their strategies on the same "platform," in other words, they are far more likely to pursue similar strategies in which advantages are short-lived and margins slim (Stalk & Webber, 1993).

Many of the traditional tools of strategic planning do little to help firms establish or maintain differentiated positions (Mintzberg, 1994). To the extent that the value of a strategic attribute becomes well understood, it ceases to offer an advantage to any one firm (MacMillan, 1988; D'Aveni, 1994). A crucial objective for firms is thus to obtain insights that are not widely shared. When these insights are used to create combinations of resources that are put together in such a way that their operations are difficult to codify, rapid imitation can be prevented, and advantage extended (Rumelt, 1987; Boisot, 1995). Where, then, do idiosyncratic insights and resource combinations stem from?

Aggressive and motivated competitors may well gain access to similar information, can hire from roughly the same pool of talent, and may have the ability to utilize similar consulting and management advisory services. Strategies derived from these sources, while often essential to keeping up with the state of the art, are thus liable to diffuse rapidly, eliminating whatever gains had been made.

In contrast, engaging in "discovery-driven" experimentation can provide information, experience, and resource combinations that are available only to the firm engaged in experimentation, because they are experientially acquired (McGrath & MacMillan, 1995; Winter, 1995). Unlike codified analytical procedures, the discoveries made through firms' trial and error learning are far more likely to embody elements of tacitness and organizational embeddedness, making them difficult for others to understand and copy. In other words, they rely upon learned combinations of organizational

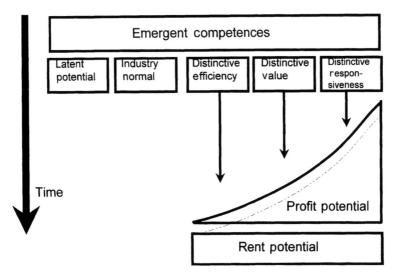

FIGURE 18.1   From competences to advantage

elements that are not readily available to competitors lacking the same experience (Dierickx & Cool, 1989). Efforts by competitors to replicate are thus hampered, and the preservation of differentiated positions enhanced.

This much being said, in a highly experimental project, many crucial variables are unpredictable at the outset. The very goal may be unclear, or may change considerably as new data emerge. How, then, are we as scholars and managers to measure progress in a manner compatible with a discovery-driven strategic philosophy? I suggest that this can be done, by measuring progress toward the achievement of a limited set of accomplishments, which almost always precedes the establishment of a competitive advantage from efforts to innovate. These are illustrated in FIGURE 18.1, which portrays the simultaneous and sequential set of steps that allows one to evaluate progress toward an as-yet-unknown advantage.

ANTECEDENTS TO COMPETITIVE ADVANTAGE

A competitive advantage allows a firm to gain access to streams of "rents," a term which typically refers to abnormally high economic returns (see Alchian, 1991). Note that it is possible for a firm to generate profits without generating rents. Profits result from the ability to charge prices in excess of costs. Rents, on the other hand, suggest that not only is a firm able to generate profits, but to do so idiosyncratically. An important source of rent is the creation of uniquely attractive products and services, or uniquely efficient operations, by combining resources in ways that other firms cannot imitate. These combinations are often termed "competences," where competence refers to "methods of doing things" (Winter, 1990, p. 274).

NEW COMPETENCES

In experimenting with new products, markets, or technologies, firms are often surprised by results that differ from prior assumptions (McGrath & MacMillan, 1995). Innovation projects, therefore, are likely to deliver performance that differs from targets, sometimes by a wide margin. Behavioral learning theory (Cyert & March, 1963; Levitt & March, 1988) tells us that the organizational response to such gaps is predictable: people will seek either to revise the target, or to improve performance. Performance gaps are evidence of a lack of ability to accomplish desired purposes, and tend to prompt change in the resources and routines deployed. They signal a lack of competence, in other words, and the need to continue to experiment.

Narrowing the gap between targets and results, on the other hand, signals that competence is improving, and will tend to prompt the organization to retain, reinforce, and extend the resource combinations producing this desired result. These qualify as competences under Teece, Pisano & Shuen's (1991) definition, meaning a combination of firm-specific resources that allow an organization to meet its objectives.

This brings us to the point at which we can begin to think operationally about measuring the emergence of new competences. A metaphor might be the creation of a path where one never existed before—it simply isn't there until someone walks on it. Only after it has been walked on over time can it be seen and followed. So, too, with competences. Only after they have been created can their form and utility be understood.

Evidence, therefore, which suggests that an organization is increasingly able to attain its objectives is evidence that it has developed competences, some of which may be distinctive due to their experiential origins. Note that it doesn't matter if the objectives have changed, or whether what the firm originally set out to do is what it is accomplishing now. Rather, as long as the firm is accomplishing something, a new competence has emerged. In more formal terms:

Hypothesis 1: Convergence between strategic intentions and results represents a necessary (but not sufficient) condition for creating a competitive advantage—absent the ability to increasingly achieve objectives, a strategy will flounder. To the extent that convergence is emerging, rent potential will increase.

COMPETENCES, LATENT COMPETENCES AND DISTINCTIVE COMPETENCES

Some competences are not all that different from those that are widely available to competitors. These are simply competences—necessary, perhaps, but unlikely to lead to rents because they are also possessed by others (these can be considered "industry normal"). Most retail banks today, for instance, must offer their customers access to automatic teller machines (ATMs). An ATM-based offering is technologically quite complex, but because most banks possess the competences required to offer the service, customers do not perceive it as a source of unusual value.

A second type of competence possessed by a firm can be considered "latent." These are resource combinations that permit a firm to do things, but their commercial value has not yet been realized. Most important innovations are in this category at some point in their development. AMR Corporation's SABRE airlines reservation system and the competences underlying the 3M "Post-it Note" are two examples. In both cases, the parent firm did not realize at the outset that it possessed competences that would later drive significant commercial success. The process of market experimentation and probing led to the discovery of these competences' ultimate value.

A third category of competences differentiates the firm from competition in ways that either allow a firm to operate with unusual efficiency or create unusual value in the eyes of customers. These competences are *distinctive*, in the sense meant by Selznick (1957) when he said "that which a firm does better than others." The emergence of distinctive competence is a further measurable antecedent to competitive advantage.

Efficiency has long received attention in the strategy literature (see Williamson, 1991; Peteraf, 1993). The essence of the argument is that when a firm is able to use its idiosyncratic resource endowments in such a way that it can create a cost advantage, it can obtain higher margins. When the nature of this cost advantage cannot be copied or imitated, it is considered to be a source for rents.

A second arena in which distinctiveness matters is in the area of value to the customer. Here, the argument is that competences of the firm are used to create product and service attributes. These can be highly valued by customers, regarded negatively by customers, or be a matter of customer indifference. When those attributes that are regarded positively outweigh those that are regarded negatively in the customers' eyes, the firm has the opportunity to capture price from that customer (MacMillan & McGrath, 1996). If in turn the price exceeds the cost to create these attributes and other firms would find it difficult to match the offering, the firm has the opportunity to capture rents. Positive attributes can be further distinguished into attributes of the product (such as features) and service attributes (such as responsiveness), which reflect the nature of the relationship between the customer and the firm.

As with the emergence of competence, emergence of distinctive efficiency, distinctive product value or distinctive responsiveness in an experimental initiative is a positive indicator of emergent competitive advantage. Again, more formally:

> Hypothesis 2: To the extent that differentiation, in the form of "distinctive" competences at (i) product value added, (ii) efficiency, or (iii) responsiveness is emerging, rent potential should be enhanced.

BUT HOW FAR FROM THE KNITTING? THE QUESTION OF EXPLORATION

A final consideration in strategies of experimentation is how far from the existing competence base of a firm experimentation should occur. March's (1991) distinction between exploration and exploitation is useful in discussing this issue. Under exploitation, the firm uses knowledge already in its possession. When exploring, in contrast, the firm must search for new knowledge.

When firms explore far from the existing competence base, what McGrath & MacMillan (1995) have called the "assumption : knowledge" ratio increases. The number of decisions, in other words, that can be made on the basis of known cause and effect relationships is smaller than the number that must be made on the basis of assumptions regarding these relationships. By implication, the advances in knowledge that derive from undertaking a more exploratory project are apt to be greater than those that can be obtained from undertaking a less exploratory one. They have a higher learning value, which should correspond to higher long-term rent potential.

Obviously, exploring far from base also has a negative aspect. This is that as fewer established skills, assets, and systems are employed, the organization is increasingly subject to liabilities of newness (Stinchcombe, 1965), which the effects of increasing uncertainty can exacerbate. The advantage, on the other hand, is that if the organization undertakes exploration in advance of competition, it can reduce this uncertainty in ways that are unique to it (McGrath, 1997). More formally:

> Hypothesis 3: The more exploratory the project, the greater the extent to which the firm will be able to create distinctiveness; in other words, there will be an interaction effect.

It is worth noting that there are two broad areas in which these dynamics of exploration might be expected to make a difference: first, when the firm is exploring new competences—new technologies, systems, assets or other resources—and second, when the firm is exploring new markets—distribution channels, customer categories, elements of customer need.

The discussion to this point suggests that renewal of competitive advantages requires innovation, but that platform oriented management processes are unlikely to suit highly uncertain new projects. Instead, a model of unfolding competitive advantage through a discovery-driven experimental process is proposed. The essence of the argument is that if a firm is not building distinctiveness in either value or efficiency terms, it is unlikely to enjoy significant potential for rent. Without clear evidence of emerging competence, it is unlikely to be able to reliably and consistently achieve distinctiveness. Finally, highly exploratory environments, while uncertain, offer the greatest opportunity for the discovery of distinctive competences. Let us turn now to the methods used to empirically evaluate this model.

METHODS

PARTICIPANTS IN THE STUDY

The firms participating in this study were contacted as part of a larger investigation of the genesis of idiosyncratic competitive advantages. The first phase comprised a major field study (including over 300 interviews and the observation of thirty-five project teams in five companies). This study, together with an extensive literature review, was used to develop a survey instrument that operationalized the constructs described here. Data from 183 innovation project teams are included. The level of analysis for this study is that of the individual project.

OPERATIONALIZATION AND MEASUREMENT

The constructs of concern in the present study are (i) emergent competence, (ii) degree of competence exploration, (iii) degree of market exploration, (iv) distinctive efficiency, (v) distinctive value, (vi) distinctive responsiveness, (vii) predicted profit potential, and (viii) predicted rent potential. The respondent set for each project was an expert reference group, consisting of those working on the project and the project leader.

Questionnaires were used largely because there is a dearth of alternatives (Clark, Chew & Fujimoto, 1987, p. 738; Day, 1994, pp. 156–157). Note that the surveys used to supply data for this study were typically part of an arrangement between the sponsoring organizations and the research team, for which the sponsors contributed financial resources and time in the expectation of receiving actionable feedback on the survey results. This distinguishes it from surveys in which contacts with companies are established through mailed requests only, and from single-informant studies.

Multiple questionnaire items were developed for each of the constructs. Individual items were derived, item-by-item, from the relevant literature. Only items that drew off at least three citations in the literature were used in the survey. Respondents scored each item on 1–5 Likert-type scales, where higher scores are always associated with higher levels of the construct. The team's average response for each item was calculated and then these average scores were totaled and averaged across items for each of the sections of the questionnaire, providing an overall grand average for each construct.

This is similar to the approach employed by Gresov, Drazin & Van de Ven (1989). A major advantage is that when scores are totaled across several items in a large sample, with group responses to large number of items, biases of individual responses are averaged out and the resulting interpretation of results is conservative. Assumptions about normality are more easily justified, increasing confidence that parametric statistical methods are appropriate. For the exploration score, only the responses of the project leader were used, since this is the individual with arguably the most information about the external conditions facing the group (Ancona & Caldwell, 1988). The project leader score for each item was totaled, and the average calculated across items.

Emerging Competence

The competence items tap how well the project is performing on a multidimensional effectiveness matrix (Jackson, 1992, p. 361; Ancona & Caldwell, 1992, p. 324; Van de Ven, Hudson & Schroeder, 1984, p. 91). The spirit of this measure follows Gresov, Drazin & Van de Ven (1989, p. 45) who note that effectiveness is often defined as degree of goal attainment, and is consonant with Doty, Glick & Huber's (1993) arguments in favor of a multidimensional performance construct. Respondents were instructed to assess the performance of the project over the previous two months. A score of 1 indicates that results were far worse than expected, and a score of 5 indicates that results were far better than expected. These scores are applied to ten generic objectives common to innovations: budget objectives, staffing objectives, major deadlines, quality objectives, reliability objectives, cost objectives, efficiency objectives, user/client satisfaction objectives, service objectives, and objectives overall.

Degree of Competence Exploration and Degree of Market Exploration

This measure assesses the degree to which a given project is new, either in terms of the technology used, market sought or product offering created, all found by previous researchers to represent important arenas of exploration (Von Hippel, 1977, 1988; Ancona & Caldwell, 1992; Block & MacMillan, 1993; Amit & Schoemaker, 1993, p. 36).

By design, all the projects in the sample are innovation projects; however, this measure attempts to capture how, and in what ways, they require new knowledge. Respondents were asked to provide a score in response to the question "To what extent are the following project characteristics or factors new to your firm at the moment?" A score of 1 means "to no extent (not new at all)" while a score of 5 means "to a very great extent (entirely new)". For competence exploration, items were: the product or service offered, the know-how of the project team, and the technology used in the project. For market exploration, the relevant items were: the market or clients served, the customer/client need to be met, and the users of the offering. The Cronbach coefficient alphas for these scales are 0.87 and 0.88, respectively.

Distinctive Efficiency

Respondents were requested to evaluate the extent to which the project would achieve the following objectives: do more work without increasing headcount, gain economies of scale, reduce the number of steps required to complete a transaction, reduce turnaround time, make better use of assets, reduce amount or cost of input resources, lower costs per unit of output, eliminate or reduce post-sales service requirements, lower fixed costs, reduce costs of distribution, reduce costs of storage or inventory, reduce costs of operation, and gain relative efficiencies. The Cronbach alpha for this measure is 0.84.

Distinctive Value

This measures the extent to which this project is supposed to increase the value customers receive from product or service attributes. Respondents were asked to respond to the following: customers/clients will get more value from our offerings than they have been getting in the past, as a result of this project customers/clients will get more value from our offerings than from competitive offerings, as a result of this project we will be able to meet customer needs we never served before, this project is likely to allow us to offer a higher quality offering than our competitors or other organizations like ours, and as a result of this project customers/clients will be willing to pay a premium price for our offerings.

Distinctive Responsiveness

This measures the extent to which the project is being seen as one which can increase the strength of the customer relationship. Items were: this project is likely to make us more responsive to customers/clients than our competitors (or other organizations like ours) are, and this project is likely to significantly improve the quality of our offerings compared to our past quality levels.

Predicted Profit Potential

This estimates the size of likely profits stemming from the project. Unlike the estimated probability of rent (rent potential), this construct simply taps whether the initiative is likely to prove a financial success, not whether it is likely to give the firm a sustainable competitive advantage. Items developed to tap this construct are: probability of contribution to unusually high profits, probability of improving margin, and probability of significantly increasing revenues.

Estimated Probability of Rent (Rent Potential)

This construct measures rent, in the sense defined by Alchian (1991) as supranormal profits which do not immediately elicit competitive appropriation. The three items developed to tap this construct are: probability of superior profits than competitors, probability of superior margins than competitors, and probability of superior revenues than competitors. In the survey, these were interspersed with a number of other items which estimate future profitability (as opposed to rent). Since this variable goes to the heart of this discussion, some effort was put into making sure that it accurately reflects the objective outcome of new initiatives, in addition to subjective estimates.

The use of a subjective performance measure, in addition to its obvious drawbacks, does have at least three clear advantages (see Covin & Slevin, 1990). First, firms are often reluctant or unable to provide "hard" objective data at project level for the issues of concern in a study like this one, which implies that more complete information can be obtained with a subjective measure. Second, objective performance data on innovation projects may be subject to deliberate and/or inadvertent manipulations, and is difficult to interpret due to inconsistent intra-firm measurement issues. Third, absolute scores can be affected by idiosyncratic differences in projects, so directly comparing the data for different projects raises its own set of measurement and analytical concerns. The Cronbach coefficient alpha for this scale is 0.85.

ADEQUACY OF THE MEASURES

Validity and reliability of the survey measures used to capture the data were tested with considerable care (for details of the procedures, please refer to McGrath, MacMillan & Venkataraman (1995) and McGrath *et al.* (1996)). Tests performed included pre-tests, Harmon's one-factor test, split sample analysis, validation of the dependent variable with an independent (objective) dataset, different country replication of results, establishment of criterion validity and longitudinal correlation.

RESULTS

TABLE 18.1 presents descriptive statistics for the variables in this study. As can be seen from the table, emergent competence is significantly and positively correlated with all three increased distinctiveness measures (distinctive efficiency, distinctive value, and distinctive responsiveness). The three distinctiveness measures are in turn significantly and positively correlated with predicted profit potential. This lends some support to the idea that as competences unfold, it becomes possible for the organization to recognize that some of these offer the promise of strategic value, by creating new opportunities for profit.

Interestingly, only distinctive value and distinctive responsiveness were significantly related to predicted rent potential, which is a measure of how much a firm will be able to outperform its peers. While distinctive efficiency was positively correlated with predicted rent potential, the correlation is not statistically significant, suggesting that while efficiency doesn't hurt, it is not a primary source for competitive differentiation in new initiatives.

Turning to the exploration measures, we see that although the projects in the sample were specifically selected to represent efforts by firms to enter new markets, develop new processes or create new products, and were all regarded as important strategic projects, they are not, on average, wildly exploratory. The means for competence and market exploration are 2.78 and 2.45, with standard deviations of 0.63 and 0.82, respectively. This suggests that firms tend to do some exploring as they undertake new initiatives, but also attempt to exploit existing resources and routines, consonant with the basic premise of the resource-based argument.

TABLE 18.1 Descriptive statistics and correlation matrix, $n = 183$

Variable	Mean	s.d.	Emergent competence	Competence exploration	Market exploration	Distinctive efficiency	Distinctive value	Distinctive responsiveness	Predicted profit potential
Emergent competence	3.22	0.52							
Competence exploration	2.78	0.63	-0.07						
Market exploration	2.45	0.82	-0.04	0.35***					
Distinctive efficiency	3.25	0.70	0.16*	0.18**	-0.18**				
Distinctive value	3.66	0.52	0.21**	0.13+	0.07	0.21**			
Distinctive responsiveness	3.81	0.62	0.13+	0.21*	-0.03	0.52***	0.63***		
Predicted profit potential	66.20	12.92	0.32***	0.08	-0.07	0.33***	0.36***	0.39***	
Predicted rent potential	60.21	22.82	0.15*	0.03	0.03	0.07	0.23**	0.21**	0.44***

$+p < 0.10$; $*p < 0.05$; $**p < 0.01$; $***p < 0.001$.

Competence exploration, in which the firms seeks to enhance its processes, products, technologies or skills, was positively and significantly correlated with all three distinctiveness measures, most strongly with distinctive efficiency. There was no significant relationship between competence exploration and predicted profits or rents, and a non-significant negative correlation with emergent competence. Market exploration, on the other hand, was significantly and *negatively* correlated with efficiency, and not significantly correlated with the other two distinctiveness measures. It was also not significantly correlated with any of the outcome measures, predicted profit potential or predicted rent potential.

TABLE 18.2 presents regression results for standardized, OLS regressions used to test the hypotheses. The first three models have potential for profits as the dependent variable. These compare the effects of distinctive efficiency (model 1), distinctive value (model 2), and distinctive responsiveness (model 3) on the potential for profits, with market and competence exploration included as control variables. Exploration in these models is not significant, while all three distinctiveness measures have a positive and significant ($p < 0.001$) effect on profit potential. This suggests support for Hypothesis 2, which postulated a positive effect upon performance from increases in the distinctiveness constructs.

Rent potential is the dependent variable in models 4, 5, and 6. Here again, as with the correlation matrix above, while increases in value and responsiveness appear to have a positive effect on the likelihood that a firm will outperform competition, the effects of increases in efficiency were non-significant, controlling for exploration. This suggests that there is a powerful difference between competitive advantages that are efficiency driven versus those that are value driven.

The remaining models test hypotheses 1 and 3, concerning the effects of competence and exploration upon the antecedents to profits and rents. Model 7 shows a positive and significant effect for competence and competence exploration on efficiency, while the effect of market exploration is negative. This suggests, firstly, that emergent competence is a predictor for whether or not distinctive efficiencies are likely to emerge, and further, that investments in new competences (for instance, in new technologies) help create greater efficiency, while the firms in this sample appeared to be unable to significantly enhance efficiencies when entering new markets.

With respect to distinctive value and distinctive responsiveness, we see a somewhat different pattern. As predicted in Hypothesis 1, emerging competence positively and significantly predicts emerging distinctive value and distinctive responsiveness. The effects of exploration were for the most part non-significant, with the exception of a positive and significant effect on responsiveness for competence exploration.

TABLE 18.2 Regression results

	Model 1	Model 2	Model 3	Model 4	Model 5	Model 6	Model 7	Model 8	Model 9
Dependent variable	Profit potential	Profit potential	Profit potential	Rent potential	Rent potential	Rent potential	Distinctive efficiency	Distinctive value	Distinctive responsiveness
R-square	0.09	0.14	0.15	0.00	0.04	0.03	0.12	0.05	0.06
F value	7.34***	10.55***	11.27***	0.54	3.31*	3.01	9.4***	4.30**	5.11**
Emergent competence	–	–	–	–	–	–	0.18* (2.52)	0.22* (3.07)	0.14* (2.03)
Distinctive efficiency	0.31*** (4.23)	–	–	NS	–	–	–	–	–
Distinctive value	–	0.36*** (5.22)	–	–	0.23** (3.10)	–	–	–	–
Distinctive responsiveness	–	–	0.38*** (5.42)	–	–	0.22** (2.95)	–	–	–
Degree of competence exploration	NS	NS	N S	NS	NS	NS	0.30*** (4.03)	0.13 NS	0.26** (3.44)
Degree of market exploration	NS	NS	N S	NS	NS	NS	−0.28*** (−3.80)	0.03 NS	NS

$+p < 0.10$; $*p < 0.05$; $**p < 0.01$; $***p < 0.001$.

Discussion and Implications

The results largely support the core arguments presented here. Given the uncertainty inherent in experimental projects, I have argued that a measure of progress is convergence between intended results and actual outcomes, and that this can be taken as a measure of emergent competence. Over time, some of these competences will create distinctiveness. The results are consistent, suggesting that emergent competence was a significant positive predictor of all three distinctiveness measures, as well as of profits and rents.

A clear implication for the management of discovery oriented projects is that unless competences are emerging, distinctiveness cannot in turn emerge. Part of the skill of managing these projects is thus to understand their sequential yet simultaneous developmental nature.

Results also suggest empirical support for a relationship that is often assumed, rather than tested. This is that rents, and to a lesser extent profits, are dependent upon the ability of the firm to create differentiation, whether these are reflected in distinctive efficiency, distinctive value in product or services, or distinctively responsive customer relationships. In the analysis of the dataset presented here, both profitability and rents showed positive and significant correlations with the distinctiveness measures.

The value of this finding for the management of discovery oriented projects is that these results suggest that it is possible to capture early evidence of distinctiveness (or lack of distinctiveness) prior to commercial execution. This gives managers data that can be used either to redirect the project or terminate it, conserving scarce corporate resources. This potentially allows a firm to undertake more initiatives, as the cost of pursuing any given one can be contained. This is consistent with a view of experimental projects as "options" on future strategies, a perspective which is gaining increasing recognition as important under turbulent competitive conditions (Bettis & Hitt, 1995; McGrath, 1997).

Interestingly, while all three measures (efficiency, value, and responsiveness) were significant drivers of profit potential, only value and responsiveness were significant in models in which the dependent variable was rent potential. What this implies is that while increases in efficiency may allow a firm to expect superior profits, relative to today, merely increasing efficiency is not enough to create a comparative competitive advantage. This provides empirical support for the contention that one cannot reengineer one's way to greatness. The clear managerial implication is to ensure that both efficiency and discovery receive adequate attention.

Finally, we come to the question of the effects of exploration. Results for Hypothesis 3, which suggested that, in general, greater exploration should be associated with greater ability to gain distinctiveness, are mixed. The argument here has been that firms can seek to extend their existing resource endowments by making investments in new competences (represented here as the degree of competence exploration) or by attempting to access new markets (represented here as the degree of market exploration). While investments in building new competences did have a positive correlation with all three distinctiveness measures, the most powerful effects were on increases in distinctive efficiency, followed by increases in distinctive responsiveness. A weak effect on distinctive value could also be seen. What this suggests is that when firms explore new competences, these investments go primarily toward improving internal processes, allowing them to function more smoothly or cost effectively and to provide better, more responsive service to their customers.

A different story emerges for investments in market exploration. Unlike investments in new competences, attempts to explore new markets had a significant and *negative* effect on the emergence of distinctive efficiency. This supports the essence of March's (1991) exploration/exploitation argument, namely that when exploring new territory it is very difficult to operate with optimal efficiency. It extends this argument, as well, providing empirical data which suggest that the broad concept of exploration can be more finely analyzed, and the effects of different kinds of exploration teased out. It suggests, for instance, that as a matter of corporate policy there may be a need to permit initiatives in which a significant objective is to explore new markets to vary from corporate overhead rates or normal operating ratios until the new markets are better understood.

This study has advanced a view of competitive advantages as *discovered* in the pursuit of strategies in which the outcome is not known at the outset. By undertaking new initiatives, I have argued, firms are able to idiosyncratically reduce uncertainty in ways specific to themselves. This specificity derives from the experiential (and therefore tacit and uncodified) nature of the knowledge acquisition in new projects (see Nelson & Winter, 1982; Boisot, 1995). Further, this firm-specific uncertainty reduction is accompanied by the creation of firm-specific, idiosyncratic resource combinations, some of which represent competences.

Progress in these two arenas, namely firm-specific uncertainty reduction and the related embeddedness in new resource combinations, can be proxied, I have argued, in a competence measure which taps convergence of intended with realized results. This is the beginning of a conceptual model for sequential and simultaneous processes that precede competitive advantage, shown in FIGURE 18.1. The framework offers a parsimonious, easy-to-use, and empirically tractable way to determine whether or not competences and competitive advantages are indeed emerging, offering managers the potential to take action earlier than if they were forced to rely on conventional measures (such as variance from plan dates or budgets).

A significant challenge for future practice and scholarship has to do with the idea of investments to increase efficiency. Increased efficiency, represented in such management practices as business process reengineering, total quality management, cycle time initiatives and the like, have consumed enormous amounts of management time and attention in many large US firms. If the results here are reliable indicators of the effects of such programs, their dangers become clear. One might indeed expect to see a relatively short-term increase in profitability (as margins improve with lower costs). The problem is that all the effort and disruption of most major efficiency drives is likely to have a negligible effect on the creation of competitive advantage, as measured by the potential to garner rents.

An opportunity suggested by this research has to do with the nature of exploration, and the effects of different kinds of exploration on the long-term viability of competitive strategies. Internally oriented investments in competences tend to generate little distinctiveness in terms of long-term value, although they do positively affect efficiency and responsiveness. Market exploration, on the other hand, has a powerful negative effect on efficiency, but negligible effects on other forms of distinctiveness.

This suggests that partitioning the nature of exploration in future studies is potentially important. It further suggests that competence exploration tends to allow a firm to reinforce advantages, but primarily with existing markets and existing products. This set of findings suggests a major challenge for the long-term robustness of strategies, namely to ensure that organizational incentives oriented toward profit and efficiency improvements do not drive out the exploration of less predictable, but potentially far more valuable, strategies in new markets or with new competences.

CONCLUSION

The purpose of making investments in an experimental discovery process is to help firms create the rare, inimitable combinations of resources thought to play such a central role in renewing competitive position. In an increasingly dynamic environment, managers will increasingly need to be able to measure and to manage these processes. The core contribution of this chapter as I see it, is to shed some light on the process through which trial and error experimentation can lead to competitive advantage, and further to offer measures helpful in determining whether a project is on track. This study proposes some specific variables that can be helpful in the prospective, as opposed to retrospective, management of the experimental process, in time for early interventions to be made.

The philosophy implicit in this study advocates a dynamic, experimental approach to strategy, and offers a theoretically grounded framework for understanding how experimentation can yield advantage. Strategy creation, I believe, must go beyond purely rational planning, but must also not fall into the trap of an undisciplined search for serendipity. Theory and metrics such as those offered here can be helpful in integrating these two concepts.

ACKNOWLEDGMENTS

I gratefully acknowledge the financial support of the Accelerating Competitive Effectiveness (ACE©) Program of the Sol C. Snider Entrepreneurial Center at the Wharton School. Ian C. MacMillan, S. Venkataraman and Max Boisot offered extremely helpful comments.

REFERENCES

Alchian, A.A. (1991). Rent. In J. Eatwell, M. Milgate & P. Newman (eds) *The World of Economics*. New York: W.W. Norton, pp. 591–597.

Amit, R. & Schoemaker, P. (1993). Strategic assets and organizational rent. *Strategic Management Journal*, **14**, 33–46.

Ancona, D.G. & Caldwell, D. (1988). Beyond task and maintenance: defining external functions in groups. *Group and Organization Studies*, **13**, 468–493.

Ancona, D.G. & Caldwell, D.F. (1992). Demography and design: predictors of new product team performance. *Organization Science*, **3**, 321–341.

Barney, J.B. (1991). Firm resources and sustained competitive advantage. *Journal of Management*, **17**, 99–120.

Bettis, R.A. & M.A. Hitt. (1995). The new competitive landscape. *Strategic Management Journal*, **16**(special issue), 7–19.

Block, Z. & MacMillan, I.C. (1993). *Corporate Venturing: Creating New Business within the Firm*. Cambridge, MA: Harvard Business School Press.

Boisot, M. (1995). *Information Space: A Framework for Learning in Organizations, Institutions and Culture*. New York: Routledge.

Clark, K. Chew, W.B. & Fujimoto, T. (1987). Product development in the world auto industry. *Brookings Papers on Economic Activity*, **3**, 729–782.

Covin, J. & Slevin, D.P. (1990). New venture strategic posture, structure and performance: an industry life cycle analysis. *Journal of Business Venturing*, **5**, 123–135.

Cyert, R.M. & March, J.G. (1963). *A Behavioral Theory of the Firm*. Englewood Cliffs, NJ: Prentice Hall.

D'Aveni, R. (1994). *Hypercompetition: The Dynamics of Strategic Maneuvering*. New York: Free Press.

Day, D.L. (1994). Raising radicals: different processes for championing innovative corporate ventures. *Organization Science*, **5**, 148–172.

Dierickx, I. & Cool, K. (1989). Asset stock accumulation and sustainability of competitive advantage. *Management Science*, **35**, 1504–1513.

Doty, D.H., Glick, W.H. & Huber, G.P. (1993). Fit, equifinality and organizational effectiveness: a test of two configurational theories. *Academy of Management Journal*, **36**, 1196–1250.

Gresov, C., Drazin, R. & Van de Ven, A. (1989). Work-unit task uncertainty, design and morale. *Organization Studies*, **10**, 45–62.

Jackson, S.E. (1992). Consequences of group composition for the interpersonal dynamics of strategic issue processing. *Advances in Strategic Management*, vol. 8 Greenwich, CT: JAI Press, pp. 345–382.

Levitt, B. & March, J.G. (1988). Organizational learning. *Annual Review of Sociology*, **14**, 319–340.

Lieberman, M.B. & Montgomery, D.B. (1988). First mover advantages. *Strategic Management Journal*, **9**, 41–58.

MacMillan, I.C. (1988). Controlling competitive dynamics by taking strategic initiative. *Academy of Management Executive*, **2**, 111–118.

MacMillan, I.C. & McGrath, R.G. (1996). Discover your products' hidden potential. *Harvard Business Review*, **74**.

March, J.G. (1991). Exploration and exploitation in organizational learning. *Organization Science*, **2**, 71–87.

McGrath, R.G. & MacMillan, I.C. (1995). Discovery driven planning. *Harvard Business Review*, **73**, 44–54.

McGrath, R.G., MacMillan, I.C. & Venkataraman, S. (1995). Defining and developing competence: a strategic process paradigm. *Strategic Management Journal*, **16**, 251–275.

McGrath, R.G., Tsai, M.H., Venkataraman, S. & MacMillan, I.C. (1996). Innovation, competitive advantage and rent: a model and test. *Management Science*, **42**, 389–403.

McGrath, R.G. (1997). A real options logic for initiating technology positioning investments. *Academy of Management Review*, **22**(4), 974–996.

Mintzberg, H. (1994). *The Rise and Fall of Strategic Planning*. New York: Free Press.

Nelson R.R. & Winter S.G. (1982). *An Evolutionary Theory of Economic Change*. Cambridge, MA: Harvard University Press.

Peteraf, M.A. (1993). The cornerstones of competitive advantage: a resource-based view. *Strategic Management Journal*, **14**, 179–192.

Rumelt, R.P. (1987). Theory, strategy and entrepreneurship. In D.J. Teece (ed.) *The Competitive Challenge: Strategies for Industrial Innovation and Renewal*. New York: Harper & Row.

Selznick, P. (1957). *Leadership in Administration: A Sociological Interpretation*. New York: Harper & Row.

Stalk, G. & Webber, A.M. (1993). Japan's dark side of time. *Harvard Business Review*, **71**, 93–102.

Stinchcombe, A.L. (1965). Organizations and social structure. In J.G. March (ed.) *Handbook of Organizations*. Chicago, IL: Rand McNally.

Teece, D.J., Pisano, G. & Shuen, A. (1991). Dynamic capabilities and strategic management, unpublished manuscript, revised 1991.

Tushman, M. & Anderson, P. (1986). Technological discontinuities and organizational environments. *Administrative Science Quarterly*, **31**, 439–465.

Van de Ven, A.H. (1986). Central problems in the management of innovation. *Management Science*, **32**, 590–607.

Van de Ven, A.H., Hudson, R. & Schroeder, D.M. (1984). Designing new business startups: entrepreneurial, organizational and ecological considerations. *Journal of Management*, **10**, 87–107.

von Hippel, E. (1988). Trading secrets over beers. *Across the Board*, June, 52–56.

von Hippel, E. (1977). Successful and failing internal corporate ventures: an empirical analysis. *Industrial Marketing Management*, **6**, 163–174.

Wernerfelt, B. (1984). A resource-based view of the firm. *Strategic Management Journal*, **5**, 171–180.

Williamson, O.E. (1991). Strategizing, economizing and economic organization. *Strategic Management Journal*, **12**, 75–94.

Winter, S. (1990). Survival, selection and inheritance in evolutionary theories of organization. In J. Singh (ed.) *Organizational Evolution: New Directions*. Newbury Park, CA: Sage, pp. 269–297.

Winter, S. (1995). Four Rs of profitability: rents, resources, routines and replication. In C. Montgomery (ed.) *Resource-Based and Evolutionary Theories of the Firm: Towards a Synthesis*. Boston, MA: Kluwer, pp. 147–178.

19

Strategic Renewal and Competence Building: Four Dynamic Mechanisms

HENK W. VOLBERDA, CHARLES BADEN-FULLER

INTRODUCTION

How do large multi-unit firms reconcile the conflicting forces for change and stability? How do they promote order and control, while having to respond, renew, and learn? Expanding worldwide competition, fragmenting markets, and emerging technologies has forced established firms to create new sources of wealth through new combinations of resources (Guth & Ginsburg, 1990). The forces for change are countered by short-term competitive forces, which require organizations to maximally exploit their existing capabilities and competencies. How do firms balance these tensions?

From an evolutionary perspective, organizations accumulate know-how in the course of their existence. They become repositories of skills which are unique and often difficult to alienate. These skills are the source of both inertia and distinctive competence. The inertia is due to sunk costs in past investments and entrenched social structures, and also to organization members becoming attached to cognitive styles, behavioral dispositions, and decision heuristics. The accumulated skills which render firms inert also

Strategic Flexibility: Managing in a Turbulent Environment. Edited by G. Hamel, C.K. Prahalad, H. Thomas and D. O'Neal.
Copyright © 1998 John Wiley & Sons Ltd.

provide opportunities for strengthening their unique advantages, and to further improve their know-how. The potential benefits include greater reliability in delivering a sound and reliable product and many economies of efficiency and routine (Miller & Chen, 1994, p. 1).

The evolutionary perspective has a close affinity with the resource-based theory of the firm. In their *Evolutionary Theory of Economic Change*, Nelson & Winter (1982) present firms as repositories of routines which endow them with a capacity to search. Yet the same routines suppress attention span and capacity to absorb new information, by spelling out behavior that permits search only for new ideas that are reasonable and consistent with prior learning. In a similar way in the *resource-based theory* the firm is seen as a bundle of tangible and intangible resources and tacit know-how that must be identified, selected, developed, and deployed to generate superior performance (Penrose, 1959; Learned *et al.*, 1969; Wernerfelt, 1984). These scarce, firm-specific assets may lead to a core competence with a limited capacity to change. Just as with the evolutionary theory of economic change, the resource-based theory assumes that *firms are stuck with what they have and have to live with what they lack*.

Teece (1984, p. 106) has also argued that a limited repertoire of available routines severely constrains a firm's strategic choice. The suppression of choice is a condition for the efficient exploitation of a core competence, and many studies show that in highly competitive environments a core competence can become a core rigidity (Leonard-Barton, 1992; Barnett, Greve & Park, 1994; Burgelman, 1994) or competence trap (Levitt & March, 1988; Levinthal & March, 1993). Firms develop core rigidities together with highly specialized resources to enhance profits at the price of reduced flexibility (Volberda, 1996b, 1998). Similarly, Utterback & Abernathy's (1975) model posits that a firm that does pursue the evolution of its processes and products to the extreme may find that it has achieved the benefits of high productivity only at the cost of decreased flexibility and innovative capacity. It must face competition from innovative products that are produced by other more flexible firms.

Teece, Pisano & Shuen (1992), therefore, have suggested that the relative superiority and imitability of organizational resources cannot be taken for granted and that, from a normative perspective, the firm must always remain in a dynamic capability building mode. It is not only the bundle of resources that matter, but also the mechanisms by which firms accumulate and dissipate new skills and capabilities, and the forces that limit the rate and direction of this process.

By synthesizing prior research, this chapter proposes a dynamic approach. It seeks to understand and investigate the managerial capabilities and organizational resources that are likely to enable a firm to renew, augment, and adapt its core competence over time. On the basis of the paradoxical tensions (Poole & Van de Ven, 1989) between core upgrading and core building, we distinguish four generic *mechanisms* by which multi-unit firms accumulate and dissipate new skills and capabilities to match firm-level distinctive competencies with industry-level sources of competitive advantage: *selection, hierarchy, time,* and *networking*.

THE SELECTION MECHANISM: RENEWAL AS A SELECTIVE PROCESS

According to the selection mechanism, the multi-unit firm's competitive environment as well as its internal environment have a major impact on the development and evolution of competencies of the firm (cf. Barney & Zajac, 1994). This "selection leads to competence" approach suggests that the intensity of internal and external selection pressures is critical for the development of potentially valuable resources and capabilities, which can give multi-unit firms important competitive advantages. Only those units of the firm that are able to match their capabilities with the internal and external selection environment will survive, while those that do not succeed will die.

Selection within the firm is typically a passive process. As described by Goold & Campbell (1987), a division may be selected-out if it fails to achieve a target rate of profit or some other objective. When a division or unit is "selected-out," it is closed, sold, or finds resources withdrawn. While spin-offs and buy-outs require an intervention of top management, they can be interpreted as a passive reaction to environmental change, not an active attempt to shape change, explored in the alternative mechanisms of hierarchy and time.

Balancing the process of selection, there is a process of the creation of new competencies by new corporate ventures. In selection, this process is not directed by top management, and we can view the pattern as akin to natural biological variation. Peters & Waterman (1982) use the term "skunk works" to highlight the absence of intervention from top management in the process of creating new competencies in many organizations. Drucker (1985, pp. 161–163) talks of the need for units with substantial autonomy from the rest of the organization, and Galbraith (1982) stresses the importance of "reservations," which are totally devoted to creating new ideas. Similarly, Van de Ven (1986) has drawn attention to part–whole relationships, and Kanter (1988, pp. 184–191) has discussed the vital role of un-directed middle managers. While we deal with the creation of new ideas by directed behaviour from top management later, under the topic of hierarchy, it is worth noting that in many situations variations will be unplanned.

In summary, the dynamics of the selection mechanism in rapidly

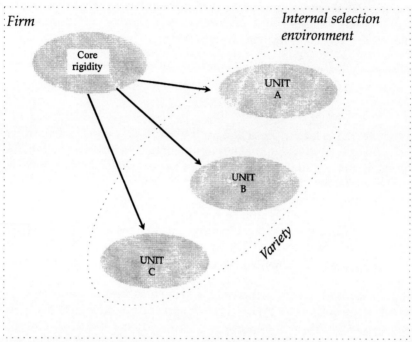

FIGURE 19.1   Selection: dissolving the paradox by selecting out core rigidities and
enhancing variety within the firm

changing environments does not really solve the paradox of renewal, but
rather dissolves it. In FIGURE 19.1, the three units, (A, B and C) are all
assumed to be different. As a consequence of environmental change, one
unit may perhaps survive, another may have to be spun out or closed
because of core rigidities and the third may transform itself by venturing.

The internal selection mechanism has an obvious parallel with population
ecology theories and organizational economics. They assume that environments are relentlessly efficient in weeding out any units or ventures that do
not closely align with environmental demands. There is little faith in
conscious initiatives by management to renew the firm. Inertial pressures
often prevent multi-unit firms from changing their core competencies in line
with industry-level sources of competitive advantage. The concept of inertia,
like that of fitness, refers to a correspondence between the behavioral
capabilities of a class of organizations and their particular environments
(Hannan & Freeman, 1984, p. 152). It is a result of the structural and

procedural baggage that organizations accumulate over time. The speed of an organization's response relative to its competitors reflects this inertia. For instance, specialization of production plants and personnel, established ideas of organizational participants, and "mind-sets" of top managers may make it impossible for organizations to engage in timely and efficient changes (Morgan, 1986, p. 67).

Variations or change may be planned or unplanned (Aldrich & Pfeffer, 1976) for the selection mechanism is indifferent regarding the source of variation or change. The general principle is that the greater the heterogeneity and number of variations in the multi-unit firm, the richer the opportunities for a close fit to the environmental selection criteria.

In line with these theories, renewal is not a managerial process, but is caused by selection of the environment of populations of organizations. For instance, Burgelman's study (1994, p. 50) of strategic business exit within Intel Corporation shows that it was not the corporate strategy but the internal selection environment that caused a shift from memory towards microprocessor business. Burgelman conjectures that the higher the correspondence between the internal selection criteria within the multi-unit firm and external selection pressures, the better the selection mechanism guarantees the co-evolution of a multi-unit firm's competencies with the sources of competitive advantage of the industry. Barnett, Greve & Park (1994) found in their empirical study of single-unit versus multi-unit firms in retail banking that multi-unit firms were able to buffer their units from the external selection environment by seeking position advantages in the market. Internal selection mechanisms replace the external selection mechanism by "soft" incentives, which are weaker than those that act on a population of single firms. They appear to inhibit learning processes that can generate distinctive competencies, but on the other hand remain immune for dysfunctional learning effects such as core rigidity or competence traps. That is, the less well-adapted multi-unit firms seem less sensitive to selection mechanisms but their development seems less path-dependent.

While the selection mechanism seems a powerful tool of ex-post explanation of renewal processes, the underlying theories represent a view of individual–organization interactions that are grounded in the assumption that the human role in organizations is essentially passive and pathological (Perrow, 1986, pp. 213–214; Bartlett & Ghoshal, 1993, p. 43). This negative assumption about human agency is manifest in extreme determinism in population ecology (Hannan & Freeman, 1984) and the assumptions about shirking, opportunism, and inertia in organizational economics (Alchian & Demsetz, 1972; Williamson, 1975). Such theories approve the breaking-up of large, complex multi-unit firms yet grounded theory has had an important role, suggesting that there is room for managerial action. Evidence from Richardson, Edwards, and Hotpoint shows that renewal can be a purposeful action to achieve leadership out of maturity (Baden-Fuller & Stopford, 1994). Furthermore, companies like Swatch were able to change their past, the rules of their sectors, and unlock hidden values. These firms combined novel approaches with stretched resources to create leading positions. These examples illustrate that we need to consider other dynamic mechanisms by which multi-unit firms match their competencies with sources of competitive advantage. Therefore, we will consider the hierarchy, time, and network as dynamic mechanisms to explore more generally how co-evolution and adaptation of the multi-unit firm come about.

THE HIERARCHY MECHANISM: RENEWAL AS AN ADMINISTRATIVE PROCESS

Most researchers believe that managers have some power over their environment, and that strategy making in large, complex firms involves multiple levels of management (Van Cauwenberg & Cool, 1982; Burgelman, 1994). The hierarchy mechanism therefore resolves the paradox of renewal by clarifying the different roles of various levels of management in the renewal process and the connections between these hierarchical levels. This approach assumes that one horn of the paradox operates at one level of analysis, while the other operates at a different level. This idea of *spatial separation* is by level and location. Level differences occur on account of hierarchy (e.g. top versus middle versus front-line managers), and location on account of geography, business unit or function. These ideas can be found in the literature on corporate restructuring (specific managerial roles for various hierarchical levels) and learning theories (types of learning related to certain hierarchical levels). Strategic renewal, in this perspective, is an administrative process in which the multi-unit firm has to spell out and manage spatial relationships.

SEPARATION BY HIERARCHICAL LEVEL: CORPORATE RESTRUCTURING AND LEARNING LEVELS

In line with the managerial perspective of classical administrative theorists such as Barnard (1938) and Selznick (1957), many researchers have considered the managerial roles of the hierarchical levels within the multi-unit firm. Originally, Schumpeter (1934) and Chandler (1962) suggested that corporate management is the primary initiator of entrepreneurial action, while front-line managers were the implementors of top-down decisions. This implies that renewal is a *top-down, deliberate managerial process*, where exploration of corporate-wide competencies created by heuristics, skill development, and fundamentally new insights or double-loop learning (Argyris & Schön, 1978) takes place at the corporate management level, while exploitation of these competencies in terms of routine proliferation or single-loop learning takes place at the business-unit or lower levels. This top-down, deliberate managerial perspective is supported by Prahalad & Hamel (1990), arguing that strategic renewal depends on the strategic intent (Hamel & Prahalad, 1989) of the CEO or corporate management based on superior industry foresight. Such grand strategy explanations in highly competitive industries are very exceptional from an evolutionary perspective (cf. Burgelman, 1994, p. 25) as well as a cognitive perspective (Cyert & March, 1963) and do not take into account that strategy in large complex firms is less centralized in top management, more multifaceted, and generally less integrated (Van Cauwenberg & Cool, 1982). That is, strategic management is an organization-wide activity in which each level has to contribute in its own way.

In reaction, building on Bower's work (1970) on the management of the resource allocation process, a rich body of literature has suggested that perhaps the most effective process of strategic renewal is through originating, developing and promoting strategic initiatives from the front-line managers (cf. Kimberly, 1979; Burgelman, 1983; Quinn, 1985; Bartlett & Ghoshal, 1993). This research finds that renewal typically emerges from autonomous strategic behavior of individuals or small groups in lower levels of the organization. Front-line managers typically have the most current knowledge and expertise and are closer to the routines and sources of information critical to innovative outcomes.

In FIGURE 19.2 we show a firm with three units, one which is mature and unaffected by the environmental change, and two other units, B and C. Unit B is renewing by autonomous behaviour of front-line managers, and Unit C by directed top-down strategic intent. Of course, our hypothetical firm is really a collage of the possibilities, which we explore further below.

Within the *reactive bottom-up, emergent perspective*, the role of top management is described as retroactive legitimizer (Burgelman, 1983) or judge and arbiter (Angle & Van de Ven, 1989) and that of middle management as supporter and intermediary of lower-level initiatives. Exploration of new competencies takes place at the lowest level by double-loop learning or generative learning (Senge, 1990); the interactions with the market and demanding clients facilitate front-line managers to call into question their norms, objectives, and basic policies. On the other hand, the exploitation of already developed competencies takes place at the upper levels by single-loop or adaptive learning; this type of learning helps the multi-unit firm to exploit previous experiences, to detect causalities, and to extrapolate to the future. It permits corporate top management to persist in its set policies and achieve its formulated objectives.

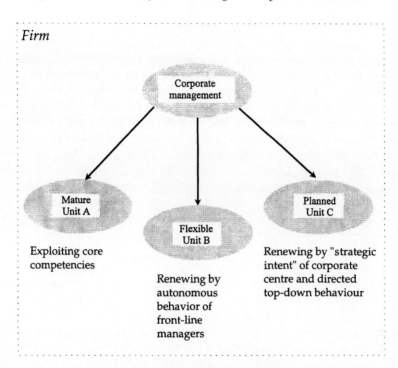

Firm

Corporate
management

Mature
Unit A

Flexible
Unit B

Planned
Unit C

Exploiting core
competencies

Renewing by
autonomous
behavior of
front-line
managers

Renewing by "strategic
intent" of corporate
centre and directed
top-down behaviour

FIGURE 19.2   Hierarchy: resolving the paradox by clarifying the distinctive roles of
multiple levels of management

By contrast, in the *proactive bottom-up, emergent perspective* the role of top
management is considered to be more than retroactive sense-making of
bottom-up initiatives but expanded towards purpose creator and challenger
of the status quo (Bartlett & Ghoshal, 1993) of the multi-unit firm. This
creative tension (Senge, 1990) at the level of corporate management forces
the multi-unit firm to balance exploitation of a core competence with the
cost of adaptability to new competencies. One could argue that in the
proactive bottom-up, emergent perspective, top management is involved in
single-loop and double-loop learning at the same time, sometimes called
deutero-learning (cf. Bateson, 1936; Argyris & Schön, 1978). That is, top
management's exploration of unknown futures and its exploitation of
known pasts balance each other (Hedberg & Jönsson, 1978, p. 50). Furthermore, middle management is concerned with horizontal linking and leveraging capabilities across the units in order to prevent fragmentation of
resources and capabilities.

Day (1994) shows in an empirical study on strategic renewal that the roles
of various management levels are diverse. Strategic initiatives arose from
lower levels as well as middle and upper levels. Moreover, she argued that

if top management follows only a reactive bottom-up, emergent perspective of strategic renewal, the chances of survival of the multi-unit firm is reduced (Day, 1994, p. 168). That is, the direct role of corporate top management is often crucial, especially in the case of strategic renewal projects which require substantial resources during development and cooperation across multiple business units.

Given these divergent views of spelling out inter-level relationships, it is difficult to give an integrated perspective on the managerial roles of different hierarchical levels. But the general assumption is that clear level separation can resolve the paradox.

THE TIME MECHANISM: RENEWAL AS A PUNCTUATED PROCESS

The paradox of exploiting existing capabilities and competencies on the one hand and their recreation on the other can be resolved by *temporal separation*, where the periods of exploitation (stability) are alternated with periods of creativity (revolution). In making the distinction between the two different phases, almost all recognize that during periods of stability, a firm can develop some new capabilities alongside the exploitation of the current portfolio. This process will be one of incremental development (such as discussed by Nelson & Winter, 1982). However, there will be moments where constructive and co-existing incrementalism is not possible; these will occur when the direction or trajectory of innovation becomes competence destroying (Tushman & Anderson, 1986). At such moments, the unit or organization cannot simultaneously exploit the old and develop the new, but has to "choose" (perhaps unconsciously) between radical change and slow decline.

The notion of competence-destroying change, where incremental change paths become radical change paths, is associated with significant unlearning (discussed by Argyris & Schön, 1978), new ways of thinking, and new mind-sets (Spender, 1980), different paths of technology (Clark, 1985; Tushman & Anderson, 1986), and particular kinds of corporate entrepreneurship (Schumpeter, 1934; Guth & Ginsberg, 1990). Although the role of time is not ignored in the discussions by those concerned with administrative heritage and selection, the question of how reversibility takes place is generally underplayed. More important, in the literature on corporate entrepreneurship, there is a different view on how the process of renewal takes place, with a greater emphasis on the whole organization changing.

DYNAMIC INNOVATION AND TIME PATHS FOR RENEWAL AND STABILITY

The concept of moving from innovation to exploitation (renewal to stability) is well accepted. The critical question is whether irreversibility is possible; that is, whether there can be "de-maturity." Burns & Stalker (1961), in their study of organizational form, have suggested that the two different phases or modes can be captured by the labels of "mechanistic" and "organic." They note that organizations may move from organic to mechanistic, and that the reverse is also possible. Other organizational theorists have undertaken a much finer and more complex categorization of possibilities, and transitions. For example, Mintzberg (1979) suggests that organizational structures can be categorized around five possibilities, for different needs and purposes. Several are concerned with the simple organization, emerging to the fully fledged complex multidivisional firm. But two modes stand out, adhocracy and bureaucracy, which are two opposing designs for the complex firm, and respectively provide models permitting renewal and exploitation.

There have been numerous studies of change from maturity to dynamism. Notable is the longer period analysis of Tushman & Romanelli (1985) which proposes a "punctuated equilibrium." They found that short periods of radical change, where revolution takes place, may be preceded and followed by longer periods of greater stability, associated with development and exploitation. Whether change is long cycled or punctuated is in part conditioned by perspective. If the time period is extended even more, the spikes will disappear and the whole path will appear more smooth.

At the level of the enterprise, Child & Smith (1987) and Pettigrew (1985) note that revolution may cascade through the organization, and that in some cases it may not always be possible to date the exact start of the managerial processes involved in starting or finishing. However, in some cases, such as British Airways (Kotter & Heskett, 1992) or Novotel (Hunt, Baden-Fuller & Calori, 1996), the moment when the process took hold is clear even if there are historical antecedents. The perception of discontinuity, or slow evolutionary processes, may also be influenced according to whether the observer is looking at tenures of chief executives, structures, systems, organizational processes or the building of knowledge and technological understanding. On some measures, such as structures, the changes may appear sharp (see for instance Mintzberg & Waters (1983) on the history of the Canadian Lady); on other dimensions such as competence building the process may seem more gradual (Burgelman, 1994; Stopford & Baden-Fuller, 1994).

Whether one has a punctuated view, or a more evolutionary view, the central premise is one of cycling through, where renewal can both precede

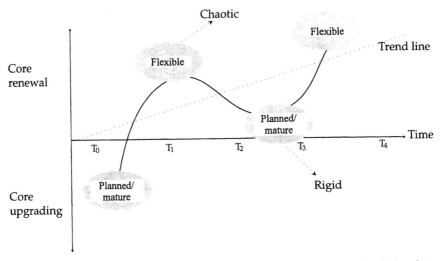

FIGURE 19.3   Time: resolving the paradox by managing temporal relationships between contrary forces

and follow stability. Not all organizations do follow these waves, for some fail and turn into rigid or chaotic forms. But a significant number do succeed, and in FIGURE 19.3, we show this process as one of oscillation between planned and flexible modes (Volberda, 1996a, 1998). In this process of change, the organization has to prevent itself from "overshooting" and becoming extremely rigid or chaotic. We do not intend to suggest that the path need be smooth or that the time periods in different states should be equal. Moreover, in some organizations the trend line will be rising, reflecting overall progress, and in others it will fall, reflecting regression.

CORPORATE ENTREPRENEURSHIP AND THE DYNAMICS OF CHANGE

The hierarchical perspective on renewal sees the process of change as driven from one administrative level to another, and the discussion is typically couched in top-down or bottom-up terms. In contrast, the corporate entrepreneurship literature suggests that renewal is a holistic exercise, which eventually involves the whole business, and it is possible to talk of the whole organization moving from one extreme (maturity) to the other (renewal).

The theories of corporate entrepreneurship typically note that the whole organization must be involved if radical change encompassing new technologies and new processes is to be accomplished (Stopford & Baden-

Fuller, 1994). It emphasizes the importance of the middle manager as entrepreneurs who connect the differing levels of the organization. This is not the case of one level driving another, but of team-working among levels and functions, as is pointed out by Kanter (1983), Hurst, Rush & White (1986), and Wooldridge & Floyd (1990), to name a few. Baden-Fuller & Stopford (1994) reconfirm the importance of complete organizational transformation in cases of mature firms renewing to achieve not only radical change for themselves, but also change for their sectors, thus linking corporate renewal to industry renewal. They point out, using examples such as Richardson in knives, and Edwards in high-vacuum pumps, that although triggers for change may have come from many quarters and may take time to gather speed, in the end the whole state of the organization can change from maturity to dynamism.

Although more entrepreneurialism is seen as being associated with faster change, too much entrepreneurialism can lead to break-up or even failure. Too great a set of aspirations compared to the resource base, and uncontrolled experimentation can lead to the taking of too great a set of risks (as was associated with Laker Airway's in their challenge to the airlines on the North Atlantic route). The organization can also be paralyzed, because the desire to be entrepreneurial creates chaos (Volberda, 1996a, 1998). While the words "corporate entrepreneurship" suggests something that recognizes and balances the forces of renewal and stability, the inherent tension for self-destruction is ever present.

The ideas of corporate entrepreneurship being extensive throughout the organization also link with the resource-based theories of competitive advantage. These identify knowledge, capabilities, and competencies as the source of success (Schumpeter, 1934; Penrose, 1959; Wernerfelt, 1984; Grant, 1991; Nonaka, 1991; Grant & Baden-Fuller, 1995). Such perspectives insist that durable advantages must reside in the heart of the organization in complex routines, systems, and hidden stores of knowledge. The development of these stores of knowledge and ability must involve, of necessity, large numbers of the organization, and cannot be confined to a single management process alone, especially that at the top. From the perspective of the complex enterprise, the process of renewal in one business unit can encourage and lead to renewal elsewhere. Examples are explored in Baden-Fuller & Boschetti (1996) and in Hunt, Baden-Fuller & Calori (1996).

THE NETWORK MECHANISM: EXTERNALIZING THE PROCESS OF RENEWAL

According to the alliance or network view, the paradox of balancing capability exploitation and renewal is resolved by interaction with other organizations. This pattern can be thought of as lying between the market selection process and that undertaken within the firm. In the market selection process, those organizations that do not adjust fail. In the hierarchy, those organizations that do not adjust are reorganized. In the alliance–network view, neither side can be wholly right, nor wholly wrong. The market, according to network analysis, is not abstract but concrete and exists everywhere as partners. In a formal or informal alliance, the market mechanism exists because the connections between the parties are mutual and voluntary, but there is a form of hierarchy as typically one party is the central firm or broker (Miles & Snow, 1986). Resolving the paradox of continuity and change can take place in an alliance because there is no longer a clear distinction between competition outside the organization and cooperation inside. Rather, the partners to the enterprise experience both competition and cooperation. Competition is a driving force for change, but cooperation helps ensure resources and stability. Competition exists between members of the alliances, because there is ultimately independence and freedom, with its associated responsibility to survive.

NETWORKS AND THE RENEWAL PROCESS

It was the Swedish school of industrial purchasing (e.g. Hakansson, 1982) which emphasized that markets are really networks, and stressed that most firms feel market forces though a network of customers and suppliers. Matsson (1987) explored strategic change in a customer network perspective. Von Hippel (1978) described in some detail how customers interacted with suppliers to ensure that new ideas for product improvement were introduced, and gave tangible meaning to the phrase market pressure.

The view that more organized networks could act as a powerful mechanism for renewal was first mentioned by Marshall at the beginning of the twentieth century, and has been echoed by Ouchi (1981) in his discussions of clans of organizations. The social pressures to aspire to higher achievement and the resources provide industrial districts and clans with powerful mechanisms for resolving the paradoxes of innovation and exploitation. (For a discussion, see Porter, 1990.) More recently, networks have been categorized and analyzed by Miles & Snow (1986) and Thorelli (1986). Miles & Snow talk of the influence of the broker in the process of change. In most of the above cases, the network or industrial districts have been informal. The same features which have given them strength, especially the social bonds, have also acted in the end to slow renewal. Industrial districts such as Lyon and Sheffield have declined, and even Prato (one of the longest running) has seen great pressures.

Alliance making and success has been the subject of a considerable volume of research, far more than can be reviewed here. It is important to note that the effectiveness of alliances in the renewal process has been seriously questioned. For example, Bleeke & Ernst (1991) and Hamel (1991) provide evidence that using the alliances is hazardous. They suggest that unless both partners are strong and balanced, the mature organization may gain relatively little from the partnering. For the weak organization, where the problem of renewal may be most acute, the risks of alliance making are the greatest.

In contrast, Lorenzoni & Baden-Fuller (1995) pay close attention to the process by which the tension between preservation and renewal takes place in a systematically organized *strategic network* which has a strong central firm (see FIGURE 19.4). The strategic network is one where there is a clear centre, which acts as a brain and strategist to its partners. The centre takes on many of the roles found in the headquarters of the large, complex vertically integrated organization. By using examples drawn from firms that have successfully employed the strategic network form over time, such as Benetton, Apple, Sun, and Corning, they show that core competencies are typically shared among the members and there is learning and teaching on a systematic basis. The authors identify two methods for the resolution of the paradox of stability and renewal. In the *learning race*, the central organization organizes a development contest between members of the network, offering a prize to the winner. However, losers also receive a reward; they can use the inventions to ensure rapid exploitation. Thus the downside is lessened without reducing the incentives to innovate. The *borrow–develop–lend* principle is more subtle. A new idea may be borrowed from one

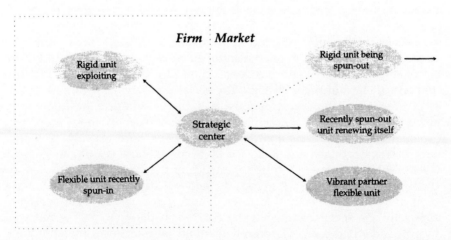

FIGURE 19.4   Network: dissolving the paradox by inter-organizational relationships

partner, or bought in from outside, development may occur in the central firm and exploitation occur elsewhere in the network.

The actual practice of these dynamic networks shows how in some cases it is not easy to separate the firm from its market. Discussing selection in an abstract sense without reference to partnerships is as dangerous as discussing hierarchical and time mechanisms without reference to the forces of competition. Firms which bridge this paradox explicitly seem to have achieved great success. But caution is in order: most of the examples are of young firms, which started as networks from the beginning. Only time will tell if this new form is better.

DISCUSSION AND CONCLUSIONS

Our chapter has many obvious limitations. In such a cursory space, the review can only draw out a set of sketchy ideas, and it does not provide a robust set of formal models which can be tested. Moreover, it sometimes gives the false impression that writers in the field only follow one strand of thought. We hope that these sins will be overlooked.

All organizations face a paradox between renewal and preservation. Stability is necessary for internal cohesion and to prevent the self-destruction of chaos. Renewal is necessary because most organizations cannot innovate as fast as the market, especially when they are stable. By examining four strands of theorizing—selection, hierarchy, time and networks—we aimed at illuminating differing insights into how these paradoxes could be resolved.

First and foremost, the review and classification gives strong support to the notion that strategic renewal is possible, and that there are multiple ways for large organizations to rebuild their competencies. Each of our mechanisms has a long, respectable history of academic work, which has developed concepts and evidence. Although individuals have often contributed to more than one strand, there are clear "schools of thought" emerging from the literature which may help researchers trying to make sense of the field. By identifying four schools of thought, we hope to aid thinking, and shed light on the heap of ideas out there.

Secondly, and perhaps more intriguingly, our themes point to important lessons for practising managers and those who teach them. By setting up the benchmark of "selection," where managers are seen as passive actors driven by path dependency in a biological game, we point out that there are three very different mechanisms for active intervention, each of which is distinctive from the other and each of which appears to have considerable potential, and within each strand there are further choices that can be made. The key mechanisms, hierarchy, time and network, are commonly recognized in the managerial literature, but rarely, if ever, discussed in the same place. Most writers, practitioners or academics advocate only one or two streams. Our review suggests that there is considerably greater latitude for managerial choice.

This brings us to our final point. What are the relative merits of the mechanisms? When is passive action better than active intervention? Is hierarchy better than network or time, and is the choice an absolute one, or one determined by history and the environment? These important questions we have not answered, although we have given clues suggesting that the potential is equal and that other factors must be used to weigh the selection. However, our answer is not definitive. It is an item of great importance to researchers and managers alike, which has not yet been addressed in the managerial literature and represents an important challenge for the future.

ACKNOWLEDGEMENTS

We gratefully acknowledge the helpful comments of participants of the EGOS Conference in Istanbul, the EMOT Conference in Reading, the Organization Science Winter Conference in Snowmass, Colorado, and the SMS Conferences in Ghent and Phoenix, Arizona, where various versions of this paper were presented. We particularly note the help of Oguz Baburoglu, John Cantwell, Yves Doz, Tom Elfring, Paul Evans, Charles Galunic, Aimé Heene, Bill McKelvey, Tammi Madsen, Ard-Pieter de Man, Alan Meyer, Sue Mohrman, Keith Pavitt and Ron Sanchez. In addition, we have received encouraging comments from other colleagues.

REFERENCES

Alchian, A.A. & Demsetz, H. (1972). Production, information costs, and economic organization. *American Economic Review*, **62**(5), 777–795.

Aldrich, H.E. & Pfeffer, J. (1976). Environments of organizations. *Annual Review of Sociology*, **21**, 121–140.

Angle, H.L. & Van de Ven, A.H. (1989). Suggestions for managing the innovation journey. In *Research on the Management of Innovation*. New York: Harper & Row.

Argyris, C. & Schön, D. (1978). *Organizational Learning*. Reading, MA: Addison-Wesley.

Baden-Fuller, C. & Stopford, J.M. (1994). *Rejuvenating the Mature Business*. Cambridge, MA: Harvard Business School Press.

Baden-Fuller, C. & Boschetti, C. (1996). Creating competitive advantage through mergers: the lens of the resource based view. In H. Thomas & D. O'Neal (eds) *Strategic Integration*. Chichester: Wiley.

Barnard, C.I. (1938). *The Functions of the Executive*. Cambridge, MA: Harvard University Press.

Barnett, W.P. Greve, H.R. & Park, D.Y. (1994). An evolutionary model of organizational performance. *Strategic Management Journal*, **15**, 11–28.

Barney, J.B. & Zajac, E.J. (1994). Competitive organizational behavior: toward an organizationally-based theory of competitive advantage. *Strategic Management Journal*, **15**, 5–9.

Bartlett, C.A. & Ghoshal, S. (1993). Beyond the M-form: toward a managerial theory of the firm. *Strategic Management Journal*, **14**, 23–46.

Bateson, G. (1936). *Naven*. Cambridge: Cambridge University Press.

Bleeke, J. & Ernst, D. (1991). The way to win in cross border alliances. *Harvard Business Review*. March/April, 78–86.

Bower, J.L. (1970). *Managing the Resource Allocation Process*. Boston, MA: Harvard Business School Press.

Burgelman, R.A. (1983). A process model of internal corporate venturing in the diversified major firm. *Administrative Science Quarterly*, **28**, 223–244.

Burgelman, R.A. (1994). Fading memories: a process theory of strategic business exit in dynamic environments. *Administrative Science Quarterly*, **39**, 24–56.

Burns, T. & Stalker, G.M. (1961). *The Management of Innovation*. London: Tavistock.

Chandler, A.D., Jr (1962). *Strategy and Structure*. Cambridge, MA: MIT Press.

Child, J. & Smith, C. (1987). The context and process of organisational transformation – Cadbury Limited. *Journal of Management Studies*, **24**(6), 565–593.

Clark, K.B. (1985). The interaction of design hierarchies and market concepts in technological evolution. *Research Policy*, **14**, 235–251.

Cyert, R. & March, J. (1963). *A Behavioral Theory of the Firm*. Englewood Cliffs, NJ: Prentice Hall.

Day, D.L. (1994). Raising radicals: different processes for championing innovative corporate ventures. *Organization Science*, **5**(2), 148–172.

Drucker, P. (1985). *Innovation and Entrepreneurship*. New York: Harper & Row.

Gailbraith, J.R. (1982). Designing the innovating organization. *Organization Dynamics*, Winter, 3–24.

Goold, M. & Campbell, A. (1987). *Strategies and Styles*. Oxford: Blackwell.

Grant, R.M. (1991). The resource based theory of competitive advantage: implications for strategy formulation. *California Management Review*, **33**(3), 114–135.

Grant, R.M. & Baden-Fuller, C. (1995). A knowledge-based theory of inter-firm collaboration. *Best Paper Academy of Management Proceedings*, Vancouver.

Guth, W.D. & Ginsburg, A. (1990). Guest editors introduction: corporate entrepreneurship. *Strategic Management Journal*, **11**, 5–15.

Hakansson, H. (1982). *International Marketing and Purchasing of Industrial Goods*. Chichester: Wiley.

Hamel, G. (1991). Learning in international alliances. *Strategic Management Journal*, **12**, 83–103.

Hamel, G. & Prahalad, C.K. (1989). Strategic intent. *Harvard Business Review*, May/June, 63–76.

Hannan, M.T. & Freeman, J.H. (1984). Structural inertia and organizational change. *American Sociological Review*, **49**, 149–164.

Hedberg, B. & Jönsson, S. (1978). Designing semi-confusing information systems for organizations in changing environments. *Accounting, Organizations and Society*, **3**(1), 47–64.

Hunt, B., Baden-Fuller, C. & Calori, R. (1996). *The Novotel Case*. Cranfield: European Case Clearing House.

Hurst, D.K., Rush, J.C. & White, R.E. (1986). Top management teams and organizational renewal. *Strategic Management Journal*, **10**, 87–105.

Kanter, R.M. (1983). *The Change Masters: Innovation and Entrepreneurship in the American Corporation.* New York: Simon & Schuster.

Kanter, R.M. (1988). When a thousand flowers bloom: structural, collective, and social conditions for innovation in organization. In B.M. Staw & L.L. Cummings (eds) *Research in Organizational Behavior*, Vol. 10. Greenwich, CT: JAI Press, pp. 169–211.

Kimberly, J.R. (1979). Issues in the creation of organizations: initiation, innovation, and institutionalization. *Academy of Management Journal*, **22**, 437–457.

Kotter, J.P. & Heskett, J.L (1992). *Corporate Culture and Performance.* New York: Free Press.

Learned, E., Christensen, C., Andrews, K. & Guth, W. (1969). *Business Policy: Text and Cases.* Homewood, IL: Irwin.

Leonard-Barton, D. (1992). Core capabilities and core rigidities: a paradox in managing new product development. *Strategic Management Journal*, **13**, 111–125.

Levinthal, D.A. & March, J.G. (1993). The myopia of learning. *Strategic Management Journal*, **14**, 95–112.

Levitt, B. & March, J.G. (1988). Organizational learning. In W.R. Scott (ed.) *Annual Review of Sociology*, vol. 14. Palo Alto, CA: Annual Reviews, pp. 319–340.

Lorenzoni, G. & Baden-Fuller, C. (1995). Creating a strategic centre to manage a web of partners. *California Management Review*, Spring.

Matsson, L-G. (1987). Management of strategic change in a "Markets as Networks" Perspective. In A. Pettigrew (ed.), *The Management of Strategic Change.* Oxford: Blackwell.

Miles, R. & Snow, C. (1986) Network organizations: new concepts for new forms. *California Management Review*, Spring.

Miller, D. & Chen, M. (1994). Sources and consequences of competitive inertia: a study of the US airline industry. *Administrative Science Quarterly*, **39**, 1–23.

Mintzberg, H. (1979). *The Structuring of Organizations: A Synthesis of the Research.* Englewood Cliffs, NJ: Prentice Hall.

Mintzberg, H. & Waters, J.A. (1983). Researching the formation of strategy: the history of Canadian Lady, 1939–1976. In R. Lamb (ed.) *Strategic Management.* Englewood Cliffs, NJ: Prentice Hall.

Morgan, G. (1986). *Images of Organization.* Beverley Hills, CA: Sage.

Nelson, R.R. & Winter, S.G. (1982). *An Evolutionary Theory of Economic Change.* Cambridge, MA: Harvard University Press.

Nonaka, I. (1991). The knowledge-creating company. *Harvard Business Review*, November/December, 96–104.

Ouchi, W.G. (1981). *Theory Z: How American Business can Meet the Japanese Challenge.* Reading, MA: Addison-Wesley.

Penrose, E. (1959). *The Theory of the Growth of the Firm.* Oxford: Basil Blackwell.

Perrow, C. (1986). *Complex Organizations—A critical essay*, 3rd edn. New York: Random House.

Peters, T.J. & Waterman, R.H. Jr. (1982). *In Search of Excellence.* New York: Warner Books.

Pettigrew, A.M. (1985). *The Awakening Giant.* Oxford: Blackwell.

Poole, M.S. & van de Ven, A.H. (1989). Using paradox to build management and organization theories. *Academy of Management Review*, **14**(4), 562–578.

Porter, M. (1990). *The Competitive Advantage of Nations.* New York: Free Press.

Prahalad, C.K. & Hamel, G. (1990). The core competence of the corporation. *Harvard Business Review*, **68**, 79–91.

Quinn, J.B. (1985). Managing innovation: controlled chaos. *Harvard Business Review*, **63**(3), 78–84.

Schumpeter, J.A. (1934). *The Theory of Economic Development*. Cambridge, MA: Harvard University Press.

Selznick, P. (1957). *Leadership in Administration – A Sociological Interpretation*. New York: Harper & Row.

Senge, P. (1990). The leader's new work: building learning organizations. *Sloan Management Review*, Fall.

Spender, J-C. (1980). *Strategy making in business*, Doctoral Dissertation, University of Manchester.

Stopford, J.M. & Baden-Fuller, C. (1994). Creating corporate entrepreneurship. *Strategic Management Journal*, 15(7), 521–536.

Teece, D.J. (1984). Economic analysis and strategic management. *California Management Review*, Spring, 87–110. *Strategic Management Journal*, 18(7), 509–533.

Teece, D.J., Pisano, G. & Shuen, A. (1992). Dynamic capabilities and strategic management. *Strategic Management Journal*, 18(7), 509–533.

Thorelli, H.B. (1986). Networks: between markets and hierarchies. *Strategic Management Journal*, 7, 37–51.

Tushman, M.L. & Anderson, P. (1986). Technological discontinuities and organizational environments. *Administrative Science Quarterly*, 31, 439–465.

Tushman, M. & Romanelli, E. (1985). Organizational evolution: a metamorphosis model of convergence and reorientation. In L.L. Cummings & B.M. Staw (eds) *Research in Organizational Behavior*, vol. 7. Greenwich, CT: JAI Press, pp. 171–222.

Utterback, J.M. & Abernathy, W.J. (1975). A dynamic model of process and product innovation. *Omega*, 3(6), 639–656.

Van Cauwenberg, A. & Cool, K. (1982). Strategic management in a new framework. *Strategic Management Journal*, 3, 245–264.

Van de Ven, A.H. (1986). Central problems in the management of innovation. *Management Science* 32(5), 590–607.

Volberda, H.W. (1996a). Toward the flexible form: how to remain vital in hypercompetitive environments. *Organization Science*, 7(4), 359–374.

Volberda, H.W. (1996b). Flexible configuration strategies within Philips Semiconductors: a strategic process of entrepreneurial revitalization. In R. Sanchez, A. Heene, & Thomas, H. (eds) *Dynamics of Competence-Based Competition*. Oxford: Elsevier, pp. 229–278.

Volberda, H.W. (1998). *Building the Flexible Firm: How to Remain Competitive*. Oxford: Oxford University Press.

Von Hippel, E. (1978). Successful industrial products from customer ideas. *Journal of Marketing*, 42, 39–49.

Wernerfelt, B. (1984). A resource-based view of the firm. *Strategic Management Journal* 5, 171–180.

Williamson, O.E. (1975). *Markets and Hierarchies: Analysis and Antitrust Implications*. New York: Free Press.

Wooldridge, B. & Floyd, S.W. (1990). The strategy process, middle management involvement and organizational performance. *Strategic Management Journal*, 11, 231–41.

Index